The Grammatical
Basis of
Linguistic Performance:
Language Use
and Acquisition

Current Studies in Linguistics Series
Samuel Jay Keyser, general editor

The Grammatical Basis of Linguistic Performance: Language Use and Acquisition

Robert C. Berwick and
Amy S. Weinberg

The MIT Press
Cambridge, Massachusetts
London, England

Copyright © 1984 by The Massachusetts Institute of Technology.

The fonts in this book are Almost Computer Modern, set using Donald E. Knuth's TEX, with help from Daniel C. Brotsky.

Printed and bound in the United States of America.

Library of Congress Cataloging in Publication Data

Berwick, Robert C.
   The grammatical basis of linguistic performance.

   (Current studies in linguistics series; 11)
   Bibliography: p.
   Includes index.
   1. Generative grammar. 2. Linguistics—Data processing.
3. Language acquisition.   I. Weinberg, Amy S.   II. Title.
III. Series.
P158.B48 1984   415   83–42550
ISBN 0–262–02192–7

Contents

Series Foreword

We are pleased to present this book as the eleventh volume in the series Current Studies in Linguistics.

As we have defined it, the series will offer book-length studies in linguistics and neighboring fields that further the exploration of man's ability to manipulate symbols. It will pursue the same editorial goals as its companion journal, *Linguistic Inquiry*, and will complement it by providing a format for in-depth studies beyond the scope of the professional article.

By publishing such studies, we hope that the series will answer the need for intensive and detailed research that sheds new light on current theoretical issues and provides a new dimension for their resolution. Toward this end it will present books dealing with the widest range of languages and addressing the widest range of theoretical topics. From time to time and with the same ends in view, the series will include collections of significant articles covering single and selected subject areas and works primarily for use as textbooks.

Like *Linguistic Inquiry*, Current Studies in Linguistics will seek to present work of theoretical interest and excellence.

Samuel Jay Keyser

Preface

In the 1960s the theory of transformational grammar generated a good deal of excitement among linguists, psychologists, and computationalists. Here was welcome relief from the "descriptivist" theories that had so long dominated linguistic theory. For transformational grammar always aimed at more than just describing language. It strove from the start for a special kind of description, designed to answer the key psychological question of how people could learn their native tongue. More than this, it was hoped that by answering the question of what it is that people learn when they learn a language, transformational grammar would lay the foundation for both theories of human sentence processing and language acquisition. This is reasonable enough; in general what you know forms a natural basis for how you put that knowledge to use.

Lately transformational grammar seems to have fallen on hard times. Researchers who once held such high hopes for it have turned their attentions elsewhere, disappointed by the apparent inability of transformational grammar to describe either sentence processing or language development.

Not only is transformational grammar not moribund, it is healthier than it has ever been. The aim of this book is to show that these reports of transformational grammar's demise are greatly exaggerated. Transformational grammar can lay the foundations for a unified, psychologically plausible, and computationally sound theory of language use and acquisition. As the tale will unfold in later chapters, in many respects transformational grammar offers the best explanations we have of language processing and acquisition.

It is easy to see why initial optimism about transformational grammar was shortlived. Many psychologists thought that experiments from the late 1960s and early 1970s showed that the rules of transformational grammar did not correspond to the mental computations people used during language understanding. Acquisition did not fare any better. Transformational grammar could not even describe early child grammars.

We have seen that both the theoretical and experimental arguments for a perceptual model in which the grammar is concretely realized appear dubious. . . . there exist no suggestions about how a generative grammar might be concretely employed as a sentence recognizer in a psychologically plausible model. (Fodor, Bever, and Garrett 1974:368)

If. . . transformational grammars represent the essence of the linguistic system captured by the child, the phenomenon of language acquisition seems to be an inexplicable mystery. (Maratsos 1978:246)

Worse still, it seemed impossible to design any kind of efficient sentence processor using a transformational grammar, psychologically plausible or not. The problem was a double-barrelled one: First, from a purely mathematical point of view, transformational grammars were too unconstrained. Second, questions of mathematical complexity aside, people were hard pressed to come up with any kind of efficient direct implementation of a transformational grammar as a sentence processing device. Researchers in artificial intelligence too turned away from transformational grammar as a model of language use. A variety of proposals sprang up to fill this perceived processing void: among them, augmented transition networks, T. Winograd's SHRDLU program, and extended context-free phrase structure grammars.

It is possible to devise abstract ideas of the logical structure of language— ideas which seem in theory to be applicable. Often, such systems, although interesting mathematically, are not valid as psychological models of human language, since they have not concerned themselves with the operational problems of a mental procedure. They often include types of representation and processes which are highly implausible, and which may be totally inapplicable in complex situations because their very nature implies astronomically large amounts of processing for certain kinds of computations. Transformational grammar. . . [is one example] of such approaches. (Winograd, in Schank and Colby 1973:167)

The analysis problem for the transformational grammar is so extremely complicated that no reasonably efficient recognition algorithm for transformational grammar has yet been found. (Woods 1970:600)

Surrounded by such apparently bleak news, our first step is simply to revive the patient. This is the job of chapters 1, 2, 3, and 4.

Given alternative but natural assumptions about the computational mechanisms used in language comprehension, transformational grammar actually can explain major psycholinguistic findings. And, discharging the fears of Winograd and Woods, this transformationally based comprehension model is computationally efficient. This result alone is enough to rehabilitate transformational grammar as a plausible component of a theory of language processing.

If we stopped here, we would simply be in the same theoretical boat as the early 1960s. Of course, we would like to do more than just turn the clock back by twenty years. We would like to advance our understanding of how grammatical representations and models of language processing and acquisition interact. This is the job of chapters 5 and 6. Chapter 5 deals with how people process sentences. It shows how the constraints of current transformational theory conspire with natural restrictions on computational power to explain why certain universal constraints on linguistic systems take the form that they do. As we will see, this explanation ties together observations about rules of natural languages that, given grammatical principles alone, would be seen as purely coincidental. To some extent then we can explain what we see in the world by blending the constraints implicit in grammars with those of a processing theory, just the kind of psychological account that transformational grammar promised from the start. And, in passing, the model answers Fodor, Bever, and Garrett's plea for a substantive theory of how to integrate transformational grammars into online sentence processors.

Chapter 6 turns to a second kind of "how" question: how transformational grammars are actually acquired over time. Here also we offer both a general computational framework and some particular proposals for child language acquisition. Traditionally, the characterization of early child grammars has been viewed as a stumbling block for a transformationally based theory of the acquisition of language. The problem is that the rules of early child grammars seem to require "semantic" predicates. Transformational theorists have always argued that categorial predicates such as "NP" or "VP" are a necessary part of grammar. They have shied away from less restrictive theories that sanction both categorial and semantic predicates. But again the difficulty is only apparent. In the particular case we look at, children actually have trouble analyzing words. When the data is re-analyzed in this way there is no need to invoke semantic predicates at all. Strikingly, this approach also predicts some typical patterns of overgeneralization in child language use. It gives a partial answer to the two key questions for any learning theory: What is a possible stage of acquisition? How is the learner driven from one stage of knowledge to another?

Along with this developmental picture, chapter 6 presents a detailed computational model for the acquisition of a subset of the transformational rules for English, the very same rules that are needed by the processing model described in chapter 5. The model has the added virtue of psychological fidelity: it uses only simple, grammatical sentences to induce the required rules and starts from a plausible initial state of knowledge. It provides a computational analogue of the informal learning theory sketched above.

The point of our story then is that the current theory of transformational grammar, combined with a healthy dose of computer science, can serve as the lynchpin for a unified theory of language use and acquisition. We see linguistics and computer science as partners of a very special kind. As every computer scientist knows, information processing models consist of algorithms that juggle very specific information structures. But algorithmic procedures for using knowledge just do not make sense without specifying the form in which that knowledge is couched. Similarly, an understanding of how language is used hinges on an understanding of what that knowledge looks like, the way it is represented. So the joint work of linguistics and computer science is like the partnership between data structures and the algorithms that use them. Linguistics is that subdiscipline of cognitive science dealing with certain structures of knowledge; computer science tells us which algorithms work best with certain data structures. Research on either side is mutually constraining. Partitioning the explanatory burden in this way allows us to gain a better understanding than having either grammar or parser go it alone.

To see this strategy at work, let us consider just one key constraint of current syntactic theory, *subjacency* (Chomsky 1981). This constraint is merely an axiom in the grammatical system: We have no explanation either for why natural languages should obey this restriction at all or why certain operations should fall outside its scope. What is subjacency? To take one example, in the first sentence below, *who* cannot denote the direct object of the verb *kiss* if this verb is embedded inside a noun phrase. But, *Howie* may co-refer with the pronoun *him*:

*Who do you believe [$_{\text{NP}}$ the claim [$_{\overline{\text{S}}}$ that Marilyn kissed]]?

Howie$_i$ believes [$_{\text{NP}}$ the claim [$_{\overline{\text{S}}}$ that Marilyn kissed him$_i$]]

Why should this be so? The grammar cannot tell us, and neither can parsing theory alone. But, as chapter 5 argues in detail, the conjunction of the two yields the necessary restrictions. Given a parsing design that is independently motivated on grounds of efficiency we can derive this distribution of data. That is, we can provide a functional explanation for subjacency. The parser simply could not operate if the grammar did not obey it.

Our strategy then is to show how the rules and representations of transformational grammar can be independently justified by the theory of language use. By assuming that mental computations are "projections" of a transformational grammar, we can actually explain part of what we observe to be true about sentence processing and language development. But we get this explanation only by blending specific linguistic results about what is computed with specific computational techniques for how to compute them. We think this partnership forges crucial links between linguistics as the study of abstract representations of knowledge and the allied fields of psychology, artificial intelligence, and cognitive science.

A Brief Tour of the Chapters

Understanding the joint linguistics-computation enterprise requires some understanding of the tools of the trade of both fields. Chapter 1 supplies the necessary background: an informal guide to computation and computational complexity and a survey of current transformational theory, the government-binding theory (Chomsky 1981).

With our analytical machinery in place, chapter 2 turns directly to the central methodological issue of the book. What role exactly should grammars play in models of language use and acquisition? As we show, the connection between grammar and external behavior is complicated because it hinges on a conjunction of three theories: an abstract linguistic theory that describes what is computed, a theory of algorithms that dictates how the computation proceeds, and a theory of implementation that says what the actual computational operations are. Earlier critiques of transformationally based parsers (Fodor, Bever, and Garrett 1974 and Bresnan 1978) assumed a fixed theory of the algorithm for language processing. They concluded that when the conjunction of the grammatical theory and the theory of the algorithm yielded incorrect psycholinguistic predictions, the source of the problem must have been the choice of linguistic theory. But there could be another culprit, the choice of algorithm. We can provide other reasonable parsing algorithms compatible with both transformational grammar and psycholinguistic experimentation.

Next we turn to questions of computational complexity. In general we can ask just what role formal mathematics has in the analysis of natural language. Mathematically, transformational grammars have been dubbed "wildly unconstrained." But is this true of current theories? Does it matter? Can we argue that the transformations of transformational grammar are computationally excessive and ought to be eliminated? What is the relationship between restrictions on linguistic systems and computational complexity? Chapters 3 and 4 probe each of these questions. We shall see that transformational grammar fits quite naturally into a computationally efficient approach. We shall also take a look at the complexity of several other current linguistic theories, including lexical-functional grammar (Bresnan 1982b), and discover that there are certain unnatural languages that lexical-functional grammars can easily generate, but that modern transformational grammars cannot generate. Finally, we apply the techniques of modern computational theory to the analysis of grammatical complexity.

Chapter 5 forms the heart of the book's new approach to the linguistics-computation partnership. We present a parser based on the government-binding theory. In order to make this parser work we must impose certain design constraints. Surprisingly, this constrained parser also predicts that a restriction like subjacency must exist, and will govern only certain lexical categories; that only certain deletion constructions must be subject to bounding conditions resembling subjacency; and that certain tree relationships must govern antecedent-anaphor/variable and quantifier-variable pairs, but not nominal or pronominal co-reference. In short, we can explain many of the "axioms" of current grammatical theory—all with an efficient parser.

Chapter 6 returns to the theme that sparked initial interest in generative grammar: language acquisition. We show formally and informally that a transformationally based learning theory predicts the stages that the child goes through while acquiring passive constructions. *This a real theory of learning: the child is forced from one stage of knowledge to the next. We illustrate our ideas with a computer model.

Acknowledgments

Finally, a word about some intellectual and personal debts. Noam Chomsky must bear the heavy burden of guilt for first suggesting that we work together. Everyone knows that two heads are better than one (as work in automata theory shows; see the first chapter) but we have been particularly fortunate in convincing almost all our friends, colleagues, and relations to give us a hand. Peter Culicover, Ken Wexler, Tom Roeper, and Edwin Williams invited us to conferences where we began to talk to each other and discuss the issues in this book. Jerry Fodor, Merrill Garrett, Lila Gleitman, Norbert Hornstein, David Israel, Elissa Newport, Jean Roger Vergnaud, Tom Wasow, and Patrick Winston encouraged us and suggested needed improvements in the early stages. Merrill and Elissa took particular care of our partial "psycholinguistic" education. Christos Papadimitriou contributed to our understanding of computational complexity. We were able to take our ideas "on the road" to McGill, the University of Pennsylvania, the Second West Coast Conference on Formal Linguistics, the MIT Cognitive Science Seminar, Georgetown University Acquisition Circle, and the Association for Computational Linguistics Annual Meeting. We thank the participants in these meetings for helpful comments and criticism. We were also fortunate to be able to publish some of this work in other places. In particular, Chapter 2 first appeared in *Cognition*, and Chapter 3, in *Linguistic Inquiry*; we would like to thank the publishers of both journals for permission to reprint those articles here. A section of Chapter 4 in different form first appeared in the *American Journal of Computational Linguistics.*

A heroic foursome waded through an entire draft of this book. Noam wanted to make sure that his first suggestion hadn't been a mistake. Many of his sharp comments have found their way into the book. Norbert Hornstein (Amy's husband) wanted to make sure that we didn't disgrace the family name and by that time had decided that this book was all that Amy would talk to him about anyway. Aravind Joshi and Ken Wexler helped guard the interests of computational linguistics, learnability theory, and much more.

Patrick Winston and Marilyn Matz constantly urged us to turn the whole thing into English. Well, nearly English. We would never have been able to carry out the research, nor do the editing and preparation of the manuscript, had it not been for the able computer resources of the MIT Artificial Intelligence Laboratory, led by its director, Patrick H. Winston. The Laboratory is supported by the Defense Advanced Research Projects Agency.

The fonts in this book are Almost Computer Modern, set using Donald E. Knuth's TEX system. Daniel Brotsky came to our aid to tame the TEX system for us. Blythe Heepe did with the artwork what TEX could not do.

A very last word for Nory and Marilyn: we promise to talk and worry about something else and become as interested in quantifiers and computer vision and *The New York Review of Books* as we should have been all along. Thanks for all the love and support.

R. C. B.
A. S. W.

Chapter 1
Computational and
Linguistic Theory

Because one of the major aims of this book is the computational analysis of modern linguistic theory, we should say what we expect the reader to know about both fields. Those who are already familiar with the rudiments of current transformational theory (the government-binding theory described in Chomsky 1981) and the basics of formal computability theory (described in Lewis and Papadimitriou 1981) may turn to the second chapter and the real beginning of our work. For the remaining readers, section 1 of this chapter gives a quick tour of the theory of computation we use, and section 2 outlines the government-binding theory.

Computational Theory

Why do we need to study computation formally at all? For us, the theory of computation forges a vital link between *what* and *how*. It tells us how hard it is to compute something—how difficult it is to process sentences, acquire language, or speak. Now this topic is an entire branch of computer science in itself, and we cannot hope to cover even a fraction of it here. What we do mean to survey includes some of the basic concepts and methods of computational complexity theory that will be relevant to later discussion.

The theory of computational complexity makes precise the intuitive notion of the "difficulty" of computing something. As the excellent survey article by Borodin 1973 makes clear, there are several subareas of the theory of computational complexity including the study of specific models of computation via tradeoff and simulation analyses and the study of specific computational problems. We will take a look at both kinds of approaches because the first will tell us about the possibility of alternative implementations (machine designs), while the second addresses specific problems (like the analysis of languages) crucial to linguistic theory.

Measuring how hard it is to compute something already presupposes much of what a theory of complexity must look like. It supposes that we are measuring the complexity of some procedure that maps a collection of inputs to desired outputs. Otherwise there is no procedure to measure. This means that the inputs, outputs, and procedure that does the input-output mapping must be precisely defined. Plainly this means that linguistic theory will have a lot to say before we even get down to the business of measuring complexity, because linguistic theory tells us what the inputs and outputs look like. In the case of parsing, for example, we could take the "input" as a segmented word or morpheme sequence, and the "output" as a labeled bracketing (a parse tree), a representation of the syntactic structure of the sentence. The procedure that carries out the mapping from input (sentence) to output (tree representation) is called a *parser*. It also makes sense that procedure taking us from inputs to outputs might not work on some inputs. In the vernacular such procedures are called *partial*. They work on part of all conceivable inputs. (On those inputs where the procedure does not work it might be natural to say that the complexity of the procedure was either undefined or infinite.)

Besides this, measuring complexity entails two things: first, a way to measure how hard it is compute something, a measure of complexity, and second, a reference machine on which to measure things, a sort of universal yardstick. Both desiderata seem appropriate. It would not be fair to say that program A is "faster" than program B simply because we ran program A on a speedy brand-new computer and program B on a painfully slow vacuum tube dinosaur.

Both machines and measures could be varied, of course; the key question is how the complexity of our procedure varies with them. For the purposes of cognitive investigation the choice of a reference computational model and measure depends on at least two factors. The first is known invariance results: Does it matter what model we pick, or does the evaluation ranking stay fixed across models? The second factor is empirical: Does the range of models considered cover the possibilities for the human cognitive system under study? It is by no means obvious that the right underlying model of the computation underlying cognitive systems should be one of the usual reference machines chosen in the mathematical study of the subject; this topic is taken up in earnest in chapter 3. For now we shall focus on some "standard" reference machine and measure.

One standard reference model used in computational complexity theory is a *Turing machine* (TM). As many readers probably already know, Turing machines are crude models of real computers. They are patterned after a "tape recorder" image of memory. In its standard incarnation we imagine a TM to be scanning one (arbitrarily) long tape that is divided into distinct cells. The TM has a single *read/write* head that scans just one cell of this tape at a time. The TM also has a finite program control. The information on the tape is written in a binary alphabet—just 1s and 0s initially, with blanks possible. Each cell holds one symbol. The basic idea of a computational step is embodied in the notion of a move or step of a TM computation. During each move, the TM (1) changes state; (2) writes a new symbol on the cell it is currently scanning (possibly a blank symbol); and (3) shifts its scanning head one cell to the right or left.[1] Its decision is made by consulting a giant (but finite) two way table cross-indexed by tape symbols and control states. That is, it looks to see what symbol (1, 0, or blank) it is currently scanning and in what state it is; this pair determines what new state it should go to and what action to take. The number of different "states of mind" of the machine is finite (unlike the states of mind of the inhabitants of Los Angeles). This has the virtue of making one dimension of the two way table finite, the one indexed by machine states. Because the other index lists different tape symbols, and because there can be only a finite number of different symbols by definition, this other dimension of the table is also finite. Thus the "control" of the machine is finite state: the next move of the machine is determined completely by a finite number of (current symbol scanned, current state number) pairs.

If the TM has just one next move (one new state and action, given some state, input pair) we say that the machine is *deterministic*, otherwise, *nondeterministic*. When a TM is deterministic, its next move mapping is a function; when it is nondeterministic, the next move mapping need only be a relation. A deterministic machine never has a choice of what to do next. Its next move and state are completely and inexorably fixed. For any given initial state and input the successive "snapshots" describing the internal state of the TM (the current cell being scanned, the symbol scanned, and the rest of the tape) will be the same, no matter how many times the computation is repeated. In contrast, a nondeterministic machine has choices: it could have any finite number of next moves, for a particular combination of current state and currently scanned input. The possible successive snapshots of a nondeterministic computation can be pictured as a branching tree with each branch corresponding to a set of possible move choices. Any one computation is represented by following a path through the tree from the root to a fringe leaf at the bottom (though a computation might not ever "bottom out" because it could keep running forever, a familiar experience to most beginning programmers).

We have left open the possibility that there might be no next state and action defined for a particular scanned cell–current state combination. In this case the machine simply halts. If the current state the machine is in at this point is one of a number of specially designated final states, we say that the machine has *accepted* the input. Otherwise, if the machine halts and its present state is not one of the final states, or if the machine never halts, we say that the machine *rejects* the input. Note that since a nondeterministic computation can take several paths we must define acceptance and rejection a bit more carefully for such a machine. We will say that a nondeterministic machine accepts an input if any one computation leads to acceptance; it rejects only if all paths never halt or never lead to final states. Given some TM, the set of all inputs defined over some alphabet that lead to acceptance is called the *language accepted* or *recognized* by the TM. For instance, we can describe informally a TM to recognize the language $0^n 1^n$ as follows. The example is from Hopcroft and Ullman 1979. We start with the TM scanning the leftmost 0. The TM replaces the leftmost 0 with an X, and then by a series of read steps scans the 1s rightward until it hits the first 0. It replaces the 0 with a Y, and then scans left until it hits the first X. It next moves right one cell, replaces a 1 with an X, and repeats. If after scanning left to find an X, it scans right one cell and finds a Y, it enters a final state from which it has no further moves.

We are now in a position to define some computational complexity measures using a TM model. These will be the number of tape cells the TM scans during its computation, the *space* the TM uses, and the number of successive primitive steps the TM makes, the *time* the TM uses. We start with some input written in coded form on the input tape and with the TM's scanning head looking at the leftmost symbol of this input. Call the nonblank length[2] of this input n. The TM then goes into operation. If the TM scans at most $S(n)$ tape cells for all inputs of length n then the TM is said to be of *space complexity* $S(n)$ for this input. The space complexity is undefined (or infinite) if the machine does not halt for some inputs of this length. The length of the input stands proxy for the complexity of the problem to solve; longer inputs mean more difficult problems.[3]

So much for space. If on any computation of length n the TM makes at most $T(n)$ moves before halting, the TM is $T(n)$ *time bounded*. If the TM does not halt, by convention it uses infinite time (as will be confirmed by practical programming experience). Because scanning one tape cell will take at least one move, the amount of time a TM takes in processing an input of length n will have to be at least as great as the amount of space it uses, perhaps more. It could loop endlessly over the same set of tape cells, another popular novice programmer's trick.

These are the two "classic" measures of computational complexity. To see how they fare in action, consider again our TM that recognizes $0^n 1^n$. What is the space complexity of this procedure? For an input of length n, the TM will eventually write down n Xs and Ys. The space complexity is just n—linear space. What about time complexity? An exact calculation is more tedious. Intuitively, the machine will have to scan a distance $n/2$ to read from the first 0 to the first 1, then $n/2$ to get back to the first X, or n moves in all. This process will be repeated n times for an accepting computation, for a total time of n^2. If the input is not in the correct form, the number of 0s does not match the number of 1s or the 0s and 1s are interspersed. In all these cases, the TM discovers this before scanning back and forth n times. The total processing time here is no more than n^2. Because this TM's time complexity is a polynomial function of the length of its input (in this case, a quadratic function), we say that this TM's time complexity is *polynomial*, or that the language $0^n 1^n$ is recognizable on a deterministic TM in polynomial (quadratic) time. Sometimes we say that the language is *polynomial time*. Of course, we could use this complexity measure as a way to classify various languages. We could collect all the languages recognizable on a deterministic TM in quadratic time or less. Other often cited language classes include the class of languages recognizable in *linear* time, or time n; the class of languages recognizable in *exponential* time (time 2^n); and the the class of languages recognizable in time n^j on a deterministic Turing machine, for some integer j. This last class, which will prove to be especially important in our discussion of complexity invariance under machine design, is called the class of polynomial time languages, denoted $\mathcal{P}$.

The reader may wonder why we have talked about complexity measures like n and n^2 but never more detailed functions like 5 or $12n^3$. The reason is simple. If we say that the complexity of a language is n^2, then that functional relationship is determined by all values of n, the length of possible inputs. But this means that the function is dominated by whatever happens when the inputs get large, since that is where "most" of the possible inputs are. For example, suppose that we arrange the possible inputs to a TM program in order of length, and that the first fifty inputs are of time complexity proportional to n^5; the remaining inputs are of time complexity n^2. Overall the time complexity of the the program is n^2 because we could store the answers to recognizing the first fifty inputs in the finite control table of the TM. In fact, we could store any finite number of answers. Finite exceptions to the functional relationship do not matter. But this means that it is only the asymptotic, infinite tail end of the input lengths that do matter, at least for the purposes of the time complexity calculation. Of course, whether this analysis is relevant for real-live cases is another matter. Some arguments that it might not matter for linguistics are given in chapter 3.

Once we have shown that the standard time complexity analysis hinges on input problem lengths "in the limit," it is a simple matter to show that constant factors do not matter. Suppose we had two different Turing machine programs to recognize a single language, one taking $5n$ steps and the other $10n$ steps. The second takes twice as long, yet as input lengths get larger and larger, in the limit the ratio $5n/10n$ approaches 1. The constant factors are "washed out" by the dominance of the functional growth itself. Thus the twice-as-slow procedure pans out the same as the faster program. Our measure here is too coarse a sieve. It is easy to show that by recoding the input alphabet we can change a procedure that has time complexity kn to one that has as close to time complexity n as we would like. We simply alter the primitive "chunks" the machine works with so that it can gobble down k tokens at a gulp instead of just one. The basic trick is simple. Where the old machine looked at one tape cell, containing, say, a 0, and moved according to some direction given by its control table indexed by (state, single symbol) pairs, the new machine will look at k cells at a time as if they formed a single new unitary symbol (101 would be different from 111, and so forth), making its move based on what the old machine would have done given that whole sequence of tape symbols.[4]

Again, whether this result is relevant for cognitive science is of some doubt; see chapter 3 again.[5] In this setting, one standard move is to talk of time complexities that are proportional to some functional form, like n^2 or 2^n—the move adopted here. Alternatively we use the standard locution of functional forms being *of order* n, n^2, and so forth.[6]

Whatever the difficulties with constants in complexity calculations, there are some standard relationships between language classes as classically defined in the formal literature and time complexity classes. We shall rehearse these here because they play a role in the sequel, especially chapters 3 and 5.

First of all what do we we mean by "classically defined" language classes? All we mean here is the familiar class of languages dubbed the *Chomsky hierarchy*. We cannot hope to provide a review of the rudiments of formal language theory here; again, see Lewis and Papadimitriou 1980 or Hopcroft and Ullman 1979. The most we can do is to repeat certain key words that are explained in those texts and hope that they trigger the proper responses (not that we actually claim to be behaviorists).

Let us ring a few bells. The Chomsky language classes are defined in terms of the structural properties of rewrite rules. Consider a general rewrite rule $\alpha \rightarrow \beta$. The narrowest class of languages in the hierarchy is defined by placing the tightest restrictions on what the rewrite rules look like. If we say that rewrite rules are either all right-linear (of the form $A \rightarrow wB$ or $A \rightarrow w$ where w is a string of terminals, possibly empty) or left-linear (the dual case with rules of the form $A \rightarrow Bw$, $A \rightarrow w$), then we obtain the class of *finite state languages*, generated by the so-called *regular grammars*. If we let the variable symbols appear on both sides of the terminal strings while still restricting α to be just one symbol, for example, NP$\rightarrow$ Determiner Noun, we get the class of *context-free languages*, "context-free" because α is rewritten "regardless of context." If we further relax what the lefthand side of a rewrite rule looks like and allow more than one symbol on the left, though keeping β at least as long as α, we get grammars that generate the *context-sensitive languages.* Unrestricted rewrite rules are what they say they are. No restrictions exist for α or β except that α is not the empty string.

That each class properly subsumes the one before it is demonstrated in introductory texts by exhibiting languages that belong to one class but not to another. For example, the language $0^n 1^n$ with n greater than 0 can be generated by some context-free grammar but by no regular grammar.

In the previous paragraph we have fallen into the standard use of the word *generate*, and we shall assume that this word also prompts the right reaction in the reader. Besides that term, we shall also distinguish carefully the *grammar*, or rule system, from language, or set of surface sentences that a grammar generates. If two grammars generate the same set of surface sentences, then the two grammars are *weakly equivalent*. Plainly there are many weakly equivalent grammars for the same language formed by simply relabeling $X \rightarrow \alpha$ to $Y \rightarrow \alpha$. Indeed, in this case something more can be said. If in addition two grammars generate the same language by means of the same tree structures (here, by a one-for-one correspondence of rule steps), then the two grammars are said to be *strongly equivalent*. There are other intermediate notions of equivalence that we will use later on but these two will be most important.

Each of the language classes so defined has an associated automaton type that recognizes exactly the languages of that class. These results are easy to prove by showing how the rewrite rules of a particular class can be used to simulate the machine, and vice-versa. The automaton type is fixed by taking as a "program control" a nondeterministic finite state automaton and then adding some kind of additional working storage. Such automata with at least one arbitrarily long tape (Turing machines) recognize exactly the languages generated by unrestricted rewrite rule systems. If the work tape is linearly bounded by the length of the input sentences, then exactly the context-sensitive languages can be recognized. Those machines with one pushdown stack (pdas) recognize precisely the context-free languages; and finite automata without any other work tapes or stacks at all of course can recognize the finite state languages. It should be a familiar story that this hierarchy of languages and machines has historically played an expository and pedagogical role in the discussion of what counts as a natural language.

Other variants of formal automata have been deployed in the

literature, mostly because of some close correspondence between the languages they recognize and a complexity class. For example, the class of auxiliary pushdown automata, where we add a push-down store to a linearly bounded tape, accept exactly the languages recognizable on a TM in exponential time. The virtue of this example is that it shows that we are not wedded to the Chomsky machine hierarchy. We are bound only by our imagination.

What is the relationship between the Chomsky language classes and time complexity classes? As it turns out, there is no clean one-to-one correspondence between them. This lack of fit is a problem for anyone who would like to argue on the basis of a time complexity result that one or another Chomsky language class is more "natural" than another; for more on this score, see chapter 3. To review the basic results here note that a finite state language (a language recognizable by a finite state automaton) can be handled completely by just the finite state control of a TM and that the machine does not need any tape moves to recognize such a language. Since we do not count the time it takes to read the input, finite state languages have complexity zero. If reading the input is counted, then finite state languages have time complexity exactly n (the input sentence length). Such languages recognizable in exactly time n are called *realtime languages*. Alternatively, we can say that a realtime language is one in which a deterministic automaton can make only a fixed number of moves m before it must read the next input token or time mn in all.[7] This constant m can be recoded so that a machine cousin of the original will take exactly time n. The intuition behind a realtime procedure is that it is "data driven": the input is fed into the machine at some fixed rate, and then vanishes forever, so that something must be done to deal with the information now rather than later. Whether this is a good model of listening to people is something for the reader to decide. Realtime procedures are also what psychologists seem to have in mind when they say that a procedure is "online." We will use the more precise term realtime.

Turning now to the other Chomsky hierarchy classes, we know that any context-free language can be recognized in time proportional to n^3 or less given a model of computation that is closer to a real computer; on a Turing machine something like time n^4 is required. Most context-free languages do not take this much time to recognize or parse. In fact, there are no constructed examples that provably take this much time. Many context-free languages take only real time or linear time for their recognition. For example, consider the language $a^n cb^n$ generated by the grammar $S \to ASB$; $S \to c$; $A \to a$; $B \to b$. This language is recognizable in real time. Context-sensitive languages take linear space for their recognition by definition and at worst exponential time. But some strictly context-sensitive languages, languages that are not context-free, are recognizable in real time; for example, the "triple counting" language $a^n b^n c^n$ is so recognizable. General rewrite languages are only guaranteed to be *recursively enumerable*; this means that a TM will recognize sentences that are in such a language, though not within any predefined time bound, and the TM might take infinite amounts of time to process sentences that are not in such a language in order to reject them. So such languages do not even have time bounded recognition procedures complete for all inputs. If the TM can accept and reject any sentence within a finite amount of time, then it is said to be *recursive*.

Plainly there is a great deal of overlap between the classical language classes and time complexity classes. As we said earlier, this alone should give one pause before drawing any conclusions about language classes based on time complexity. Yet another stumbling block is the difference between just recognizing a language and parsing it. Recognizing a language is easier. All the TM has to do is accept or reject sentences. Parsing is at least this hard. Not only does the machine have to say whether or not a sentence is in a given language, but also it must write down a representation of how that sentence was derived with respect to some fixed grammar. For example, if the productions of the grammar were numbered, we could just output an ordered list of the productions used to derive the sentence.[8] Parsing, then, is grammar relative; recognition is not. We are free to pick whatever grammar we want in order to recognize a language. Because parsing is more restrictive, one might expect it to be more difficult and it is. For example, as we have seen, all finite state languages are recognizable in real time. But are such languages always parsable in real time, given a grammar? The answer is no. Consider a language consisting of a c followed by one or more as followed by either a d or an e. Suppose we have a grammar for this language like $S \to cX$; $S \to cY$; $X \to aX$; $X \to aD$; $D \to d$; $Y \to aY$; $Y \to aE$; $E \to e$. In order to know how to parse the language with respect to this grammar, we must be able to look at the trailing d or e (because we must know whether the rule $S \to cX$ or $S \to cY$ has applied). But this cannot be done in general without relying on arbitrary lookahead or rescanning of the input. Parsing would take more than real time in this case. We can verify, however, that the strictly context-free language described in the previous paragraph is parsable in real time. We see then that being a finite state language is neither necessary nor sufficient for realtime parsability. Again, results like these immediately dash any hopes of establishing a line of deduction from efficient parsability (here, realtime parsability) to one of the Chomsky hierarchy languages; there is no reason why a language must be finite state in order to be efficiently parsable.

We have now illustrated a machine model, defined complexity measures, and given an example of complexity calculations. We have postponed the question of invariance over models. Evidently a Turing machine is quite unlike "real" computers in some ways and quite like them in others. Like all models, what matters is whether it is faithful to what we want to understand. In this case what we want to understand about computation. For instance, suppose we are currently scanning some "middle" portion of the input tape. In order to access the information written in some sequence of tape cells way off to the left, the TM must laboriously lumber one cell at a time to the left. In contrast, "real" computers are usually constructed so that this kind of access to (at least some) information is instantaneous. It is written in some central high-speed memory or at worst on a spinning magnetic disk. Then too, the number and kinds of operations seem severely straitjacketed. There is nothing like the complex numerical operations, shifting, or complementation and test juggling that one finds upon turning to any text on "machine language." The question is: Do these deficiencies matter? The answer is no if our complexity results are invariant across TMs and real computers. Better still, precisely because of the simplicity of TMs, it is easier to establish their mathematical properties. We have nothing to lose if invariance holds, and much to gain.

The TM menagerie is crowded indeed. We can envision multiple tapes, multiple read (or write) heads. We can propose that any m cells be accessible in constant time (this would be a "random access" model). We can come even closer to a normal computer: We can adopt a model like a random access machine (RAM). A RAM has a flashier instruction set than a Turing machine. In one typical version, it has a finite set of registers that can hold numbers of arbitrary size and that are instantly accessible; a set of memory location that can be accessed like the cells in a TM tape; and a program counter that keeps track of the next instruction to execute.[9] As for instructions, it can add or subtract a number from that stored in a register; load a register with a number; store the number in a register in another memory location or register; read what is in a memory cell; and jump to a specific memory address if the contents of some register are 0.

Finally we can relax our insistence that the machine make exactly one move at a time, in serial order. We can have a machine that executes any finite number of instructions at once, a parallel computer. There are a variety of formal models of parallel computation that have been advanced. No one candidate has emerged as the right model here in the way that even the Turing machine or RAM is considered to be right as a model of serial computation, but it would be well to mention some of the alternatives here, as they will play a role in chapter 2.

As the excellent survey by Cook 1980 makes clear, there are two broad classes of parallel machine models analogous to TMs on the one hand and modifiable RAMs on the other. Both classes of models are grounded on the notion of synchronous parallel computation where there is some global co-ordination of the multiple machine moves (the machine is "synchronized"). We shall not investigate the question of asynchronous parallel models (like the models of independently operating procedures that compete for common resources); but see chapter 2 for some discussion of this choice.

The "fixed" parallel models are like TMs in that their storage structure is invariant. We can write on a TM tape but cannot change its basically linear array nature. One fixed storage parallel model that we will look at is the uniform circuit model described by Borodin 1977. We imagine a function being computed by a finite arrangement of *and* and *or* gates, a circuit. The input of length n to the circuit is entered into a set of n designated input gates. We can imagine gate x_i being assigned either a 0 or a 1, according to what the input looks like in the ith position. The gates are wired up in such a way that when the input is placed on the input gates, the Boolean combination of values propagated through the network is such that the right function output value appears on certain designated output gates. We can bound the gate network so that each gate only gets inputs from just two other gates, so as to make the device physically realistic. We can also limit things so that each gate has just two wires leading from it, without changing complexity results a great deal; see Cook (1980:7). Clearly, in this scheme of things we need a different circuit to compute each differently sized input. We actually need an infinite family of circuits to handle all the possible inputs to a function. Unless we are careful about this, strange things can happen. We want each size circuit to be related to the next, in some sense. One useful but still tentative definition of "related" is to say that given the circuit we have for an input of size n we can easily build the next sized circuit. Here "easily" means in some small amount of time (as a function of n). This uniform circuit definition is one that we shall use in chapter 2.

The circuit model has two natural complexity measures: *size*, or the number of gates required to compute a function of length n and *depth*, the longest path from input to output as a function of n. Depth corresponds in an obvious way to the amount of time it will take to compute something. It is a proxy for parallel time. Size is a proxy for parallel space. There is one pitfall. These natural measures of parallel time and space do not neatly correspond to measures of serial time and space (Cook 1980). One must be cautious in extrapolating results from the serial world to the parallel one. We shall take up a concrete case in point in chapter 2.

Given this plethora of models the key question is: Does this variation matter? On some counts, yes, on others no. Not unexpectedly, it depends how fine we are willing to slice the complexity pie. The finer grained the complexity analysis, the more precisely we can separate computational models; the coarser the analysis, the more one brand of computer looks like another.

For instance, suppose we are interested in linear time complexity classes. Then the number of tapes on our Turing machine matters, because we can show that there are languages recognizable in linear time on a 2-tape Turing machine but unrecognizable in linear time on a 1-tape machine. In the worst case, such languages could take quadratic time on the 1-tape machine; see Hopcroft and Ullman (1979:292). More generally, if we look at languages recognizable in real time, then the number read-write heads matters; "k heads are better than $k - 1$"(Aanderaa 1974). But suppose we are just interested in the class of languages recognizable in polynomial time (the class $\mathcal{P}$). Then it does not matter whether we pick a RAM, a one tape TM or a multi-tape TM. The reason is that every one of these models can simulate each other using just (small) amounts of polynomial time.

That is, if we can recognize context-free languages in, say, time n^3 on a RAM, then we can build a deterministic TM that will simulate the RAM doing this, instruction by instruction, with the simulation itself taking just a small extra amount of polynomial time.[10] The class P is invariant with respect to such shifts in underlying machine model. It even seems stable if the machine model is a "constructible" parallel machine, realizable in physically imaginable hardware.[11] Because all the parallel models can simulate each other in cubic time (Cook 1980), it does not matter which parallel model we pick. Given this invariance, it is not surprising that computationalists have traditionally identified as "tractable" those languages that can be recognized in polynomial time on a deterministic Turing machine, and as "intractable" those languages that take exponential time on such a machine.[12]

The boundary line between the two is fuzzy. While languages recognizable in deterministic polynomial time are tractable and languages recognizable in exponential time are not, languages recognizable in nondeterministic polynomial time (the class NP) currently inhabit a no-man's land in the middle. In fact it is not yet provable whether there are languages recognizable in nondeterministic polynomial time that are not recognizable in deterministic polynomial time, that is, whether P is a a proper subset of NP. It is widely suspected that these two classes must be unequal. Otherwise there would be whole host of problems for which no known polynomial time algorithm currently exists that would immediately become tractable. As of this date no one knows how to prove this.[13]

To end our quick tour, we shall blend together several of the concepts sketched in this section to describe one of the methods used later on to analyze formally the complexity of one theory of grammar, lexical-functional grammar (Kaplan and Bresnan 1982). The demonstration of the computational complexity of lexical-functional grammar draws upon the standard complexity theoretic technique of *reduction.*

The idea behind the reduction technique is to take a difficult problem, in this case the problem of determining the satisfiability of Boolean formulas in *conjunctive normal form* (CNF), and to show that this problem can be quickly transformed into the problem whose complexity remains to be determined. Here the problem is to decide whether a given string is in the language generated by a given lexical-functional grammar. Before the reduction proper is reviewed, we must do some definitional groundwork. A Boolean formula in conjunctive normal form is a conjunction of disjunctions of literals, where a literal is just an atom (like X_i) or the negation of an atom ($\overline{X}_i$). A formula is satisfiable just in case there exists an assignment of "true" (Ts) and "false" (Fs) to the atoms of a formula that forces the evaluation of the entire formula to be true; otherwise, the formula is unsatisfiable. For example, the following formula is satisfiable because the assignment of $X_2 = T$, $X_3 = F$, $X_7 = F$, $X_1 = T$, and $X_4 = F$ makes the whole formula evaluate to true:

$$(X_2 \vee X_3 \vee X_7) \wedge (X_1 \vee \overline{X}_2 \vee X_4) \wedge (\overline{X}_3 \vee \overline{X}_1 \vee X_7)$$

The actual reduction we use follows a more restricted format where every term is comprised of the disjunction of exactly three literals, so-called 3-conjunctive normal form (3-CNF).[14]

How does a reduction show that the lexical-functional grammar recognition problem must be at least as hard (computationally speaking) as the original problem of Boolean satisfiability? We can use any decision procedure for lexical-functional grammar recognition as a correspondingly fast decision procedure for 3-CNF, as follows:

(1) Given an instance of a 3-CNF problem apply the transformational algorithm provided by the reduction; this algorithm is itself assumed to execute quickly in polynomial time or less. The algorithm outputs a corresponding lexical-functional grammar recognition problem, namely: (i) a lexical-functional grammar and (ii) a string to be tested for membership in the language generated by the lexical-functional grammar. The lexical-functional grammar recognition problem mimics the decision problem for 3-CNF in the sense that the yes and no answers to both satisfiability and membership problems must coincide. If there is a satisfying assignment, then the corresponding lexical-functional grammar recognition problem should give a yes answer, and conversely; similarly for unsatisfiable formulas.

(2) Solve the lexical-functional grammar recognition problem output by Step 1. If the string is in the language generated by the lexical-functional grammar, the original formula is satisfiable; if not, it is unsatisfiable.[15]

Let us see what a reduction reveals about the worst case time or space complexity required to recognize whether a string is or is not in a lexical-functional language. Suppose that the decision procedure for determining whether a string is in a lexical-functional language took only polynomial time. Because the composition of two polynomial algorithms can be readily shown to take only polynomial time (Hopcroft and Ullman 1979 chapter 12), the entire process sketched above from input of the CNF formula to the decision about its satisfiability will take only polynomial time.

However, CNF (or 3-CNF) has no known polynomial time algorithm, and indeed, it is considered exceedingly unlikely that one could exist. Therefore, it is just as unlikely that lexical-functional recognition could be done in general in polynomial time. What the reduction shows is that lexical-functional recognition is at least as hard as the problem of CNF. The latter problem is widely considered to be difficult; the former inherits the difficulty.

The theory of computational complexity has a much more compact term for problems like CNF. CNF is $\mathcal{NP}$-complete. This label is easily deciphered:

(1) CNF satisfiability is in the class $\mathcal{NP}$, as defined earlier. To see that CNF is indeed in $\mathcal{NP}$, note that one can simply guess all possible combinations of truth assignments to literals and check each guess in polynomial time.

(2) CNF is complete. All other problems in the class $\mathcal{NP}$ can be quickly reduced to some CNF formula. Roughly, Boolean formulas can be used to simulate the computations of any nondeterministic Turing machine.

The class of problems solvable in polynomial time on a deterministic Turing machine is trivially contained in the class so solved by a nondeterministic Turing machine. Therefore, the class $\mathcal{P}$ must be a subset of $\mathcal{NP}$. Because all of the several thousand $\mathcal{NP}$-complete problems now catalogued have thus far proved recalcitrant to deterministic polynomial time solution, it is widely believed that $\mathcal{P}$ must indeed be a proper subset of $\mathcal{NP}$. Further, the best possible algorithms for solving $\mathcal{NP}$-complete problems must take more than polynomial time. In general, the algorithms now known for such problems involve exponential combinatorial search in one fashion or another, simulating a nondeterministic machine that "guesses" possible answers.

To repeat the force of the reduction argument, if all lexical-functional recognition problems were solvable in polynomial time, then the ability to reduce CNF formulas to lexical-functional recognition problems would imply that all NP-complete problems were solvable in polynomial time, and that the class $\mathcal{P} = \mathcal{NP}$. This possibility seems extremely remote. Hence, our assumption of a fast, general procedure for determining whether a sentence is or is not in the language generated by an arbitrary lexical-functional grammar must be false. In the terminology of complexity theory, lexical-functional language recognition must be $\mathcal{N}P$-hard, as hard as any other $\mathcal{N}P$ problem. This means only that lexical-functional recognition is at least as hard as other $\mathcal{N}P$-complete problems. It could still be more difficult.

Modern Transformational Theory: The Government-Binding Theory

Throughout this book, we shall draw on features of the government-binding framework that are important to the theory of language use. First, we shall discuss government-binding theory on its own terms. We shall try to give non-linguistic readers a feel for the research goals of the theory and the various technical devices that are deployed to achieve these aims. We shall also discuss the similarities and differences between government-binding and earlier transformational frameworks with particular attention to the question of what psycholinguistics can expect to get from each.

Not surprisingly what follows can be only the barest sketch of the government-binding theory. Our aim is to provide enough of a mooring in modern grammatical theory so that readers do not feel overwhelmed. The theory will not be extensively justified, and many interesting consequences and theoretical problems will be ignored. Our discussion of the various subtheories of government-binding theory will be quite incomplete because some of the subtheories are not used in later chapters. For a full exposition and defense of the government-binding framework interested readers should consult Chomsky 1981 (and references therein). For a good summary of the general rationale behind the generative approach see Hornstein and Lightfoot 1981.[16] We begin with a central puzzle that has been at the heart of transformational grammar: language acquisition.

The Logical Problem of Language Acquisition

From its inception transformational grammar has wrestled with the logical problem of language acquisition. Why is this a logical problem? First, the term is used to distinguish this theory from one that seeks to chart the actual stage-by-stage course of language development.[17] Logical acquisition theory assumes that language acquisition works as if it were instantaneous. Our claim is that linguistic data appears to native speakers in an enormous variety of different orders. No matter in what order the data is presented, speakers converge on the same final state. We want our theory to do the same. Therefore, we abstract away from the order of data presentation. Other properties of the environment cannot be so easily dismissed. In fact, they heavily shape what counts as an acceptable solution for generative grammar. Properties of the linguistic environment together with the rapidity of language acquisition force us to posit innate structures as part of the theory of language learning. A fundamental feature of the generative approach has been the belief that speakers could not learn their native language on the basis of environmental evidence alone. There must be a substantive body of innate principles that shape the linguistic environment for the child, restricting the hypotheses that are made. These are evidently quite specific to language learning. Unlike many empiricist models that posit very general innate principles such as general schedules of reinforcement or a Quinean quality space, generative grammar assumes that there must be particular innate linguistic structures.

Two key features of the linguistic environment are its degeneracy and deficiency. By *degeneracy* we mean that children do not receive data tailored for language learning. Grammatically relevant information may be available only by inspection of utterances that are simply too long for the child to remember. In addition, the linguistic sample contains many incomplete and ungrammatical sentences. The evidence for an analysis may be available in the linguistic environment but not displayed perspicuously enough to be useful to the child. Besides, correction by caretakers does not facilitate language learning (Brown 1973). We conclude that children must form their hypotheses on the basis of incomplete positive evidence.[18] *Deficiency* refers to the ability of speakers to converge on knowledge that is simply not provided by the linguistic sample. Consider the following example. In the sentence below we can use a pronoun to co-refer with the object *a statement*:

(1) Ronald Reagan finally issued a statement without contradicting it.

Generalizing, we might conclude that a pronoun can co-refer with the subject as well, as (2) shows.

(2) Ronald Reagan finally issued a statement without
    contradicting himself.

We can also form questions from the first part of this sentence yielding (3) and (4).[19]

(3) Who finally issued a statement?

(4) Which statement did Ronald Reagan finally issue?

One can form complex questions from (1), replacing both objects with "gaps" denoted by e_i:

(5) Which statement$_i$ did Ronald Reagan issue e_i without contradicting e_i ?

However, unlike (2) above, the corresponding complex question where both "gaps" refer to the constituent moved from subject position is ungrammatical:

(6) *Who$_i$ e_i issued a statement without contradicting e_i?

What is the basis for the knowledge that sentences like (6) are ungrammatical? It cannot simply be that these sentences are novel because even for many persons reading this book (5) is equally novel. Novel sentences are not universally treated as ungrammatical. Did anyone ever explicitly teach you that sentences like (6) are bad? No. Nor can (6) be ruled out on semantic grounds. Semantically (6) is much the same as (2). The problem is clear. Judgments are firm and speakers even crosslinguistically tend to converge on them. Nonetheless, there seems to be no evidence in the linguistic environment that speakers can use to forge this knowledge. Therefore, speakers must come equipped with this knowledge for language learning.[20]

Attribution of tacit knowledge then is necessary to explain both the possibility and rapidity of the attainment of adult linguistic competence. Even for cases where the linguistic sample provides evidence for a piece of linguistic knowledge, this evidence may equally well support a host of alternative generalizations. The choice between competing linguistic analyses for a given construction might necessitate extensive testing.[21] In an environment of fragmentary evidence where utterances are not designed primarily for the step by step acquisition of a particular construction we would expect the sifting through a potential host of hypotheses to be both painstaking and time consuming. Nonetheless the bulk of adult linguistic knowledge is attained extraordinarily rapidly.[22] Tacit linguistic knowledge explains this startling ability. While there may be an enormous number of logical possibilities compatible with any given data sample, the child will only consider those compatible with the innate schemata given to her by Universal Grammar. Thus an enormous amount of *a priori* testing is eliminated. If a small enough number of hypotheses are compatible with the linguistic environment, then the rapidity of language learning is explained. It is therefore no surprise that since the earliest days the goal of transformational theories has been to constrain the class of possible grammars.

Unfortunately, early theories of transformational grammar were extremely powerful and generated a very large set of possible grammars. They allowed large inventories of rules, in some cases almost one rule for every grammatical construction. Rule form was also extremely complicated and arbitrary because the context in which a rule applied was exhaustively specified in the structural description of each rule. This had to be done to insure that rules would only apply in their proper domains.

As an example consider early transformational treatments of the passive construction. It is well known that the ability of the semantic object of the verb to appear preverbally is roughly correlated with its appearance in a position directly adjacent to the verb or at most a verb and preposition in the active form. The verb in question also undergoes a morphological change, in English the addition of the *en* morpheme. Thus both (7) and (8) below are ungrammatical while (9) and (10) are correct.[23]

(7) *John hit by Fred. (meaning "Fred hit John")
(8) *John was talked to Fred about.
(9)   John was hit.
(10) John was talked to.

In earlier theories this array of facts was handled by exhaustively specifying the proper context for the rule's application in the rule's structural description and structural change. The NP preposing rule applies only to sentences whose verbs have passive morphology; the only phrase that this rule preposes is adjacent to the verb. The problems with this formulation for language acquisition should be plain. How does the child know that passive meaning implies passive morphology? Given that the child overgeneralizes in other cases, why not overgeneralize NP preposing to NPs adjacent to nonpassive verbs? Here is an example of what children would have to learn. One can see immediately how complex the resulting rule is.

(11) NP Postposing structural description and change:

X	NP	V	(P)	NP	(Y)
1	2	3	(4)	5	6	$\rightarrow$

X	NP	$be+en$	V+pas	(P)	NP	(Y)	(by NP)	Z
1	$\emptyset$		3	(4)	5	6	2	7

(12) NP Preposing structural description and change:

X	$\emptyset$	$be+en$	V+pas	NP	by NP	(Y)
1	2	3	4	5	6	7	$\rightarrow$

X	NP	$be+en$	V+pas	$\emptyset$	by NP	(Y)
1	5	3	4		6	7

Another problem with older theories of transformational grammar is that the description of the terms permissible in the transformational vocabulary was almost arbitrary. For example, quantificational and Boolean conditions were allowed in structural descriptions.[24]

Finally, a rule's mode of application (whether obligatory or optional or blocked) was merely stipulated. Put in the context of language acquisition, this meant that the child would have to determine from positive evidence which of the arbitrary concatenations of constants and variables actually specified a particular rule's context. Because the conditions on a rule's form and function were not general and had to be specified rule by rule, the child would have to figure out by trial and error whether the predicates for a given rule were unary, Boolean, or quantificational and what the rule's mode of application was. In many cases it is difficult to believe that the evidence for making such decisions could be found in the evidence the child would get. Worse still, the more possibilities that have to be tested by the child, the more mysterious the rapid course of acquisition becomes.[25]

The basic strategy for dealing with this problem has been to replace the various *ad hoc* stipulations on an individual rule's form and function with universal conditions that apply to the entire class of transformational rules. If the conditions are universal, rather than learning from the data how they apply to each rule we can assume that no learning is involved at all. Instead these conditions form part of the innate endowment. As such they form general constraints on the type of hypotheses that the child can formulate about the linguistic environment. In the example cited above, we shall see that the nonapplication of NP preposing to verbs without passive morphology derives from independently motivated principles of θ theory and Case theory.[26]

Over the past fifteen years each of these problems has been eliminated. Chomsky (1965) suggested that there was no need for quantificational terms to write transformational rules.[27] He also (1977a) banned Boolean conditions from transformational rules. Buttressing this conclusion, Bresnan (1976) pointed out that Boolean conditions allow options that we do not find in the rule inventories of natural languages. This is no loss, because Bresnan also shows how to replace arbitrary Boolean terms with natural unary predicates. This move allows us to delimit correctly the class of possible rules; rules that have no natural expression in terms of unary predicates are not attested in the world's languages. Even the English auxiliary verb system, a thorny problem that was once a major motivation for Boolean conditions, has yielded to assault. Lasnik (1980) shows that one may avoid such conditions and still arrive at a good description of the distribution of auxiliary verbs in English.[28] Given this mass of evidence and argument, we shall assume a more restricted theory where rules may only refer to unary predicates with no Boolean or quantificational terms attached to them.

Besides paring down the structural descriptions of rules, linguists have reduced the types of rule actions. Chomsky (1977b) showed that many superficially dissimilar rules in fact share many important properties at a more abstract level. One can reduce much of the large rule inventory to a general rule called Move α, a rule that simply takes a complete phrase and moves it anywhere. This rule subdivides into two main parts: Move NP, subsuming the so-called passive and raising transformations of English, and Move wh, subsuming English question, relative, and comparative clause formation, topicalization and clefting.[29] Chomsky (1977a) observed that this rule could be stated without using complicated contexts. Rather, rule misapplications could be handled via a series of universal conditions on derivation outputs. This enormously simplifies what a child has to learn. There are no individual rules to acquire, and the basic Move α rule is given.

How do the constraints work? In English, certain movements of noun phrases never take place out of a tensed sentence. Nor do they occur when a subject is present in the clause. (13), (14), and (15) contrast with (16) and (17).

(13) I expect that John likes Bill.
(14) I expect John to like Bill.
(15) John was expected to like Bill.
(16) *John$_i$ was expected e_i likes Bill.
(17) *Bill$_i$ was expected John likes e_i.

One could rule out the bad outputs by exhaustively stipulating all the conditions that block the Move α rule from applying in its structural description. But then we would have to explain how the child learned this without recourse to negative evidence, without being overtly told that (16) and (17) are ungrammatical. In addition, this stipulation must be duplicated in the statement of other rules with no explanation for why the same conditions applied in these cases. Reciprocals, lexical items like *each other*, and reflexives, words like *herself*, are banned from the same environments, as shown by (18)–(22) below.

(18) The men expected John to come.
(19) The men expected each other to come.
(20) *The men expected each other would come.
(21) *The men expected Renee to kiss each other.
(22) Each of the men expected Renee to kiss the others.

Chomsky (1973) proposed separating these conditions from the actual rule system, thus allowing them to apply as a universal filtering mechanism on both noun phrase movement and reciprocal binding. These filters were dubbed the *Tensed S* and the *Specified Subject Conditions*. Generally speaking, these conditions state that elements in the following structures may not be linked to each other:

$$[\ldots X \ldots [_\alpha \ldots Y \ldots] \ldots X \ldots]$$
where α contains a subject or is tensed

These conditions are the precursors to the binding theory of Chomsky's government-binding approach (Chomsky 1981). This subsequent work attempts to clear up empirical and conceptual problems with the formulation of the two filter conditions. For example, one might ask why the restrictions "is tensed" and "contains a subject" should naturally co-occur. The binding theory proposed in Chomsky 1981 is an attempt to show that this co-occurrence is natural because the two conditions can be unified into a single, more general opacity condition. The unification uses the notions *bound, free,* and *minimal governing category.* An element is bound if it is linked to a *c-commanding* antecedent. C-command is defined in Reinhart 1976 and refers to a structural relationship between two nodes in a syntactic tree. A node α c-commands a node β if α does not dominate β, and the first branching node that dominates α dominates β. For example, in the tree below, NP_1 does c-command NP_2 because the first branching node that dominates NP_1, namely S, also dominates NP_2. NP_2, on the other hand, does not c-command NP_1 because the branching VP dominates it first.

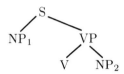

An item's minimal governing category is the least maximal category where that item has a *governor*. Assuming that the inflection of tensed clauses and verbs acts as a governor, the desired unification of the opacity conditions follows. According to binding theory:

A. An anaphor must be bound in its minimal governing category.

B. A pronominal must be free in its minimal governing category.

C. An *r-expression* (basically a name) must be free.

It follows that anaphors that are objects of any clauses and subjects or objects of tensed clauses must be bound inside their own clause, because in all cases the object of a clause will be governed by the verb. Subjects of tensed clauses are also governed by the inflection marker. But this gives the effect of both the tensed S and specified subject conditions. It allows clause external binding only for the subject position of a nontensed clause.[30]

We might also ask whether the class of rules governed by these conditions is arbitrary. The *trace* theory of movement is partially motivated by just this ability to explain why rules form a natural class and would be treated similarly by language learners. Trace theory asserts that a category leaves a phonologically null structural residue in any position from which it has been moved. Thus the structure of a passive sentence like (23) would be (24):

(23) John was hit.

(24) John$_i$ was hit e_i.

John, thematically the affected object of the verb *hit*, would have been inserted in the direct object position in deep structure. The Move α rule carries it to its surface position, leaving a trace marked e (symbolizing that the element is phonologically *empty*). NP traces semantically mimic anaphors, receiving their designation by co-reference with an overtly expressed noun phrase. Thus we may reasonably argue that they are syntactic anaphors. It follows that the opacity conditions are expected to apply to the now natural class of anaphors.[31]

Traces are not identical to lexical anaphors though. There are restrictions that apply to the antecedent-trace relation that do not apply to other antecedent-anaphor pairs. These relationships are the meat of bounding theory, covered by the *subjacency* condition.

Ross (1967) noted that movement cannot occur across certain syntactic configurations, for example, relative clauses or clauses with previous applications of question formation. Sentences (25)–(27) illustrate.

(25)   a.   I believe [$_{NP}$ the claim [$_{\overline{S}}$ that [$_S$ Fred knows Sue]]]
      b. *Who$_i$ do you believe [$_{NP}$ the claim [$_{\overline{S}}$ that Fred knows e_i]]
(26)   I wonder who$_i$ e_i saw the sailboat?
(27) *What$_i$ do you wonder who$_j$ e_j saw e_i?

Ross also observed that this condition, like the binding phenomena, held of all syntactic movement rules, both *wh* and NP movement. Again this seemed to hold crosslinguistically, with exceptions explainable by other, independently motivated, components of the grammar. Presumably this restriction should not be stated on any particular rule. Instead Ross proposed that each of the syntactic structures that were barriers to movement should be listed as part of the child's innate endowment. This explains how the child knows which environments form barriers to movement without extensive and implausible testing.

Still we are faced with the problem of naturalness. Why do these environments cluster together for the purposes of stating constraints? Subsequent work by Chomsky (1973) claims that bounding domains really share structural features. There is only one bounding condition, subjacency. The subjacency condition states that no category may be bound over more than one "bounding node," where a bounding node is defined as a category such as NP or S that defines a domain of movement (Chomsky 1973, 1977a). Formally the condition is (28):

(28) X_i cannot be bound to Y_i in the configuration:
      $Y_i \ldots$ [$_\alpha \ldots$ [$_\beta \ldots X_i \ldots$] $\ldots$] $\ldots Y_i$
      where α and β are bounding nodes.

In the previous examples movement is ruled out because too many bounding nodes must be crossed and subjacency is violated, as in (29) and (30).[32] (Crossed nodes display the violation.)

(29) What$_i$ $\cancel{}$ do you believe $\cancel{}_{NP}$ the claim [$_{\bar{S}}$ that Mary saw e_i]]]

(30) What$_i$ $\cancel{}$ do you wonder [$_{\bar{S}}$ who$_j$ [$_S$ e_j saw e_i ?]]

Surprisingly, not all binding relationships are shackled by subjacency. Pronominal and anaphoric binding occur in the same environments as the ungrammatical (25b) and (27).

(31) The men$_i$ accepted [$_{NP}$ a proposal [$_S$ to like each other$_i$]]

(32) The men wonder whether they like each other.

This raises the question of naturalness again. Why do traces of *wh* and NP movements form a natural domain for bounding? One answer is there is one movement rule subject to one bounding constraint, with NP and *wh* movement being particular instances of that rule. This is basically the proposal made in Chomsky 1977b. There is still one nagging problem. Although this account tells us why certain constructions behave alike, it still cannot say why certain unmoved categories are subject to bounding. We can say,

(33) John hit Mary, and Bill, Sue.

But we cannot cross another S:

(34) *John hit Mary, and I don't believe Bill Sue.

In chapter 5 we shall provide a solution for this remaining puzzle.

Case Theory

Chomsky and Lasnik (1977) and Rouveret and Vergnaud (1980) attacked the problem of why certain rules of grammar *must* apply by dividing complex rules into simpler counterparts subject to specific principles. Consider the following sentences:[33]

(35) [e] was hit John.

(36) John was hit.

It is clear that the Move NP rule must apply to (35). (35) is not an acceptable output nor is (37), the result of applying *it* insertion to (35).

(37) *It was hit John.

Case theory allows us to derive the obligatoriness of the rule's application for cases like these without *ad hoc* stipulation on the rule itself. Chomsky (1981), following Rouveret and Vergnaud (1980), proposed a universal principle forcing every lexical NP to receive a case in surface structure. What do we mean by case? In many languages, a noun's case assignment is morphologically marked on the surface, in English, the familiar subject—*he* object—*him* distinction. The "case" that Rouveret and Vergnaud have in mind is a representation of case at an abstract level, a Case marking principle that holds even in languages like English that have an impoverished surface case system. In other words, there is a more abstract case system in all languages that makes its presence felt, even if it is morphologically unmarked, by its interaction with rules. The principle is stated as a filter, the *case filter*. (The "*" denotes an unacceptable surface outcome):

(38) *lexical NP (unless case marked with one and only one case)

Combined with evidence from Chomsky 1981 and Rouveret and Vergnaud 1980 showing that only verbs and prepositions assign case, the case filter is sufficient to explain why adjective phrases (APs) cannot occur with NPs directly following them at surface structure.[34] We can see that APs cannot in fact have postadjectival NPs by examining sentences like (39)–(41):

(39) *The man was angry John.
(40)   The man was angry at John.
(41)   The man hit John.

Beyond this, the case filter explains why nominals with NP heads insert a semantically null prepositional *of* phrase between heads and complements:

(42) *The destruction Rome
(43)   The destruction of Rome

In both the adjectival and nominal situations a preposition must be inserted to assign a case to the NP that appears to the right of the head adjective or noun. If the preposition were not present, the NP would not receive a case and the structure would be ruled out by the case filter. An element may be assigned case in two ways. Either it is assigned case in virtue of a structural relationship (the relationship of being "governed" by an element that assigns case) or it receives case via special case assigning rules that can transmit case to a position even

when no government relationship obtains. Genitive case assignment
to the subject position of an NP like *John's book* is an instance of
the latter type of case assignment.[35] The major configurations for
structural case assignment are:

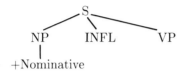

The subject NP is assigned [+nominative] case by the inflectional
element, the tense or agreement marker, and the postverbal NP is
assigned [+objective] case by the verb.

An interesting property of passive participles is their quasi-adjectival
character. For example, unlike their active counterparts they can occur
in the prenominal position usually reserved for true adjectives:[36]

(44) a. The happy lawyer
     b. The respected carpenter
     c. *The respect carpenter

These participles can occur with modifiers and affixes usually reserved
for adjectives. The *un* prefix in English is an example:

(45) a. John was *un*happy.
     b. John was *un*impressed.
     c. *People began to *un*impress John.

Rouveret and Vergnaud (1980) and Chomsky (1981) point out that
passive participles, like adjectives, would not assign case to their
complements. We would expect a sentence like (46) to be ruled out
because the complement would not receive a case from the passive
participle. The sentence would surface as a lexical NP without a case,
violating the case filter.

(46) *It was hit John.

If the NP moved to the pre-inflectional position it would get nominative case from the inflection and the case filter would be satisfied. Hence the grammatical surface form *John was hit.*[37] Obligatory movement in passive sentences results from the need to satisfy the case filter. In brief, this account gives us the effects of conditioning the rule to apply obligatorily without the need for a direct and *ad hoc* stipulation. Obligatory rule application falls out from universal conditions the child does not have to learn.

The θ Criterion and the Projection Principle

In comprehending a sentence, a given predicate clearly calls for various NPs to distribute the thematic roles that it requires. This is just the difference between *kiss* and *walk*, for example. Government-binding theory claims that this distribution must satisfy (at least) two criteria, the *θ criterion* and the *projection principle*. The θ criterion says that every NP in a sentence must receive one and only one thematic role and that each thematic role associated with a predicate must be assigned. The θ criterion explains why sentences like (47) and (48) are ungrammatical:

(47) *John kissed.

(48) *John kissed Mary Sally.

The verb *kissed* obligatorily subcategorizes a direct object that is interpreted as its patient (the affected object). In (47) there is no NP in the string to fulfill this function. In (48) there are two unconnected NPs that need thematic roles. The verb *to kiss* takes only direct objects and instrumental or locative phrases. *Sally* has no way of combining with this predicate to receive a proper thematic interpretation. We also know that active verbs (or their verb phrases) subcategorize for thematic subjects. We see this because nonthematic subjects (so-called *pleonastic elements*) are not permissible in this position.[38]

(49) a. *There pushed John.

b. *It pushed John. (pleonastic *it*)

Interestingly enough, predicates containing passive participles do not select thematic subjects. *Believe* subcategorizes for a direct object and its verb phrase for a thematic subject. Consider (50):

(50) a. *John was believed that Fred was a fool.

b. It was believed that Fred was a fool.

In (50a) *John* cannot be interpreted as the object of *believed* because the proposition *that Fred was a fool* fulfills this role. But it cannot be interpreted as the agent in the sense of "the one who believes" in this sentence. On the other hand athematic pleonastic elements like *it* or *there* can occur in this position, as in (50b).

The choice of a thematic or nonthematic subject by a predicate also explains why an NP movement rule may not apply in an active sentence. We cannot surface with a sentence like (51) by applying the Move NP rule:

(51) John$_i$ kissed e_i

Because *kissed* subcategorizes for a thematic direct object, *John* must be able to serve this function (as it is the only NP). Because *kissed* also takes a thematic subject (an agent), *John* takes on this thematic role as well. The derivation will thus violate the θ criterion. Given that the θ criterion is part of Universal Grammar, we allow the passive rule or any other subcases of NP movement to apply freely, disregarding the morphological type of verb because the derivation will only survive the θ criterion in the cases where no θ role is assigned to the subject position. Once again, the discovery of general conditions allows us to factor out *ad hoc* conditions on individual rules.[39]

There is one other hurdle that derivations must cross on the road to well-formedness, the projection principle. Chomsky states the projection principle as follows, with our expansions of his abbreviations:

Representations at each syntactic level (i.e., LF [the level of logical form], D-[eep] and S-[urface] structure) are projected from the lexicon in the sense that they observe the subcategorization properties of lexical items. (1981:29)

This means that if a verb subcategorizes for a direct object there must be an element in direct object position at every level of the derivation. As Chomsky points out, trace theory may be seen as one way of fulfilling this function. Whenever a subcategorized category is moved, it leaves a trace in the position subcategorized for by the verb. By being indexed to this position, the category is interpreted as the verb's direct object at every level of the derivation.

The motivation for the projection principle is in part slightly different from that of the other principles at which we have looked thus far. It does not directly restrict rule format or functioning. Rather, its role is to remedy a redundancy in the lexical and categorial components of the base. The lexicon states the contexts in which a verb may appear, that *hit* takes an NP object. But this information is duplicated in the expansion of the base phrase structure rules. A phrase structure rule for a VP also states that a verb like *hit* occurs with a postverbal NP (for example, the rule $VP \rightarrow V\,NP\,(PP)$).

With the projection principle we can check whether a predicate's subcategorization restrictions are satisfied at every level without the addition of phrase structure rules. Chomsky (1981) and Stowell (1981) show that the projection principle, a minimal theory of phrase structure (the $\overline{X}$ theory), and a few other natural assumptions about Case assignment suffice to eliminate the "core" phrase structure rules entirely. This is a startling result. Contrary to many other current approaches, there are no context-free base phrase structure rules in a modern transformational grammar.

The projection principle should come as no surprise to people familiar with parsing theory. The principle has been implicitly assumed in many previous parsing models as a way to detect expected noun phrase arguments or "gaps." Many researchers working with augmented transition networks (ATNs) have proposed that a parser could detect the presence of gaps by consulting a verb's lexical properties. Verb recognition entails retrieval of its full lexical entry, including its subcategorization frame. If this frame revealed that the verb was obligatorily transitive and there was no overt lexical element in the sentence to play this role, the parser could automatically insert such an element.[40]

$\overline{X}$ Syntax

Another proposal to make phrase structure acquisition easier is known as the $\overline{X}$ theory (Chomsky 1970, Jackendoff 1977). $\overline{X}$ theory eliminates the need for special rules dictating that a noun will be dominated by a noun phrase, or a verb by a verb phrase. Instead this information is placed in a universal constraint that a phrase of type "X" will be grounded on a lexical item of the same type. Further, the theory permits a natural description of cross-categorial similarities, explaining why a lexical item in verbal or nominal form will have more or less the same complement structure. This eliminates the need for category-changing transformations (see Chomsky 1970 for details). The net effect is that far fewer rules must be learned.

The central notion of $\overline{X}$ theory is that of *head*. Roughly speaking, an NP inherits the properties (singularity, plurality, and so forth) of the noun it dominates; this noun is the phrase's head. This privileged relationship does not hold for all categories dominated by a phrase. In a more complex nominal we do not say that a dominating NP would inherit properties from the prepositional phrase it dominates. $\overline{\text{X}}$ theory captures this privileged relationship by decomposing lexical categories into features, transmitted from the head of the phrase to the major category. This enforces a distinction between the head and *complement* of a phrase. Complements are divided into two types. There are true complements, which can themselves be major categories, and specifiers like determiners or prenominal adjectives that are usually considered *modifiers* in more traditional grammatical terms.

In this theory the phrase structure expansion for English would be something like this:

XP $\rightarrow$ Specifier $\overline{\text{X}}$ Complement
$\overline{\text{X}}$ $\rightarrow$ Specifier X Complement

Here *XP* stands for a generalized phrasal expansion; *X* stands for an "ordinary" lexical category—a noun, verb, preposition, or adjective.[41]

$\overline{\text{X}}$ theory is also meant to capture regularities of phrasal structure within a language. If a language places prepositional complements to the right of the prepositional head, it will also tend to place adjectival complements to the right. The claim of $\overline{\text{X}}$ theory is that the child comes equipped with a set of templates that do not mention particular categorial types. The child chooses one of the templates as relevant for whatever language it finds itself in. But since no categories are mentioned, the schema will apply across the board, for prepositional phrases as well as verb phrases. Learning the phrase expansion of one category gives the child much information about how the other categories in the language are expanded.[42]

Summary: Modern Transformational Grammar

What are the key features of modern transformational theory? First, it should be clear that the research aims of transformational grammar have not changed. The emendations to the earlier approaches are motivated in large part because they restrict the class of possible grammars. Second, the theory is highly modular. There is no one construction–one constraint correlation as in previous theories. The passive construction is a perfect illustration. The distribution of passive sentences is regulated by Case theory, θ theory, binding theory, and the projection principle. All conspire to force the existence of an apparent rule like English passive. Now because we have concentrated on explaining one example, this may make government-binding seem rather baroque. Why should so many principles be invoked to regulate one construction? This appearance is but an artifact of our effort to explain just one example at a time. To give an analogy from another scientific domain, any particular explanation of, say, the chemical bonding of hydrogen to oxygen, demands a large array of principles for its success. But this does not mean that the theory is flawed; rather, the power of the theory comes from the ability to use the same principles over and over again to explain many different examples. The same holds true for the government-binding theory. We must look at a whole range of syntactic constructions to get a feel for the theory's power to explain more examples via a single set of principles.

The government-binding theory does work this way. The case filter forces movement from uncase marked postparticipial to the case marked preverbal positions in passive constructions. But it also explains the distribution of the semantically null preposition *of.* In addition, because Case is assigned under government, we would predict that the case filter rules out other structures as well, since they would contain a lexical NP in an ungoverned and hence non-case marked position. Thus the case filter also explains why (52) and (53) contrast in acceptability.[43] There are many other examples of this kind. It would take a book in itself to describe them in sufficient detail (see Chomsky 1981). Although we may need to invoke a seemingly large array of principles for any given case, the overall grammar remains quite simple because these principles each handle a host of other cases as well.

(52)   I said [$_\overline{S}$ that Louella should get a grant.]
            [+nominative]
(53)   *I said [$_S$ Louella to get a grant.]
            [−case]

One final point. In line with its emphasis on interacting systems of constraints, the government-binding theory represents a shift away from a system of rules to a system of principles. The bulk of the explanatory burden is shouldered by universal principles that derivations must satisfy. No theoretical work is done by writing down complicated structural descriptions and changes as rules. We shall see in the next chapter that this change dramatically alters the conception of a parser that "follows" the government-binding theory. Earlier work assumed that a parser "followed" a grammatical theory if and only if it employed the same rules as that theory (though perhaps in inverse order). The explanatory shift to principles entails a new conception of what parsing comes to: A parser that satisfies these principles is a government-binding parser even if the algorithm it uses only roughly resembles a government-binding type Move α rule.

Chapter 2
Grammars and Models of Language Use

A key point of contact between experimental psycholinguistics and the theory of generative grammar has been the natural link between theories of knowledge representation and theories of knowledge processing, the grammatical basis of linguistic performance. Although the link has always seemed natural enough, it has proved difficult to forge. On the one hand, the rules and representations of generative grammar serve as a description of knowledge representation, a system independently justified by the role it plays in guaranteeing language learnability. In contrast, very little is known about the machinery actually governing sentence processing.

As a starting point, it was hoped that the theory of grammar could fill in some of the details about how this machinery worked. It is easy to see the logic of this. If we could show that the independently justified grammar plus some processing theory could predict external behavior, then we would have some support for the proposed processing model, and additional evidence for the proposed grammar. Of course, since processing evidence is not veridical, its power to evaluate grammatical theories can only be as strong as the confidence we have in it. If the processing theory and grammar predict only a partial and unnatural class of linguistic behaviors, then support for the processing theory must be correspondingly weak. Similarly, failure to predict behavioral data does not automatically foretell a grammar's doom; this is so only if we can show that there is no processing theory–grammar pair that can produce the right external behavior. There is then one big hitch. A given theory of grammar might be compatible with a variety of parsing models. Unfortunately, the more flexible the grammatical system with respect to implementation, the weaker its ability to constrain what the parser looks like.

We might also ask if the constraint could work the other way. Logically, the answer is yes. We ought to be able to recruit sentence processing results to tell us something about what the grammar should look like. If we had some independently justified parsing model, we could reject grammars that were incompatible with it. In practice though, because very little is known about the details of the syntactic parser, confidence in constraining the choice of grammatical theory via this route must be correspondingly weak. If the parsing theory has no independent motivation, we can always change it to suit the grammatical format.

Even so, some have argued that experimental results are the most important, perhaps the only, road to psychological justification of a theory of grammar. On this view, informant judgments and other evidence standardly used to justify linguistic analyses do not bear on the question of "psychological reality"

I am assuming...that use and understanding of a language can profitably be described at one level...in computational terms. If we wish to claim...that the language user actually performs these computations...then each step must take some time. Hence, a crucial test of adequacy for such a model is its ability to make correct real-time predictions.... real-time tests provide the most versatile and potentially the most finely calibrated measure of complexity; hence, they also constitute the acid test for claims of psychological reality for grammars. (Wasow 1978:83–84)

It is a rare linguist indeed who would say that only informant judgments determine the psychological adequacy of grammars. The real question is whether this evidence has been very illuminating up to the present.[1] Chomsky, for one, certainly claims that experimental results may bear on our theories about a speaker's linguistic representations:

In the real world of actual research on language, it would be fair to say, I think, that principles based on evidence derived from informant judgments have proved to be deeper and more revealing than those based on evidence derived from experiments on processing and the like, although the future may be different in this regard. If we accept—as I do—...[the] contention that the rules of grammar enter into the processing mechanisms, then evidence concerning production, recognition, recall, and language use in general can be expected (in principle) to have bearing on the investigation of rules of grammar, on what is sometimes called "grammatical competence" or "knowledge of language." (1980b:200–201)

Chomsky insists then that informant judgments are at least legitimate as evidence for a psychological theory of language.[2] He imagines a situation where a linguist has just finished providing an argument based on informant judgments for a particular mental construct. The linguist is then asked to provide real evidence (that is, evidence bearing on psychological reality) for such a construct. Chomsky points out that in this situation:

We observe what people say and do, how they react and respond, often in situations contrived so that this behavior will provide some evidence (we hope) concerning the operative mechanisms. We then try, as best we can, to devise a theory of some depth and significance with regard to these mechanisms, testing our theory by its success in providing explanations for selected phenomena. Challenged to show that the constructions postulated in that theory have "psychological reality," we can do no more than repeat the evidence and the proposed explanations that involve these constructions. Or...we can search for more conclusive evidence, always aware that in empirical inquiry we can, at best, support a theory against substantive alternatives and empirical challenge; we cannot prove it to be true. (Ibid.:191)

This "more conclusive evidence" could, of course, be reaction time data or further informant judgments. On this view a theory that could handle both informant judgments and online processing data is preferred to one that merely handles judgment facts. This point has often been misconstrued. For example, Bresnan and Kaplan (1982:xxi), citing a fragment of the last passage, conclude that Chomsky has explicitly denied the possible relevance of experimental results for linguistic theory when in fact he has explicitly affirmed it: "On Chomsky's view, then, a grammar is psychologically real if it contributes to the explanation of linguistic judgments and the other verbal behavior studied by linguists, and nothing more need be said."

In a related argument, Bresnan and Kaplan claim that Chomsky's notion of psychological reality forces us to accept a phonological derivation of *baritone* and *grieve* from the same underlying form:

This however, is a much weaker conception of psychological reality than we would like.... For example, the English words *baritone* and *grieve* derive from an Indo-European root *gwer*–'heavy'.... Now it is possible to construct a formal system of morphophonemic rules and abstract representations for these historical relations. By such rules one can formally derive English words from their Indo-European roots. Thus the labiovelar *gw* is the source of both the initial *b* in *baritone* and the initial *g* in *grieve*.... Would such a formal rule system be psychologically real? With Chomsky's conception of psychological reality, we could answer affirmatively. (Ibid.:xxi)

Is this true though? Assume that native speakers come equipped with a universal grammar that allows them to shape the phonological stimulus. Does this stimulus include information about the historical derivation of the words of their native language? Only if native speakers are equipped with a racial memory for the derivational history of their language. This is perhaps bizarre enough, but things are worse. Any person can become a native speaker of any language, via transfer at birth. But then speakers would have to be innately endowed with the derivational histories of all the world's languages, which seems absurd.

The apparent paradox dissolves if we realize that sometimes common historical derivation is reflected in the synchronic rule system of a person's native language, as a residue of things past. Latinate words have predictably different stress patterns from words of Germanic origin (Chomsky and Halle 1968). Chomsky and Halle argue that these words must be marked as belonging to two different classes. It is a mere historical accident—one that is not to be captured by generative phonology—that these classes correspond to different historical sources (that we, as outside observers, label with convenient, perhaps misleading, names). The same logic applies to the example that Bresnan and Kaplan cite. Chomsky has always claimed that informant judgments are relevant only insofar as they contribute to our understanding of how speakers learn their native language. Insofar as the notion of racial memory plays no role in this enterprise, commonality of historical source plays no role in determining an underlying representation of a phonological form (though it may appear to do so, as an historical by-product).[3]

We have two questions here. Can we use the theory of grammar to constrain the choice of possible parsers and vice-versa? How can we use the theory of grammar to constrain parsers? Logically, of course, the more evidence bearing on a theory the better. Practically speaking though, we must remember it might turn out that two systems can be made compatible in a large variety of ways. The more parsing machines that can be made compatible with a grammar and with behavioral results, the less initial constraining power that the grammar has for the theory of parsing. In particular this holds for the case where any single theory of parsing has weak or inconclusive independent justification.

Nonetheless, the simplest answer to the second question is that competence and performance are connected as directly as possible. This answer was tried first. Miller and Chomsky (1963) identified rules of the grammar with computational operations of the parser in a one-to-one fashion. This identification led to specific behavioral predictions, collapsing grammatical with processing complexity; the more transformations needed to derive a sentence by the grammar, the more computational steps needed to parse a sentence. Again, this simple first attempt was the natural one. If it had been correct, we would have learned a lot about the parsing device; namely, that it was a serial machine that actively computed the inverse of transformational rules on-the-fly. We would also have fresh confirmation, from an entirely different source, for transformational grammar.

The psychological plausibility of a transformational model of the language user would be strengthened, of course, if it could be shown that our performance on tasks requiring an appreciation of the structure of transformed sentences is some function of the nature, number, and complexity of the grammatical transformations involved. (1963:481)

Miller and Chomsky's original (1963) suggestion is really that grammars be realized more or less directly as parsing algorithms. We might take this as a methodological principle. In this case we impose the condition that the logical organization of rules and structures incorporated in a grammar be mirrored rather exactly in the organization of the parsing mechanism. We will call this *type transparency*.

The intuitive appeal of the type transparency condition is easy to understand. The demand for a direct relationship between the theoretical objects of grammar and those of parsing would seem to allow experiments that tap into actual online processing to bear equally directly on the choice of both grammars and parsers for natural language. The claim that we now know enough about the grammar-parser relationship for experimental data to bear on the choice of grammars has been expressed, for example, by Bresnan: "But the grammatical realization problem can clarify and delimit the grammatical characterization problem. We can narrow the class of possible theoretical solutions by subjecting them to experimental psychological investigation as well as to linguistic investigation" (1978:59).

But, as with all experimental paradigms, reaction time experiments do not have any *a priori* methodological status. We do not start out knowing that this paradigm will reveal deep properties about language use. We must find out that this is so.[4] Type transparency helps guarantee that the reaction time paradigm has the requisite constraining power, but we obviously need independent arguments that this principle holds. We might try to provide a methodological argument for type transparency. That is, we might claim that in principle the rules and representation of a grammar should be token-token identical to the corresponding components of a parsing algorithm. This argument seems unreasonable. As Chomsky has repeatedly noted, the grammar describes only what knowledge a speaker/hearer has of language; it does not prescribe any one particular parsing algorithm for how that knowledge is put to use. Even though one should expect a natural connection between what you know and how you put that knowledge to use, the connection may be rather indirect:

it is important to distinguish between the function and the properties of the perceptual model PM and the competence model G that it incorporates.... Although we may describe the grammar G as a system of processes and rules that apply in a certain order to relate sound and meaning, we are not entitled to take this as a description of the successive acts of a performance model. (1968:117)

Even if we cannot make the direct mapping a logical necessity, we might ask if there are other arguments favoring such an approach. Bresnan and Kaplan (1982) try to make such an argument from simplicity and uniformity:

If it is uncontroversial that stored knowledge structures underlie all forms of verbal behavior, the question arises of how these different components of linguistic knowledge are related. To reject the competence hypothesis [the Bresnan and Kaplan version of type transparency rcb/asw] is to adopt the theoretical alternative that a different body of knowledge of one's language is required for every type of verbal behavior.... it is the weakest hypothesis that one could entertain since it postulates multiple stores of linguistic knowledge that have no necessary connection. In contrast, the competence hypothesis postulates an *isomorphic* [our emphasis rcb/asw] relationship between the different knowledge components and is thus the strongest and simplest hypothesis that one could adopt. (1982:xix)

This position seems perfectly reasonable. It assumes that grammars are mentally represented and justified by their ability to describe a native speaker's acquisition of language. Beyond this, grammars do double duty in that they contribute to a theory of why speakers find sentences acceptable or ungrammatical (assuming that speakers use the mentally represented grammar to make such judgments). If we postulated another system of mental representation to handle language processing we would be advocating an odd redundancy. One system of knowledge would be for learning and another would be for parsing.

Even so, the uniformity argument does not guarantee isomorphism between the linguist's representations and those that people use for online processing. After all, the linguist does not typically ponder the issues of computational implementation that must be faced squarely by online processors, be they people or machines. Still Bresnan and Kaplan are right in the weak sense that we certainly want reasons for claiming that one system of linguistic knowledge is not sufficient to govern all types of verbal behavior. Any difference between the knowledge representation used in one domain and that used in some other should be justified. In principle, we would like to show that the modifications to the linguist's representational format are motivated functionally from below or above—from below by the language using mechanism (sentence producer or comprehension device) and from above by the peculiarities of the subtask that the machinery and grammar must perform. These conditions may force us to entertain less direct mappings between the grammar and parser. Starting from the strongest position, we could require an isomorphism between rules and operations of the grammar and the corresponding rules and operations of the parser. In its most literal interpretation this means that if a grammar derives a sentence using four transformations, then the parsing mechanism must take four operations to analyze the sentence.[5]

Plainly, far weaker conditions are still compatible with the requirement of "direct realization." For instance, we might insist that the parser merely preserve distinctions made in the grammar (allow a homomorphic mapping); then the parser would be free to make additional distinctions. But the spirit of even this weakened condition still requires that more complex derivations in the grammar map over into more complex parsing operations in an order preserving way; a derivation that takes five steps in the grammar should take, say, seven or eight steps for the parser.

We could weaken the condition on homomorphism still further, as is done in Bresnan 1978. The mapping that Bresnan has in mind is weaker than token transparency between rules of the grammar–parser pair. Rather, the distinctions between types of grammar and parser rules is preserved. Once this type–type relationship is acknowledged we can admit many positions intermediate between, on the one hand, absolute type transparency, and on the other hand, a weak form of association between grammar and parser where the grammar specifies only the extension of the function that the parser computes. We will outline some of these alternatives later in this chapter. Both the type transparency and the Chomskyan approaches take the grammar as at least specifying the function to be computed by a parsing algorithm. That is, the grammar spells out which sentences input to the parser are to be considered members of a given language and provides structural descriptions for these sentences.[6]

On either view, the speaker/hearer's knowledge of language guides the use of language. At the broader theoretical level, theories about the system of linguistic knowledge (the grammar) guide the construction of theories of parsing. Both positions constrain the theory of parsing to choose among algorithms that are capable of computing the function specified by the grammar.

Weakening the relationship between grammars and parsers still further, we might demand that partial descriptions of such levels of representation as deep structure or surface structure must be preserved either isomorphically or homomorphically by the parser while allowing computational operations mapping between these levels to vary freely. This is effectively the position that Fodor, Bever, and Garrett (1974) maintained.

Under any of these interpretations we could still say that the parser operates so as to "interpret or generate sentences of L in the manner of G," to use Chomsky's phrase (1963:399).

In the rest of this chapter we shall sort out all these proposals. We begin by examining two approaches that have made crucial use of the type transparency condition. First we consider the derivational theory of complexity (DTC), which assumes the type transparency condition. Next we take up the extended lexical theory as outlined in Bresnan 1978. Both approaches presume that transformational rules are only weakly realizable.[7] Assuming that type transparency acts as an *a priori* methodological principle, sanctioning only direct mappings between grammars and parsers, it follows that transformational grammar is undermined as a description of linguistic competence.

Bresnan's criticism of transformational grammar opens by examining the failure of the direct explanatory connection between grammar and parser proposed by Miller and Chomsky. The experiments that forced a retreat are reported in Fodor, Bever, and Garrett 1974. Bresnan observes that the failure of the DTC has convinced many psychologists that "no model of language use that incorporates a transformational grammar, or indeed any grammar, is reasonable" (1978:2).

In fact, Fodor, Bever, and Garrett (1974) argued for retaining a transformationally based knowledge representation for learning while adopting "heuristic" or nongrammatically based representations to handle parsing facts. Bresnan adopts Fodor, Bever, and Garrett's conclusions and argues that since lexical-functional grammar permits an isomorphism between grammar and parser rules it is to be preferred to a transformational grammar. We will scrutinize this position in some detail below and judge it unfounded for the following reasons:

It is not clear that the reported psycholinguistic results are in fact problematic for current transformational theories.

The Bresnan system can handle the relevant psycholinguistic results only if it is allowed a homomorphic mapping between grammar and parser. This homomorphism can in fact be duplicated by a transformationally based parser.

In short, type transparency only favors lexical-functional grammar when it is combined with a particular view of human computational capacities. We shall show that we can provide a model for the type transparent realization of a transformational grammar simply by embedding the grammar in an alternative parsing system. By an alternative parsing system we mean an alternative measure of computational complexity that can be embedded in a machine. We outline one such proposal that employs the parser of Marcus 1980. Type transparency does not guarantee that psycholinguistic results can choose between competing grammars. Both transformational grammar and extended lexical grammar can meet the demand of type transparency, while retaining compatibility with the relevant psycholinguistic evidence.

More broadly, we conclude that the evaluation of psycholinguistic experiments is perhaps more complicated than has previously been thought. The proper evaluation of competing parsing procedures only makes sense if we supply two things: (1) the procedures to be compared written in a uniform language (an algorithmic language) and (2) an underlying theory of computational complexity, that is, a machine specification (its architecture plus explicit costs for each primitive operation of the machine), and how the procedures specified in the algorithmic language "execute" on that machine. In using psycholinguistic experiments to choose between grammars it is not sufficient to present one parser (incorporating some grammar) that can perform a certain task. Rather, we must justify at least in a preliminary way both the grammar and the theory of human computational capacity underlying the parser. The computational moral is even more pointed in the particular case at hand. In order to use psycholinguistic evidence to show that one grammar is more highly valued than another we must have an independently plausible theory of computational capacity that yields the correct predictions for the experimental data most naturally when coupled with that particular theory of grammar. We will see that none of this has been shown. Current parsing evidence is neutral with respect to the choice between candidate grammars for natural languages.[8]

Arguments against transformational grammar are also flawed in their assumption that adequate grammars must meet the type transparency condition. We claim that even if a transformational grammar could not meet this condition this should not be construed as a decisive argument against the grammar. As we shall show, it is unwise to grant *a priori* methodological preference to theories that comport with type transparency.

The last section of this chapter deals more directly with the notion of type transparency as a theoretical principle. In this section we outline how a theory that does not assume type transparency may still express the relationship between a theory of knowledge of language and a theory of language use. We present a formal way of stating this relaxation of transparency via a device that has some currency in the study of parsers for programming languages, the notion of a *covering grammar*.

The Derivational Theory of Complexity

We turn first to theories assuming type transparency. The classic view of a direct relationship between theories of grammar and parsing is the derivational theory of complexity, or DTC. At the core of the DTC is a simple set of theses about human sentence processing. The first is about what representation is constructed during a parse, the second about how that representation is constructed, and the third about the complexity of the computation itself. These are the three necessary components of any complete computational model that links grammar to external behavior: a representation, an algorithm, and a complexity metric.

What representation is computed:
The so-called Standard Theory (outlined in *Aspects of the Theory of Syntax*) was taken as the optimal theory of grammar. By type transparency, this means that sentences must be analyzed by a direct processing analogue of the Standard Theory.

How that representation is computed:
The sentence parser recovers both the deep and surface structure representations of the input string of words. The surface structure is built up by consulting the phrase structure rules of the grammar and matching them against the input string. The deep structure is derived from the surface structure by applying "inverse transformations," if any; otherwise, the deep structure is just "read off" the corresponding surface structure.

The measure of computational complexity:
Every grammatical operation has a unit time cost. That is, in order to be counted as an "active" component of the computation, each grammatical operation must take a unit of time to compute. A parser containing a grammar that maps between deep and surface structure by applying inverse transformations would thus assign a unit cost to each one. Because each inverse operation counts in the final complexity tally, we see that the model is implicitly serial. Two operations take two units of time. Thus the total cost of constructing the deep and surface structures is simply the sum of the total number of rules involved in the derivation of the sentence. Note that surface behavioral complexity reflects processing time, rather than processing space as measured by memory load.

So much for the theory. What about the experimental results testing it? Under the assumptions of the DTC a passive sentence would cost one more time unit than an active sentence because there would be an extra operation, the passive transformation, involved in the mapping between deep and surface structure for passive sentences.[9]

This hypothesis was investigated experimentally, and early work (experiments by McMahon 1963, Gough 1965, and Savin and Perchonock 1965) apparently supported it. However, later investigation evidently disconfirmed the DTC. Slobin 1966 and Walker et al. 1968 dealt the final blows. All experiments found no correlation between sentence processing time and length of transformational derivation. Fodor, Bever, and Garrett (1974:369–370) concluded that "the grammar is probably not concretely realized in a perceptual model."

There are four obvious ways out of this dilemma:

Question the theory of grammar. Either transformational grammar as a whole is wrong or the individual transformations contributing to results disconfirming the DTC are wrongly formulated.

Question the behavioral results. The experiments disconfirming the DTC are irrelevant to the theory of online sentence comprehension.

Question the notion of direct realization. The direct embedding of a transformational grammar into the online sentence processor is wrong.

Question the complexity measure. The direct association between unit time costs and sequential (serial) inverse transformational operations is wrong.

Each of these four "escape hatches" has been tried; we will survey the first three before turning to a detailed discussion of the last one, the question of alternative complexity measures.

In exploring the first alternative we consider a set of experiments that suggest minor modifications of the grammar (the Standard Theory) assumed by the DTC but otherwise leave the DTC unscathed. The theory of grammar underlying the Standard Theory is maintained but independent evidence is adduced to show that details about the rule format are incorrect or that there are distinctions among rules that were ignored when the early experiments were performed.[10]

The basic problem with the grammatical theory underlying the DTC is that the only formal operations it allowed were transformations. Subsequent work has shown that this restriction yields an unnatural class of transformations. It lumps together rules that have very different grammatical properties.[11]

As a case in point, Fodor and Garrett (1967) performed an experiment contrasting sentences whose noun phrases were modified by a series of prenominal adjectives with sentences containing only bare noun phrases. They assumed a theory that derived prenominal adjectives from relative clauses by a reduction and preposing operation called *whiz* deletion.[12] Under this analysis a phrase like (1a) derives from (1b) by first deleting the *wh* and verb sequence and then preposing the adjective to prenominal position:

(1) a. The red book
    b. The book which is red

Assuming that *whiz* deletion is a transformation, constructions with prenominal adjectives should take more total time to parse than those containing basic noun phrases. Fodor and Garrett found though that prenominal modification produced no complexity effect: "The sentences with adjectives exhibited no tendency to inhibit subjects' accuracy on the paraphrase task" (Fodor, Bever, and Garrett 1974:325). Their results indicate that prenominal adjectives are not transformationally derived.

Williams (1975) independently reached the same conclusion. He provides a host of purely syntactic arguments against the *whiz* deletion analysis, offering an alternative theory where prenominal adjectives are simply generated in place. He then shows how this analysis fits with the kind of transformational grammar proposed by Chomsky 1970.[13] Assuming Williams's analysis, we may predict the complexity results of Fodor and Garrett while staying entirely within the framework of the Standard Theory.

Another purported counterexample to the DTC is reported in Watt 1970. Watt presupposes a theory advanced by many linguists in the 1960s whereby "short passives" (such as *John was hit*) are derived from "long passives" (*John was hit by Fred*) via deletion of the agentive *by* phrase. Watt (following Fodor and Garrett 1967) claims that short passives take no longer to parse than their longer counterparts, a problem for the DTC on the assumption that the deletion operation involved in generating short passives adds time complexity to the analysis of these sentences. But current linguistic theory generates short passives directly; no deletion of a *by* phrase is required.[14]

The next set of experiments seemingly impugning the direct embedding of a transformational grammar in a processing model deal with so-called particle and adverbial movements. In unpublished experiments (reported in Fodor, Bever, and Garrett 1974 and Mehler 1963) the following sentences were compared:

(2) a. John phoned up the girl.
    b. John phoned the girl up.

Bever and Mehler (Bever 1968) compared sentences like (3a) and (3b):

(3) a. Slowly the operator looked the number up.
    b. The operator slowly looked the number up.

At one time both of the (b) examples were supposedly derived transformationally from the corresponding (a) examples. (2b) was derived from (2a) by particle movement (Emonds 1976), and (3b) from (3a) by adverb preposing (Emonds 1976 and Keyser 1968). Given the assumptions of the DTC we would predict that the (b) examples would

be more complex than the (a) examples. No such complexity effects
appeared.

The problem is that these rules do not look like ordinary
transformations. In (2) and (3) above there is no reason to suppose
that the (a) sentences represent canonical thematic structures and (b)
derived thematic structures. In some cases relating a sentential adverb
back to a postverbal position would even give the wrong semantic
interpretation. There is no semantic reason to say that any of the
adverb or particle positions are canonical deep structure positions.
Neither the particle nor the adverb receives its semantic interpretation
by being related to another position. Rather, the semantics for these
elements read directly off the surface structure. Further, these rules do
not apply successive cyclically. They cannot move a constituent out of
the clause from which it originates, again unlike NP movement rules.
Contrast, for example, (4b) and (4d). (The "[e]" denotes an empty
position):

(4) a. I said that the operator quickly dialed the number.
    b. I said quickly that the operator [e] dialed the number.
    c. [e] seems [e] to have eaten the yogurt.
    d. The yogurt seems [e] to be eaten [e].

Although (4b) is grammatical, it cannot be derived from (4a) because
in (4a) the adverb modifies the verb *to dial* while in (4b) it modifies
said and has no relation at all to the lower verb. It seems reasonable to
assume then that the adverbs in these sentences simply originate in the
clauses where they are found in surface structure. Adverb movement
is only clause internal. In contrast, (4d) is derived from (4c) by the
iterated application of NP movement.

In the case of particle movement, the particle cannot even be moved
from the verb phrase from which it originated. Compare:

(5) a. I called the operator up yesterday.
    b. *I called the operator yesterday up.

(5b) is ungrammatical because *yesterday* is a sentence adverb. Its
derivation requires movement of the particle *up* out of the verb phrase
and into a slot directly under the S. This is impossible if we assume
that the domain of particle movement is strictly "local" or internal to
the verb phrase (Emonds 1976).

These properties contrast sharply with those of the so-called passive
rule and with the properties of noun phrase and *wh* movement in

general. Consider the derivation of (6a) from (6b) via step (6c):

(6) a. John was believed to have been seen by Bill.
   b. [e] believed [e] to have been seen John by Bill.
   c. [e] was believed John to have been seen by Bill.

Starting with deep structure (6b), we apply the passive rule to get (6c); the passive rule applies once more to the next higher sentence to derive (6a).

In contrast to the particle and adverb movement cases, it is clear that we must relate *John* back to its deep structure position because the proper interpretation of this sentence requires that *John* be construed as the logical object of *be seen*.

Because rules like particle movement and adverb placement have properties that are so different from passive, it has been proposed that these rules be classified as stylistic (Chomsky and Lasnik 1977 and Dresher and Hornstein 1979). They are cordoned off from the class of "core" transformations.

Under such a proposal we could still cling fast to the DTC by claiming that transformations but not stylistic rules are actually computed during sentence processing and therefore add to its complexity. Because particle movement and adverb placement do not influence semantics, we could perhaps claim that "detransforming" operations need not apply in these cases; the particles or adverbs are simply left in place, as they appear in the input string. This would accord with the DTC hypothesis that the sentence processor need only recover structure relevant to semantic interpretation.[15]

To summarize: The important point is that even the Standard Theory provides the distinctions needed to make the DTC compatible with the cited psycholinguistic complexity results.

Turning now to the actual behavioral data, the most devastating psycholinguistic evidence against the DTC comes from Slobin's experiment (1966). Slobin presented subjects with pictures of action scenes that were described by either passive or active sentences. Subjects were asked to verify whether the supplied sentences truly described the corresponding pictures. Given the DTC, pictures described with passive sentences should be associated with longer verification times. Presumably, the task forced subjects to retrieve a representation of the deep structure level, a structure presumably one unit harder to construct in the passive than in the active case.

Unfortunately for the DTC though, this expected difference showed up only in the verification of pictures described by reversible passive sentences, that is, sentences such as *John was loved by Mary*, where either argument *John* or *Mary* may be reasonably interpreted as the subject or direct object of the sentence. These sentences contrast with nonreversible passives such as *The cookies were smelled by John*. Here only the animate *John* can be interpreted as the subject of the sentence because *cookies* are incapable of smelling. Because both reversible and nonreversible passives have the same syntactic structure, any account of the complexity difference between these two sentence types cannot be syntactic. Some other component of the grammar or processing system must account for the difference; Slobin suggested a hypothesized semantic component. Unfortunately, these results disconfirm the DTC particularly when one compares reversible passive sentences against active sentences. According to the DTC both reversible and nonreversible passives should take longer to compute than their active counterparts because both involve the same number of transformations from deep to surface structure.

Following the familiar pattern of debate in the psycholinguistic arena, researchers have recently questioned the validity of Slobin's results. Forster (1976) has noted that "using other experimental techniques (the RSVP presentation, Forster and Olbrei 1973), reaction times for passives were found to be significantly *longer* than those for actives when subjects were asked to decide whether sentences were 'intelligible and grammatical'" (1976 quoted in Bresnan 1978:49). If Forster is right then the correct parsing theory for English should predict that passives are more complex than corresponding active sentences. These results confirm the DTC. Forster and Olbrei's experiments showed no reversibility effects once sentences were controlled for their semantic plausibility.

Results aside, Forster has also argued that the RSVP technique is a better probe into online sentence behavior: "The problem with this [Slobin's rcb/asw] experiment is that it used a picture verification technique.... Unfortunately, this technique appears to have little to do with on-line sentence processing" (1979:47). We agree with Forster's criticisms. Because we are interested in the conceptual issue of Slobin-type results as a barrier to transformationally based models, for purposes of discussion we are going to ignore them. The issue raised by the Slobin results will surely emerge anyway if the computational models of psycholinguistic theories are not identical to those people actually require. Even if it is false, the Slobin data can help us to prepare for this eventual day of reckoning.[16]

Fodor, Bever, and Garrett (1974) decided that the way to accommodate results like Slobin's was to revise the way that grammar and parser are related. In their model online sentence comprehension does not normally make use of a transformational component. Parsing functions previously attributed to transformations are in fact performed by "heuristic strategies" (1974:356ff.). The purpose of the heuristic strategies is to reduce or eliminate the amount of online computation involved in sentence comprehension.[17]

Instead of repairing transformational grammar piecemeal, we could do away with it entirely. This is the position taken in Bresnan 1978. The remainder of this section shows just why this position is unnecessary. First we discuss the assumption that extra computation must necessarily be associated with added time complexity in experimental tasks. This assumption also underpins Bresnan's 1978 critique of transformational grammar and guides the design of a computational model associated with her alternative theory of grammar. Next we show why this assumption need not hold. We present a model allowing simultaneous computation (relaxing DTC thesis 3 above) while directly realizing a transformational grammar in the parsing mechanism.

The Extended Lexical Theory

We have seen that Slobin's refutation of DTC led to his rejection of transformational grammar as a "realized" component of sentence processing. Bresnan 1978 has also apparently taken these results to mean that the DTC has been effectively refuted. But rather than exploring alternative computational organizations, Bresnan has opted for modifying the grammar so that it is compatible with the parsing organization.

The Bresnan 1978 approach differs from transformational grammar in essentially two ways.[18] First, Bresnan claims that no noun phrase movement transformations[19] are part of the grammar or a model of sentence processing. Rather, these transformational rules are reformulated as rules of lexical-functional interpretation. Bresnan 1978 presents one way for these rules to be embedded in a parser, as precomputed templates rather than "active" computations. This allows Bresnan to embed the modified grammar (extended lexical grammar, or ELG) in a parsing model organized along the lines of DTC assumption 3 above. She claims that the compatibility of this particular grammar-parser pair with results like Slobin's provides a strong reason for preferring the ELG theory of grammar to a transformational one.

In order to understand exactly how these claims about grammar interact with those about parsing, it will be necessary first to outline the kind of grammar that Bresnan envisions and then to sketch one way of realizing it in a parsing model.

The main difference between transformational grammar and extended lexical grammar is the method by which these theories relate the thematic argument structure of predicates to surface syntactic structure. Consider the following three sentences:

(7) John sang *the Messiah*.

(8) What did John sing?

(9) *The Messiah* was sung by John.

Here, *the Messiah* serves as the patient of the verb *sing*. Transformational grammar encodes this via a representational level of deep structure. In all three sentences *the Messiah* will be in the direct object position at this level of representation.[20] Transformations take care of mapping deep structure to surface syntactic structure.

The lexical-functional approach eliminates the deep structure level and the transformations for all the noun phrase movement cases, deriving thematic argument structure directly from the surface structure representation of a sentence.[21] This is done by "defining a set of lexical-functional structures that provide a direct mapping from the logical structure of a verb into its various syntactic contexts" (Bresnan 1978:23).

Let us provide a clarifying example. In English, positions in the phrase structure tree are associated with certain functional roles, telling us whether a noun phrase should be the subject, direct object, and so forth. Noun phrases in English receive functional interpretations as indicated: an NP directly dominated by S is a subject; an NP directly dominated by VP is an object; and an NP directly dominated by a PP is a prepositional object. Following Bresnan 1978, we abbreviate these NPs as NP_1, NP_2, and NP_P.

Returning now to sentence (7), the lexical theory enters *sing* into the lexicon like this:

(10) *sing*: NP_1 sing NP_2 (*to* NP_3)

This "template" tells us that whatever NP fills the NP_1 slot in the phrase structure tree will act as the subject, whatever NP is in the NP_2 slot will be the direct object, and so on. The functional structure template is matched with the phrase structure tree that corresponds to sentence (7). *John* is interpreted as the subject of this sentence because it is the NP dominated by S; likewise, *the Messiah* gets dubbed the functional direct object because it is the NP dominated by VP.

On the other hand, the mapping deriving the correct thematic interpretation of the passive counterpart of (7) differs from the one needed for active sentences. The grammar must encode that the position associated with the surface grammatical subject is athematic, and that the element in this position picks up the thematic role associated with the direct object position. In our running example, a rule like the following will do the trick:

Eliminate NP_1 ...
Replace NP_2 by NP_1 ...
(Bresnan 1978:21)

To encode the athematicity of the subject position Bresnan suggests that we bind a variable to this position.[22] The argument in surface structure is then no longer associated with the thematic role normally given by the NP under S position. It has been de-thematized and has no thematic role to be given. Following the rule above, this argument is associated with the thematic role of the NP_2 position. *The Messiah be+past sung by John* is interpreted as,

$(\exists x \;[\; x$ be sung *the Messiah* by John])

That is, in sentence (9) the noun phrase in the surface subject position is associated with the thematic role interpreted as the functional direct object of *sing*.[23]

How is this modified grammar embedded in a parsing model? To ensure the most direct mapping one could proceed in the following way: for the passive case we would need evidence from the input string that the "typical" interpretation is to be blocked. This trigger can be supplied by the lexical entry associated with the form *sung*. Then we would force the right noncanonical interpretation via the application of the above lexical relation. Given the phrase structure tree, we interpret sentence (9) by locating the NP directly dominated by S and removing any functional arguments associated with this position. The element in the NP_1 position is placed and thematically interpreted in the direct object position (the NP_2 position).

But the theory-grammar pair as presented so far still does not square the extended lexical grammar with psycholinguistic results like Slobin's, assuming now that the lexical redundancy rule mentioned above is an active computation performed by the parser. The interpretation of passive sentences still costs one unit of time more than their active counterparts. The difference is exactly the processing cost of the lexical redundancy rule. We are still left with a model equivalent to the DTC transformational version with respect to Slobin's timing results.

In order to make the model compatible with Slobin's results one could assume that the interpretation of passive sentences works by comparing the surface string to a functional structure template that is listed in the lexicon as part of the entry of the corresponding verb, just as in active sentences. This is the method that Bresnan 1978 suggests. The effect of the lexical redundancy rule rather than the rule itself is encoded into the form of the functional template associated with a passive verb. An example may make this clear. The functional template for the passive verb form of *sing* is:[24]

Be+sing:

$(\exists y \ [\ y \ sing \ \text{NP}_1 \ (to \ \text{NP}_3)])$

As this sentence is parsed, the same matching operation would be carried out as in the active case, but now the passive lexical form would be retrieved and the noun phrase in the structural subject position would be placed in the functional object position (as dictated by the template). The system interprets this noun phrase as the direct object. Since the same matching operation is involved in both the active and passive sentence, namely, the retrieval of lexical templates, the processing of active and passive sentences will now take the same amount of time.[25]

In this model the complexity distinction between reversible and nonreversible passives is not due to the relative complexity of retrieving the lexical templates. Rather, interpretation of noun phrase functional roles is harder in all passives. Passives cause the parser to stumble because one cannot provide a direct assignment between NPs in the phrase structure tree and argument positions in functional structure; some kind of additional manipulation is demanded. We might expect then that any extra cues indicating which NP matches with which argument position could potentially speed up comprehension. Nonreversible passives contain such cues by virtue of the verb's selectional restrictions, such as whether a verb takes an animate or inanimate subject. Such verbs permit only a single well-formed mapping between NP positions in the phrase structure tree and functional structural positions. For example, in a sentence like *the flowers were sniffed by John* once the verb *sniff* is recognized, its selectional restrictions become available to the parser. The parser has an additional cue to tell it that the NP_1 in the phrase structure tree cannot be the NP_1 of the functional structure, because only animate NPs may appear first in the functional structure associated with *smell*.[26]

Finally it should be noted that in the extended lexical grammar both actives and passives contrast with *wh* movement constructions, in that they are derived by lexical rules rather than by the transformations used to derive sentences with *wh* movements. Therefore, the recognition of actives and passives need not involve the same computations required to analyze *wh* constructions. Thus Bresnan assumes a weaker version of type transparency. There is no one-to-one grammar–parser rule correspondence. There is a type of grammatical rule–type of parsing computation correspondence. Because Bresnan 1978 treats *wh* movement and passive separately in the grammar, she justifiably assigns these two rules to different processing components. In contrast, she argues by implication that transformational grammar retains both these rules as transformations, and so must parse them by the same type of algorithm. Conclusion: the lexical theory can capture similarities between actives and passives and differences between passives and *wh* movement that transformational grammar cannot.[27] Bresnan claims that the theory of language use

should map distinct grammatical rules and units into distinct processing operations and informational units in such a way that different rule types are associated with different processing functions. If distinct grammatical rules were not distinguished in a psychological model under some realization mapping... the grammar could not be said to represent the knowledge of a language user in any psychologically interesting sense. (1978:3)

It is important to point out that the ability to distinguish two rules by their contribution to "time complexity" does not automatically follow from this argument. Rather this depends on their association to different "informational units" and a particular choice of computational organization. Given that the assumed parsing organization is so crucial to the argument against transformational grammar, it is important to investigate whether the same conclusions hold under alternative assumptions about computational organization. In the next section we shall show that by allowing a rudimentary kind of parallel computation we can bring a transformationally based parser into line with existing psycholinguistic reaction time results. In particular we claim that if the Slobin data holds up it merely suggests a processing model that allows passive morphology to act as a local cue, telling the parser that a certain computation must take place. The computation is either movement or binding, depending on whether the parser uses the Standard Theory or Extended Standard Theory. In addition, we must assume that this computation can be carried out concurrently with the recognition and attachment of the verbal element, and thus need not require any additional externally measured reaction time. If, on the other hand, Forster 1976 and Gough 1965 are correct, then we can maintain the "local cue" hypothesis within a more serially based model.

Alternative Parsing Models

In this section we shall see that by holding the transformational grammar constant and varying the other two "parameters" of the DTC, we can readily accommodate Slobin's psycholinguistic evidence. First we consider modifications to the computational organization of parsing. Our basic approach is to introduce a slight amount of nonseriality (concurrent processing) into the execution schedule of parsing rules. We show how the crucial nonconcurrent processing can be triggered in the "passive cases" upon recognition of the predicate of a passive sentence and how this triggering can be reasonably integrated into the machine architecture we have in mind.

We shall illustrate the impact of this nonserial processing by exhibiting parsing models for two transformational theories, the Standard and the newer Extended Standard Theories (Chomsky 1977a). Thus modified, both models will prove to be compatible with the DTC timing results.

A Parsing Model for the Standard Theory

For the purposes of constructing a parsing model we need to briefly review the key premises of the Standard Theory (ST). ST assumes that there is one level of linguistic representation relevant to phonetic interpretation and one to semantic interpretation. Phonetic interpretation is "read off" the surface structure of a sentence, while semantic interpretation is determined by the deep structure configuration. Even though the theory specifies that two representations must be recovered from the input string, it does not specify in what order they must be recovered. Deep structure may be "computed" after the entire surface structure tree is built, or, more to the point, it may be built in parallel with the ongoing construction of the surface structure tree. It is this last alternative that we shall adopt: surface structure and deep structure are built in tandem.

We shall use the parsing model designed by Marcus 1980. We adopt this parser to be concrete. The concurrency scheme to be sketched is compatible with any number of parsing models. The added benefit of this parser is that one can show that it is compatible with a transformational grammar. One last caveat: we are not interested in justifying all the details of the Marcus parser. Rather, we are interested in showing that by assuming different machine architectures we can radically alter what a particular grammar-parser pair predicts vis-a-vis reaction time and other measures of complexity.

The Marcus parser mimics the important properties of a transformational grammar in the following way. First of all, it is equivalent to a transformational grammar in the sense that for every surface string (sentence) it associates the same annotated surface structure (annotated by traces) that would be paired with that sentence by a transformational grammar. One might dub this a condition of "input-output" equivalence.[28] Note that this definition of equivalence leaves open the question of how it is exactly that the annotated surface structure gets computed.[29] That is, a parser could reconstruct the right underlying representations using principles entirely unrelated to the grammar and yet still be input-output equivalent to that grammar. The Marcus parser uses a transformational grammar much more directly than this; some of its "internals" are similar. It maps between levels of representation in accordance with each of the principles discussed in the first chapter. It is constructed to respect both parts of the opacity conditions and the subjacency condition; and it crucially makes reference to the lexical properties of items at every level of representation, in accordance with the projection principle.

To understand the following discussion, all one has to know is that a Marcus-style parser operates by making decisions based upon two sources of information. First, it uses the features of the parse tree node currently under construction plus the features of a noun phrase or sentence phrase (cyclic node) immediately higher in the parse tree.

This information is clearly useful in determining what the parse tree already built looks like, and hence what should be built next. Second, it uses the features of items in the input stream not yet attached to the parse tree, up to a limit, almost always, of three items (though this last constraint can be relaxed in some circumstances to a "lookahead" of five items). Together predicates defined over (1) and (2) determine the parser's next move. The evidence the parser uses is strictly local, amounting to the examination of the features of nodes and input tokens in the "immediate vicinity" of the parser's activity.[30] At any given step in a parse the Marcus parser can access the contents of five "cells" in order to decide what to do next, two for the nodes corresponding to partially or completely analyzed phrases that will become part of the parse tree and three for the lookahead. We will assume that access to each of these five cells takes only constant time. The contents of these cells may be retrieved, examined, or modified, all in constant time.

Parsing an active sentence in this model is straightforward. Words enter the input stream, three at a time under most circumstances.[31] The surface structure and deep structure trees are built in parallel, elements in the input stream being placed simultaneously in their proper positions in each one. First the parser assembles the subject noun phrase and attaches it to the S node. Next, it builds the verb phrase and attaches it to the budding parse tree. A sentence such as,

(1) The girl kissed the boy.

parses in roughly eight steps of the parser: two steps to assemble the NP, and one to attach the NP to the S; five to build the VP and one to attach the VP to the S (one for the verb, one to attach the verb to the VP, and three to build the NP and attach it to the VP). In a simple active sentence the deep structure tree is isomorphic to the surface structure tree. Let us assume that recognition of the predicate of a sentence also entails the retrieval of its subcategorization frames (see Marcus 1980 for one way that this proposal may be carried out). This is the parsing analogue of the projection principle. Experiments that tap online processing support this assumption. There are significant complexity differences between the comprehension of "anomalous" and fully well-formed sentences (Forster 1979). These two classes of sentences are often distinguished solely because the "anomalous" cases fail to meet a predicate's thematic or selectional restrictions. One way to explain these results is to assume that subcategorization frames are available for online processing.

We now turn to a mechanism for analyzing passive sentences. The approach in Bresnan 1978 uses lexical lookup to analyze both passive and active structures. The extra complexity of reversible passives follows from the extra complexity in assigning the proper functional roles to NPs in the phrase structure representations of such sentences. Nonreversible passives have complexity compensating extra cues guiding the NP–functional role mapping.

We may adapt this approach to a computational model based on transformational grammar. By using a modest amount of parallel processing whereby two parsing actions can take place simultaneously, we shall show that the analysis of passive structures takes the same amount of time as the recognition of corresponding active structures.

This model can then be modified so that finding the proper NP is more difficult for passives than actives (the resolution is by actual movement in the Standard Theory or binding in EST). In previous work (Berwick and Weinberg 1983) we explained the reversibility effects in terms of properties of the online sentence processor. Bresnan and Kaplan (1982) also explore this possibility. On further reflection this alternative should be rejected. This is because Slobin found reversibility effects in active as well as passive sentences.[32] This rules out a purely syntactic processing explanation that makes all actives faster than passives. It follows that the form of the explanation for the reversibility facts should be more explicitly along the lines Slobin suggested. That is, some sort of semantic processing adds complexity to the picture matching task. The syntactic processing of active and passive sentences matched for reversibility should be equally difficult. Let us see how this might work in detail.

In almost all cases, the ability of the Marcus parser to look at three words or constituents will allow rules to simultaneously access the subject, auxiliary verb, and verbal material of the predicate. To take a concrete example consider the following sentences:

(2) The eggplant was kissed.
(3) The boy was kissed.
(4) The girl kissed Fred.

During the parse of the first sentence, the parser's input buffer will
first be filled as follows:

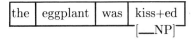

| the | eggplant | was | kiss+ed |

[__NP]

The NP frame below the verb says just that *kiss* requires an NP
object. The *ed* is the residue of prior morphological analysis that has
stripped off the affix of the verb and added the appropriate feature
information that the verb is marked *ed*. We have also taken the liberty
of filling four buffer cells for the sake of illustration. In reality *kiss*
would not enter the buffer until slightly later, after the NP has been
completely built and entered into the first buffer cell as a unit.

Here is a quick rundown of the sequence of parsing steps that would
be initiated. The parser determines the categorization of the first item
in the buffer cell. We assume with Marcus that recognition of the first
category as a noun phrase is tied to the recognition of the determiner.
The termination of the noun phrase with *the eggplant* can be deduced
by looking at the item in the second buffer cell, the verbal element
was. Because tensed verbs cannot be part of an NP, the parser knows
that the NP is complete, closes it off and prepares to attach it to its
mother node. The input buffer will now look like this:

| [the eggplant]_{NP} | was | kiss+ed |

The parser must now fix the category of the subject NP. In the Marcus
parser this is confirmed by the contiguity of a noun phrase and verb.
The verb appears within the lookahead window of the device. The
participle-verb sequence and particularly the morphological features of
the verb signal to the parser that this predicate is passive. We assume
that the passive morphology tells the parser that the preverbal noun
phrase has to be inserted in postverbal position. While the parser
attaches the NP to the sentence initial position in the surface structure
tree, it also holds this element in the buffer of the deep structure tree
that it is concurrently building. Next, just as in the active case, the
parser assembles the VP by joining auxiliary and verb nodes together.
Again, the ability to use morphology to recognize the predicate as
passive is crucial. Upon recognition of this morphology, the parser
simultaneously (1) labels the predicate +*passive* and (2) attaches the
V to the VP node under construction. The passive morphology as
encoded by the feature +*passive* signals the parser that the predicate

must have a postverbal NP at the deep structure level. Consequently, the parser moves the NP previously unattached at the deep structure level into postverbal position in the deep structure tree. The reader may verify that this parse of a passive takes exactly the same number of steps as the parse of a corresponding active sentence, precisely the Slobin result.[33]

The two key properties of the passive rule that permit us to achieve this speedup by concurrent processing are first, the passive expresses a local dependency and second, this dependency can be detected by examination of surface verb morphology. The detection of passive morphology within the buffer window allows both nonattachment of the NP to the tree and its appropriate postverbal insertion. It is crucial that the preverbal NP not be attached to the tree. Otherwise, moving it to its proper position would take an extra step. Put another way, the passive rule can be expressed in terms of the local, five cell "vocabulary" of the parser's lookahead and items in the current cyclic clause. Because access to any of the five cells within the parser's field of view takes constant time, given a strictly sequential execution the total time for the verb attachment and object relocation associated with a passive would be at most some multiple of the primitive execution time of parsing operations, say, three operations vs. one for the active form (one to attach the verb; one to locate the NP under the S; one to attach the NP under S as the object). This multiple cost is "recoded" into a unit cost by assuming the simultaneous attachment of the verb and the (pseudo) movement of the true object NP.[34]

More generally, such a result demonstrates that external, real world time measured by the experimenter need not bear any simple relationship to algorithmic time (the number of steps used by some procedure under some simple model of computation like a Turing machine). In fact, as we discuss directly below, the time observed via reaction time probes may be more closely related to parallel time, which corresponds more closely to the space that a serial Turing machine uses.

A bounded rule like passive is very different from a rule that operates over seemingly unbounded domains, such as *wh* movement. If the "speedup" analysis is accurate, then our inability to apply local recoding to a rule like *wh* movement implies that the processing of *wh* movement sentences should take ever longer amounts of time as the structural distance between the displaced *wh* clause and its underlying position grows. In fact, this complexity distinction between local and unbounded dependencies is just that suggested by the extended lexical theory of Bresnan 1978. This approach aims to eliminate as transformations precisely those rules that are expressible as local dependencies (passive, *there* insertion, so-called raising, and the like), retaining only "unbounded" rules like *wh* movement. Intriguingly, just those rules alleged to be not realistically captured by transformational grammar are amenable to local analysis, hence to concurrent speedup in certain parsing models. The nonreality of these rules can be attributed to particular assumptions about the organization of processing, rather than any failure in principle of transformational grammar.

A Parsing Model for the Extended Standard Theory

Like the Standard Theory, the Extended Standard Theory (EST) is a model incorporating both a deep and surface structure and a transformational mapping between these levels. In contrast to the Standard Theory, EST holds that both phonetic and semantic interpretations can be read off a single representation, namely, annotated surface structure or *s-structure*. In the Standard Theory, the only way to recover the thematic relations of a given noun phrase (such as *John* in *John was kissed*) is to recover the deep structure. This is because the information that *John* functions as the object of the predicate *be kissed* is only accessible at the level of deep structure. In an EST framework when a category is moved it leaves behind a structural residue, a trace, in the position from which it originated. We can use the trace to tell us what has happened.

A parser must do just the reverse of this. It must "undo" the effects of movement, determining where traces are in the input stream. This is a nontrivial task because traces have no phonetic content. It must also link displaced constituents to the traces in an appropriate way. Such a parser starts with the representation of a sentence in phonetic form (PF) and derives an annotated surface structure representation. Annotated surface structure provides an initial format for semantic interpretation, whatever that may be.

Marcus's parser builds a close variant of the EST annotated surface structure and so provides a ready-made format in which to illustrate the potential for concurrent processing. Specifically, wherever a trace is required in the parse tree, the Marcus parser creates and attaches a noun phrase node labeled *trace*, co-indexing the trace to the constituent to which it corresponds. For instance, the output representation for the passive sentence, *John was kissed by Mary* would look like,

$$[[\text{John}]_{\text{NP}} \; [[\text{was kissed}][\text{trace}]_{\text{NP}}]]$$

If a base generated active form has no movement rules applied and hence no traces, its analysis via the Marcus EST parser proceeds just as in the parsing version of the ST model; the annotated surface structure tree will look just like the surface structure tree built by the ST parser. Likewise, the EST parse of the passive sentence *John was kissed by Mary* parallels the construction of the ST surface structure tree up to the point after the passive verb morphology *was sung* is detected in the input stream and labeled as passive. Then, instead of next attaching the verb form and locating and moving the noun phrase *John* as in the ST analysis, we shall assume that the parser attaches the verb and simultaneously places a dummy element, a co-indexed trace, into the input stream:

NP-trace$_i$	by	Mary

The NP now in the input stream (the trace) functions syntactically as if it were a true lexical NP, that is, as if it were any ordinary noun phrase like *John* or *Mary*. As a result it attaches in the next step as the syntactic object of the verb. The remainder of the parse proceeds as in the ST model. The *by* phrase attaches to the annotated surface structure tree, as required. The essential point again is that the passive rule expresses a local dependency, visible even in the surface string because it is associated with specific verbal morphology within with the limited lookahead of the Marcus device.

Bresnan and Kaplan (1982) claim that this local dependency property is not enough to guarantee speedup by recoding. They suggest that the feeding relationships between transformations in a grammarian's derivation pose insurmountable problems to parallel computation:

to successfully mimic the results of the LFG-based model, however, they [Berwick and Weinberg rcb/asw] would have to demonstrate that the operations specified by *all* of the sequences of standard transformational operations—Dative, Dative–Passive, Dative–Passive, *There* insertion, etc.—can be executed in unit time. But because these operations are in true feeding relationships, in which the necessary input of one operation is created by the output of another, it is simply not possible to execute them in parallel. (1982:xxxvi)

This criticism has two major flaws. First, it assumes that the "feeding relationships" established when mapping from deep to surface structure (as in the grammarian's derivation of sentences) remain intact when one maps from surface to deep structure (as one does in parsing). Is this really so? Consider the case of passive–*there* insertion. These rules are in a feeding relationship if the structural description for *there* insertion is not met until passive has applied. Assume that the description of *there* insertion is roughly this:

(5) Structural description and change:

NP	(Aux)	be	X	→	*There*	Aux	be	NP	X
2	3	4	5		1	3	4	2	5

Given a deep structure like (6a), we see that the structural description for *there* insertion is not met until passive applies, yielding (6b).[35]

(6) a. [e] was being eaten an apple.
  b. An apple$_i$ was being eaten e_i.
  c. There was an apple being eaten.

There is a feeding relationship for generating such sentences. But in the corresponding parse we know that *there* insertion has applied because we can recognize the lexical item *there*.[36] We also know that this element must be linked to the postposed subject. Consequently, *there* insertion can be recognized independently of passive. There is no feeding relationship for the purpose of parsing.[37] Besides, all these operations are local. *There* insertion is marked by the presence of a specific lexical element. The relationship between it and the postposed element is also a local dependency; the parser can link this element directly upon its recognition of *there* in the subject position. There is no problem in parallel parsing here at all.

The feeding critique has another problem. It is grounded on an outdated *Aspects* style transformational theory, but many of the rules of that theory have long since gone the way of the dinosaur. For example, a problem is supposed to occur when passive interacts with dative movement, as in a sentence like, *Politicians are being given too many gifts.* The problem is that the structural description for dative is not met until the passive transformation is undone.[38] We agree that this might cause problems if we were to interpret dative as an active computation, because in this case we would have to wait until we undid the passive before we could undo the dative, thus adding to time complexity.[39]

The principles of transformational grammar however, or at least recent versions of transformationally based theory, point to dative as a lexical rule. The first empirical argument in a transformational framework to this effect appears in Oehrle 1975. Unlike passive, a transformational dative rule would violate most otherwise well-motivated principles governing the class of transformational rules as a whole. Dresher and Hornstein 1979 provide another set of arguments that would rule out a transformational treatment for the dative in English. Dresher and Hornstein motivate the "trace erasure principle," stating that only designated NP elements like *it* or *there* can erase traces. A dative rule would violate this principle. More recently the θ criterion and the projection principle of government-binding theory supplant the trace erasure principle and prohibit a dative rule. In short, many recent transformational treatments prohibit a dative transformation. Because passive and dative must be distinguished by the principles of a transformationally based grammar, we are free to treat dative as a lexical template while treating the passive as a different kind of computation. In the sentence above we could simultaneously insert the trace of *the politicians* and look up the dative subpart of the lexical entry triggered by the recognition of the verb *give*. In other words, recognition of dative constructions could proceed exactly as in the lexical-functional framework.[40]

Two Views of Cognitive Capacity

Let us take stock of what has been discussed so far. The DTC conjoins several hypotheses: (1) a certain type of grammar, for example, a transformational grammar; (2) a transparent relation between grammatical and processing operations, for example, grammatical rule types and operations mirrored by parsing operations; (3) a certain computational organization of parsing; and (4) a particular computational complexity measure. There are then at least four easy ways in which to modify the grammar–parser relation to accommodate the DTC results. One could alter the theory of grammar, changing either the theory itself (Bresnan's approach) or the way the grammar is embedded into the sentence processor (Fodor, Bever, and Garrett's choice). One could retain a transformational grammar and make the complexity measure give way, changing initial assumptions about available computational power. This was our approach above. Surprisingly straightforward modifications suffice to accommodate the parser to the reaction time data. We simply assume that the parser is able to perform a small finite number of grammatical operations simultaneously, rather than just one at a time. Then a rule like passive "costs" roughly the same as any other bounded rule.[41]

The concurrency model does not necessarily imply that a multi-component operation like "passive" fails to take extra computational effort.[42] The associated operations are more complex, but the difference in complexity is not measured in terms of time, but rather in terms of the extra "hardware" that is engaged to effect the computation. By expanding the computational power of the processor, increasing the amount of work we can get done per unit of externally measured time, we can make a once time intensive computation less so. In the case of passive we need not expand computational power in an unlimited way. We have assumed only that a small finite number of operations per unit time can be carried out. This is a quite modest use of the computational power of parallelism. As we shall observe below, the general use of parallel machinery admits much broader variation in the apparent time complexity of computations than this.

Stepping back a moment from the details of the fray, we can see that this approach is quite different from that of Bresnan 1978. Instead of assuming deeper computational power, Bresnan 1978 removes supposedly costly operations such as passive from "active" processing and replaces them with the retrieval of lexical forms. These "forms" reproduce the effect of rules like passive. Instead of a single lexical entry for each passivizing verb plus a single passive rule to generate or recognize corresponding passive lexical forms, Bresnan 1978 substitutes two separate lexical forms for each verb.[43] The effect of the passive rule is "precomputed" by expanding the rule over all verbs in the lexicon before any sentence is processed. Implicit in this view is the assumption that it is easier to look up a precomputed result than to compute it using some rule. Memory storage is large and retrieval is fast and nearly costless:

Finally, I assume that it is easier for us to look something up than it is to compute it. It does in fact appear that our lexical capacity—the long-term capability to remember lexical information—is very large. (1978:14)

The underlying assumption here—that memory far exceeds computational capacity—leads directly to a theory of parsing that attempts to maximize the use of memory resources relative to computation.

We now have two divergent views on human cognitive capacity in sentence processing. On the one hand, the parser-modification approach suggests that the computational power of the language faculty is possibly quite deep and that significant resources are available for parsing. On the other hand, the Bresnan 1978 proposal implies that what can be rapidly computed is quite limited and that previously stored "remembrances of words past" are required. These two views seem to be empirically indistinguishable, at least for the restricted domain of psycholinguistic results for which any comparisons are available. We might, however, uncover other empirical reasons for choosing one approach over the other. For instance, the amount of parallel computation required might exceed any reasonable upper bound on human computational capacity.

The modest parallelism invoked earlier is unlikely to be beyond the limits of what is humanly possible. First of all, the parallel computation required is indeed quite modest, because only a small, finite number of operations need be computed at the same time. Second, by looking at other cognitive domains in which rapid processing is at a premium and in which we have some hard knowledge about the associated neural "implementation" we find that the neural hardware involved actually implements parallel computational power far beyond that required for syntactic analysis.

Consider the results on early visual processing in primates, as discussed by Marr and Poggio 1977, 1979; Marr and Hildreth 1980; Grimson and Marr 1980; Ullman 1979; Richter and Ullman 1980 and many others. It is reasonable to suppose that the primate nervous system's computational solution to such problems as finding the edges of objects, detecting motion, and matching points from left and right retinal images so as to obtain a fused stereo image involves a rich, highly parallel network of nerve cells interconnected in a quite specific fashion to compute exactly those functions demanded of it according to the theoretical account.

The same may be true for motor control. Early studies emphasized the power of memory. Horn and Raibert 1978 is a representative approach. More recently it has been shown that changes in representational format may eliminate the need for memory driven motor control (Armstrong 1979 and Silver 1981).

Interestingly then, the history of scientific investigation in two domains, visual processing and motor control, has been roughly the same. In each case the very first computational accounts of how a particular human competence should be "realized" rested on looking up "precomputed" answers, remembering past visual, auditory or motor control "templates." In each case "look up the answer" theories now compete with theories assuming a richer computational power. These are often schemes that are more closely tailored to the particular domain under investigation. We would not be surprised if the investigation of syntactic processing turns out to recapitulate this history. Of course, we do not suggest that syntactic processing models must rely on deep computation. Whether memory-intensive or computationally-intensive methods are used in linguistic processing is an open question. Even so, recent results in neurophysiology call into question a blind reliance on memory. Poggio stresses that memory retrieval is quite slow compared to the computation that even a single neuron could carry out. This is particularly true given his discovery with Torre (Poggio and Torre 1980) that one neuron can encode many thousands of states:

Any consideration of a tradeoff between memory and computation time applied to the brain is unlikely to give the same result when applied to computers.... On the one hand, memory access may be a relatively slow process involving several synaptic delays, while on the other, a large number of nerve cells acting in parallel may be capable of performing a large amount of processing quite quickly. The processing power of a single neuron is still largely unknown, but is probably much greater than the traditional view maintains (see Poggio and Torre, 1980). (Poggio and Rosser 1982:5)

We should, of course, be extremely cautious about generalizing these findings across cognitive domains; the computational problems the visual system solves presumably do not include the syntactic analysis demanded by the language faculty. But we can conclude from an examination of the powerful hardware in the visual system that such computational power is available at least in principle to the language faculty.

Let us attempt then to make precise the concepts "depth of processing" and "parallelism" considered informally in the previous section. First, these notions make sense only with respect to some reference model of computation. Otherwise, we cannot properly compare the resource use of one procedure relative to another. But does the choice of reference machine really matter? Many psychologists suspect that "parallel computation" might radically alter the view of what is or is not easy to compute; it is an informal aphorism that parallelism naturally allows one to compute faster.[44] This result is a familiar story to computer scientists. By expanding the amount of hardware or space allowed, the amount of time taken to compute a given function often decreases. But we do not have in mind this standard and straightforward demonstration of the interchangeability of time and space resources. The following two results are apparently less well known. First, the standard theorems demonstrating the power of parallel speedup hold only if one posits computational circuitry that is not necessarily physically realizable.[45] Second, notwithstanding the difficulty of translating mathematical results to the real world, a similar kind of radical exchange of time for space does still hold for models assuming physically constructible parallel devices, in fact, for all such reasonable parallel models that have so far been proposed.

In a network model of "and" and "or" gates, parallelism is captured by being able to perform any finite number of gate operations ("ands" and "ors") at any single step. This formalizes the sense of "doing more than one thing at a time" mentioned in the previous section. The total time (number of steps) taken by the computation is clearly equal to the length of the longest path in the circuit from input to output; this is the depth of the circuit. Depth is one natural complexity measure of the computational work done by a circuit, one that corresponds to a measure of parallel time. We can also measure the complexity of a circuit by the amount of "hardware" (the number of gates) required to construct it. By convention this is called the size of the circuit.

These two measures, circuit depth (parallel time) and circuit size (amount of hardware), relate to the methods used to speed up parsing time at the expense of increased parallelism. Take the demonstration that the rule of passive could be incorporated into a fast parser if the amount of work allowed at any single "step" were expanded. This is just the sort of expansion captured by a circuit model. The circuit also permits the amount of hardware required to compute the answer for any particular input to vary. We are allowed to use more gates to parse a sentence ten words long than five words long. A trade-off between parallel time and hardware thus arises quite naturally in the context of the circuit model. By changing the "wiring diagram" of our machine we can effect substantial speed-up of certain computations.

This poses a specific problem for those who have already fixed upon a serial computational organization as the "right" underlying model to judge an algorithm's complexity. Suppose that the assumption of seriality is incorrect and that the function is realized using parallel circuitry. The time it will take to compute an output is mirrored by circuit depth. If this is so, a reaction time probe (a measure of external clock time) will measure circuit depth and hence parallel time. This makes sense. If an operation is underlyingly parallel, then its execution time as measured externally should be identified with internal parallel time.[46] We can now formulate the key question. What happens if we use the wrong algorithmic model for a computation? Is there any cause for alarm? Is there any distinction between serial and parallel time possibly causing problems if we confused one with the other?

We would claim that it is potentially misleading to use a serial reference machine where a parallel one would be correct. The reason is that parallel time (circuit depth) does not map over into serial time as clocked by a Turing machine in the natural way one might expect. A circuit of size $T \log T$ can simulate a Turing machine using serial time T. T is some function of n, for example, n^3, where n is the length of the input.[47]

In brief, the "time cost" of an algorithm measured using a serial computational clock need not directly reflect the amount of externally measured time necessary for a person to carry out the procedure. Rather, the cost might be more closely allied to the amount of hardware (circuit size) engaged. The relation between externally clocked time and algorithmic time is lost because external time maps in a more complicated way to the size of a circuit. A circuit can often compute the same result as the Turing machine in less external time by becoming "wider," thus keeping its size to within the required $T \log T$ bound but compressing the needed depth. The exact compression possible would depend upon the number of gates allowed at any one level of the circuit, the number of wires feeding into and out of gates and exactly what problem was being "solved" by the circuit. The externally observed time behavior of such circuits could be diverse, ranging from little apparent difference with the serial algorithm to an apparent exponential increase in speed. In short, ticks on the external, experimental clock would no longer necessarily correspond to ticks of the internal, algorithmic one. We could have unluckily picked the wrong model for timekeeping. This is the abstract counterpart of the situation discussed above. Experimentalists have generally equated externally measured, phenomenal time with serial algorithmic time, assuming that external time complexity for sentence processing must be proportional to the number of grammatical rules involved in the derivation of a sentence. The lack of fit between grammatical model time steps and external time steps has then been taken to imply a weakness in the theory of grammar, and a demand for more suitable theories. But this conclusion does not necessarily follow; the simplest remedy could be to move to an appropriate parallel clock.

We must bear in mind that these speed-up results hold under models of synchronous parallel computation, that is, models where the machine has been designed from the start to concurrently compute some function. The parser described in the preceding section is one such machine. It is meant to compute one basic output representation with some of its operations taking place simultaneously. These machines should not be confused with models of asynchronous parallelism, where several machines vie independently for a common set of computational resources. The submachines might or might not be computing the same function. A paradigmatic type of asynchronous parallelism is a time sharing system; here, many different programs run by different users all demand central resource use. As users of time sharing systems are well aware, there may be no speedup at all in some asynchronously designed systems. Indeed, it is often the case that as more programs compete for limited resources, the time it takes for each individual program to execute rises dramatically.[48] This distinction is crucial because many of the studies demonstrating people's rather limited abilities to "process in parallel" have assumed, probably rightly, an asynchronous model of parallelism. This assumption is natural because the tasks that have been tested are intermodal in nature, and thus naturally fall under the "operating system" rubric of competition for common resources (see notes 34 and 46 above and Posner and Mitchell 1967).

In contrast synchronous parallelism most naturally operates only intramodally, within some single component like a syntactic parser. The resource competition paradigm is not necessarily appropriate; results like Posner's indicating the apparent lack of parallel speed-up in people need not apply. Indeed, distinguishing between synchronous parallel and serial computation appears to be a difficult experimental task, as described in note 34. For example, as Anderson observes, the usual Sternberg additive componential paradigm "analyzes information processing into a sequence of stages, specifies which factors affect the time for each stage, specifies the time parameters for each stage, but does not analyze in computational detail why each stage takes as long

as it does or why it is affected by factors in the way that it is"
(Anderson 1979:404–405). This means that the "inside" of any stage is
opaque to further computational decomposition; one is free to choose a
serial or parallel mechanism to "realize" the computational machinery
of any stage, subject only to constraints of externally observable time
behavior. But as we have just seen this means that the time observed
via the Sternberg analysis for individual stages might actually be
parallel circuit time, not Turing machine serial time, and parallel
circuit time maps over into Turing machine space. If true, models
based on serial time must be judged in terms of the space efficiency,
not their time efficiency.

Let us sketch more carefully just how, even under the Sternberg
assumptions of linear stage decomposition, parallel computation might
make the interpretation of competing processing models more difficult.
Suppose that the response time for some isolated stage varies as the
square of the input problem size, n^2. Thus phenomenally observed time
is quadratic. Suppose further that there are two processing models
proposed to account for the computation of this stage and that the
complexity of both models has been evaluated with respect to a serial
reference machine. Model A uses quadratic time and linear space,
model B uses cubic time and quadratic space. With respect to an
assumption of seriality, model A comports with the psycholinguistic
evidence, model B is too slow. But if a parallel circuit reference base
is adopted, then B can run in parallel quadratic time n^2 (its old space
requirement); model A, in parallel linear time. Model B is now closer
to the psychological evidence, model A is now perhaps too fast.[49]

The parallel circuit model urges caution when we claim that one
procedure is "better" than another in a cognitive domain. Claims
about cognitive capacity and the trade-off between time and space
resources depend upon both a precise specification of the algorithms
to be compared and an underlying model of computation to be
used as a reference base for comparisons. A judgment of algorithmic
superiority may be empty without confidence in the fidelity of the
reference model. We cannot simply stipulate an underlying model
of computation on which to base our predictions of the amount
of externally measured time a procedure takes without substantial
support for that model. Otherwise we may be favoring certain kinds of
procedures capriciously at the expense of others. Even though it may
seem intuitively plausible that it is easier to "look things up" than

to compute them, it is not a logically necessary solution; in fact, the evidence from the domain of early visual processing points in quite the opposite direction. This makes it clear that cognitive science is, in the end, an empirical, biological science. While we may speculate about what is or is not the "right" computational organization of the brain (based on whatever psychological, engineering or computational biases we may have), ultimately there is a fact of the matter rendering such speculation moot. If the brain uses parallel computational power to process sentences rather than memory lookup, then that is what it uses; no stipulation can change this fact. If our aim is to discover what computational organization the brain does have, then stipulation again seems unwise. Given our current lack of understanding it would seem best to keep all (so far indistinguishable) computational organizations available, lest we rule out by fiat the "right" theory of processing.

There is one further point to discuss before concluding our comparison of extended lexical grammar and the Extended Standard Theory. In the preceding discussion we have assumed along with Bresnan that the transformations postulated by EST should be thought of as "active," time-consuming computations. We then provided a machine architecture that would make an EST based sentence processor compatible with certain psycholinguistic results. However, the necessity of this assumption is unclear unless there is also insistence upon some strong version of transparency and we state the Move NP rule and its parsing correlate in exactly the same form. If transparency is relaxed, it is possible to embed an ST or EST based parser in a serial computational model. We could do this by "precomputing" the effects of the transformational component and storing the results in the lexicon. Note that this in no way disconfirms transformational grammar either as a grammar or as a central component of a parsing model; it says merely that the way in which a grammar may be embedded as part of a model of language use is less than straightforward.

In order to understand why this is so we must be sure to distinguish the claims that a grammar makes about the system of knowledge incorporated in the language faculty from the implications of those claims for a theory of parsing. Let us make this point clear with a concrete example. Assume that psycholinguistic results show that passives and actives take less time to parse than *wh* movement constructions. In an extended lexical grammar a context-free base component derives simple active sentences, lexical rules derive passives, and structural movement rules or their interpretive counterparts derive *wh* questions. Lexical rules and movement rules are quite distinct. "Functional" criteria govern lexical rules while structural principles govern movement. This distinction in the grammar—plus transparency—warrants a corresponding distinction between these two sorts of rules in the parser.

In contrast a transformational grammar treats both passive (NP movement in current theories) and *wh* movement as parts of the same component of the grammar, as subcases of a more general Move α rule. Consequently, certain critics of transformational grammar assume that we cannot draw any formal distinctions between NP and *wh* movement. Given a strong version of type transparency we should not be able to distinguish between these two sorts of rules in the parser either. We cannot have one parsing procedure for NP movement and another quite distinct computational routine for *wh* movement. The conclusion is that we cannot embed a transformational grammar in a parsing model of the sort Bresnan envisages.

The way out of this difficulty is to note that transformational grammar has long recognized that there are important formal differences between NP and *wh* movement. For example, Emonds 1970 argues that NP movement rules are structure preserving,[50] while *wh* movement rules are not.[51] Even in the most recent theories where NP and *wh* movements are taken to be special cases of a more general rule the theory posits different relations between a moved element and its trace. For example, the trace of NP movement cannot be case marked, while the trace of a *wh* movement must be in a case marked position. There are then criteria to distinguish NP movement from *wh* movement in the grammar. We are licensed to precompute the effects of NP movement and store them in the lexicon, while continuing to "realize" *wh* movement as an active computation. This is so even in a transformationally based parser. Given the assumptions of transformational grammar though, one should note that the precomputed lexical templates associated with NP movement would necessarily be governed by purely structural principles, unlike the templates of extended lexical grammar.[52]

Let us summarize. First of all, there seems to be no reason to adopt the particular machine architecture envisioned in Bresnan 1978. The psycholinguistic evidence does not force this choice. Second, there is no inherent link between a lexically oriented grammar and a precomputed memory retrieval scheme for the processing of active and passive sentences. Transformational grammar also provides the necessary principles to distinguish among rule types so as to permit some rules to be handled by memory retrieval and others by active computation, all within a machine architecture like that assumed in the DTC or in Bresnan 1978.

Type Transparency and the Theory of Grammar

Our story so far can be put as follows: Miller and Chomsky's assumption of a direct grammar-parser relationship seems to have foundered on confrontation with the DTC experimental results. The token-token identity between parsing and grammar rules must give way. What replaces it is a weaker type–type correspondence via the lexical-functional or revised Marcus parser approach. But have we lost anything by giving up this strict version of type transparency? We can assess any potential loss from either a logical or an empirical perspective:

(1) Logical: Is type transparency the most preferred relationship between grammar and parser?

(2) Empirical: Given what we know, is strict type transparency likely to constrain the choice of parsers or grammars?

Consider the logical perspective first. We would prefer that grammars be type transparently related to their corresponding parsers. Why? Simply because we could then use facts about the grammar to constrain directly what the parser looks like. Unfortunately this correspondence is not logically necessary.

If we insisted on strict type transparency we should reject the Bresnan system. Bresnan argues quite reasonably however that she can provide independent motivation for the rules of her system. This plus the understanding that a uniform representation for grammar and parsing must be grammatically based forces a weakening of the transparency thesis. Unfortunately even Bresnan's minimal weakening precludes the use of reaction time data to choose between her system and transformational grammar.

In any case, this discussion is premature because we know so little about the actual machinery engaged in human sentence parsing. This shortcoming greatly weakens the constraining power of type transparency. Even in the examples cited we can always change the underlying computational architecture so that otherwise well justified theories may be transparently embedded in it. As things stand then, there is a continuum of more to less direct parsing "realizations" of grammars as parsers. There is not just an "all or none" choice between a grammar embedded directly as a computational model (the DTC model) and a total decoupling between grammatical rules and computational rules, with the structural descriptions of the grammar computed by some totally unrelated "heuristic strategies," the Fodor, Bever, and Garrett conclusion.

We might ask though just why one needs to specify a level of purely grammatical characterization at all. Why not simply dispense with grammar and just look at parsing algorithms directly, incorporating notions of computation from the start? Why should theorists interested in language use be concerned at all with a level of grammatical description? Indeed, some have suggested abandoning grammar as the proper subject matter for psycholinguistic investigation: "The proper task for the psycholinguist is not, at the moment, to determine the relationships between linguistic theory and psychological process, but to try to acquire the kind of psychological processing data which will allow the construction of a genuinely psychological theory of sentence recognition" (Tyler 1980:58).

The problems with jettisoning grammar altogether should be obvious. First of all we can use competence theory to constrain parsing theory. The choice of one parsing algorithm over another depends on a great many factors, including what structural descriptions the parser is supposed to compute and what computational organization is presumed to carry out the computation. As we have tried to make clear, very little is known about what computational organization is actually used for human language processing. We cannot even specify its basic structure with any degree of certainty. Though we have much firmer evidence about the correct characterization of linguistic knowledge, even that characterization is presumably far from the millenial theory of grammar. Consequently, we must build parsing theory on a doubly incomplete knowledge about the language faculty and human computational machinery.

Even if the grammar does not specify the exact computation or representation employed by the parser, it delimits a class of possible operations. Take the Marcus parser again. The Marcus parser's analogue of the "passive transformation" amounts to dropping a trace after a verb with passive morphology. The government-binding theory derives the obligatoriness of this rule by the conjunction of the projection principle, θ theory, and Case theory. The projection principle ensures the parser will couple transitive verbs with postverbal NPs. θ theory links the postverbal NP to the phonologically realized NP in the subject position. Case theory insists that a postverbal NP of a passive participle will not normally be phonetically realized except where an independent nonverbal case assigner occurs in the right structural environments. The Marcus parser does not mention any of these subtheories explicitly. Nonetheless we claim that it realizes a transformational theory in a way that the heuristic strategies of Fodor, Bever and Garrett do not. The Marcus parser precomputes the effects of these principles. The ultimate consequence of the three subtheories forces a trace linked to the subject position in certain environments. Because certain sequences of deductions always apply we can precompute their effects by automatically dropping a trace upon recognition of a verb with passive morphology. This is the key insight behind the Marcus system.[53]

We claim that this system is still a "realization" of a transformational system. Only by reference to a transformational theory do we provide a principled answer to the question of why the machine performs the trace dropping automatically in such an environment. The heuristic strategy approach does not measure up. Rather, it matches passive structures directly against the following template:

Logical Object   Verb+en (Preposition Actor)

The template would work if argument structures are linked directly to surface categories. This is true in lexical-functional grammar. But it would also work if argument structures are linked to deep structure positions and then interpreted, as in transformational grammar. So matching does not crucially depend on the assumptions of either of the two theories although it can be made compatible with either. It is this sense in which the heuristic strategy approach does not depend on the government-binding theory, and is not explained by it.

To summarize, the Marcus parser represents a fairly direct embedding of a transformational grammar in a model of language use. Logically speaking, there are other possibilities. The parser could use a very different set of representations than the grammar, yet still "realize" that grammar. In the next section we outline a general mathematical means of characterizing this kind of grammar-parser relationship, the theory of grammatical covering.

Grammatical Covering and Type Transparency

The notion of grammatical cover appeared informally for several years prior to formalization by Reynolds 1968 and Gray and Harrison 1969. The idea that covering grammars could have value in developing parsing models for natural languages is not new. In fact, Kuno (1966) suggests precisely this. Intuitively, one grammar is said to *cover* another if the first grammar can be used to easily recover all the parses that the second grammar assigns to input sentences. This being so, the first grammar can be used instead of the second grammar itself to parse sentences of the language generated by the second grammar. More importantly, the cover relation provides a rich stock of cases where two grammars generate trees that do not necessarily look very much alike. Yet one grammar can serve as the "true" competence grammar for a language because it generates the proper structural descriptions while the other can be used for efficient parsing because of certain special structural characteristics of the trees it generates. In short, this approach allows us to hold the structural descriptions of a grammar fixed and then consider variations in parsing methods. The theory of grammar will limit the class of possible parsers to just those that cover the original competence grammar. This is possibly a strong limitation, hence of potential interest to parsing theory.

Such cases provide real examples of the existence of nontransparent ways to incorporate grammars into models of language use. Having settled the question about the existence of such grammar-parser pairs, the next question concerns the potential advantage of explicitly separating out the levels of grammar and parser in this manner. In the remainder of this section we shall advance some reasons as to why separation is advantageous. In brief, explicit decomposition into grammar, parser, and implementation permits a modular attack on the explanation of a complex information processing system, the language faculty. In addition, there are explanations of inherent psychological interest, such as accounts of language acquisition, that make crucial reference to a separate level of grammatical representation.

Returning now to the notion of grammatical cover, it is easy to show that there are well known but degenerate examples of pairs of grammars covering each other. Consider a grammar strongly equivalent to another grammar. By the usual definition of strong equivalence this means that the first grammar generates exactly the same set of structural descriptions as the second, and so covers the second grammar.[54]

If this were the only example of grammatical covering, then the cover relation would collapse to the usual notion of strong equivalence. But it is also true that one grammar can cover another under far less stringent conditions of similarity. Informally, one grammar G_1 covers another grammar G_2 if (1) both generate the same language $L(G_1) = L(G_2)$, that is, the grammars are weakly equivalent; and (2) we can find the parses or structural descriptions that G_2 assigns to sentences by parsing the sentences using G_1 and then applying a "simple" or easily computed mapping to the resulting output. We shall be more precise shortly about what is meant by "simple." Note that these two grammars need not be strongly equivalent, and yet the first can still parse sentences generated by the second; for the purposes of parsing, such grammars are equivalent.[55]

Given some "correct" grammar for a language that is, a grammar generating the right structural descriptions, why would we want to parse sentences using a different but covering grammar rather than the correct grammar itself? The reason is that the covering grammar may be more "suitable" for parsing along any one of a number of dimensions (efficiency of processing in terms of time or space use, perspicuity, compatibility with fixed hardware, and so forth). On this view the "true" grammar provides the right structural descriptions for rules of semantic interpretation while the covering grammar provides the right format for algorithmic instantiation. These two grammars might be the same, in which case we obtain strict transparency, a one-to-one grammar-parser relation. The cover mapping takes trees generated by the covering grammar into trees generated by the "correct" grammar. Thus, if one grammar covers another, then whatever the rules of semantic interpretation either grammar can be used to pair exactly the same input strings and meanings.

What is meant by a simple mapping in the definition of grammatical cover? The mapping from parse trees to parse trees must be tightly restricted, or else any grammar could cover any other weakly equivalent grammar. The usual definition of "simple" drawn from the formal literature is that of string homomorphism (Aho and Ullman 1972:275). That is, if the parse of a sentence with respect to a grammar G_1 is a string of numbers corresponding to the rules that were applied to generate the sentence under some arbitrary numbering of the rules of the grammar and some canonical derivation sequence, then the translation mapping that carries this string of numbers to a new string corresponding to another parse must be a homomorphism under concatenation. Note that the homomorphic recovery can proceed online, incrementally and left to right as the parse proceeds, and that if the mapping is fixed in advance the computation can be done quite rapidly.[56] What this means is that the desired parse tree can be recovered with little computational loss.[57] The covering grammar could look very different from the original grammar, however; the notes explore this matter in more detail.

Covering grammars provide an abundant source of examples illustrating that the grammar used by the parser or sentence processor need not directly generate structural descriptions isomorphic to those specified by the grammar of the competence theory. Indeed, the sets of structural descriptions directly constructed by the parser and generated by the grammar can look quite different, and yet the parser can still faithfully mirror the competence grammar by incorporating a cover homomorphism that recovers the proper structural descriptions as required. As far as parsing is concerned, both the theory and practice of parser design have made considerable use of a nontransparent relation between grammar and parser, that of grammatical cover.

But why should the notion of covering grammar play a role at all? That is, given that the mapping between grammar and parser may be quite abstract, why should we connect them at all? Why not just build a possibly nonlinguistically based parser? The answer is that by keeping the levels of grammar and algorithmic realization distinct, it is easier to determine just what is contributing to discrepancies between theory and surface facts. For instance, if levels are kept distinct, then one is able to hold the grammar constant and vary machine architectures to explore the possibility of a good fit between psycholinguistic evidence and model. Suppose these results came to naught. We can then try to covary machine architecture and covering mappings, still seeking model and data compatibility. If this fails, one could then try different grammars. In short, modularity of explanation permits a corresponding modularity of scientific investigation. For a complex information processing system like the language faculty, this may be the investigative method of choice. This has been the research strategy adopted by D. Marr and others in their study of early visual processing, a strategy that has paid off with impressive results:

In a system that solves an information processing problem, we may distinguish four important levels of description.... At the lowest, there is basic component and circuit analysis—how do transistors (or neurons), diodes (or synapses) work? The second level is the study of particular mechanisms: adders, multipliers, and memories, these being assemblies made from basic components. The third level is that of the algorithm, the scheme for a computation; and the top level contains the theory of the computation.... [T]ake the case of Fourier analysis. Here the computational theory of the Fourier transform—the decomposition of an arbitrary mathematical curve into a sum of sine waves of differing frequencies—is well understood, and is expressed independently of the particular way in which it might be computed. One level down, there are several algorithms for computing a Fourier transform, among them the so-called Fast Fourier Transform (FFT), which comprises a sequence of mathematical operations, and the so-called spatial algorithm, a single, global operation that is based on the mechanisms of laser optics. All such algorithms produce the same result, so the choice of which one to use depends upon the particular mechanisms that are available. If one has fast digital memory, adders, and multipliers, then one will use the FFT, and if one has a laser and photographic plates, one will use an "optical" method. (Marr and Poggio 1977:470)

In contrast, a theory that collapses grammar, parser, and machine together cannot decouple these levels of description so as to settle independently what and how questions. Should discrepancies between external facts and theory arise, we must either reformulate the entire theory or backtrack and attempt to extract properties invariant with respect to algorithmic or machine instantiation. Given our current limited understanding, we would expect many such discrepancies between data and model. Thus the "constant reformulation" strategy seems fruitless. The other route amounts to what Marr suggested. We must separate out the levels of abstract theory, algorithm, and implementation to carve out at least roughly the results at each level in a more independent fashion.

Besides the tactical advantage of a modular approach, there are basic questions of psychological interest whose answers refer to grammatical descriptions. For example, most questions of "language learning" are most perspicuously answered by reference to grammars. Confounding even the pessimists, there are even examples connecting the theories of language use and language acquisition.[58] For instance, assume that the theory of extended lexical grammar provides the optimal grammar for English, and that the processing model outlined in Bresnan 1978 is in fact the one embodied by the language faculty.

Now assume that at some stage of acquisition we encounter a new verb, say, *to disambiguate*, in the sentence: *The context disambiguated the meaning of the sentence*. Within the framework of the extended lexical theory the lexicon stores this verb with its functional representation: *disambiguate*: $[NP_1\_\_NP_2]$. It is clear that a native speaker could easily recognize the passive counterpart to the above sentence, even without having met an example: *The meaning was disambiguated by the context of the sentence*. How? The extended lexical theory would claim that the lexicon also associates a passive template with the lexical entry for *disambiguate*. But on what basis? Presumably there is some sort of active-passive relation, perhaps captured by a lexical redundancy rule, that constructs the passive entry once the active entry is built. However, note that this active-passive relation is not part of the parsing algorithm itself. The lexicon encodes its effects independently. This relation is statable only at a level of grammatical description. In order to show how new lexical forms are integrated into the parser, a problem of obvious psychological interest, we must refer to a level of grammatical representation. We could cite other such examples drawn from the study of acquisition, but they would take us far beyond the scope of this chapter. Chapter 6 explains in more detail just how linguistic theory can account for actual language acquisition.

Three major points emerge from this investigation of the connection between grammars, parsers, and machine implementations. First, given our limited knowledge about possible machine implementations it is ill advised to specify directly a theory of parsing for natural language without first having a good theory of grammar. Second, the theory of grammar goes a long way to delimit the class of possible parsing algorithms because it specifies the function to be computed by the parser. Finally, some questions relevant to the theory of language use have answers only by direct appeal to a level of grammatical representation. Each of these conclusions points to a single moral. The development of an adequate theory of language use depends on a firm characterization of linguistic knowledge, a grammar. We cannot build a theory of language use directly, but must rely on theories of competence, algorithms, implementations, and the proper mappings between these explanatory levels.

Chapter 3
Generative Power and Linguistic Theories

Traditionally, an adequate theory of language use has been one in which the sentences generated by a particular grammar are at least efficiently recognizable. This demand for efficient recognizability has a two-pronged appeal. On the one hand, a fast recognition procedure could be pressed into service as a psychological model of sentence processing on the assumption of a transparent embedding of the grammar as a processor. Quite naturally then, a grammatical system demanding less in the way of computational resources for recognition has been considered a more promising candidate for psychological plausibility. As we saw in chapter 2, and as we shall see in this chapter, this argument from efficiency holds only under a constellation of auxiliary assumptions. Second, there is a correlation between the richness of a grammatical rule system and the computational resources required to recognize the language it generates. Chapter 1 reviewed this link. Broadly speaking, the more powerful the rule system, the more computational resources might be required to recognize sentences of the language generated by that rule system. If we now claim that the more restricted a rule system the more easily it is learned, then it seems that we should avoid such excess computational power, both on grounds of parsability and learnability.

What then of the theory of transformational grammar? Historically, the theory has been judged as computationally "unrealistic" on both counts. Perhaps the first formal indictment lies with the results of Peters and Ritchie 1973b. They demonstrated that the transformational theory presented in *Aspects* was powerful enough to specify a grammar for any recursively enumerable set of strings. This was and is regarded as a serious problem for transformational grammar, as the following passages show.

In *Aspects* Chomsky states that the set of possible transformational grammars is the set of hypotheses which a child learning a language has available concerning the linguistic data he must explain.... the theory formulated in *Aspects* makes available to the child a hypothesis to explain any recursively enumerable set of data.... we must consider the possibility that the child can actually learn any grammar made available given some set of data. (Peters and Ritchie 1973b:71)

The reliability constraint [a speaker's ability to judge the grammaticality of any sentence] further requires that these rule systems specify languages within the class of recursive sets, thereby ruling out arbitrary standard transformational grammars. (Bresnan and Kaplan 1982:xlviii)

The proposals of Gazdar 1981 are similar in spirit. The idea here is to eliminate all transformational rules in favor of a context-free rule system. Again, one presumed advantage is that the class of resulting languages is more restricted, hence a step towards the explanation of language learnability and processability.

In the face of the "profligate" transformational theory of *Aspects*, some have suggested eliminating transformations in favor of just context-free rules (Gazdar), while others have suggested eliminating the notion of transformations in favor of a distinct mapping between surface constituent structure and a representation of grammatical relations (lexical-functional grammar). There are two other possibilities, though.

First, we might supplement the *Aspects* theory of transformational grammar with additional formal principles guaranteeing efficient parsability. Peters and Ritchie (1971) and Peters (1973) pursued just such an approach; Rounds (1973, 1975) refined their results. We shall return to their story in chapter 4. Second, we might discover linguistically justified principles guaranteeing learnability that incidentally also ensure efficient parsability. These are not just idle strategies. After all, the transformational theory as set out in *Aspects* has been significantly modified in the past few decades, and perhaps these changes affect the complexity of the language classes describable by transformational grammar. In fact Lapointe (1977) did show that Extended Standard Theories could only specify grammars for recursive languages. The next chapter explores some of these changes and their effects. We see then that even if we accept their assumptions, Bresnan and Kaplan's critique is outdated; it simply does not even apply to the theory of transformational grammar in its current incarnation since about the mid 1970s. There is even some debate about the requirement that natural languages be recursive (Chomsky 1980b).

Still, we might ask an even deeper question. Does constraining the languages that grammatical theories generate actually bear on the theory of linguistic performance at all? For it has been intermittently proposed that the usual linguistic research scenario be inverted. The idea is to gain insight into the nature of the system of knowledge that makes up the language faculty by considering how that knowledge is put to use or acquired in real time. In particular, because different grammatical theories are associated with different parsing models, some of which will be plausible and others less so, we can exploit a theory of language use to constrain the class of possible grammars by insisting that a grammar is "possible" just in case it has an associated plausible parsing model.

For instance, as we described in detail in the previous chapter, we can argue that the class of natural languages, more precisely, grammars for those languages, be constrained by insisting that parsers associated with putatively possible grammars reproduce the time complexity of human sentence processing. Sentences complex under some measure of psychological resource complexity are to be correspondingly complex for the processing model. A strengthened version of this condition might require that the complexity metric preserve the ordinal ranking of psychological sentence processing complexity.

In this chapter we focus on general proposals suggesting that we can constrain the class of possible grammars by imposing just such a cognitive fidelity requirement on the class of possible grammars, a criterion of efficient parsability. It is generally assumed that people can process sentences quite rapidly. By imposing a condition of efficient parsability then, we claim that sentence processing models should reproduce this aspect of human behavior. This is the requirement advanced, for example, by Marcus:

But there is another fact about language behavior that is only slightly less marvelous: that language works at all. It is far from apparent how the mind, given only the speech waveform, or even a string of written words, can reconstruct linguistic structure in something like real time. From this, it seems reasonable to assume that language must be constrained in ways which make it amenable to efficient generation and recognition. (1980:240–241)

Couched at this informal and general level, such a quasi-functional view seems untendentious. If the "language faculty" is even roughly analogous to other organs of the body then we might reasonably expect, just as in the case of other systems of the body, that it has been "well designed" according to some as yet undetermined criteria of efficiency. This scenario clearly takes for granted the usual backdrop of natural selection. Because one of the evolutionary "design criteria" could well have been ease of language processing, it is certainly conceivable that efficient parsability has played a role in the shaping of the language faculty.

It is another question entirely to argue that considerations of parsing efficiency allow us to restrict the class of possible grammars to just those capable of generating certain mathematically defined classes of languages, because these languages, and no others, can meet the demand of efficient parsability. Perhaps we should deliberately restrict our study to phrase structure grammars generating only context-free languages. This is because there are known efficient parsing algorithms to recognize and parse any language that is context-free; in contrast, there is no way to guarantee that all context-sensitive languages can be as efficiently parsed as the context-free languages, and of course broader classes of languages beyond the context-sensitive need not even have algorithmic recognition procedures.

Such a line of reasoning appears to provide a simple *a priori* way to reject the theory of transformational grammar as a "psychologically realistic" account of the language faculty. Because otherwise unrestricted transformational grammars can generate all the recursively enumerable languages (Peters and Ritchie 1973b) and because moderately restricted transformational grammars generate languages that cannot be parsed in less than exponential (2^n) time, (Rounds 1975), we can apparently conclude that there are theories of transformational grammar that generate languages for which we have no known efficient general parsing algorithms. Therefore, as some researchers conclude, a theory of grammar generating only languages for which there are known efficient parsing algorithms has an important leg up on the theory of transformational grammar. In this view, if we restricted attention to the study of systems generating only context-free languages, (perhaps for independently motivated reasons such as the usual linguistic reasons) then we get an important benefit because the entire class of context-free languages is already known to have "efficient" parsing algorithms. This is the view that Gazdar, for one, has advocated:

Suppose, in fact, that the permitted class of generative grammars constituted a subset of those phrase structure grammars capable of generating context-free languages.... we would have the beginnings of an explanation for the obvious, but largely ignored, fact that humans process the sentences they hear very rapidly. Sentences of a context-free language are provably parsable in a time which is proportional to the cube of the length of the sentence or less (Younger (1967), Earley (1970)). But no such restrictive result holds for the recursive or recursively enumerable sets potentially generable by grammars which include a transformational component. (1981:155)

The form of Gazdar's argument is simple enough:

(1) People parse sentences rapidly.

(2) The sentences of any context-free language can be parsed rapidly.

(3) Gazdar's phrase-structure grammars generate only context-free languages.

(4) Not all languages generated by transformational grammars can be parsed rapidly.

Conclusion: The theory of transformational grammar cannot provide an explanation of how people parse sentences; in contrast, a theory that can weakly generate only context-free languages can provide such an explanation.[1]

But is this line of argument valid? We believe not. In the first part of this chapter we show that when the relevant formal language theory results are set in their proper real world context they do not choose between context-free phrase structure and transformational grammars in the manner suggested by this argument. What the property of context-freeness supposedly buys is a guarantee that transformational grammar cannot meet, that of efficient processability. But the identification of all and only the context-free languages as the "efficiently processable" languages is misleading. On the one hand, strict context-sensitivity is not an absolute barrier to efficiency in the manner implied by the argument above. Many strictly context-sensitive languages can also be efficiently analyzed. On the other hand natural languages plainly do not include all the context-free languages. Therefore, even if we adopt a context-free hypothesis we must still impose additional constraints, beyond mere context-freeness, in order to characterize all and only the natural languages. Because we have to investigate additional characterizing constraints even in the context-free case, it would seem just as legitimate to look at those strictly context-sensitive languages efficiently processable, given additional constraints. As it turns out, there are such languages and constraints. We conclude then that the actual mathematical results do not rule out transformational grammar.[2]

In the second part of the chapter we consider more carefully the application of general mathematical results to a cognitive domain. We shall see that biologically relevant parsing efficiency need not be primarily determined by general, mathematically defined measures of efficiency. Therefore, although mathematical efficiency measures may apply in an abstract, formal sense to rank context-free phrase structure grammars as "better" than transformational grammars, this ranking may be relevant only in formal theory, not in biological practice. The commonly used mathematical measures of efficiency, including the one cited by Gazdar, by and large abstract away from the structural features of parsing algorithms that may actually dominate the efficiency of a procedure in the biologically relevant sense. In particular, we shall see how the size of a grammar as embedded in a parsing procedure can contribute to the efficiency of a parsing algorithm, and how, because grammar size shrinks as we move to more powerful descriptive formalisms, there is a possible trade-off between parsing efficiency and descriptive apparatus.

Our investigation of the use of "computational complexity" arguments to choose among alternative grammars also calls into question more generally the applicability of general mathematical results in a narrow cognitive domain. We shall see that because parsing efficiency clearly depends upon the representational format chosen for computation, it may well be that narrow, highly tailored representations for the particular grammatical formats associated with natural languages may allow correspondingly particular and nongeneral algorithms to be quite efficient, as opposed to whatever general purpose parsing algorithm we might propose. It seems likely that some of the computational work formerly done by the parser could be shouldered by the narrowness of the restricted set of representations under consideration. Chapters 4 and 5 examine specific constraints in the government-binding theory guaranteeing efficient parsability.

We find arguments such as the one sketched above to be symptomatic of an all too common confusion about the role of mathematics in linguistic theory. Consider the Peters and Ritchie result that an unrestricted transformational theory can specify a grammar for any recursively enumerable set. Some have taken this as proof that transformational grammars cannot be "psychologically real." Because some recursively enumerable sets do not even have algorithmic parsing procedures, unrestricted transformational grammars can generate languages for which no parsing procedure even exists, let alone an efficient one. The context-free language/efficient parsability argument is really just a subrecursive analogue of this more general argument.[3]

While our aim is to dispel certain technical confusions about the applicability of mathematical results to the domain of linguistics, we should stress that we are not implying that mathematical argument is worthless for the study of language. On the contrary, when the results of mathematical analysis are evaluated in the proper empirical context they can and have provided insights of enormous depth. The point of the chapter then is not to furnish a simple, sweeping conclusion that all purely *a priori* arguments about language based on mathematical results are invalid, or that thinking about parsing efficiency is a worthless enterprise. There is no difficulty with admitting additional valid sources of evidence bearing on theories of language, be it from the domain of mathematics, reaction time experiments, or observations of child development. The problem is that such arguments seem to be quite difficult to make properly, at least given our current understanding. In short, the moral of this chapter reinforces the one of chapter 2. Mathematical insights culled from the study of formal languages must be tempered with a sensitivity for the biological and empirical situation to which they are applied. In this we can do no better than to recall Kripke's observation regarding the role of mathematics and formalization in philosophical thinking:

Logical investigations can obviously be a useful tool for philosophy. They must, however, be informed by a sensitivity to the philosophical significance of the formalism and by a generous admixture of common sense, as well as a thorough understanding of both the basic concepts and of the technical details of the formal material used. It should not be supposed that the formalism can grind out philosophical results in a manner beyond the capacity of ordinary philosophical reasoning. There is no mathematical substitute for philosophy. (1976:416)

Context-Free Languages and Efficient Parsability

To begin our analysis we rehearse chapter 1's summary of the parsing time results for context-free languages. An amount of time proportional to roughly the cube of the number of input words is known to be sufficient to recognize the sentences of any context-free language.[4] Cubic time is known to be sufficient but is not known to be a necessary bound on the amount of time required. We shall see below why this is the case. Indeed, all known context-free languages are recognizable in linear time.[5] Even if the cubic bound were shown to be necessary for some context-free language, it does not then follow that all context-free languages would take that much time to parse; only some "hardest" language need take that much time. Similarly, it is known that an amount of time proportional to an exponential function of the length of the input string, k^n, is sufficient to parse any context-sensitive language, but this too is an upper bound; many context-sensitive languages do not require that much time for parsing. We discuss some explicit cases immediately below.

It is important to keep in mind just what these sorts of results show when applied to the case of natural languages. In its usual mathematical formulation, the "efficiency rating" of a given class of languages is determined by the "worst case" language for that class, that is, the language in the class that requires the most time to parse. Formally, if we let P_i be the parsing time with respect to language i, index i ranging over some class of languages L, then the parsing complexity of L is $max(P_i)$. For example, if we say counterfactually that the class of context-sensitive languages is of exponential time complexity, this means that at least one context-sensitive language requires exponential time; many of the other strictly context-sensitive languages in the class might require much less time, and indeed this is the case, as noted in the first chapter. This is the reason for the "sufficiency vs. necessity" distinction noted above. If such "worst case" theorems about mathematically defined classes of languages are to be applied directly to the class of possible natural languages (NL), then one must assume that the particular language used to demonstrate property P is itself in NL. This requirement is a sensible one to enforce, because, after all, we are clearly aiming to use property P as a partial characterization for what it means to be a natural language, and the proposed property would not be a very appropriate one if no natural language possessed it. A characterization based on parsing efficiency obviously is successful insofar as it helps us to characterize all and only the natural languages.

With this background in mind, consider again the argument to restrict the study of language to the study of rule systems that generate only context-free languages, because efficient general parsing methods exist for any context-free language. On this view, the property of "efficient parsability" (EP) that all context-free languages enjoy is a partial characterization of what it means to be a natural language. Languages that do not possess property EP are simply not natural languages. Our characterization now looks like this. The class NL has been identified with the class EP. Because all members of the class of context-free languages (CFL) are also efficiently parsable under our current definition of "efficient," CFL is identified with EP as well. Depending upon whether we impose additional characterization constraints on the class NL, NL might be a proper subset of the CFL class, a matter to which we return shortly; we also ignore the question of just where the class NL is bounded from below.

Strictly interpreted, this particular "state of the world" diagram is misleading. EP is not a property unique to the context-free languages because many strictly context-sensitive languages share the property of efficient parsability. Given that our sole criterion is efficient parsability, we had better include the strictly context-sensitive languages with property EP in our diagram, expanding the class NL beyond the strictly CFL boundary.

Pursuing the parsability characterization, recall that the theorems also tell us that any context-free language is efficiently parsable. Hence, all the unnatural languages that are context-free are also in the class EP, no matter how bizarre. On this account, mirror image languages, generating only palindromes like *abbaabba*, are also candidate natural languages because they are easily analyzable. Because these are apparently not natural languages, it is clear that we must rule out some context-free languages as natural languages based on criteria other than that of efficient parsability. Thus we must alter our diagram once more, redrawing the class NL so that it excludes some members of the class of context-free languages, and yet runs outside that class. Let us also assume that natural languages exceed the weak generative capacity of finite state grammars.[6]

We might argue that the reason the Chomsky language hierarchy has not been a fruitful classification is because we arbitrarily picked the wrong criterion for "efficient," namely, cubic time recognizability. But the same inappropriateness arises if we pick more rigid criteria. Suppose, for example, that we insisted on recognition in real time as the criterion of "efficient." As chapter 1 defined it, a realtime algorithm can make at most k steps before it is forced to read the next input element to process. Does the Chomsky language hierarchy map cleanly over into this criterion? Again, the answer is no. There is one obvious containment. Because realtime language recognition can take no more than time kn on an input of length n, it can take no more than space n. Such languages are context-sensitive. But beyond this the alignment is not very good. First, there are some strictly context-sensitive languages that are recognizable in real time, for example, ww and $a^n b^n c^n$. There are also inherently ambiguous context-free languages that are recognizable in real time. On the other hand, there are deterministic context-free languages that are not recognizable in real time. See Rosenberg 1967 for this last example and proofs of the other claims. So once again, the classical language hierarchy does not work well as a proxy for "efficient."

Yet another possible definition of "efficient" might be a restriction to realtime parsability, rather than just recognizability. It might then be suggested that only certain classes in the Chomsky hierarchy, for example, the finite state languages are realtime parsable. But this too is false. Chapter 1 gave an example of a finite state language not parsable in real time. On the other hand, chapter 1 also gave an example of strictly context-free languages with grammars whose productions are "self-embedding" that are realtime parsable. We see then that being a finite state language is neither necessary nor sufficient for realtime parsability, and any simple identification of finite state languages and efficient processability cannot work. This implies that one cannot impose the condition that languages be regular on grounds of efficient processability because nonregularity is no barrier to efficient parsability.

What has the efficient parsability criterion in this case bought us then? We can say for certain only that the class NL cuts across the context-sensitive and context-free language classes in some as yet undetermined fashion. But this is precisely what has generally been observed since the earliest mathematical work on the subject. The class of natural languages is suspected to be some subset of the class of context-sensitive languages, including, perhaps, some non-context-free languages. Even this much is not certain; it is an open question whether there are natural languages that are, for example, nonrecursive or even nonrecursively enumerable (Hintikka 1974 and Chomsky 1980b have a discussion).[7] In this case then, the imposition of the parsability criterion has told us nothing new at all; if our goal is to obtain as narrow a characterization of the class of natural languages as possible, then requiring that all natural languages possess property EP does not advance us beyond what has been suspected since the early 1960s.[8]

Summarizing the discussion, the problem with the identification of context-free languages with the class of natural languages is that it is at once too broad and too narrow. It is too broad in that it includes too many languages. Not all context-free languages are natural languages. But it is also too narrow. If the efficient parsability argument is only that natural languages be efficiently parsable, then there would seem to be no reason to exclude by fiat that subset of context-sensitive languages whose members are also efficiently parsable. In short, the fault lines of "efficient processing" do not fall neatly into place along the context-free/context-sensitive/recursively enumerable language boundaries.

The Relevance of Computational Complexity to Linguistics

The preceding discussion raises the first important point about the use of mathematical results in cognitive science. What the previous discussion has shown is that we cannot simply assume that a class of languages derived via a consideration of purely mathematical properties will correlate in a neat one for one fashion with the class of natural languages. A mathematically relevant class need not be coextensive with a cognitively relevant one. In the case above, the mathematical property of context-freeness could not be shown to be coextensive with the assumed cognitively relevant property of efficient parsability. We might summarize this problem by the slogan, mathematical relevance need not imply cognitive relevance.

A further question of cognitive relevance arises with the mathematical results because of the way in which results in the complexity literature are couched. The typical measure of complexity used in the theorems most often cited to back up efficient parsability arguments is the notion of asymptotic complexity, and it is not clear whether asymptotic complexity is a biologically relevant measure of computational complexity. Let us run through an example of the use of asymptotic complexity measures to see just what is at stake here. Because context-free languages are recognizable in time of order n^3, the "exact" recognition complexity would be kn^3, where k is a constant of proportionality. Suppose we wish to compare the time complexity for this algorithm against some other procedure of time complexity say, $k'f(n)$. For instance, $f(n)$ might be n^2. As n approaches infinity the ratio of the two complexities

$kn^3/k'f(n)$ will in the limit be dominated by the functional terms alone, and hence could be expressed more simply as just $n^3/f(n)$. This is because the constant factors, though possibly large, are fixed.[9] In contrast, the two functional terms n and $f(n)$ get larger and larger as the input sentence length n increases. Unless n^3 and $f(n)$ are equal, no matter how large the constant terms were to begin with the $n^3/f(n)$ ratio will grow many times larger or smaller than the constants. The constants will play no role in the comparison of one complexity formula against another. Hence the term "asymptotic complexity" for this kind of evaluation measure of computational efficiency.

Evidently if we use asymptotic complexity the constant terms in front of functional forms may be dropped for comparative purposes. We say that an algorithm runs in time n^3 or in linear time, without specifying the constant of proportionality; conversely, whenever such terminology is used, it has been tacitly assumed unless stated otherwise that the notion of asymptotic complexity is the relevant one.

Why would anyone adopt such a rough measure, one that can only distinguish between gross functional form differences? The reason is that the constants in front of the functional forms, k and k' in the example above, are parameters that are independent of the length of the input sentence but highly dependent on such "details" as the size of the grammar (total number of symbols required to write down the grammar), the representation of the grammar as a data structure (as a list, an array, a special look-up table); how rules are accessed and manipulated by the control structure of the parsing procedure; and the primitive operations available in the instruction repertoire of the assumed underlying machine. In short, the constants in front of the functional forms depend upon all those idiosyncratic "implementation details" that vary from particular machine to machine. The use of an asymptotic measure is intended to deal with precisely this problem; by comparing procedures only in the limit of input lengths, we have abstracted away from such details of implementation.

From one standpoint then, the use of asymptotic complexity measures is widely considered to be an appropriate solution to the problem of how to deal with variation in computational models. A mathematical theory of computation would not be of much use if its results could be invalidated simply by purchasing someone else's computer. Invariance over changes in computational model is a desirable property.

Turning now to the domain of cognitive science, it is much less clear that asymptotic measures are as appropriate. The problem is that in the case of human sentence processing we are studying one particular machine, though which one we do not know, and if we assume that the "design" of this machine has been optimized at all, then it has been optimized with respect to that machine. It is not necessarily optimized with respect to some abstract mathematical measure of complexity that considers all possible machines of a given type.[10] In particular, consider the claim that an algorithm that runs in time n^3 is "better" than one that runs in time 2^n. This is one of the senses of "more efficient" that an advocate of context-free parsing would rely upon. This comparison uses the notion of asymptotic complexity. The domination of n^3 over 2^n is guaranteed only asymptotically, in the limit as the length of sentences approaches infinity. But if sentences long enough to ensure the domination effect never arise in biologically relevant sentence processing, then the theoretical difference in parsing times will simply never amount to a practical difference. All those features ignored by adopting an asymptotic complexity measure may be precisely those that are most important for the range of problems that the organism must actually solve.

The difference could not be clearer. Asymptotic measures ignore the range of input sentence lengths and the constant factors in front of the functional forms specifying the computational complexity of an algorithm. In contrast cognitive measures must focus on what range of input sentence lengths are actually encountered in biological practice, for the "constant" values in front of the functional forms are proxies for the mental representations that parsing algorithms presumably are to use.[11] Note that these detailed problems are not those that are encountered when we consider the efficiency of algorithms at the most abstract level; they arise only when we start to address the question of how a grammar might be actually put to use in the human language faculty. We shall call the first problem, determining whether asymptotic theoretical complexity differences occur in practice, the *relevant range* problem; the second we call the *implementation problem*.

Let us consider first then the relevant range question and its quasi-biological import, ignoring for the moment the question of the constant values in front of the functional forms in asymptotic complexity measures. In particular, let us assume the constants in front of the functional forms to be equal, say, 1. Then the value of an exponential form like 2^n would not begin to exceed a polynomial form like n^3 until n is greater than nine. Given the operative assumptions, only sentences ten or more words long would distinguish between a parsing method that runs in time 2^n and one that runs in cubic time.[12]. In other words, given the assumptions above, an argument based on algorithmic superiority only goes through if one adds the following assumptions. (1) Sentences of the break-point length or greater actually occur; (2) it actually matters that one procedure can parse a single sentence 11 words long in half the time of another, presumably for reasons of expressive power; and (3) the language faculty has been "shaped" by natural selection primarily on the basis of the selectional advantage conferred by more efficient sentence processing, leaving aside the question whether this is indeed the primary "role" of the language faculty. But it is actually difficult to see under what conditions this alleged parsing advantage could arise. Not only are we forced to envisage a case where the speedier parsing of a long sentence matters, and matters in some selectional sense, but this difficult to parse sentence can have no two sentence expressive substitute. Otherwise it would come under the functional umbrella of the "slower" exponential procedure as well.[13]

Thus, the distinction between, say, cubic time and exponential time procedures is possibly of no import in biological practice, depending upon the range of sentence lengths that actually mattered in the evolutionary "design" of language. This is a potential outcome even in the restricted case where as we assumed the procedures to be compared had time complexities of n^3 and 2^n, that is, identical constant terms of 1 entering into the calculation of their execution times. If one weakens this assumption to include a broader class of cases where the constant factors in front of the functional forms like n^3 or 2^n can vary radically, then it is obvious that the range of input sentence lengths over which an exponential time bound may actually be of practical superiority to, for example, a cubic time bound could be vastly greater. Suppose an exponential time algorithm executed in exactly 2^n time steps while a competing cubic time algorithm is known to take $1000n^3$ steps to do the same processing job. Then the exponential algorithm will now be superior to the cubic one for sentences of 20 words in length or less.[14]

Evidently the constant factors that are quite properly ignored in asymptotic complexity analyses may actually be crucial to the analysis of complexity in a cognitive setting.[15] As a case study of this possibility, let us examine more carefully the complexity of general context-free parsing. Recall that for any context-free language the time to parse a sentence of length n is kn^3. The constant k, as mentioned, is a function of many other factors, including the size of the grammar, $|G|$; thus the "true" complexity is something like, $k'f(|G|)n^3$. Clearly, if the size of the grammar is very large compared to the typical range of input lengths, then it is the grammar size that dominates the overall complexity of the procedure.[16]

To say anything more specific, we must talk about a specific algorithm. Consider the "standard" cubic-time context-free recognition algorithm, Earley's algorithm (Earley 1968, 1970).[17] Earley shows that the time his method takes on an input sentence of length n is $k|G|^2n^3$, proportional to the square of the size of the grammar and the cube of the length of the input sentence.[18] Roughly speaking, the bigger the grammar, the more time the algorithm spends running through its list of potential recognition rules, deciding which one is applicable next. Which factor, grammar size or sentence length, dominates the time complexity for processing sentences? The outcome of the analysis clearly depends upon the relative size of the grammar compared to the range of sentence lengths. If the grammar is of a size adequate to describe natural language, then we might expect there to be many hundreds of rules; however, the sentences input to the recognizer will almost invariably be 20 words long or less. For example, if $|G| = 500$, and $n = 10$, then the parsing time complexity according to the Earley algorithm is 2.5×10^8. Neglecting the constant k, about two-thirds of this total is contributed by the grammar size, and the remaining third by the input sentence length.[19] Grammar size can dominate processing complexity for a "relevant" grammar size and a relevant range of input sentence lengths.

We might also consider whether directly reducing the size of the grammar has a telling impact on the overall efficiency of an algorithm. The potential advantages of a succinct representation are familiar to the linguist. More compact grammars are generally assumed to capture generalizations better than their bloated relatives, and are often taken to be more easily learnable as well. From the preceding paragraph we see that the linguist's intuition also has some computational support. If we can reduce grammar size "easily enough," then this kind of reduction may be more advantageous than a reduction on the exponent of input sentence length. As an illustrative example, consider a case where the size of the grammar $|G| = 500$, and the maximum length sentence analyzed is 10 tokens long. Now suppose that we are faced with a new alternative grammar, grammar B, that is a bit more than triple the size of the old grammar ($|G_B| = 1600$), but runs in only quadratic (n^2) time in the length of input sentences. In this situation the first grammar with an input sentence of length 10 will take time $k \times 2.50 \times 10^8$ to process, whereas Grammar B, although processed by an asymptotically faster algorithm than Grammar A, will take time $k \times 2.56 \times 10^8$. Given this particular set of assumptions about the range of input sentence lengths and algorithmic complexity functions, the more succinct grammar is more efficiently processed.[20]

Clearly an exact tradeoff between grammar size and exponent on input sentence length cannot be calculated without a specific set of grammars in hand. It would be a pointless exercise to show that succinctness is a potential advantage if we cannot reduce grammar size at all. In this regard it is important to observe that as we move from weaker to more powerful rule systems we can express languages more succinctly. This informal suspicion has some formal mathematical backing. Meyer and Fischer (1971) have shown that as we move up in expressive power from deterministic finite state automata, to nondeterministic finite state automata, to pushdown automata or context-free languages, to context-sensitive languages and beyond, there are always languages lower down in the hierarchy that can be expressed more succinctly via the more powerful rule systems.[21] For example, the gain in economy of pushdown automata over finite automata for describing finite and trivially regular sets can be exponential. Surprisingly, the amount of "compaction" achieved by using a nondeterministic pushdown machine to describe an infinite regular set can be arbitrarily large. Succinctness gains can also be unbounded as we move from context-free to context-sensitive languages. Formally we can reproduce this extra power by proposing a theory with multiple levels of representation and systematic mappings between these levels. This would be essentially the theory of transformational grammar as laid out in Chomsky's *Logical Structure of Linguistic Theory* (Chomsky 1955). Such a multiple-level theory obtains an enormous succinctness advantage over a theory that encodes linguistic descriptions via one level. Berwick 1982 and Borgida 1983 have a formal analysis.

Thus, although a set of strings may be perfectly well describable in the weak generative sense by a system of low expressive power, it may actually be advantageous in terms of parsing efficiency to capture the structure of that set by a more powerful formalism. The reason is simply that if in one formalism parsing time is some linear function of the length of the input and the size of the grammar, that is, is proportional to $k \times |G|n$, and if we can move to, say, a context-free formalism and reduce the size of the grammar exponentially, then the price of using the n^3 context-free parsing algorithm could be well worth it. A reduction in the size of the grammar could more than make up for the increase due to the linear to cubic exponent change.[22] Note that this advantage of succinctness is quite different from the usual linguistic claim that a more compact grammar is more easily learnable; we are claiming that it is possible that a more compact grammar, expressed by a more powerful formal system, is more efficiently processed as well.[23]

Analyzing the complexity of a parsing procedure as some joint function of grammar size and sentence length is but the first crude step in a more detailed comparison of parsing procedures. The unanalyzed grammar size term itself covers a multitude of implementation details. Besides reducing the sheer size of the grammar, we could also try to discover alternative representational formats for the grammar rules that are more easily coupled to the demands of parsing routines; perhaps we could reduce the exponent on the grammar size contribution from quadratic to linear. The success of this effort in turn depends upon both the exact form of the grammar and available representational formats or what primitive operations and structures the brain actually has available or can "quickly" simulate. This is an important concomitant and almost inevitable effect of moving away from abstract analysis and towards more fine grained efficiency analysis. Our comparisons become more attuned to the relevant cognitive details, but we lose the ability to say that our comparisons will remain fixed over all possible variations in primitive machine operations. If the human cognitive machinery does not have the requisite operating characteristics that we have assumed for our low level detailed efficiency analysis, then the comparison is simply beside the point. As we saw earlier in chapter 2, if we have concluded that algorithm A is faster than algorithm B on the assumption that the primitive instruction set of the underlying computational machinery includes a unit operation to multiply two numbers together, but the actual machinery provided includes only addition operations, then it may well be that the superiority of algorithm A is just academic. Similarly, detailed complexity analyses of variations in one or another parsing algorithm that are based upon differences in the details of computer organization seem problematic without independent verification that the relevant differences in computer organization are reflected in the cognitive domain. A careful complexity analysis must ride a thin line between over-abstraction and over-specialization.

The possibility of arranging for the "internalization" of grammar rules in a wide variety of formats as matrices, linked lists, or more complicated arrangements would be of little interest for efficiency analysis if it were true that modifications of this kind had little impact on overall parsing efficiency. As it turns out, variation in such "data structures" can have a significant practical effect on the efficiency of an algorithm. Quite often merely changing the way in which rules are accessed can make order of magnitude differences in algorithmic efficiency. To take a concrete example, Ruzzo and his colleagues (Ruzzo 1978, Graham, Harrison, and Ruzzo 1980) have shown that the Earley algorithm can be made more efficient by a combination of actual changes to the algorithm plus a palette of "implementation" techniques. These include shifts to alternative representational formats for storing grammar rules and how those rules are "looked up" as the parse progresses; alternative primitive machine operations whether we have parallel operations available for certain tests; and whether "preanalysis" of the grammar is permitted so as to compute in advance commonly used derivational steps. As Graham, Harrison, and Ruzzo point out, these changes can speed up the same algorithm ten times or more, and may well dominate the algorithm's execution time for practical sized inputs. "Implementation details," far from being safely ignored, may actually be crucial in the practical evaluation of an algorithm's complexity. Importantly, Graham et. al. point out that some of these format "tricks" are not available if we use the original Earley algorithm.[24]

Because different representational formats can make for quite significant differences in parsing efficiency for the case of context-free parsing, it seems reasonable to conclude that the proper practical evaluation of an algorithm is a sophisticated task. It requires careful attention to alternative data structures and the underlying organization of the computer that has been assumed. In the cognitive domain the task is even more difficult, because the attendant computational assumptions are more likely to be lacking independent support. For example, if the primitive parallel operations demanded by the most efficient of the Graham, Harrison, and Ruzzo techniques have no analogue in cognitive machinery, then we cannot exploit the efficiency gains of this method.[25] In short, we again discover that we must have a theory of implementation and some specific knowledge of the computational capabilities of the brain.

A stronger case for a particular algorithm's superiority could be made if we were able to show that its efficiency was preserved for input sizes of practical interest over many or all conceivable implementations. Then we might be more confident that, no matter what particular "implementation" the brain had picked, our algorithm would still be superior. It still does not necessarily follow that the brain would pick that particular algorithm. It is this property of invariance over implementation that lends at least some credibility to the distinction between procedures that run in some polynomial function of the length of their inputs, such as n^3 in the case of context-free recognition, versus those that take some exponential amount of time. As chapter 1 pointed out, we know that procedures that take polynomial time on a Turing machine still take polynomial time under any other natural model though the exponent may be larger or smaller. For instance, Earley's algorithm takes n^3 time on a random access machine, but n^4 time on a Turing machine under the straightforward simulation of one machine by the other. The important point is that the asymptotic superiority of polynomial over exponential algorithms will be maintained across all "natural" machine implementations.

Unfortunately, as we have seen, this invariance is again an asymptotic property, and hence its relevance for cognitive analysis is not clear. It seems just as likely that it is the constant multipliers that dominate the usual execution time of parsing algorithms for natural language. Consequently, we suggest that the proper analysis of parsing algorithms will have to wait upon the as yet undeveloped theory of implementation or perhaps even some hard but still abstract information about the computational abilities of the language faculty/brain. Compare Marr's work on visual processing (1982); this work depended crucially on "hard" information about the visual system.

The Empirical Significance of Mathematical Linguistics

Let us summarize our examination of the efficient parsability assumptions. The conclusion that context free languages form a privileged class because of parsing efficiency requires both a functional and a mathematical argument. The mathematical argument that has appeared in the literature rests on the direct use of computational complexity results apparently without a proper consideration of either the domain of application of the relevant theorems or a proper evaluation of the efficiency condition in a realistic biological setting. There is a distinction to be drawn between relevant cognitive complexity and the mathematical complexity of a language. It is relevant cognitive complexity that is actually of interest to linguists and psychologists. But this measure must be couched at a level of detail incorporating many implementation factors. To determine relevant cognitive complexity we must determine the range of inputs that will be encountered, the size of the grammar, its internal representation, and the basic architecture of the machine actually instantiating a parsing algorithm that makes use of the grammar. Languages that are quite "high up" in the Chomsky hierarchy, for example, context-sensitive languages, may in fact be parsed more rapidly than context-free languages lower down in the hierarchy if the gain in succinctness is enough to offset the possible increase in parsing time.

There is nothing in principle that prevents the theory of language use from constraining the class of possible grammars. Apparently though, a parsing efficiency criterion as defined via the class of context-free languages is not much of a criterion at all. The entire class of context-free languages plus many other languages that are strictly context-sensitive are efficiently parsable. Indeed, it seems likely that when implementation factors are taken into consideration, including the possibility of parallel hardware, and when we realize that it is only of interest to consider sentences of "practical" size, then it actually seems likely that any of the languages proposed under current linguistic theories will be efficiently parsable for a relevant range of inputs. Consequently attention to the criterion of efficient parsability alone can do little to advance us toward our goal of constraining the class of possible grammars.[26] This apparent fact was noted by Chomsky where the difference between mathematical and biological relevance is also pointed out:

It is important to keep the requirements of explanatory adequacy and feasibility in mind when weak and strong generative capacities of theories are studied as mathematical questions. Thus one can construct hierarchies of weak and strong generative capacity, but it is important to bear in mind that these hierarchies do not necessarily correspond to what is probably the empirically most significant dimension of increasing power of linguistic theory. This dimension is presumably to be defined in terms of the scattering in value of grammars compatible with fixed data. Along this empirically significant dimension, we should like to accept the least "powerful" theory that is empirically adequate. It might conceivably turn out that this theory is extremely powerful (perhaps even universal, that is, equivalent in generative capacity to the theory of Turing machines) along the dimension of weak generative capacity, and even along the dimension of strong generative capacity. It will not necessarily follow that it is very powerful (and hence to be discounted) in the dimension which is ultimately of real empirical significance.... It is important to realize that the questions presently being studied are primarily determined by feasibility of mathematical study, and it is important not to confuse this with the question of empirical significance. (1965:62)

Chapter 5 shows how we can join parsing criteria with independently motivated principles of grammar in a way that does constrain what grammars look like. Beyond this, it seems reasonable that "empirical significance" might demand criteria above and beyond that of efficient parsability. One possible criterion comes from research into the class of grammars that are learnable. Chapter 6 probes more deeply into this question.[27]

Chapter 4
Transformational Grammar: A Formal Analysis

The previous chapter had one simple moral: What is natural mathematics need not be natural linguistics. Because our goal is to study natural languages, not mathematics, this means that in the tug of war between mathematics and linguistics, mathematics must give way. The "restrictiveness" of linguistic theories is measured against how well they characterize exactly the natural grammars. Context-free languages are more restricted than context-sensitive languages in a formal sense, but this is a different sense of "restrictive" than the one we are after. We can ask an even broader question. Why study natural language formally at all? The answer here is no different than in the other sciences. Formalisms can tell us what the implications of a theory are. Because it is by comparing the implications of different theories that we edge closer to what is right, formalisms can sometimes guide us along this path. But they also do no more than this. If a formalism clarifies otherwise murky predictions of a theory, then well and good; but if it does not, or if the implications of the theory are already all too apparent, then a formalism is of little use except as something of purely mathematical interest.

This is the same rationale behind our critique of weak generative capacity analyses. A weak generative capacity analysis is profitable if it serves as a "diagnostic" for what ails a theory of grammar. It has no restorative powers beyond this. In particular, weak generative capacity tells us only about the set of sentences generated by a grammar. We can use this as a handy guide to why that grammar is "unnatural," but only if the sentences really suggest what underlying rules are going awry. It is the grammar, the system of principles, that we want to study.[1] What really matters to us is whether the rule system itself is "unnatural," that is, whether it draws on machinery that is never attested in natural languages. This unnatural machinery can in turn lead to "predictions" about unnatural sentences, and these can be checked against observations of natural languages, but it is the internal machinery that is central, not the surface effects.

This same concern with grammar also underpins our study of the computational complexity of languages. It does not matter if a language has an efficient recognition procedure, if that procedure does not implicate an independently justified system of grammatical representation. It matters still less if we argue indirectly that a language has an efficient recognition procedure because it is at one or another level of the Chomsky hierarchy. If we are interested in time complexity, what matters is the direct study of the computational time complexity of the specific language class we are interested in, not some poor proxy for it. What matters even more is the study of efficient parsers that use the same operating principles as the grammar. There is one sense in which recognition complexity can be an aid. Chapter 1 observed that parsing was always at least as hard as recognition. But this means that if there is no efficient recognition procedure for a language there is not a ghost of a chance for an efficient parsing procedure. So recognition complexity puts a lower bound on what we can expect for parsing complexity.

The next two chapters will take to heart this admonition to study directly the naturalness of rule systems and parsing complexity. The next chapter turns to specific parsing models for the government-binding theory. In this chapter we shall see whether weak generative capacity can be put to use as a diagnostic aid for deeper maladies in theories of grammar. As it turns out, weak generative capacity does give us a clue that the lexical-functional theory is unnatural. It is easy to write a lexical-functional grammar that generates the language $L_2 = \{a^i | i$ is a power of $2\}$ What is more important, though, is the causative agent lurking behind the scene here. We can trace this unnaturalness to a particular rule writing capability of lexical-functional grammars: the ability to check entire trees for compatibility, what Kaplan and Bresnan 1982 dub "functional structure compatibility." This power, which must be crucially invoked by Kaplan and Bresnan in order to describe the well-formed sentence structures of Dutch (Bresnan, Kaplan, Peters, Zaenen 1982), unfortunately leads directly to an ability to describe unnatural grammars, rule systems quite unlikely ever to be attested.[2]

We should be explicit about this point, because it differs from the usual weak generative capacity analysis. It is not simply that the machinery of lexical-functional grammar, combined in perverse ways, can simulate a computationally complex device. This was the substance of Peters and Ritchie's proof that a transformational grammar could be used to simulate arbitrary Turing machine computations. Rather, the building blocks of the lexical-functional theory combine in grammatically natural ways to form a grammar that looks almost exactly like a natural grammar, except that it could not be one.

The comparison here is between a system that is unnatural because it simulates a Turing machine and a system that is unnatural because it represents a grammar that forces object "control" by a preceding NP just in case both the NP and object are equally deeply embedded. It is not that one system is unnatural and the other is not. Both are unnatural. No one has found a grammar for a natural language that simulates an arbitrary TM computation, and likewise no one has found a grammar for a natural language that insists on object control based on depth of embedding. The difference is that the TM simulation establishes unnaturalness by looking at just input-output behavior, namely, the set of sentences that can be generated. The object control simulation establishes the same point by looking at an unnatural grammatically based construction, namely, the set of structures allowed. The unnaturalness of certain lexical-functional grammars is diagnosed by the unnatural languages it can generate, but the difficulties are caused by its rule writing powers. Importantly, we shall see that the government-binding theory does not suffer from the same problems. The unnatural rule systems and languages that lexical-functional grammars can encode cannot be written in the government-binding theory.

This chapter will also consider directly the question of computational complexity. Rather than relying on weak generative capacity results we will take a look at the time complexity of lexical-functional language recognition. Our finding will be that lexical-functional grammars are powerful enough to encode any Turing machine computation that takes nondeterministic polynomial time. Such power is widely considered to be a sign of computational intractability. Because such results are also invariant under translation to another computer reference model, this means we cannot remedy things by moving to a "more powerful" machine, even a parallel one.

To sum up the theme of this chapter, we believe that what should be avoided is a commitment to mathematical formalism that ignores the proper role of mathematics or empirical results. This is Kripke's warning once again. The problem is that natural languages look seductively "like" certain elegant mathematical constructs. Natural languages are "like" context-free languages, in that they exhibit hierarchical phrase structure, but, as we have suggested, context-free languages are not exactly the natural languages. Marr's words on the analysis of the human visual system are appropriate here:

No longer are we allowed to invoke a mechanism that seems to have some features in common with the problem and to assert that the mechanism works like the process.... Stereo matching, for example, is like a lot of other things, but it is not the same as any of them. It is like a correlation, but it is not a correlation, and if it is treated like a correlation, the methods chosen will be unreliable.... the enterprise of looking for structure at different scales... is reminiscent of ideas like filtering the image with different band-pass filters.... The point is once again that, just as for gray-level correlation and stereopsis, these ideas based on Fourier theory are like what is wanted, but they are not what is wanted. (1982:76)

Applied to the study of language, Marr's suggestion is that we look at what natural languages are like first, and only then turn to consider possible mechanisms. This is the goal of chapters 4 and 5.

Unnatural Languages and Linguistic Theory

If weak generative capacity is to tell us anything at all, then it must bear some relationship to what is a "natural" or "unnatural" language. Our first claim is this. The power of 2 language L_2 is not a natural language. We shall simply take this as given. Below we discuss just why this is an unnatural language. L_2 is a lexical-functional language however, for the following lexical-functional grammar generates it:

(1)
$$A \rightarrow \quad A \qquad A$$
$$(\uparrow f) = \downarrow \quad (\uparrow f) = \downarrow$$

(2)
$$A \rightarrow \quad a$$
$$(\uparrow f) = 1$$

Because this grammar may well be the reader's first exposure to the lexical-functional notation, and because we shall require this machinery throughout this chapter, this would be as good a place as any to summarize the formal apparatus of lexical-functional grammar.

As we saw in chapter 2, a lexical-functional grammar associates with each generable surface string or sentence a number of distinct representations. For our purposes we need to focus on just two of these, the constituent structure of a sentence or its "c-structure," roughly a labeled bracketing of the surface string annotated with certain feature complexes; and the functional structure of a sentence or its "f-structure," roughly a representation of the underlying predicate-argument structure of a sentence described in terms of grammatical relations such as subject and object. Unlike a transformational grammar, a lexical-functional grammar does not generate surface sentences by first specifying an explicit, context-free deep structure followed by a series of categorially based transformations like Move NP. Rather, predicate-argument structure is related directly to c-structure on the basis of predicates grounded upon grammatical relations like subject and object. The conditions for this mapping are provided by a set of so-called functional equations associated with the context-free rules for generating permissible c-structures, along with a set of conventions that in effect convert the functional equations into well-formedness predicates for c-structures.

In more detail, a lexical-functional c-structure is generated by a base context-free grammar. A necessary condition for a sentence to be in the language generated by a lexical-functional grammar is that its c-structure can be generated by this base grammar. Such a sentence is then said to have a well-formed constituent structure. For example, if the base rules included $S \rightarrow NP\,VP$; $VP \rightarrow V\,NP$, then, glossing over details of noun phrase rules, the sentence *John kissed the baby* would be well-formed but *John the baby kissed* would not. This assumes the existence of a lexicon that provides a categorization for each terminal item, for example, that *baby* is of the category N, *kissed* is a V, etc.[3] Importantly then, this well-formedness condition requires us to provide at least one legitimate structure for the candidate sentence that shows how it may be derived from the underlying lexical-functional base context-free grammar. There could be more than one legitimate tree if the underlying grammar is ambiguous. Note further that the choice of categorization for a lexical item may be crucial. If *baby* was assumed to be of category V, then both sentences above would be ill-formed.

A lexical-functional grammar consists of more than just a base context-free grammar, however. As mentioned, a second major component of the theory is the provision for adding a set of so-called *functional equations* to the base context-free rules. The functional equations define an implicit functional structure associated with every c-structure, and this functional structure must itself be well-formed. Part of the linguistic role of functional structures is to account for the co-occurrence restrictions that are an obvious part of natural languages, for example, subject-verb agreement.

How exactly do the functional equations work? Their job is to specify how the functional structure of a sentence gets built. This is done by associating possibly complex features with lexical entries and with the nonterminals of specified context-free rules. These features have values. The features are pasted together under the direction of the functional equations to form functional structures associated with the subconstituents of the sentence; these now possibly complex functional structures are in turn assembled to form a master functional structure associated with the root node of the sentence.

In this theory a "feature" can be something as simple as an atomic object that is binary valued. For example, a subject feature could be either plural or singular in value. But an atomic feature can also have a range of values, and, more crucially for the purposes of the demonstration here, a feature can itself be a complex, hierarchically structured object that contains other features as subconstituents. For example, the "feature" that eventually becomes associated with the root node of a sentence is in fact a functional structure that represents the full propositional structure of the sentence. Thus if the surface string was the sentence, *The girl promised to kiss the baby* then the functional structure associated with the root node of the sentence is a complex "feature" that itself contains an embedded functional structure corresponding to the embedded proposition *the girl kisses the baby*.

As mentioned, well-formedness is also determined by functional equations dictating how feature complexes are to be assembled. By and large the functional structure complex at a node X is assembled compositionally in terms of the functional structure complexes of the nodes below it in the constituent structure tree. For example, the root node of a sentence will have an associated functional structure with subject and predicate subfeatures. These structures are themselves complex. They include the entire subject NP and verb–verb complement structures, respectively. For instance, the subject NP in turn has a subfeature *number*; the predicate contains complex subfeatures corresponding to the verb and verb complements. The basic assembly directive is the notation ($\uparrow=\downarrow$). When attached to a particular node X, it states that the functional structure of the node immediately above X is to share all the functional structure of the nodes below X. The effect is to merge and "pass up" all the functional structure values of the nodes below X to the node above X. We can also pass along just particular subfields of the functional structure below X by specifying a subfield on the righthand side of the expansion rule.[4] As an example, the notation $\uparrow=$ ($\downarrow$ number) attached to a node X states that the functional structure of the node above X is to contain at least the value of the number feature. This "value" may itself be a functional structure. Similarly, a particular subfield of the functional structure above a node X may be specified by providing a subfield label on the lefthand side of the arrow notation. For example, the notation, ($\uparrow$ subject) $=\downarrow$ means that the subject subfield of the functional structure built at the node above X must contain the functional structure built below X.

A basic constraint on functional structure is that the functional structure assembled at X must be uniquely determined; that is, it cannot contain a feature F_1 with conflicting values. This entails, for example, that the subject subfunctional structure that is built at a root S node cannot have a number subfield that is filled in from one place beneath with the value *singular* and from another place with the value *plural*. More generally, this restriction means that two or more functional structures that are "passed up" from below according to the dictates of an arrow notation must be unifiable. Any common subfields, no matter how hierarchically complex, must be mergeable without conflict in their values.

For example, consider subject-verb agreement and the sentence *the baby is kissing John*. The lexical entry for *baby* considered as a noun might have the *number* feature, with the value singular. The lexical entry for *is* might assert that the number feature of the subject above it in the parse tree must have the value singular, via the annotation ($\uparrow$ subject) = singular attached to the verb. Meanwhile, the feature values for *subject* are automatically found by the annotation ($\uparrow$ subject) $=\downarrow$ associated with the noun phrase portion of $S \rightarrow NP\,VP$ that grabs whatever features it finds below the NP node and copies them up above to the S node. Thus the S node gets the subject feature with whatever value it has passed from *baby* below, namely the value singular. This agrees with what the verb *is* demands, and all is well.

In contrast, in the sentence, *the boys in the band is kissing John, boys* passes up the number value plural, and this clashes with the verb's constraint; as a result this sentence is judged ill formed.

It is important to note that the feature compatibility check requires (1) a particular constituent structure tree; and (2) an assignment of terminal items or words to lexical categories. For example, in the first subject-verb agreement example above, *baby* was assigned to the category N, a noun. The tree is obviously required because the feature checking machinery propagates values according to the links specified by the derivation tree. The assignment of terminal items to categories is crucial because in most cases the values of features are derived from those listed in the lexical entry for an item, just as the value of the number feature was derived from the lexical entry for the noun form of *baby*. One and the same terminal item can have two distinct lexical entries, corresponding to distinct lexical categorizations; for example, *baby* can be both a noun and a verb. If we had picked *baby* to be a verb, and hence had adopted whatever features are associated with the verb entry for *baby* to be propagated up the tree, then the string that was previously well-formed, *the baby is kissing John* would now be considered deviant. If a string is ill formed under all possible derivation trees and assignments of features from possible lexical categorizations, then that string is not in the language generated by the lexical-functional grammar.

Finally, lexical-functional grammar also provides a way to express the familiar patterning of grammatical relations, such as "subject" and "object" in natural languages. For example, transitive verbs must have objects. This fact of life, expressed in an *Aspects* style transformational grammar by subcategorization restrictions, is captured in lexical-functional grammar by specifying a so-called predicate (pred) feature with a verb; the pred can describe what grammatical relations like "subject" and "object" must be filled in after feature passing has taken place in order for the analysis to be well-formed. For instance, a transitive verb like *kiss* might have the pattern, *kiss* $\langle (subject)(object) \rangle$, and thus demand that the subject and object, now considered to be features, have some value in the final analysis. The values for subject and object might of course be provided from some other branch of the parse tree, as provided by the feature propagation machinery; for example, the object feature could be filled in from the noun phrase part of the VP expansion. But if the object were not filled in, then the analysis is declared functionally incomplete and is ruled out. This device is used to cast out sentences such as *the baby kissed.*

Having completed our brief tour of the lexical-functional formal machinery, we can now understand how the grammar generating the power of 2 language works. The $(\uparrow f) = \downarrow$ functional structure constraints on the nonterminals enforce the restriction that the same number of A expansions be taken on each subtree. Expansions are symmetric all the way down to the "words," the a's. It is an easy proof by induction that this generates exactly L_2. Consider for example the following derivations, one where the A's are expanded equally down all spines of the constituent structure tree, and one where they are not. In the first case consider the functional structure built up at the highest A node. This functional structure is governed by the functional equations of the first rule of the grammar, because it was this rule that must have applied to generate the first two A's. This means that the functional structure of the highest A node is formed by merging the functional structures built up at the subtrees immediately dominated by this topmost A. The functional structure of the leftmost A subtree is just $[f[f[f\,1]]]$, with the number of f's corresponding to the number of times the first rule was applied to build up subtree A, plus the final application of the second rule. By the definition of the functional structure unification procedure this functional structure must be compatible with that built up by the righthand A subtree. But this means that it must have been built up by the same number of A expansions via the two rules. Continuing this reasoning, we see that at all subtree levels the number of left and right A subtrees must be identical. This property holds just in case the number of a's generated at the bottom is a power of 2. Here is an unequal expansion:

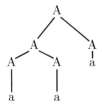

Languages like L_2 violate another property that might be taken as a useful proxy for a natural language. If we arrange the sentences of this language in order of increasing length, we see that they become farther and farther apart. In fact, for any fixed set of constants C, we can always find a sentence of L_2, w_i say, such that there is no w_j in L_2, with $|w_i| = |w_j| + c$, for $c \in C$. But, we might claim that in any natural language we never obtain sentences that are that "far apart." In other words, natural languages possess a "constant growth" property, as defined by Joshi 1983. We can define this property as follows:

Definition. A language L is said to *possess the constant growth property* (or be constant growth) if and only if there exists a constant M and a set of constants C such that for all sentences $w_k \in L$ with $|w_k| > M$, there exists another sentence in L, $w_{k'}$, such that w_k is at most a constant longer than $w_{k'}$, $|w_k| = |w_{k'}| + c$, for $c \in C$. A grammar is said to possess the constant growth property iff the language it generates is constant growth.

Lexical-functional grammars, then, are not constant growth.[5] In contrast, government-binding grammars cannot generate such languages. One of our results below will be to show that government-binding languages are constant growth, and that therefore no government-binding grammar can generate L_2, or any nonconstant growth language.

First, though, we would like to turn from this weak generative capacity symptom to diagnosis. Our diagnosis has two parts. First, what is it about lexical-functional grammars that allows them to generate difficult languages? Second, why is this power invoked elsewhere in the lexical-functional system? We shall also exhibit a lexical-functional grammar that uses this extra power to define a rule system unlike anything ever seen in natural grammars.

First then, what is it that gives lexical-functional grammars their ability to define languages like the power of 2 language? Intuitively it is because lexical-functional grammars can test complete subtrees for compatibility in terms of their functional structures. At a dominating node we can check whether an entire hierarchical structure is feature compatible with another structure. This follows from the account of functional structure unification defined by Kaplan and Bresnan 1982. Functional structures are hierarchical in nature. They are directed, acyclic graphs. Functional structure well-formedness is defined by the condition of functional structure uniqueness. Roughly speaking, there can be no conflicts in the assignment of feature complexes, even if those features are in fact hierarchical structures. Note that this kind of feature compatibility test goes well beyond that required for the checking of "ordinary" agreement, as in subject-verb number agreement. When

we test a subject and verb for agreement, all that we do is check
an unordered list of features for compatibility. The number, gender,
and so forth of the subject NP must agree with that of the verb, as
percolated through the VP. It is a far cry from this kind of agreement
checking to the "agreement" of two entire tree structures, but this is
what is implied by the lexical-functional unification procedure.

As we saw in our earlier example, this unification procedure is
sufficient to generate the power of 2 language. A natural question to
ask then is whether this ability to compare entire functional structures
is necessary. For if all cases of functional structure unification can
be replaced by unordered feature agreement tests, then there is no
motivation for adopting the more powerful mechanism, at least on
these grounds.

Of course, from one standpoint, the lexical-functional theory is already
committed to the ability to test hierarchical functional structures for
compatibility. For functional structures are certainly hierarchical in
nature. They must encode the hierarchical relationships between root
and embedded propositions, for example. A functional structure is used
as the input to semantic interpretation, and so must reflect hierarchical
dependencies. Otherwise we cannot decipher the relationships in a
complex sentence like *John expected Mary to persuade Bill to win.* The
feature checking machinery must be designed to test for functional
structure compatibility because that is the only level of representation
where features like the number of the subject are to be found. But
once we permit feature checking of functional structures at a single,
unembedded level for the number of a subject NP, it is hard to see
how we can rule it out for a more complex functional structure.

In fact, there are cases in natural languages where it is necessary
to check one complex functional structure for compatibility against
another one. Just such a case has been discussed by Bresnan, Kaplan,
Peters, and Zaenen 1982, in the analysis of certain Dutch sentences.
We will not review all the details of their proposal here except to
establish the point that hierarchical functional structure comparisons
are crucially implicated. The data Bresnan et al. want to account for
is this. Dutch contains infinitely many sentences of the following sort
(examples from Bresnan et al. 1982:614):

(1) ... dat Jan de kinderen zag zwemmen
     ... that Jan the children saw swim
     ... that Jan saw the children swim

(2) ... dat Jan Piet Marie de kinderen zag helpen laten zwemmen
     ... that Jan Peter Marie the children saw help make swim
     ... that Jan saw Piet help Marie make the children swim

To quote Bresnan et al.:

Arbitrarily many of these sentences can be formed simply by inserting
into the string a noun phrase and a verb that is subcategorized for both a
noun phrase and an infinitival complement without the complementizer
te. The verb in the first position is formally distinguished by its
marking for tense and its person and number agreement with the first
NP. The verb in last position is distinguished from the others by its
subcategorization restrictions.... provided that the number of verbs
matches the number of noun phrases, and provided that the agreement
constraint between the first NP and the first verb is respected and
the subcategorization restrictions between the final NPs and final verb
are satisfied, all permutations of the NPs within the NP sequence
and all permutations of the verbs within the verb sequence produce
grammatical sentences. (1982:614–615)

These Dutch sentences must have a certain constituent structure. Their
proposed structure consists of two branching "spines," one a right
branching tree of VPs containing objects and complements, the other
a right branching tree of V̄s containing verbs without their objects and
complements. Sentence (2) comes out looking like this:

(3)

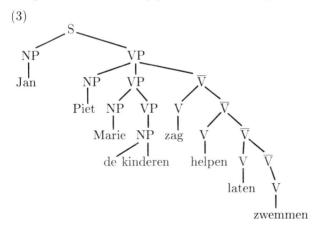

The crucial constraint that must be encoded is this. Every verb uses its lexical argument structure to demand certain NP objects or that the verb complement's subject be controlled by the verb's object or subject. For example, the verb *zag* demands that its object control the subject of *zag*'s verbal complement. This is analogous to the English case where the object of a verb, for example, *persuade*, controls the subject of *persuade*'s complement, as in, *We persuaded John to leave*.

In the lexical-functional system we can encode this by forcing an identification between the functional structure of the object of *zag* and the functional structure of the verb complement of *zag* (denoted Vcomp). The "equation" is written ($\uparrow$ Vcomp subj)=($\uparrow$ obj). The problem, of course, is that if we have three verbs then we have three such constraints, but the associated NPs that satisfy them lie along a distinct VP "spine" of the constituent structure tree that is separated from the verbs along the $\overline{V}$ spine. In other words, the "control" equations are built up along the rightmost, $\overline{V}$ spine of the constituent structure tree, but the NPs that satisfy these equations lie along the left side. How can we assemble the NP functional structures for proper checking against the control equation demands? Because feature checking can occur only at some common dominating mother node, the first place where all elements are "visible" to each other is at the first VP node completely dominating both right and left subtrees. The way that Bresnan et al. accomplish this task is to build up along the rightmost subtree a functional structure representation that encodes all of the control equations, in the form of a hierarchical functional structure with unfilled slots (denoted by "____") standing for the subjects and objects mentioned by the controlling verbs. Note that the structure is indeed hierarchical, containing embedded components.

Along the lefthand side of the constituent tree Bresnan et al. build up a second hierarchical functional structure that "merges" successfully into the righthand one just in case the number of NPs and their assignment to controlled positions meshes with the "slots" left remaining in the righthand functional structure.

The way to visualize the unification procedure is to imagine overlaying the first hierarchical structure on top of the second. One can see that they "fit" together, with the embedded object functional structure for the second one filling the object slot of the first, the Vcomp object meshing as well, and so on, all the way down the line.

(4) Functional structure from righthand side spine:

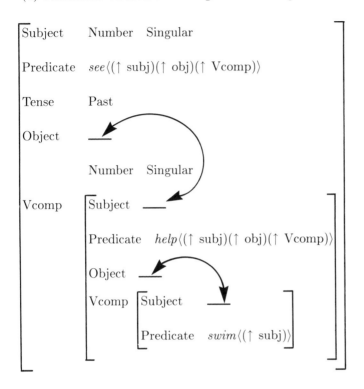

(5) Functional structure from lefthand spine:

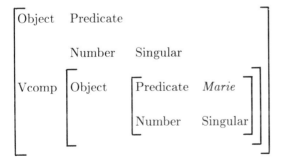

We see then that what Bresnan et al. do is build up a functional
structure feature chain that is tested for compatibility against another
such chain. They must build up and check a hierarchy of features
for two reasons. First, from a linguistic point of view, that is the
natural propositional structure that should be passed along. Second,
in order to encode the possibility of an arbitrary number of controlled
NPs below the dominating VP node, we must adopt some means of
encoding a potentially arbitrary number of features (denoting each of
the NPs and their associated verbs). But given that the functional
structure "equations" annotating the underlying context-free grammar
are fixed once the grammar is written down, the only way to do that
is by building up some recursive structure that mimics the constituent
structure derivation as a chain. (With only a finite number of features,
we can only encode an infinite number of different cases by means
of chains or trees.) This means that Bresnan et al. are forced to
adopt hierarchical feature checking as the means to describe the Dutch
sentences.

In contrast, the government-binding theory represents argument
structure restrictions like subcategorization at a specific level of
representation, d-structure. These restrictions may then be stated
"locally," without the need for potentially unbounded functional
equations. In the case at hand, the relevant d-structure is this:

(6)

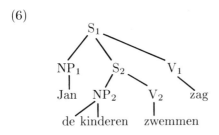

Evers 1975 motivates a cyclic rule of "V raising" moving the V_2
zwemmen to the right of the matrix verb *zag*. This rule, together with
a pruning principle that applies to NPs, produces structure (7):

(7)

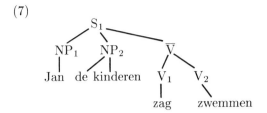

The actual dependency between the verb and its complement is stated locally at d-structure. There is no need for a mechanism that checks for tree structure compatibility over long distances.[6] In other words, the only kind of "compatibility test" allowed involves the flat connection between predicates and arguments. In contrast, the lexical-functional system really asks for too much. Not only does it establish a "flat" relationship between verbs and arguments, it also requires that the tree relationships among the arguments and verbs be of a certain sort. This extension is required in order to account for simple agreement tests where the features are unordered sets, as in subject-verb agreement, while retaining a notion of "local" checking. The test is done at some common mother node dominating two subnodes. Unfortunately, it is this extension that goes beyond what is actually observed in natural languages.

The problem for the lexical-functional machinery is that once hierarchical checking is admitted for this one example, there is nothing to bar it in other cases. But then the power of 2 language can be generated. Worse still, we can build unnatural lexical-functional grammars using just the linguistically motivated control equation apparatus and phrase structure rules proposed in the lexical-functional theory. The same linguistically motivated rules used for Dutch, combined in slightly different ways, lead to grammars quite unlike anything ever attested or likely to be attested in natural rule systems. The example we give uses almost precisely the Dutch control equations, and a slightly different context-free base. The idea behind our unnatural grammar is this. We will build a grammar where a verb controls a higher object NP just in case both the verb and that NP are essentially equally deeply embedded along different "spines" of the constituent structure tree. This we take to be a highly unnatural system. There is no natural language where a control property "counts." Here is an example of the structure we want:

(8)

```
                 VP
           _____/_____
        NP₁         VP              V̄
              _____/\          ____/\____
           NP₂        VP      V₁         V̄
                     /                 __/\__
                   NP₃               V₂      V̄
                                            /
                                          V₃
```

As we can see, the tree structure itself is just like that in Bresnan et al.'s Dutch examples. We need in addition these context-free rules and their functional structure annotations:

(9)

$$\text{VP} \rightarrow \quad \text{NP} \qquad\qquad \text{VP} \qquad\qquad (\overline{\text{V}})$$
$$(\uparrow \text{ subj})=\downarrow \quad (\uparrow \text{ Vcomp})=\downarrow \quad \uparrow=\downarrow$$

(10)

$$\text{VP} \rightarrow \quad \text{NP}$$
$$(\uparrow \text{ obj})=\downarrow$$

(11)

$$\overline{\text{V}} \rightarrow \quad \text{V} \qquad\qquad \overline{\text{V}}$$
$$(\uparrow \text{ Vcomp})=\downarrow$$

(12)

$$\overline{\text{V}} \rightarrow \quad \text{V}$$

(13)

$$\text{NP} \rightarrow \quad \text{N}$$

Rules (10)–(13) are precisely those used by Bresnan et al. Rule (9) is different. (9) has the associated equation $(\uparrow \text{ subj})=\downarrow$ attached to the NP node instead of the equation $(\uparrow \text{ obj})=\downarrow$. We must also add new lexical entries:

V3: $(\uparrow \text{Vcomp subj})=(\uparrow \text{obj})$
      $(\uparrow \text{pred})=V_3\langle(\uparrow \text{subj})(\uparrow \text{obj})(\uparrow \text{Vcomp})\rangle$

V2: $(\uparrow \text{pred})=V_2\langle\ (\uparrow \text{subj})(\uparrow \text{Vcomp})\rangle$
V1: $(\uparrow \text{pred})=V_1\langle(\uparrow \text{subj})(\uparrow \text{Vcomp})\rangle$

The effect of this modest change is a rule system that has exactly
the effects we claimed. Consider first the functional structure built up
along the lefthand VP branching spine. The last NP expansion will
have the associated equation $(\uparrow \text{obj})=\downarrow$. Each VP demands that the
Vcomp functional structure component associated with the node above
it be identified with the functional structure built up at that VP. The
effect is to build up a hierarchical arrangement of Vcomp functional
structures, one for every VP node that is generated except for the
top and the bottommost VP. This again is exactly the same as in
the Bresnan et al. grammar. Compare functional structure (5) above.
In addition, a subject functional structure component is passed up
from all NPs but the last one. The resulting lefthand spine functional
structure corresponding to the example constituent structure tree (8)
would look like this, with two levels of Vcomp embedding:

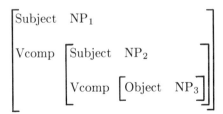

What about the righthand spine? Again, the functional structure built
up will look almost like the Dutch example. But only the last verb
in the sequence will be a control verb, demanding that its object
be the same as the subject of its Vcomp. The other predicate and
subject slots, though not filled in, will also be passed up. Again, "___"
denotes a slotholder to be filled in later by the lefthand functional
structure. The lowermost subject functional structure is linked to the
higher object, via the control equation on V_3.

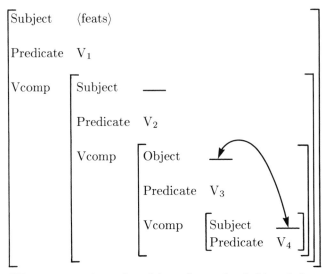

We can see that the object from the lefthand functional structure merges into this righthand structure successfully if and only if it has one level of embedding less than the righthand structure. This is our desired result. Otherwise the object structure cannot be laid on top of the righthand structure and overlap properly; it must coincide with the empty object slot on the righthand side.[7] For example, suppose we interchanged V_2 and V_3 in constituent structure (8). Then the control verb V_3 is less deeply embedded than the object NP it is supposed to control. This structure should be ruled out, and it is. The lefthand functional structure will be as before. But now the righthand functional structure will look like the following, as the reader may verify.

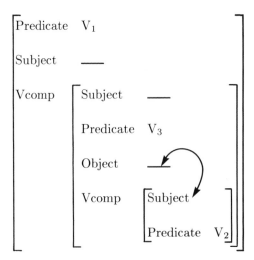

This will not merge properly with the lefthand functional structure because that functional structure demands that the object be embedded inside two Vcomps, whereas the righthand structure calls for an object embedded inside just one. Similarly, if V_3 were embedded one more level down, the number of Vcomps would not match. Only when the number of embeddings is the same on both left- and righthand sides is the structure well-formed.

If we can build such "unnatural" rule systems using lexical-functional grammars, a parallel question to ask is what we can do in the government-binding framework. Here again we can start with a weak generative capacity "diagnostic" result, and then move on to a deeper consideration of just why this result holds.

Our intuition is this. The government-binding theory contains no general unification procedure that is defined over anything more than unordered sets of features (as for subject-verb agreement). The basic identification statement is co-indexing (binding), expressed by the subscripting of two NPs at the topmost syntactic level. That is, we cannot "dive down" inside an NP to determine whether it may be properly co-indexed with another NP. Likewise, syntactic dependencies such as control relationships, verb subcategorization, and the like are defined over a local domain of government, never over arbitrary tree structure.

These limitations hint at less power than the lexical-functional framework. Again intuitively, in the government-binding theory, sentences are generated via a context-free ($\overline{X}$) base, and transformed sentences are produced from these canonical predicate-argument sentences by means of movement. Constituents are just rearranged, hopping into one of a finite number of "landing sites" in each cyclic domain (see Baltin 1982). This suggests three things. First, government-binding grammars should not be able to generate languages like the power of 2 language. Second, government-binding languages should be constant growth. There is no way for the sentences of such a system to be very far apart from one another. The deep reason for this is that there is no general means of feature checking, as in the lexical-functional approach. Third, government-binding annotated surface structures are at most linearly larger than their associated surface sentences. This implies that the well-formedness of government-binding sentences can be checked by a nondeterministic linear bounded automaton, in turn implying that the languages so generated are context-sensitive. Again, the deeper reason for this is that government-binding surface sentences are essentially generated by a context-free base plus movement.

These intuitions are confirmed by the following results. First we will establish the constant growth property, and then turn to the question of annotated surface structure size.

Theorem. Given a government-binding grammar G and its corresponding language $L(G)$, for every sentence w_k in $L(G)$ larger than some predefined constant M, there exists (a distinct) sentence $w_{k'} \in L(G)$ such that $|w_k| = |w_{k'}| + c$, where c is a member of a finite set of constants depending on $L(G)$.

It follows that the difference in length between any two sentences of a government-binding language must be equal to some constant, fixed in advance. The language L_2 does not meet this property. Hence, this language cannot be generated by a government-binding grammar. Intuitively, the sentences of L_2 are "too far apart". The difference between sentence w_i and w_{i+1} if w are the sentences arranged in order of increasing length (not counting sentences of duplicate length) is more than any fixed constant. Similarly, $\{a^i | i$ is a perfect square$\}$, or $\{a^i | i = 2^{2^n}\}$ cannot be government-binding languages.

In order to prove this result, we must say what we mean by a "government-binding grammar." We take a government-binding grammar to consist of:

1. D-structures generated by a base context-free grammar meeting the constraints of $\overline{X}$ theory.

2. Derived surface structures formed by moving base generated constituents into "landing sites." Movement consists of adjunction to a landing site, and leaves behind an empty category. In particular, movement does not consist of copying followed by deletion.

3. Movement obeying the constraints of government-binding theory: the strict cycle; subjacency; proper binding.

4. Simple local filters like the case filter that operate at the phonological level, but no other surface filters.

5. Deletion rules governed by the "across the board" condition of Williams 1978.

Given this definition of government-binding theory, we can now continue. The proof is by cases on the type of government-binding sentences and is unilluminating. The faithful may proceed boldly to the next section; the enthusiastic may consult appendix A.

The implications of this result have already been drawn. To repeat them, it follows that government-binding grammars cannot generate the unnatural power of 2 language, nor any similar arithmetic predicate language whose sentences are "far apart."

If government-binding grammars cannot generate unnatural languages like the power of 2 language, but lexical-functional grammars can, we might wonder whether the extra power of lexical-functional grammars is necessary in order to handle certain natural languages like the Dutch sentences described earlier. Then there would be at least some reason for adopting the stronger machinery, even though it leads to difficulties elsewhere, as we have seen.

The source of lexical-functional grammar's extra power is its ability to build up a hierarchical functional structure and test it for compatibility against another functional structure. In Dutch, this extra power is used to pair up object NPs in the lefthand constituent structure spine with controlled subject positions in the righthand spine. As we saw, this is done by constructing a chain of embedded structures. This device is required because the lexical-functional system does not make use of an underlying level of categorial representation. The lexical-functional constituent structure is just a labeled bracketing of the surface sentence with no underlying empty categories. Any functional comparisons must be based directly on constituent structure. The system must be able to compare constituents that are arbitrarily far apart from each other at the constituent structure level. As we mentioned earlier though, government-binding does away with this mechanism by positing an additional level of categorial representation, annotated surface structure. In the Dutch case the relevant constituents are in the same clause at this level of representation and so may be compared locally, without recourse to the hierarchical comparison machinery of lexical-functional grammar.

The Complexity of Government-Binding Languages

We have shown that certain unnatural languages cannot be generated by government-binding type grammars. Even so, some complex constructions in natural languages can be generated by government-binding grammars. What can we say about languages generated by government-binding grammars generally? One way to look at this problem is to think of the minimum machinery required to enforce the co-occurrence restrictions of government-binding theory. Here there

seem to be two major components: (1) a (context-free) phrase structure
grammar; and (2) a pattern of co-indexing relationships indicating
the binding between antecedents and empty categories, anaphors, and
reciprocals.

Intuitively, because government-binding grammars have context-free
bases plus allowable movements that simply displace constituents, they
should be "nearly" context-free. We have already seen evidence for this
claim. Government-binding grammars cannot generate some strictly
context-sensitive languages, such as the power of 2 language. But how
can we make this claim precise? Our strategy will be as follows. First we
shall eliminate a central "problem" with *Aspects* style transformational
grammars, potentially unbounded deletion. The remedy here is simple.
Because the problem is that deep structures can be too large compared
to surface structures, we see whether we can shorten the representation
of underlying structures that must be recovered. Replacing literal
copying with co-indexing meets this need. More precisely, we show that
given the principles of government-binding theory, annotated surface
structures at most linearly larger than their corresponding surface
strings. This implies that a nondeterministic linear bounded automaton
can recognize the sentences of a government-binding language. Given
a putative sentence, it can guess all possible associated annotated
surface structures, and then check each one in turn to see if the
annotated surface structure meets the conditions on well-formedness to
be associated with the surface sentence. Such languages are context-
sensitive.[8]

The key obstacle to overcome here is the problem of unbounded
deletion. The reason is that the efficiency of a parsing procedure
depends in part on just what we take the job of parsing to be.
The parser's job by definition is to build some output representation
of the sentences input to it. Therefore the parser must do at least
as much computational work as it takes to write down this output
representation. If this representation is complex, for example, if it is
extremely large compared to the size of input sentences, then just the
task of writing down the output make take a significant amount of time
compared to the length of input sentences. For instance, suppose that
given a sentence of length n, the parser had to construct an output
representation of length 2^n. Then at least this many computational
steps would be required to parse such sentences.

It has long been recognized that this is at the root of the complexity of *Aspects* style transformational theories. If what the parser must recover given a surface string is a deep structure, and if it is also the case that deep structures can be arbitrarily large compared to the surface strings derived from them, then the recognition procedures for such languages are not even recursive. More formally, the general result established by Peters and Ritchie (1973b) that connects recognition complexity to the possible difference in length between deep structures and surface strings may be stated as follows:

Let G be a transformational grammar. Let f_G be the cycling function of G, where $f_G(x)$ is 0 if x is not in $L(G)$, and otherwise is the least number s such that G assigns x a deep structure with s subsentences. If f_G is bounded by an elementary (primitive) recursive function, then $L(G)$ is elementary (primitive) recursive. (In fact, if f_G is linear, then $L(G)$ is in a still smaller class.) If the cycling function is not bounded, then $L(G)$ is not even recursive.

Now, as has also long been known (see Lapointe 1977 for a review) it is primarily arbitrary deletion that results in an unbounded cycling function. To quote Lapointe:

Putnam noted that early theories of transformations allowed grammars which could generate any r.e. language (whether recursive or not). The chief reason for this was that early theories allowed arbitrary deletions and substitutions in the course of a derivation. Arbitrary permutations or copying could never cause a grammar to generate a nonrecursive set, for if τ_i and τ_{i+1} are successive steps in a derivation such that τ_{i+1} arises through the application of a permutation or copying rule [from] τ_i then...the number of terminal symbols in τ_{i+1} will be at least as great as [the number of] terminal symbols in τ_i. But this property, that successive steps in a derivation do not "shrink" in length, is the basic defining characteristic of context-sensitive grammars. Therefore only the application of rules which reduce length (that is, deletions and substitutions) could cause a grammar to generate a non-CS [context-sensitive rcb/asw], and perhaps a nonrecursive, language. (1977:228)

The whole argument here hinges on the assumption that the job of the parser is to recover a literal copy of deleted NPs. If this assumption is not needed, then the job of the parser could well be easier, as observed by Peters 1973 and in Peters and Ritchie 1973a:

even if English is a context-sensitive language, and is therefore the language accepted by some nondeterministic linear bounded automaton, no linear bounded automaton...accepts the set of English sentences by "reconstructing" their underlying structures. For an infinite number of inputs, even the "smallest" underlying structure is too "large" to be written down on the tape available to such an automaton. Of course, this does not establish that English is not accepted by a linear bounded automaton (using some other computational strategy). (Peters 1973:379)

In earlier *Aspects* type theories, linearity could not be preserved because many of the operations mapping between deep and surface structure involved extensive copying and deletion. For example, the Equi analysis of sentences cited in Peters 1973 claims that the sentence,

(1) Their sitting down promises to steady the canoe.

has the underlying representation,

(2) $[_S [_{NP}$ Their sitting down]] promises $[_S [_S [_{NP}$ their sitting down] to steady the canoe]]

Note that this sentence consists of three S phrases: the root S and two embedded S phrases (the subject NP of the matrix clause and the subject NP of the complement of the VP). The subject NP of the VP complement is deleted under structural identity with the matrix subject NP. Peters next builds a surface string that has a large associated deep structure by embedding this sentence recursively in a construction of the same type, that is, a sentence that has a matrix subject NP structurally identical to the subject NP of a verb complement. Because by construction the subject NP had more than 2 S phrases (three, in fact), and because deletion occurs under conditions of structural identity, it follows that at the level of deep structure the subject NP of the complement must have the same number of subsentences as the subject NP of the matrix, more than 2. Thus, the new sentence must have a deep structure with more than $2^2 = 4$ S phrases in all:

(3) Their sitting down promising to steady the canoe threatens to spoil the joke.

Each time that this embedding construction is carried out the number of deep structure subsentences is at least doubled, because of the assumption that the complement NP subject is identical to that of the matrix subject. In other words, the number of deep structure subsentences grows as an exponential function when compared to the length of the surface string, exactly the sort of sentence that was to be constructed.

But the argument does not go through under current versions of transformational theory. Here, in place of the literally duplicated subject complement NPs we have an empty category placeholder, Pro, indexed to the proper antecedent NP as appropriate. The empty category is Pro rather than trace because the subject NP position in the complement is not governed by tense or the matrix verb.

(4) $[_{\text{S}}\ [_{\text{NP}}$[Their sitting down]$_i$ promising [Pro$_i$ to steady the canoe]]$_j$ threatens [Pro$_j$ to spoil the joke]]

Crucially, the indexed Pros are not "nested." Pro$_j$, indexed to the entire matrix subject NP *their sitting down promising to steady the canoe*, does not contain, as a subpart, the Pro corresponding to *their sitting down* (although it may be indexed to a subpart of a long antecedent string). We can reconstruct underlying predicate-argument structure without building up an explicit representation of antecedents in the embedded clause.

As a result, the length of the annotated surface structure does not grow exponentially with respect to the length of associated surface strings. Assuming that empty categories cannot be nested and that they correspond only to displaced NPs, then there can be at most only a fixed number of such empty categories in each S. In fact, the number of underlying subsentences of the annotated surface structure will be proportional to the length of the input surface string. If an input sentence is of length n, and if there can be at most k empty categories in each S, then its corresponding annotated surface structure will be at most of length proportional to $(kn)\log(n)$. The additional factor of $\log(n)$ is required because of the space needed to write down the indices for the Pros, $i = 1, 2, \ldots, kn$. The use of indices on NPs rather than explicit tree copying does two things. (1) It prohibits tree comparisons of the detailed sort allowed in the lexical-functional system; and (2) it lets us build an implicit representation of tree structure without explicitly reconstructing it.[9] Peters and Ritchie have already described the implications of this result:

Putnam proposed that the class of transformational grammars be defined so that they satisfy a "cut-elimination" theorem. We can interpret this rather broadly to mean that for for every grammar G_1 in a class there exists G_2 such that (i) $L(G_1) = L(G_2)$ and (ii) there is a constant k with the property that for every x in $L(G_2)$, there is a deep phrase marker ϕ underlying x with respect to G_2 such that $l[d(\phi)] < kx$. (1973b:81–82)

Here, the notation $l(x)$ stands for "length of," while $d(\phi)$ is the "debracketization" of the deep structure. The debracketization consists of terminal elements *sans* right and left brackets, but with traces and Pros. As Peters and Ritchie go on to say:

We now see that any grammar satisfying such a cut-elimination theorem generates a language which more than being recursive is context sensitive. This is so because a nondeterministic linear bounded automaton can determine both that a labeled bracketing ϕ is strongly generated by a context sensitive grammar and that it underlies a given string x if the automaton has enough tape to write ϕ. (1973b:82)

Formally, we want to prove this:[10]

Theorem. Let G be a government-binding grammar, and $L(G)$ the language it generates. Let AS_i be the annotated surface structure structure) associated with sentence w_i in $L(G)$. (If there is more than one such annotated surface structure, then AS_i is a set of annotated surface structures; AS_i is a singleton set if there is just one annotated surface structure.) Then there is a constant k such that for all sentences w_i in $L(G)$, and for all annotated surface structures AS_i underlying w_i, $|AS_i| < k|w_i|$.

The proof, which again proceeds by cases, is in appendix A. What constraints does the proof depend on? The key restrictions are (1) no nesting of traces, (2) the strict cycle, (3) landing site theory, (4) conjunction reduction operating at just the "topmost" constituent level, and (5) co-indexing subscripts incorporated into the grammar's terminal vocabulary. The first constraint bans hierarchical feature co-indexing, of the sort allowed in the lexical-functional theory. The second and third guarantee that there are at most a finite number of empty categories in each cycle, and that intercyclic interactions can be calculated by looking just at the movements from cycle i to cycle $i + 1$. The fourth constraint ensures that deletion is bounded. The last, described at length earlier, allows co-indexed NPs to be written down in linear space.

Having established that annotated surface structures are bounded by linear functions of surface sentence lengths in government-binding grammars, then, as Peters and Ritchie note, we can use that bound to get a nondeterministic recognition procedure for government-binding languages that uses only linear space as a function of input sentence length. The procedure uses "analysis by synthesis," using its nondeterministic power to "guess" all possible annotated surface structures less than a certain length, and checking each one in turn.

Computational Complexity and Natural Language: A Modern Approach

So far we have seen that modern transformational grammars are not as computationally unwieldy as has sometimes been suggested. Following up a weak generative capacity symptom, we have seen that lexical-functional grammars can be written for unnatural rule systems. The last goal of this chapter is to study the time complexity of lexical-functional grammars directly. The elimination of transformational power and the use of a different kind of underlying representation for sentences naturally gives rise to the hope that a lexical-functional system would be computationally simpler than a transformational one. But is this hope realized? If the recognition time complexity for languages generated by the basic lexical-functional theory can be as complex as that for languages generated by a moderately restricted transformational system, then presumably lexical-functional grammar will also have to add additional constraints, beyond those provided in its basic theory, in order to ensure efficient parsability. Just as with transformational theories, these could be constraints on either the theory or its performance model realization.

The main result of this section is to show that certain lexical-functional grammars can generate languages whose recognition time is very likely computationally intractable, at least according to our current understanding of algorithmic complexity. Briefly, the demonstration proceeds by showing how a problem that is widely conjectured to be computationally difficult can be re-expressed as the problem of recognizing whether a particular string is or is not a member of the language generated by a certain lexical-functional grammar. The computationally difficult problem is whether there exists an assignment of 1s and 0s (or Ts and Fs) to the atoms of a Boolean formula in conjunctive normal form that makes the formula evaluate to 1 (or "true"). This "reduction" shows that in the worst case the recognition of lexical-functional languages can be just as hard as the original Boolean satisfiability problem. Because it is widely conjectured that there cannot be a polynomial time algorithm for satisfiability (the problem is $\mathcal{N}P$-complete), there cannot be a polynomial time recognition algorithm for lexical-functional grammars in general either. This result sharpens that in Kaplan and Bresnan 1982. There it is shown only that lexical-functional grammars (weakly) generate some subset of the class of context-sensitive languages. This means that in the worst case exponential time is sufficient to recognize any lexical-functional language. The result in Kaplan and Bresnan 1982 does not address the question of how much time is necessary to recognize lexical-functional languages. The result of this section indicates that in the worst case more than polynomial time will probably be necessary. The reason for the hedge "probably" will become apparent below; it hinges upon the central unsolved conjecture of current complexity theory. In short then, this result places the lexical-functional languages more precisely in the complexity hierarchy of languages.

It is instructive to ask just why the lexical-functional approach can turn out to be computationally difficult, and how computational tractability may be guaranteed. Advocates of lexical-functional theories may have thought, and some have explicitly stated, that the banishment of transformations is a computationally wise move because transformations are computationally costly. Eliminate the transformations, so this casual argument goes, and we eliminate all computational problems. Intriguingly though, when we examine the proof to be given below, the ability to express co-occurrence constraints over arbitrary distances across terminal tokens in a string (as in subject-verb number agreement), when coupled with the possibility of alternative lexical entries, seems to be all that is required to make the recognition of lexical-functional languages intractable.

The Complexity of Lexical-functional Grammars

The demonstration of the computational complexity of lexical-functional languages depends upon the technique of reduction. The idea is to take a difficult problem, in this case the problem of determining the satisfiability of Boolean formulas in conjunctive normal form (CNF), and show that this problem can be quickly transformed into the problem whose complexity remains to be determined, in this case the problem of deciding whether a given string is in the language generated by a given lexical-functional grammar.

To carry out the reduction in detail we must explicitly describe the transformation procedure that takes as input a formula in CNF and outputs a sentence to be tested for membership in a lexical-functional language and the lexical-functional grammar itself. We must also show that this conversion can be done in polynomial time with respect to the length of the original formula.

One caveat is in order before embarking on a proof sketch of this reduction. The grammar that is output by the reduction procedure will not look very much like a grammar for a natural language, although the grammatical devices that will be employed will in every way be those that are an essential part of the lexical-functional theory.[11] In other words, although it is most unlikely that any natural language would encode the satisfiability problem and hence be intractable in just the manner outlined below, no "exotic" lexical-functional machinery is used in the reduction. Indeed, some of the more powerful lexical-functional notational formalisms (long distance binding or existential and negative feature operators) have not been exploited.

To make good this demonstration we must set out just what the satisfiability problem is and what the decision problem for membership in a lexical-functional language is. Recall that a formula in conjunctive normal form is satisfiable just in case every conjunctive term evaluates to true, that is, at least one literal in each term is true. The satisfiability problem is to find an assignment of Ts and Fs to the atoms at the bottom (note that complements of atoms are also permitted) such that the root node at the top gets the value T (for true). How can we get a lexical-functional grammar to represent this problem? What we want is for satisfying assignments to correspond to well-formed sentences of some corresponding lexical-functional grammar, and nonsatisfying assignments to correspond to sentences that are not well-formed. Here we must exploit the lexical-functional machinery for capturing well-formedness conditions on sentences.

The ability to have multiple derivation trees and lexical categorizations for one and the same terminal item plays a crucial rule in the reduction proof. It captures the satisfiability problem of deciding whether to give an atom X_i a value of T or F.

What then does the lexical-functional representation of the CNF satisfiability problem look like? Basically, there are three parts to the satisfiability problem that must be mimicked by the lexical-functional grammar. First is the assignment of values to atoms, for example, $X_2 \leftarrow T$; $X_4 \leftarrow F$. Second is the consistency of value assignments in the formula; for example, the atom X_2 can appear in several different terms, but we are not allowed to assign it the value T in one term and F in another. Finally, CNF satisfiability is preserved, in that a string will be in the lexical-functional language to be defined just in case its associated CNF formula is satisfiable. Let us now go over these.

(1) Assignments: The input string to be tested for membership in the lexical-functional grammar will simply be the original formula *sans* parentheses and the operators $\vee$ and $\wedge$; the terminal items are thus just a string of X_i's. The job of checking the string for well-formedness involves finding a derivation tree for the string, solving the ancillary co-occurrence equations (by feature propagation), and checking for functional completeness. Now, the context-free grammar constructed by the transformation procedure will be set up so as to generate a virtual copy of the associated formula, down to the point where literals X_i are assigned their values of T or F. If the original formula had n terms, then, denoting each by the symbol $E_p, p = 1, \ldots, n$, this part of grammar would look like the following:

$$S \to E_1 E_2 \ldots E_n$$
$$E_p \to Y_i Y_j Y_k; (p = 1, 2, \ldots, n)$$

The subscripts i, j, and k correspond to the actual subscripts in the original formula. Further, the Y_i are not terminal items, but are nonterminals that will be expanded into one of the nonterminals T_i or F_i.[12]

Note that so far there are no rules to extend the parse tree down to the level of terminal items, namely the X_i. The next step does this and at the same time adds the power to choose between T and F assignments to atoms. We add to the context-free base grammar two productions deriving each terminal item X_i, namely, $T_i \to X_i$ and $F_i \to X_i$, corresponding to an assignment of true or false to the atoms of the formula. It is important not to get confused here between the atoms of the formula—these are terminal elements in the lexical-functional grammar—and the nonterminals of the grammar. Plainly, we must also add the rules $Y_i \to T_i$ or F_i, for each i, and rules corresponding to the assignment of truth values to the negations of literals, $T_i \to \overline{X}_i$ and $F_i \to \overline{X}_i$. Note that these are not "exotic" lexical-functional rules. The same sort of rule is required in the *baby* case, that is, $N \to baby$ or $V \to baby$, corresponding to whether *baby* is a noun or a verb. Now, the lexical entries for the T_i categorization of X_i will look very different from the F_i categorization of X_i, just as we might expect the N and V forms for *baby* to be different. Here are the entries for the two categorizations of X_i:

X_i: T_i ($\uparrow$ truth-assignment)=T
                   ($\uparrow$ assign X_i)=T

X_i: F_i ($\uparrow$ assign X_i)=F

Putting aside for the moment the truth-assignment feature in this entry, the feature assignments for the negation of the literal X_i must be the complement of this entry:

$\overline{X}_i$: T_i ($\uparrow$ truth-assignment)=T
                              ($\uparrow$ assign X_i)=F

$\overline{X}_i$: F_i ($\uparrow$ assign X_i)=T

The upward directed arrows in the entries reflect the lexical-functional feature propagation machinery. Remember that T_i and F_i are just nonterminal categories like noun and verb. For example, if the T_i categorization for X_i is selected, the entry says to make the truth-assignment feature of the node above T_i have the value T, and make the X_i portion of the assign feature of the node above have the value T. This feature propagation device reproduces the assignment of true and false to the CNF literals. If we have a triple of such elements, and at least one of them is expanded out to T_i, then the feature propagation machinery of lexical-functional grammar will merge the common feature names into one large structure for the node above, reflecting the assignments made; moreover, the term will get a filled in truth-assignment value just in case at least one of the expansions selected a T_i path. Features are passed transparently through the intervening Y_i nodes via the lexical-functional "copy" device, ($\uparrow=\downarrow$); this simply means that all the features of the node below the node to which the "copy" up and down arrows are attached are to be the same as those of the node above the up and down arrows.

It should be plain that this mechanism mimics the assignment of values to literals required by the satisfiability problem.

(2) Coordination of assignments: We must also guarantee that the X_i value assigned at one place in the tree is not contradicted by the value of an X_i or $\overline{X}_i$ elsewhere. To ensure this, we use the lexical-functional co-occurrence agreement machinery. The *assign* feature bundle is passed up from each term to the highest node in the parse tree. We simply add the ($\uparrow=\downarrow$) notation to each E_i rule to indicate this. The assign feature at this node will thus contain the union of all assign feature bundles

passed up by all terms. If any X_i values conflict, then the resulting structure is judged ill-formed. Only compatible X_i assignments are well-formed.

(3) Preservation of satisfying assignments: Finally, we reproduce the conjunctive character of the 3-CNF problem. A sentence is satisfiable if and only if each term has at least one literal assigned the value T. Part of the disjunctive character of the problem has already been encoded in the feature propagation machinery presented so far. If at least one X_i in a term E_l expands to the lexical categorization T_i, then the truth-assignment feature gets the value T. This is just as desired. If one, two, or three of the literals X_i in a term select T_i, then E_l's truth-assignment feature is T, and the analysis is well-formed. But how do we rule out the case where all three X_i's in a term select the F path, F_i? And how do we ensure that all terms have at least one T below them?

Both of these problems can be solved by resorting to the lexical-functional grammar functional completeness constraint. The trick is to add a predicate feature to a dummy node attached to each term. The sole purpose of this feature will be to refer to the feature *truth-assignment*, just as the predicate template for the transitive verb *kiss* mentions the feature *object*. Because an analysis is not well-formed if the "grammatical relations" a predicate mentions are not filled in from somewhere, this will have the effect of forcing the truth-assignment feature to get filled for every term. Because the F lexical entry does not have a truth-assignment value, if all the X_i's in a term triple select the F_i path (all the literals are assigned *false*) then no truth-assignment feature is ever picked up from the lexical entries, and that term never gets a value for the truth-assignment feature. This violates what the predicate template demands, and so the whole analysis is thrown out. The ill-formedness is exactly analogous to the case where a transitive verb never gets an object. Because this condition is applied to each term, we have now guaranteed that each term must have at least one literal below it that selects the T path. To add the new predicate template, we simply add a new but dummy branch to each term E_i, with the appropriate predicate constraint attached to it. (The new nonterminal is labeled *Dummy*.)

There is one final subtle point here. We must also prevent the predicate and truth-assignment features for each term from being passed up to the head S node. The reason is that if these features were passed up, then, because the lexical-functional machinery automatically merges the values of any features with the same name at the topmost node of the parse tree, the lexical-functional machinery would force the union of the feature values for the predicate and truth-assignment slots over all terms in the analysis tree. The result would be that if any term had at least one T and so satisfied the truth-assignment predicate template in at least one term, then the predicate and truth-assignment features would get filled in at the topmost node as well. The string below would be well-formed if at least one term were T. This would amount to a disjunction of disjunctions (an *or* of *or*'s), not quite what is sought.

To eliminate this possibility we add a final trick. Each term E_i is given separate predicate, truth-assignment, and assign features, but only the assign feature is propagated to the highest node in the parse tree as such. In contrast, the pred and truth-assignment features for each term are kept "protected" from merger by storing them under separate feature headings labeled $E_1, \ldots, E_n$. Just the assign feature bundle is lifted out by using the lexical-functional analogue of the natural language phenomenon of subject or object "control," whereby just the features of the subject or object of a lower clause are lifted out of the lower clause to become the subject or object of a matrix sentence. The remaining features stay unmergeable because they stay protected behind the individually labeled terms.

To actually "implement" this in a lexical-functional grammar we can add two new branches to each term expansion in the base context-free grammar, as well as two control equation specifications that do the actual work of lifting the features from a lower clause to the matrix sentence. A natural language example of this phenomenon is the link between the object of *persuade* and the subject of an embedded complement. The lexical entry for *persuade* encodes this as follows:

persuade: ($\uparrow$ Vcomp subject)=($\uparrow$ object)

According to this lexical entry, the object feature structure of a root sentence containing a verb like *persuade* is to be the same as the feature structure of the subject of the complement of *persuade*, a control equation. Because this subject is *the baby*, this means that the features associated with the NP *the baby* are shared with the features of the object of the matrix sentence.

The satisfiability analogue of this machinery is quite similar to this. A control equation may be attached to an A_i node that forces the assign feature bundle from another node, C_i, to be lifted up and ultimately merged into the assign feature bundle of the E_i node (and then, in turn, to become merged at the topmost node of the tree by the usual full copy up and down arrows):

($\uparrow$ C_i assign)=($\uparrow$ assign)

The satisfiability analogue is just like the sharing of the subject features of a verb complement with the object position of a matrix clause.

To finish off the reduction argument, it must be shown that, given any 3-CNF formula, the corresponding lexical-functional grammar and string as just described can be constructed in a time that is a polynomial function of the length of the original input formula. This is not a difficult task, and only an informal sketch of how it can be done will be given.

All we have to do is scan the original formula from left to right, outputting an appropriate cluster of base rules as each triple of literals is scanned: $E_i \rightarrow A_i C_i$; $C_i \rightarrow Dummy\, Y_i Y_j Y_k$; $Y_i \rightarrow T_i$ or F_i (similarly for Y_j and Y_k); $T_i \rightarrow X_i$; $F_i \rightarrow X_i$ (similarly for T_j and T_k). Note that for each triple of literals in the original input formula the appropriate grammar rules can be output in an amount of time that is just a constant times the length of each triple. If n denotes the length of the original input formula, then because there are fewer than n such triples, the total amount of time to output these grammar rules is just a constant times n. In addition, we must also maintain a counter to keep track of the number of triples so far encountered. This adds at most a logarithmic factor, to do the actual counting. At the end of processing the input formula, we must also output the rule $S \rightarrow E_1 E_2, \ldots, E_m$, where m is the number of triples in the CNF formula. Because m is less than n, this procedure too is easily seen to take time that is a polynomial function of the length of the original input formula. Finally, one must also construct the lexical entry for each X_i and $\overline{X}_i$. This too can be done as the input formula is scanned, left to right. The only difficulty here is that we must check to see if the entry for each X_i has been previously constructed. In the worst case this involves rescanning the list of lexical entries built so far. Because there are at most n such entries, and because the time to output a single entry is constant, at worst the time spent constructing a single lexical entry could be proportional to n. Thus for n entries the total time spent in construction could be at most of order n^2. Because the time to construct the entire grammar is just the sum of the times spent in constructing its production rules and its lexicon, the total time to transform the input formula is bounded above by some constant times n^2.

Implications of Complexity Results

The demonstration of the previous section shows that lexical-functional grammars have enough power to "simulate" a probably computationally intractable problem. But what are we to make of this result? On the positive side, a complexity result such as this one places the lexical-functional theory more precisely in the complexity hierarchy. If we conjecture, as seems reasonable, that lexical-functional language recognition is actually in the class $\mathcal{NP}$ (that is, lexical-functional language recognition can be done by a nondeterministic Turing machine in polynomial time), then the lexical-functional languages are $\mathcal{NP}$-complete. This is a plausible conjecture because a nondeterministic Turing machine should be able to "guess" all candidate feature propagation solutions using its nondeterministic power, including any long distance binding solutions (a lexical-functional device not discussed in this section). Checking candidate solutions is quite rapid. It can be done in n^2 time or less, as described by Kaplan and Bresnan 1982. This means that recognition should be possible in polynomial time on such a machine. Comparing this result to other known language classes, note that context-sensitive language recognition is in the class polynomial space (PSPACE), because (nondeterministic) linear space bounded automata recognize exactly the class of context-sensitive languages. As is well known, for polynomial space the deterministic and nondeterministic classes collapse together because of Savitch's result (see Hopcroft and Ullman 1979) that any function computable in nondeterministic space n can be computed in deterministic space n^2. Furthermore, the class $\mathcal{NP}$ is clearly a subset of PSPACE (because if a function uses space n it must use at least time n) and it is suspected, but not known for certain, that $\mathcal{NP}$ is a proper subset of PSPACE, this being the $\mathcal{P} = \mathcal{NP}$ question once again. Our conclusion is that it is likely that lexical-functional grammars can generate only a proper subset of the context-sensitive languages, including, as is shown in Kaplan and Bresnan 1982, some strictly context-sensitive languages.

On the other side of the coin, how might we restrict the lexical-functional theory further so as to avoid potential intractability? Several escape hatches come to mind; these will simply be listed here. Note that all of these "fixes" have the effect of supplying additional constraints to further restrict the lexical-functional theory.

1. Rule out worst case languages as linguistically, that is, empirically, irrelevant.

The probable computational intractability of lexical-functional language recognition arises because co-occurrence restrictions (compatible X_i assignments) can be expressed across arbitrary stretches of the terminal string in conjunction with potential categorial ambiguity for each terminal item. If some device can be found in natural languages that always filters out or removes such ambiguity locally, so that the choice of whether an item is T or F never depends on other items arbitrarily far away in the terminal string, or if natural languages never employ such kinds of co-occurrence restrictions, then the reduction is theoretically valid, but linguistically irrelevant.

2. Add locality principles for recognition or parsing.

We could simply stipulate that lexical-functional languages must meet additional conditions known to ensure efficient parsability, for example, Knuth's LR(k) restriction, suitably extended. This approach is typified by Marcus's work (1980). Marcus supposed that people normally construct only a single derivation for any given sentence and proposed other conditions that turn out guaranteeing that Knuth's LR(k) restriction will hold. Chapter 5 examines this proposal in detail. We shall see that besides guaranteeing computational efficiency, this kind of proposal can be used to actually explain certain observed constraints in natural grammars.

3. Restrict the lexicon.

The reduction argument crucially depends upon having an infinite stock of lexical items and an infinite number of features with which to label them. This is necessary because as CNF formulas grow larger and larger, the number of distinct literals can grow arbitrarily large, and we require an arbitrarily large number of distinct X_i features to check for co-occurrence conditions. If for whatever reason the stock of lexical items or feature labels is finite, then the reduction method works for only finite sized problems. This restriction seems *ad hoc* in the case of lexical items (why could there not be an infinite number of words?) but less so in the case of features. If features required "grounding" in terms of other subsystems of knowledge, for example, if a feature had to be in the spanning set of a finite number of some hypothetical cognitive or sensory-motor basis elements, then the total number of features might be finite.[13]

Of course, constraints may be drawn from all three of these general classes in order to make the lexical-functional theory computationally tractable. Even then, it remains to be seen what additional constraints would be required in order to guarantee that lexical-functional language recognition takes only a small amount of polynomial time. Here it may well turn out to be the case that something like LR(k) restrictions suffice.

Even if the lexical-functional system can be restricted along these lines, the problem of unnatural rule machinery remains. The unnatural Dutch-like control rule system described earlier is not eliminated by any of these changes. Just how the lexical-functional theory should be restricted so as to rule out these possibilities, while ruling in grammars like Dutch, remains an open question.

Chapter 5
Parsing and Government-Binding Theory

Linguistic theory has long sought to reduce complicated subsystems of facts to a limited set of axioms and their consequences. Almost invariably this drive toward explanation has been justified on grounds of learnability. The idea is to take the linguistic axioms as some presumed initial state of a learner, combine these axioms with "reasonable" sets of input data contributed by the external environment, and derive a limited set of consequences, the observed array of natural rule systems covering the class of natural languages. The properties of natural grammars are then explained by the limiting characteristics of the axioms from which they are derived. We might take this line of reasoning one step further, however. While the axioms of grammar must be irreducible within the grammatical system itself, we might ask whether properties of these axioms can be explained in terms of extragrammatical factors, for example, parsing.

In this chapter we shall show how this can be done. In order to obtain an efficient parser based on the government-binding theory we must impose certain design constraints. Surprisingly, this constrained parser also predicts:

That traces (as opposed to other binder–bindees) must be governed by subjacency;

That gapping constructions but not VP deletion must be subject to bounding conditions resembling subjacency;

That c-command restrictions must apply to antecedent-anaphor or antecedent-variable and quantifier-variable pairs;

That certain interpretations of so-called "parasitic gaps" will be preferred to others;

That grammatical rules may refer to root or nonroot contexts, but to no other more deeply embedded contexts (chapter 6).

Because these constraints are actually observed to hold in natural languages, we see that a variety of otherwise disparate facts can be functionally unified in the domain of parsing.

Although the results in this section are new, this style of explanation is not. Miller and Chomsky 1963 present an early example of this research strategy. They noticed that a grammar would be significantly complicated if center- and self-embedded structures were to be ruled out directly by grammatical principles. But, they claimed, this complication is unnecessary. These sentences can be ruled out on the extragrammatical grounds of parsing complexity. Center-embedded sentences force a natural parsing model to retain large amounts of uncompleted left context, thus overloading the memory of such a device (see Miller and Chomsky 1963 for details). In this case two simple subtheories easily explain data that a unitary theory can explain only with great difficulty. In this chapter we shall see a similar explanation for the form of certain axioms of the grammatical system in terms of extragrammatical principles.

It is reasonable to expect principles of grammar to be compatible with parsing and learning. A particularly well designed system would be constructed in such a way that all of the subtasks of the language faculty could be handled by a unified set of principles. The results of this section suggest that this is the case. Principles demanded for language parsability are also those required to guarantee language learnability.

Echoing chapter 2, there are many other possible relationships between grammar and parsing model than strict type transparency. These range from the relatively uninteresting case of input-output mimicry to more interesting models that respect the division of labor specified by the grammar. On this latter view the parser is a kind of natural implementation of the rules and representations of the grammar. Unlike the grammar, the parser is a device designed to perform a specific task, and hence the particular exigencies of parsing can influence implementation details. This is the view that we shall adopt. First we shall show that a modified Marcus parser makes crucial reference to the principles of transformational grammar (analogues of the projection principle and the θ criterion) in order to guarantee deterministic parsing. This is a central feature of Marcus's system that will be discussed in more detail below. We conclude that a simple extension of a Marcus parser goes beyond mere input-output mimicry and in fact embeds many of the basic principles of a transformational grammar fairly directly.

Second, we shall show that this extended parser can handle cases of pronominal and full NP anaphora in a way that is both linguistically and psycholinguistically justified and compatible with the government-binding theory. First of all, the autonomy of grammar is respected. The parser separates decisions that can be made given structural and lexical information from decisions that require more general inferential processing. In addition, the proposed representation for syntactic processing provides a natural format for the binding theory of Chomsky 1981.

The two submodules of the parser may be viewed as a particular type of parser, a restricted LR(k) parser or bounded context parser, conjoined to a search procedure for co-indexing. The basic theory of LR(k) parsing is discussed below; for present purposes, the point is that such parsing devices are guaranteed to run in time proportional to the length of input sentences. Efficiency is guaranteed both by specific properties of the grammar and by specific properties of the parsing device. Note that this is a performance oriented complexity analysis that is to be contrasted with the more typical complexity analysis of linguistic systems grounded in the study of generative capacity. As discussed in chapter 3, a generative capacity analysis focuses on the mathematical properties of the set of sentences specifiable by the grammar, abstracting away from considerations of online language processing. It is just these details of implementation that could be fixed to guarantee efficient parsability in real cases. This chapter presents specific and independently justified proposals to do this.[1]

In contrast with earlier views, this approach makes transformational grammar a rather plausible component of a theory of language comprehension. Earlier criticisms insisted that there were at least two major obstacles to a transformational grammar as a part of a theory of language use. The first was that the amount of "active" computation demanded by a transformationally based model did not appear to comport with what was assumed to be the structure of the online sentence processor. Chapter 2 showed that this objection was unfounded because it was based on unjustified assumptions about possible computational machinery underlying short term memory. The second objection centered around the generative capacity of the languages specifiable in unrestricted theories of transformational grammar. This objection is likewise unfounded if, as shall be shown, generative capacity analyses must be supplemented with specific proposals about how a grammar is embedded into a parser so that the functional demands of a system are guaranteed. These results reinforce the general point made in chapters 3 and 4 that generative capacity analyses of linguistic systems may be largely irrelevant to the actual efficiency of parsing systems. In the case at hand, the set of sentences that can be handled by the parsing model is quite "complex," and yet the theory's individual components are simple. In short, if the proposed parsing model is correct, it seems that a theory of implementation using a transformational grammar is particularly well designed. The functional demands of learnability and efficient parsability can be guaranteed, at least in part, by a unified set of principles.

Transformational Grammar and the Marcus Parser

In this section we shall quickly review the relevant details of the Extended Standard Theory and of the Marcus parser, showing the Marcus parser in fact realizes an Extended Standard Theory.

We shall first rehearse some relevant properties of the Extended Standard Theory (EST). EST claims that thematically relevant linguistic information is encoded at one level of representation, namely deep or D-structure. D-structure is related to other levels via the operation of Move α. The level of D-structure essentially represents the output of the lexicon, in that it encodes relevant subcategorization information such as *believe*'s ability to appear with a nominal or sentential complement but not an adjectival one:

(1) a. $[_S$ I $[_{VP}$ believe $[_{NP}$ John]]]
    b. $[_S$ I $[_{VP}$ believe $[_{\bar{S}}$ that $[_S$ John is a fool]]]]
    c. $[_S$ I $[_{VP}$ am $[_{AP}$ happy]]]

Such properties are captured by generating a verb such as *believe* with an immediately postverbal NP or S at the D-structure level.

According to the government-binding theory of Chomsky 1981, this subcategorization information is available not only at the D-structure level but at every level of linguistic representation. The availability of this information is guaranteed by the projection principle, as discussed in chapter 1: "Representations at each syntactic level (i.e., LF [logical form rcb/asw], D- and S- structure) are projected from the lexicon

in that they observe the subcategorization properties of lexical items"
(Chomsky 1981:29). EST uses the mechanism of trace insertion to
guarantee that the projection principle is respected. When a category
is moved from the position that it occupied at deep (or D-structure),
it leaves behind a phonologically null element in this spot identified
with the moved category by the notational device of co-indexing. For
example, a sentence such as (2a) would be derived from the deep
structure (2b) by Move α, leaving a trace as shown in (2c):

(2) a. Who do you believe?

   b. $[_{\bar{S}}[_{Comp}\ \ ][_{S}\ You\ [_{VP}\ believe\ [_{NP}\ wh]]]]$

   c. $[_{\bar{S}}[_{Comp}\ wh_i\ ][_{S}\ You\ [_{VP}believe\ [_{NP}\ e_i\ ]]]]$

Trace theory plus the conditions on rule form and functioning
outlined in chapter 1 enforce the shift from complicated rule formats
to a system of simple rules plus general constraining principles. Of the
several conditions mentioned in chapter 1, the subjacency constraint
will be most relevant, and we shall review it again briefly.

Subjacency limits the distance that a category may move from its
D-structure position. By "distance" we mean the number of nonterminal
phrases that may intervene between a category's D-structure position
and the position to which it moves. Alternatively, we may think of this
condition as limiting the distance between an antecedent and its trace.
Consider sentence (2a) above. In the derivation of (2b) from (2c) the
category wh moved into the Comp position from its position inside
the VP and S containing the verb believe. The subjacency condition
defines a subclass of nonterminal nodes that act as "bounding nodes."
In English, these are S, NP, and, perhaps, PP. Subjacency says that a
given movement may cross at most one of these nodes. Formally, the
condition may be stated as follows (Chomsky 1977a:108):

No rule may relate X and Y in the configuration

$[\dots X \dots [_{\alpha}\ \dots [_{\beta}\ \dots Y \dots]\ \dots\ ]\ \dots X \dots\ ]$ (α, β bounding)

The derivation in (3) is blocked because the movement of the wh
phrase must cross both an NP and an S as it moves into the Comp
node, violating subjacency.

(3) a. *Who do I believe the claim that Bill likes?

   b. *$[\ [_{Comp}\ \ Wh_i]\ [_{\bar{S}}\ I\ believe\ [_{NP}\ the\ claim\ [_{\bar{S}}\ Wh_i\ that\ [_{S}\ Bill$
      $likes\ e_i\ ]]]]]$

As mentioned in chapter 1, this condition applies only to movement rules. It does not govern the relationship between a lexical anaphor and its antecedent, as shown by sentence (4):

(4) The men$_i$ expect [$_S$ [$_{NP}$ pictures of each other$_i$] to be on sale]

In this case, the anaphor *each other* is separated from its antecedent *the men* by two cyclic nodes, S and NP.

The Marcus Parser as a Transformationally Based Model

How does the Marcus parser mimic the important properties of a transformational grammar? First of all, it is equivalent to a transformational grammar in the sense that for every surface string (sentence) it associates the same annotated surface structure (annotated by traces) that would be paired with that sentence by a transformational grammar. We might dub this a condition of "input-output" or black box functional equivalence.[2] Note that this definition of equivalence leaves open the question of how it is exactly that the annotated surface structure gets computed. That is, a parser could reconstruct the right underlying representations using principles entirely unrelated to the grammar, and yet these structures could be the same as those generated by the grammar. The Marcus parser uses a transformational grammar much more directly than this, though. It maps between levels of representation in accordance with each of the principles of government-binding theory. It is explicitly constructed to respect both parts of the opacity conditions and the subjacency condition. Further, it crucially makes reference to lexical properties of items at every level of representation, in accordance with the projection principle. Each of these properties will be exemplified as we discuss the Marcus parser below. In addition to these conditions on rule functioning the Marcus parser also mimics conditions on rule form, as proposed in current theories of transformational grammar.[3]

It is important to stress that it is adherence to these principles rather than the details of the rule system itself that determines the potential implementation of a transformational grammar. We want to say that a parser "implements" a grammar when we can ground its organizing principles by looking at the grammar. For example, a parser's automatic dropping of a trace in a post-passive participial position may be rationalized as the expression of the constraint that only nonphonetic elements may appear in this position, a constraint in turn explained by the various subtheories of the government-binding theory. In this case, the grammar's principles are not transparently related to the parser's operation. It takes a few deductive steps to go from the government-binding principles to the "insert trace" action. This point is important because the actual rules and organization used by the Marcus parser are in no sense direct translations of the rules and organization proposed by transformational theorists except in the sense that the parser respects the principles discussed above. Nonetheless, we would like to claim that the Marcus parser implements an extended EST grammar, because it uses the representations of EST and mimics its constraints.

Given these preliminary remarks about the general relationship between EST and the Marcus parser, we now turn to a more detailed consideration of the actual implementation of the Marcus parser. For the purposes of this chapter, the most important property of the Marcus parser is that it is assumed to operate deterministically. Marcus explains this notion by presenting several properties of his parser that he claims prevent it from simulating nondeterminism:

First, all syntactic substructures created by the grammar interpreter are permanent. This eliminates the possibility of simulating [non]determinism by "backtracking," that is, by undoing the actions that were done while pursuing a guess that turns out to be incorrect. In terms of the structures that the interpreter creates and manipulates, this will mean that once a parse node is created, it cannot be destroyed; that once a node is labeled with a given grammatical feature, that feature cannot be removed; and that once one node is attached to another node as its daughter, that attachment cannot be broken.

Second, all syntactic substructures created by the grammar interpreter for a given input must be output as part of the syntactic structure assigned to that input ....

Finally, the internal state of the mechanism must be constrained in such a way that no temporary syntactic structures are encoded within the internal state of the machine. (1980:12–13)

The main stumbling block for the construction of a deterministic parser is local ambiguity in natural language. For example, there are many cases of lexical ambiguity where a lexical element can take multiple subcategorization frames, and these cause problems because a parser must decide which of these frames is relevant in a particular case. In contrast, a nondeterministic machine can handle this problem because it has the power to "guess" which of these alternatives is correct, at no apparent cost.

A nondeterministic device is just a convenient mathematical fiction. There are several ways to actually implement such a procedure, either by pursuing all possible pathways at once or by ordering hypotheses from most to least likely and then testing these hypotheses against the actual input string in turn. Returning to the problem of multiple subcategorization, this means that upon encountering a lexical item a parser could begin to form parse trees for all possible complements of this item, in parallel, erasing or otherwise marking the incorrect complements as irrelevant based on information encountered later in the parse. Alternatively, a parser could test the complement judged most likely to occur (based, perhaps, on frequency or other criteria, stored with the lexical entry for each item), discarding this single hypothesis if it does not pan out and proceeding to the next most plausible hypothesis in its list of candidates. In this case, a parser is said to be able to backtrack, because it is permitted to withdraw previous decisions about the structure of sentences.[4]

In contrast, the Marcus parser is assumed to operate strictly deterministically, in that (i) it builds a single labeled syntactic tree representation of a sentence, from which relevant thematic information can be extracted; and (ii) it does not carry along in parallel a representation of multiple possible parses. Each structure that is built is assumed to be part of the final, single structural description of the input sentence. Thus any part of the parse tree structure that is created, either node labelings or tree structure, is never discarded. This means that if the parser guesses that a postverbal NP is the direct object of a verb, as would be shown by attaching the NP directly underneath the VP, then that attachment can never be undone. This ensures, by fiat, that no backtracking ever occurs; the real trick, of course, is to show that even if this constrained course is adopted then the parser's guesses will be correct for those sentences that people can also analyze without evident guessing.

The net effect of these constraints is that the parser can only compute one derivation at a time, and that at each step its next move is completely determined. It is this property that forges the close connection between the Marcus parser and the deterministic parsing algorithm to be discussed below.

Plainly, if a deterministic parser did not contain some way to ensure that the guesses it makes are the right ones, then it could not be made to work deterministically at all. For if a mistake were made the parser would have to wind its way laboriously through alternative hypotheses until the right one was discovered. We would have to add some kind of backtracking machinery. So there must be some way to guarantee that the right choices are always made.[5]

How then does the Marcus parser resolve cases of local ambiguity? We will have to examine how the Marcus parser works in some detail. There are two key sources of information that the Marcus parser exploits to decide what to do next:

1. It can examine a representation of the parse tree that it has built so far. We will call this the "left context," because the tree is built roughly left to right.[6]

2. It can examine a (finite) portion of the input string yet to be analyzed, its lookahead.

Assume that the parser is currently scanning item w_j of the input sentence. Then the left context, the parse tree including the terminal items w_1 through w_{j-1}, is assumed to have already been analyzed by the parser. For example, by the time the Marcus parser is reading *kissed* in *the boys thought that Sue had kissed them*, it has already built up a parsed representation of the sentence like this:

$$[_S [_{NP} \text{ The boys}] \text{ Infl } [_{VP} [_V \text{ think}][_{\overline{S}}[_{Comp} \text{ that}] [_S [_{NP} \text{ Sue}] \text{ Infl}$$

Besides this portion of the parse tree, the parser can also "look ahead" to examine items in the input stream, up to a limit of 5 such items. In the case above, the tokens *kissed* and *them* will be accessible.

The particular way in which the Marcus parser encodes left context and lookahead information is as follows. The left context is stored in a particular data structure that Marcus calls the active node stack. It is called active because the items in it represent phrases that have not yet been completely built. For example, the S in the above structure is still active because it has not yet been completely built; the VP must still be completely analyzed and attached to it. Likewise, the VP itself has not yet been built, because its complement structure is yet to be completed. In contrast, the NP attached to the root S is completely built, hence is inactive. A constituent is complete when the argument structure of a predicate is filled. The list of active phrases is also organized as a stack, in that the most recently built (but not yet completed) phrase is the first one that is accessible, the next most recently built phrase is the next most accessible, and so forth:

1   INFL   (most recently built, uncompleted phrase)
         /
        had

2   S   (next most recently built, uncompleted phrase)
          /
        NP
         |
        Sue

3   S̄
          `Comp
          /
        that

4   ‚VP
        V
         |
      thought

5   ⎯S   (least recently built, uncompleted phrase)
       NP INFL
      / | |
   the boys Past

The active node stack is simply a convenient representation of the labeled bracketing.

By stipulation, the original Marcus parser's operating rules are restricted to have access to just the features of items in the lookahead (what Marcus calls the lookahead buffer) and just two items in the active node stack, namely the top item in the stack itself and the next cyclic node down in the active node stack. Here cyclic node means cyclic in the linguistic sense, that is, an NP or S node for English. We will modify this assumption below.

A parse proceeds in roughly the following fashion. Words enter the parser's domain of action via the lookahead buffer, usually three words at a time. The parser can perform three basic actions. First, it can bundle up one or more words into a complete constituent. For instance, it can take the items *the* and *boy* and determine they are both part of a larger phrase, a noun phrase. Second, it can predict that a certain larger phrase will eventually be found. For instance, if it sees the item *the*, it can safely posit the existence of an NP. Third, the parser can co-index noun phrases with empty noun phrases or with other anaphoric elements in accordance with the principles of the government-binding theory.

In all of this, left context and lookahead play a vital role in ensuring that the parser's actions will always be uniquely determined and correct. Consider, for example, a construction where an item is no longer in its proper thematic position, as in (5) and (6) below where the italicized elements are interpreted as direct objects but do not appear in this position at the surface.

(5) *The man* was expected.
(6) *Who* did you expect?

The Marcus parser can create a representation for these sentences where the NP elements are linked to their proper thematic position via the mechanism of trace binding:

(7) The man$_i$ was expected e_i.
(8) Who$_i$ did you expect e_i?

This linking is carried out in part by exploiting a parsing analogue of the projection principle. The parser has access to the lexical entries for elements it encounters in its lookahead buffer. For example, upon recognition of the verb *expect* in the sentences above, the parser would have access to the information that *expect* subcategorizes for either an NP or an S:

(9) I expect [$_{NP}$ John]
(10) I expect [$_{S}$ John to be home soon]

Thus the parser respects a machine analogue of the projection principle. Subcategorization information is available at all levels of representation. The Marcus parser assumes that subcategorization information is available to guide an ongoing parse. In this way, lexical information is "projected" through syntactic structure.

Finally, lookahead information plays a key role in the Marcus parser via its ability to disambiguate locally uncertain context. Consider for the example the following pair of sentences, and assume that the parser has analyzed this input up to the tokens *his sister*.[7]

(11) John believes his sister.
(12) John believes his sister is smart.

The first sentence has an NP VP complement, the second a propositional ($\bar{S}$) complement. If the parser could not look ahead there would be no way to disambiguate between these two parses. However, because the NP in the first case is followed by nothing and in the second case by a verb (plus additional material), the proper distinction can be made easily by simply looking at the next token in the input beyond *his sister*.

In fact, the modified Marcus parser is really just an informal machine version of an LR(k) parser, specifically, a bounded context parser. The relevant properties of such a machine are:

1. An LR(k) parser computes a rightmost derivation in reverse.

2. It computes this derivation deterministically using a finitely bounded lookahead.

3. The parsing rules that it uses are stored in a finite control table. Therefore, they must be finitely representable. In addition, a bounded context parser's rules are stated just in terms of terminal or nonterminal symbols. For example, if the grammar has just the symbols S, NP, VP, then the parser can use only these symbols.

The second property is trivially satisfied by Marcus's device. The first property is also satisfied by the Marcus parser, if we look at the order in which phrases are completed. A rightmost derivation goes from the fringe (the terminal symbols) to the root (the topmost S of the tree) from right to left. This, of course is not particularly helpful for natural language parsing, because it is assumed that material is input from left to right. A rightmost derivation in reverse mimics the left to right order. The third property is crucial to our explanation of subjacency. It states that for rules to be finitely representable in the LR(k) device's finite control table, they must be representable by a literally finite number of terminal and nonterminal symbols. We cannot bundle up arbitrary strings of symbols using essential variables because these symbols are uninterpretable in a finite control table. Again, the Marcus parser's grammar rules are trivially finite; if we also insist that they refer to just unalloyed grammatical symbols, we can satisfy the second part of property (3).

Parsing and Subjacency

So far we have described a machine solution but no problem. The hurdle for deterministic parsing is unbounded syntactic dependencies. Assuming that the parser must be able to access an element's antecedent, the amount of information a procedure must keep track of is apparently unbounded. Because the material between an antecedent and its trace can be arbitrarily long, how can the machine store all the context to the left of the token it is currently analyzing? This problem can be solved if we can guarantee that the left context required for parsing decisions is finitely representable. This demand, plus the assumption that the grammar is directly embedded in the parsing model, will be all we need to derive the existence of a central constraint of current grammatical theories, subjacency. In other words, the functional demand of deterministic parsing can be used to derive an "axiom" of the grammatical system. Moreover, this derivation explains why subjacency governs only a subset of the superficially unbounded dependencies. It also explains why some dependencies may be strictly unbounded.

This functional explanation does not go through if we assume that all parses are carried along "in parallel." For example, the classic fast parsing methods for context-free grammars, such as Earley's algorithm, use pseudoparallelism in this way. In these models, all possible alternative derivations are carried along in a parse. Subjacency also cannot be derived this way in a theory that posits generalized phrase structure categories, rather than just the "bare" $\overline{X}$ categories. This is true of the generalized phrase structure grammars of Gazdar 1981. In such models subjacency remains a mystery, rather than a necessity, at least given the functional derivation presented here.

Before going into the details of the functional derivation, let us review which binding relationships are strictly bounded and which are not. Here is subjacency:[8]

(1) No rule may relate X and Y in the configuration:
$$[\ldots X \ldots [_\alpha \ldots [_\beta \ldots Y \ldots] \ldots] \ldots] \ldots X \ldots]$$
where α and β are bounding nodes.

The bounding nodes for English are S, NP, and perhaps PP. In chapter 1 we showed that complex noun phrase and *wh* island constraint violations fall out of subjacency. The diagnostic for these constraints is simple. We just check whether binding out of a complex NP or *wh* island yields a grammatical or an ungrammatical sentence. For instance, the following elements obey subjacency and can be only boundedly far from their antecedents. The crossed nodes show violations of subjacency (where S and NP are bounding).

(2) *wh* trace:
    a. *$[_{\bar{S}}$ What$_i$ $\not\times_{\bar{S}}$ did John believe $\not\times_{NP}$ the claim
       $[_{\bar{S}}\ e_i\ [_S$ Harry would like to eat $e_i]]]$
    b. $[_{\bar{S}}$ What$_i\ [_S$ did Harry claim ...
       $[_{\bar{S}}\ e_i\ [_S$ he would like to eat $e_i]]]]$

NP trace:
    c. *$[_{\bar{S}}$ John$_i$ seems $[_{\bar{S}}$that $\not\times_S\ \not\times_{NP}\ [_S\ e_i$ feeding himself$]]$
       will be difficult$]]]$
    d. $[_{\bar{S}}$ John thinks $[_{\bar{S}}$ that $[_S\ [_{NP}$ Pro$]$ feeding himself$]]$
       will be difficult$]]]$

In (2a) and (2c) the appearance of unbounded movement is derived from the iterative application of bounded movements. In (2d) the unbounded relationship is allowed because it is not produced by movement.

Gapping is also strictly bounded, as noted by Koster 1978. Because gapping cannot apply iteratively, in part because it is not a movement rule, its strict boundedness is apparent even from direct examination of the surface representation.

(3) Gapping:
    a. John kissed$_i$ Mary and Bill $[_V \emptyset]_i$ Sue.
    b. *John kissed$_i$ Mary and $[_S$ I don't believe $[_S$ Bill $[_V \emptyset]_i$ Sue$]]$

In contrast, the following cases of lexical anaphor, pronominal, nominal or Pro binding, and VP deletion are unbounded. The antecedent in these cases may be indefinitely distant from the element it binds:

(4) Lexical Anaphors:
    a. The men$_i$ thought $[_{\bar{S}}$that $[_S\ [_{NP}$ pictures of each other$_i]$
       would be on sale$]]$

Pronominal binding:
    b. John$_i$ was pleased $[_{\bar{S}}$that $[_S$ Mary believed $[_{NP}\ [_{NP}$ the claim$]$
       $[_{\bar{S}}$that $[_S$ he$_i$ was courageous$]]]]]$

Nominal Binding:
    c. The woman that John$_i$ adored made $[_{NP}\ [_{NP}$ the proposal$]$
       $[_{\bar{S}}$that $[_S$ John$_i$ take her to dinner$]]]$

Pro:

d. Fred$_i$ believed [$_{\overline{S}}$that [$_S$ [Pro$_i$ shaving himself]
   would make him a hit at the party]]

VP deletion:

e. John [$_{VP}$ kissed Mary]$_i$ and Frank thought that John said
   that Harry would have [$\emptyset_i$] too.

We have seen before how local subcategorization information can be
used by a Marcus type machine to correctly decide what parsing action
to take, both in simple sentences and in sentences where constituents
have been moved from their canonical thematic positions:

I kissed John.
Who did you kiss e_i?

Recognition of the verb *kiss* entails retrieval of this element's
subcategorization frame as well. Given that *kiss* is a transitive verb,
the parser will enter a state where it expects to see an NP object next.
If there is an actual NP in the string, the parser will eventually attach
it as the direct object of *kiss*. If there is no such phonological element,
the parser will insert an empty NP, and attach it as the direct object
NP. In contrast, if the verb encountered is intransitive, then the parser
should enter a state where it would not expect to find an NP. In these
cases, the expansion of the parse tree is unambiguously determined
using just subcategorization information and a limited lookahead. We
do not have to look for the presence or absence of an antecedent in
order to build the next part of the parse tree correctly. Transitive
verbs must have NP direct objects. The parsing decision for this case is
fixed by this lexical fact, which is obtained by consulting the parser's
dictionary.

There is still one problem, however. Not all verbs are unambiguously
transitive or intransitive. The correct expansion of the parse tree cannot
always be determined simply by looking at the subcategorization frame
of a verb. The parser must also check whether an actual antecedent is
present. Suppose we have a verb that is either transitive or intransitive,
such as *eat*. We can embed this verb in the following kind of *wh*
question. Note that the trace can be arbitrarily far from its antecedent.

(5) What$_i$ did John say that Frank believed that Sue said ...
    ... that Bill would like to eat e_i?

At the point where the parser is analyzing the predicate *eat*, it must decide whether *eat* is to be taken as transitive or intransitive. If it is transitive, then because there is no overt NP object, a trace must be inserted; if intransitive, then this should not be done. Further, given the assumption of determinism, this decision cannot be tentatively advanced and then retracted; the parser must decide what to do correctly on its first try as it encounters the predicate online. But the determination of the transitivity of. *eat* clearly depends upon whether there is an appropriate antecedent. If no such antecedent is present, then the intransitive reading will automatically be selected:

(6) Did John say that Frank believed that Sue said ...
    ... that Bill would eat?

Therefore, if the parsing decision to insert a trace or not is to be made correctly, the relevant parsing rule would have to refer to a potentially unbounded left context in order to determine whether or not an antecedent was present. In effect, such a rule would have to be written in the following form:

IF   lookahead string is:

$[_{\overline{S}}$Wh $[_{VP}$ $[_{\overline{S}}$ $[_{VP}$ $\cdots$ $[_{VP}$ eat

THEN
        insert a *trace*;

ELSE
        do not insert a *trace*.

While such a rule can perfectly well be finitely stated in terms of an essential variable, this option is not open for the finite control table of a parser. The reason is that the finite control table of such a parser uses actual input and context symbols, not variables. In order to actually implement the effect of an essential variable, we would have to store a potentially unbounded left context of actual symbols, and then search through this stored material to see if it matched the *wh* trace rule.[9]

How can this difficulty be overcome? There are two obvious solutions to this problem. First, the dilemma would be avoided if the machine's actions always depended on some literally finite left context. Then, by fiat, the machine's rules would be representable in a finite state control.[10] Second, we can posit a particular kind of nonliteral representation of left context designed to get around precisely this difficulty. This is in fact the proposal made by Gazdar 1981, in his generalized phrase structure grammars. We will consider this alternative below, showing that it is apparently not the one that natural parsing systems have adopted.

For now though let us assume that the nonliteral context alternative is not at our disposal and that left context must be literally bounded. By literal context we mean that the parser can use only the unalloyed categories given by $\overline{X}$ theory, subject to one caveat, discussed below. Transformational grammar enforces this restriction on left context via the constraint of subjacency. Given that subjacency holds, there can be at most a finite amount of literal, constituent material separating an antecedent and its trace.[11] This restriction ensures that any parsing rules involving the proper expansion of a tree containing traces can be stored in a finite control table. The presence of a grammatical condition like subjacency can be understood as a deterministic parser's adaptation to the problem caused by ambiguity in natural language.[12]

In short, assuming that the parser operates deterministically and that left context includes only symbols of the grammar like S, NP, and VP, there must be some bounding condition on trace insertion, because this is a parsing decision.

But why *subj*acency? The requirement that left context be literally finite explains why some bounding condition must be imposed on antecedent-anaphor dependencies, but does not explain why it takes the form that it does. Any finite bound on the number of S (or X^{max}) domains to be searched would enforce the required condition. Why should this limit be one, rather than ten? The reason is that natural grammars cannot "count." Evidently, natural rule systems cannot express predicates like "ten" or "fifteen."[13] In other words, we suppose that the search for an antecedent can be stated only as follows, where we use just predicates that are naturally available.

(7) Look for the nearest c-commanding NP, satisfying all additional grammatical constraints.

The grammar cannot express a rule like the following, that uses an unnatural predicate:

(8) Look for the c-commanding NP in the seventh S domain above the current one, satisfying all additional grammatical constraints.

The rules and principles of grammar make reference to structures and categories, rather than any precise number of such structures. But now observe that there is precisely one situation where a purely structural characteristic coincides with a purely numerical one, namely, in the case of the structural property of "next to" or "adjacent." The next higher S domain is adjacent to the current one. "Adjacent" is presumably a primitive that the grammar can exploit. It appears again and again in the statement of syntactic and phonological rules. We can write a rule like (7), but not a rule like (8).[14] This means that if the grammar is not allowed to count clauses, it must express a "nearest NP" search without specifying any bound on the number of S domains that may be crossed, just as in the case of other kinds of co-indexing. The co-indexing rule will still look something like: find the nearest c-commanding NP meeting constraints "..." where the constraints "..." refer to purely structural properties of the intervening derivation. But then, this is a rule that could make reference to unbounded left context again. "Nearest" could be as far away as we would like. We conclude that there is precisely one constraint stable within the vocabulary of the grammar that can enforce the desired bound of left context: subjacency. Neither parsing nor grammatical constraints alone suffice to explain the existence of subjacency; rather, it is the compound effect of interacting rule writing structure and parsing functions that does the trick.

So far we have motivated subjacency for sentences involving *wh* movement. In chapter 2 we mentioned that passive morphology could be used as an indicator that a trace should be inserted postverbally. This would seem to cause problems for our explanation of subjacency because subjacency applies to cases of NP movement (including passive) as well as *wh* movement. If the presence of the trace can always be locally detected using passive morphology, then it is difficult to see why there must be a search for the trace's antecedent to insure the proper syntactic expansion of the tree. But the need for bounded search is what functionally grounds subjacency.

While it seems that in the normal case passive morphology is a reliable indicator of NP movement, it is not foolproof. There are sentences where we find passive morphology but no NP movement and no NP trace. These sentences are predicted by case theory, as discussed by Chomsky 1981. Case theory predicts that NP movement is forced by a lexical NP's requirement to receive Case and the absorption of

Case by passive morphology (see chapter 1 for full details). If a verb takes a constituent that does not require Case, then there should be no movement. (9) and (10) illustrate.

(9) John believed that Bob told great stories.
(10) It was believed that Bob told great stories.

In lieu of movement in (10), a pleonastic *it* is inserted in the athematic subject position. The relevant problem comes from verbs that optionally subcategorize an NP, S or S̄. *Ask* is such a verb, as (11) and (12) show.

(11) The press asked Jody Powell whether Carter would go
     back to the farm.
(12) The press asked whether Carter would go back to the farm.

Both (11) and (12) can passivize, yielding (13) and (14):

(13) Jody Powell was asked by the press whether Carter would go
     back to the farm.
(14) It was asked (by the press) whether Carter would go
     back to the farm.

(13) and (14) are problems because in the local environment of the passive verb phrase there is no way to tell which subcategorization frame is involved. The surface sequence $V+ed$ [$_S$ could result from either NP movement of the immediately postverbal trace assuming that the sentence was the passive of (11) or it could result from simple insertion of *it* in the athematic subject position. We can only resolve the ambiguity by determining whether the NP subject is pleonastic or not. As in the *wh* case we must assure the boundedness of this search or else it will not be statable within the finite control format of the parser. Subjacency helps. Given subjacency alone though, we would still have problems because even though each successive cyclic movement is bounded by subjacency, the net effect is to remove the lexically specified material, as opposed to intermediate antecedents that are traces, to a position that is potentially indefinitely far from its deep structure source. This apparent cloud does have a silver lining, because it allows us to explain some otherwise puzzling facts first noticed by Postal (as cited in Dresher and Hornstein 1979:81). Postal observed that pleonastic NPs are not subject to successive cyclic movement:

(15) a. There was believed to be a fire in the yard.
     b. *There seems to be believed to be a fire in the yard.

Dresher and Hornstein claim that this distribution of data follows from a designated element property of these items. Indices are not left on the categories designated items fill if they are moved from those categories. Therefore, any successive cyclic movement will yield a structure with unbound NP positions. The problem with this solution is that Dresher and Hornstein appeal to an independently motivated principle (numbered 38 in their text), stating that only designated elements can erase traces. This principle assumes an analysis of *there* insertion where a preverbal subject is first moved to the right and then replaced with the designated NP *there* or *it*. The problem is that Dresher and Hornstein's principle can be subsumed under the θ criterion and the derivation that Dresher and Hornstein assume is inconsistent with both the θ criterion and the projection principle. The θ criterion does not make reference to erasure. This removes the independent motivation for Dresher and Hornstein's nonindexing convention. Actually, the subjacency story provides the needed grounding. If designated elements can only be moved once, and if the first movement is bounded by subjacency, then the parser needs only a finite search to distinguish between cases like (13) and (14). If (14) is the relevant structure, then there will be a lexically specified pleonastic element in a subjacent domain.[15] If (13) is the source then there will be either a lexically specified referential element or a trace in the NP subject position of the subjacent sentence. This trace can only be the trace of a referential element and so the parser knows that the relevant subcategorization frame is NP, S.[16]

There are other questions to ask. Because it is ambiguity that apparently drives the subjacency restriction, we might wonder why subjacency applies to all cases of *wh* and NP movement instead of just the ambiguous cases. Again we appeal to the necessity of stating this condition within the rule writing vocabulary of the grammar. To handle just the ambiguous cases, subjacency would have to explicitly stipulate these environments. The stipulation would involve the use of existential quantification. Such predicates are not available to the rule writing system for natural language and so the more general solution where subjacency applies to all movements is the one that the grammar selects. This argument is not quite sufficient, however, because it may be argued that the ban on existential quantification is motivated by learnability. That is, a rule system that allows predicates of this kind presents the language learner with too much leeway as to the choice of suitable terms for rules. Still, subjacency is a universal condition and is taken as part of the language learner's innate endowment. It is hard to see why the ban on such terms would apply to subjacency, as it is not learned at all. The answer is that this condition is stated in the parser as an explicit rule of parsing. If we assume that the constraints on the rule writing vocabulary sanctioned by the grammar apply to the parsing rules as well, as is reasonable if we want to say that the parser implements the grammar, then a condition banning existential quantification will apply to the parsing rule of subjacency as well. What this means is that the rule writing system will mechanically incorporate constraints that must be built into it without regard for the source of those constraints. Thus, even though the subjacency condition cannot be the source of any learnability problems (as it is innate), once it is written as a rule of the parsing grammar, it must respect the general constraints on all grammatical rules. This drives home our point that the system we are dealing with is really a very unified one that can simultaneously deal with all of the functional demands placed on the language faculty. In such a system it is not surprising that constraints motivated by one functional demand should influence the way the system can meet the other functional demands imposed on it.

Confirmation of the subjacency explanation comes from studying the boundedness of gapping constructions. As has been noted by Koster 1978 and others, gapping is strictly bounded. Thus (16a) is grammatical while (16b) is not.

(16) a. John hit$_i$ Mary and Bill [$_V$ $\emptyset$]$_i$ Sue.

b. *John hit$_i$ Mary and I don't believe Bill [$_V$ $\emptyset$]$_i$ Sue.

Formally, this is surprising. The boundedness of *wh* and NP movement rules can be seen formally as the result of principles applying to what we can independently establish as a unified class of rules. That is, NP and *wh* movements share many properties and are formally rather distinct from each other. In contrast, gapping is not easily viewed as a movement rule. It differs from the former two rules in its formal properties (see Koster 1978 for discussion). It is better characterized as a deletion rule, but bounding conditions do not govern most deletion rules. VP deletion contrasts with gapping in this respect. The apparent puzzle can be resolved by showing that gapping and movement are functionally alike with respect to parsing and left context, and hence it is to be expected that gapping and movement should both be bounded.

The demonstration is simple. Gapped constituents can be locally ambiguous in ways analogous to the local ambiguities that result from movement; this ambiguity can only be resolved by inspection of the gapped constituent's antecedent. Then, by the same arguments given above, we conclude that the distance between the gapped constituent and the antecedent must be finite and so the boundedness of the construction is derived. It is this functional similarity, we argue, that leads to the similar bounding properties of gapping and movement.

For gapping, the relevant cases of ambiguity involve the attachment of complements around gapped constituents. We cannot always determine the proper attachment of a complement from its phonological shape. In (17) the complement PP *after Bill* is attached as a sister to the V node:

(17) Mary $[_{VP}$ $[_{V}$ ran $][_{PP}$ after Bill]]

But in (18) it is attached to the $\overline{VP}$.

(18) Mary $[_{\overline{VP}}$ $[_{VP}$ $[_{V}$ arrived]] $[_{PP}$ after Bill]]

Extraction possibilities from within complement clauses are affected by the place of attachment of the complement clause. Roughly, if the complement clause attaches to VP, extraction is possible; if the complement attaches higher in the tree, extraction is blocked. See Hornstein and Weinberg 1981 and Kayne 1981 for discussion. The following examples, shown with their relevant structures, illustrate.

(19) It was Mary that Bill ran after.

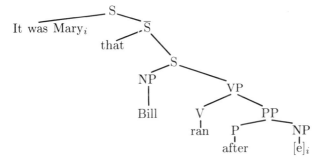

(20) *It was Mary that John arrived after.

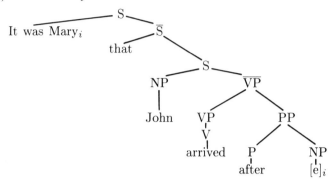

In these examples, the attachment of the complement is governed both
by its phonological shape and by the subcategorization properties of
the verb that it potentially attaches to. This is a parsing decision. In
gapped constructions, though, the verb is not locally present. The only
way to retrieve the subcategorization features is to find the identical
antecedent:

(21) a. John ran$_i$ after Sue and Frank [$_{VP}$ [$_V$ ∅]$_i$ after Mary]

 b. John arrived$_i$ after Sue and Bill [$_{\overline{VP}}$ [$_{VP}$ [$_V$ ∅]$_i$] after Mary]

But if the antecedent is to be found it can only be some bounded
distance away from its target; otherwise the rule telling the parser how
to expand the tree at the postgapped position would not be finitely
specifiable (assuming a literal representation of left context). Again we
find the same complex of properties, a potentially ambiguous parsing
decision and a resolution via literally bounded context.

This situation contrasts with VP deletion. VP deletion deletes the
entire verb phrase. But verb phrases are unambiguously parts of
sentences. The parser never has to see if there is an antecedent VP to
know that one is called for in the sentence it is currently considering.
Therefore, VP deletion is predicted to be free of a bounding constraint,
because there is no parsing ambiguity here. (22) confirms this prediction.

(22) John [$_{VP}$ kissed Mary]$_i$ and I think that Frank said that
 Mary thought that Harry would have [$_{VP}$ [∅]$_i$] too.

Summarizing, exactly in those cases where we can have a parsing
ambiguity, we find a local bound; exactly in those cases where parsing
decisions can proceed unambiguously, we find allowable unbounded
relationships.

Let us now return to consider the second way of handling unbounded dependencies we deferred earlier. Instead of insisting on a literal bound on left context, we could adopt an alternative representation ensuring finite representability for parsing rules. Roughly speaking, we can create a derived representation that makes the antecedent locally available at all times. This is the type of mechanism associated with the generalized phrase structure grammars (GPSGs) of Gerald Gazdar and his colleagues.[17] A GPSG can "remember" that a displaced constituent has been encountered by using complex nonterminal symbols. This information can be stored during a parse until the source position of the displaced category has been reached. For example, consider the sentence:

(23) Who did Mary tell John that Bill liked?

In GPSG, the *wh* element's presence is encoded in the grammar by means of the complex nonterminal XP/NP, where X is any category defined by the $\overline{X}$ system. The slash notation effectively serves as a memory cell. Here, the "slash NP" notation tells the parser that it must expand some context-free rule (in this case VP/NP) with an empty NP on the righthand side. This information is available locally because the finitely representable (though complex) nonterminal label directly dominates the expansion site. Therefore the relevant parsing rules can all be finitely representable in a control table, and all is well.[18]

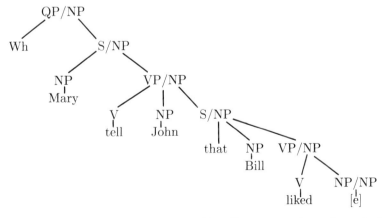

Instead of representing left contexts literally as a string of symbols or a tree, we could choose to represent them generatively via a finite state automaton, and still be assured that no information is lost.

Given the properties of context-free grammars cited in the previous note, it should be apparent that finitely representable parsing rules can be written in a GPSG no matter how far the actual distance between an antecedent and its trace. In other words, given a GPSG grammatical framework, there is no functional derivation in terms of parsing for a constraint like subjacency. So for example, a GPSG system could perfectly well represent a parsing rule to handle this sentence:[19]

(24) *Who do you wonder who remembers who likes?

The first *who* would be encoded into slashed nonterminals as usual, carried along via the sequence Q/NP, V/NP, and S/NP. Then, the second *who* would be encountered, and passed along. Because there are now two nonterminals, this would have to be done by a context-free rewrite rule and complex nonterminal system such as, $\overline{S}$/NP→ S/NP-1 NP-2, where NP-1 and NP-2 denote the first and second *who*s encountered, respectively. Next, the complex S would be expanded as an empty NP (corresponding to the missing subject NP filled by the second *who*) and VP/NP-1 (corresponding to the continued "transmission" of the first *who*). Then the third *who* would be picked up, and analyzed just like the second *who*; the first *who* would be passed along via a complex nonterminal VP/NP-1 as before. Finally, the object NP would be expanded as an empty element, with a rule like VP/NP-1→ V NP[e]. Note that no problem would be encountered in carrying out the parse, no matter how far away the first *wh* constituent is from its argument position, and no matter how many complete S nodes with filled complementizer positions must be crossed.

This negative result does not mean that subjacency could not be functionally grounded in a GPSG. As chapter 3 observed, there are many possible "functional" constraints that could have played a role in the shaping of language. Foremost among these, at least traditionally, is learnability. Even though subjacency does not have a functional explanation in GPSG, it could still be demanded on account of its role in learnability. For example, it could be that something like the Degree-2 constraints of Wexler and Culicover 1980 play a role in the learnability of a GPSG.[20] In any case, the failure of a parsing account of subjacency means that GPSG will lack a certain uniformity of explanation. The optimal case is that the linguistic system will be designed for both easy learnability and easy parsability, and it is reasonable to expect constraints that are grounded in both.

Still another objection to a GPSG grammar follows from the actual use of the nonterminal symbols themselves. The system of complex nonterminals is explicitly introduced to salvage the mathematical property of context-freeness; at least part of the point of the salvage operation is the bonus that the resulting system is efficiently parsable. But we have just seen that if complex nonterminal grammars were used in natural systems, then we would not expect to find the patterning of locality constraints with ambiguous subcategorizations that we do observe. The same point holds for other "unbounded" models of constituent displacement, for example, the "hold cell" model employed in ATN systems. Further, the use of complex nonterminal symbols plainly expands the entities postulated by the grammar, because we admit symbols such as "S/NP" and "S/NP-1 NP-2" to the ranks of full fledged constituenthood. These categories are not motivated by the $\overline{X}$ theory. Because the only point in introducing complex nonterminals was to solve the problem of unbounded dependencies and because that problem may be solved, and evidently is solved, in some other way by natural grammatical systems, we may conclude that complex nonterminals represent an unwarranted expansion of the stock of grammatical entities. What we observe is that parsers need to use just the simplest categories handed over by grammars, units like S, NP, and VP. The parser needs to use at least these categories; what the subjacency analysis shows is that no more than these are needed. This is the optimal situation and one that actually explains the existence of subjacency as a real bonus.

Finally, explanatory power and simplicity aside, the complex nonterminal solution might fail at the level of descriptive adequacy. It would then fail to account correctly for observed grammatical constraints. For example, if the analysis proposed by Bresnan et al. 1982 for Dutch is correct, then a context-free grammar cannot even properly describe certain tree structures exhibited by natural languages. See chapter 4 for a comparison of the derivation of these Dutch sentences in the lexical functional and government-binding theories.

It is reasons like these that lead us to rule out the possibility of a generative encoding of left context, and allow only a literal encoding. This would mean, for example, that the left context,

$$[\mathit{Wh}\ [_S\ NP\ [_{VP}\ [_S\ NP\ VP\ [_S$$

would be represented as such or by its tree equivalent.

Summarizing the story so far, the functional account of subjacency depends on three key assumptions. First, parsing is not parallel. Second, generative encoding of left context is disallowed. Third, the linking of traces or other elements to their antecedents is done online. This means that the existence of subjacency actually constitutes an argument for these assumptions. Take the first assumption. If parsing were nondeterministic, in the sense that the parser had the luxury of storing all possible analyses of ambiguous sentences, then at the point where it is unclear whether a trace is to be inserted or not such a machine can simply store all possible alternatives, delaying the search for an antecedent until the entire sentence has been analyzed. In this model, there would be no reason why a constraint like subjacency should exist at all. Likewise, if a general context-free parsing model is assumed, for example, Earley's algorithm, then its generative encoding of left context will allow trace binding over literally unbounded domains, and subjacency remains a mystery. Finally, suppose that antecedent recovery as it pertains to parsing decisions need not be done online. This would imply that we could reprocess a sentence via a series of several "scans." But then, we could always delay an ambiguous parsing decision by effectively rereading the input sentence.

On our assumptions then, imposing the subjacency restriction is necessary in the case of antecedent-trace binding. But our story is not over; we have not exhausted the possible dependency relationships observed in natural languages. In the next few sections we will take up several interesting subcases of "binding" relationships, exploring how each of them fits into the model of parsing that we have sketched. We will see that these examples also support our functional account.

Parallel Processing and Subjacency

Our prediction of which rules must be governed by subjacency depends crucially on the assumption that the underlying parser is deterministic. This is true in two senses. The first is the sense that ambiguity causes problems for the deterministic parser, problems that must be resolved online as the parser may only take one path at a time. It should be noted that there is one nondeterministic model that simulates this aspect of determinism. The ATN models of Woods 1970 or Kaplan 1974 also allow the parser to pursue only one path at a time. The difference between these models and Marcus's approach is that when an ATN finds that it has misparsed an ambiguous verb, it is allowed to undo its previous actions. By contrast, the Marcus parser is not allowed to do any backup at all.

Both of these machines contrast with models that allow parallel computation of alternative parses. Such machines allow a parser encountering an ambiguous lexical item to compute a representation of all possible parsing paths at once.[21] But then, there should be no contrast between antecedent–trace/gapping constructions and antecedent/(pro)nominal and Pro binding. If the parser were able to store all possible paths, then it would be able to delay the search for an antecedent in the ambiguous cases until after the sentence has been fully analyzed. Only after the parse was fully complete would the search for an antecedent begin. However, if this were true, then there would be no distinction between the two classes of cases. The parsing decisions could be made in both cases without reference to the presence or absence of the antecedent. There can be no question of the finite representability of the parsing rules for these cases. But it was precisely the matter of finite representability that forced us to invoke bounding conditions in the first place. We see then that if all parsing alternatives can be carried along in parallel then there is no argument for subjacency along the lines that we we sketched.

True Long Distance Binding

At first glance, we might think that our derivation of subjacency creates more problems than it solves. How, for example, could any long distance binding be possible? We dealt with cases of unbounded VP deletion rules above. We will now turn to two outstanding classes of problems, nominal/pronominal and anaphor binding. Either a pronoun or a name can be arbitrarily distant from its antecedent:

(25) a. The man that John$_i$ liked said that Mary believed ...
     ... that John$_i$ would make a great date.
   b. The man$_i$ said that Mary believed ...
     ... that he$_i$ loved her.
   c. The men$_i$ wanted [$_S$ [$_{NP}$ pictures of each other$_i$] to appear in the newspaper]

Plainly, if the entire left context tree were to be stored here then the amount of context that could be required might be unbounded. But there is a crucial difference between trace insertion/co-indexing and nontrace co-indexing that eliminates the problem of finite left context for nontraces. First of all, the decision to insert a nontrace element in the parse tree does not depend on the presence or absence of an antecedent. There are two reasons for this.

First, nontrace elements are either phonetically realized in the input sentence itself or can be inferred from purely local context. This is true of Pro. Pro is only inserted in ungoverned contexts, as described in chapter 1. But the notion of ungoverned context is a strictly local one. A category is ungoverned if and only if there is nothing in its local domain (its immediate S̄) to serve as its governor. Note that the decision to insert a trace or not cannot be based on just the local environment; the same local context that sanctions a trace also permits intransitive subcategorizations (for ambiguous verbs).

Second, unlike traces, pronominal and nominal elements need not have antecedents, so their insertion cannot depend on the existence of antecedents. The decision to insert a Pro or leave it out of a parse can be made independently of the existence of an antecedent. To see that pronominal and nominal elements (including Pro) can lack antecedents, consider the following examples.

(26) John said that *she* was nice.

(27) *Pro* eating peas can be bothersome.

Now, the decision whether to insert a trace or not is a parsing decision. The outcome of the decision determines what the annotated surface tree will look like, because in some cases an NP trace is attached to the tree, and in others it is not. But in the case of pronouns and lexical anaphors we know what the parse tree will look like. Other grammatical principles tightly constrain where Pro is to be inserted. Pro is ungoverned, and so is found in subject position, but only if a literal subject is missing. If the parser runs across a subject position with no lexical material, it can insert an empty category, interpreting the empty category as Pro if it is ungoverned. This decision is fixed. Note that this is a situation where parsing and competence part ways. Lexical anaphors must always have antecedents. However, their occurrence in an input string does not depend on the presence or absence of such antecedents, because their mere phonetic shape will trigger their correct attachment. If an antecedent can be found, the sentence will be grammatical, otherwise not; in both cases the sentence will be parsable.

Still, we do not know what the index of the pronoun or lexical anaphor is. The co-indexing of nontraces is not part of the parsing process per se. By this we mean that it is defined over the already built syntactic parse tree. Co-indexing can be thought of as a search procedure imposed on a fixed parse tree that takes place after relevant parsing decisions have been made. It is not a part of the construction of the tree itself. Let us call this the "second stage" of the analysis of the sentence. Co-indexing is defined not by any single finite rule of the second stage, but rather by a computation defined by the entire second stage procedure itself. That is, we may imagine a separate finite state control device, operating with a pushdown stack, that reads as input a "string" representing the annotated surface structure corresponding to the parse of the sentence, with empty categories (traces, Pros, and so forth) in place, but without indices. The machine outputs a representation with indices. The entire set of operating rules, along with the stack data structure, constitute an algorithm for co-indexing. The use of a stack means that co-indexed antecedents can be arbitrarily far from each other.[22] Note that since co-indexing is not a parsing process, it may be assumed to be distinct from first stage parsing. But because the syntactic tree has already been built, indexing can proceed rapidly; we discuss how rapidly at the end of this chapter.

Given this division between parsing and non-parsing processes, we can now account for the different behavior of trace vs. nontrace NP constituents. Syntactically nonambiguous constituents are predictably not subject to bounding conditions, while traces must be subject to bounding conditions and, given noncounting, subjacency. We predict this division to hold uniformly. As far as we can tell, it does seem to hold. We will consider a final example, that of parasitic gaps.

Parasitic Gaps

Parasitic gaps pose yet another potential stumbling block for our analysis. Here are some examples of parasitic gaps. We distinguish parasitic gaps from "real" gaps by labeling them "p."

(28) Who did Matilda see [e] without greeting [p]?

(29) These are the people who you like [e] without knowing [p].

(30) I saw [e] without recognizing [p], my favorite uncle from Detroit.

Parasitic gaps occur in the following environment: First, the sentence containing the gap must also contain an antecedent (an $\overline{A}$ antecedent as defined by Chomsky 1982). Second, the antecedent must be bound to an independent empty category that is subjacent to it. Finally, the parasitic gap must not be c-commanded by the other gap.

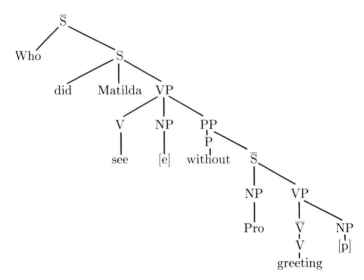

Our approach predicts that parasitic gaps, given that they are not subjacent to their "antecedents," must be inserted without reference to the presence or absence of these antecedents. Otherwise, we would not be able to guarantee the finite representability of left context in these cases. This in turn predicts that for an ambiguously transitive/intransitive verb the parasitic gap interpretation should always be optional (assuming neutral context), because local subcategorization information will not be able to distinguish between transitive and intransitive readings. Unlike normal *wh* movement then, the parasitic gap of an optionally intransitive verb should permit an intransitive interpretation in this position. The following examples show that this prediction is correct.

(31) A dish [that people [who enjoy eating [(p)]] dislike [(e)]]]
(32) Which sonata can you listen to [e] while reading [(p)]]?

Plainly, there are two possible interpretations for each of these sentences. On one reading, the parasitic gap refers to the same entity as the real gap; on the other, intransitive reading, what is being described is some general activity such as eating or reading. But the existence of an ambiguity here shows that the parsing decision to insert an [e] or not need not be made on strictly the basis of left context.

(33) What$_i$ did John say that Frank believed that Sue said ...
       ... that Bill would like to eat e_i ?
(34) Did John say that Frank believed that Sue said ...
       ... that Bill would like to eat? (intransitive)

These two sentences are not ambiguous, indicating that the left context information is available in these cases. And it is precisely these [e]'s that are subject to subjacency, as expected. In short, the possibility of (structurally) ambiguous readings and subjacency violations fall together, as would be anticipated from the parsing model that we have sketched. The parasitic gap is either inserted or not based on the lexical properties of the verb. After the parse is completed, the tree may be searched for a possible antecedent, but this does not affect the actual parsing decision.[23]

A Functional Account Of C-Command

While traces and nontraces diverge with respect to bounding conditions, traces and some of the nontrace categories are similar in that they both obey c-command. Traces, pronouns bound by some quantifiers, and lexical anaphors must be c-commanded by their antecedents.

Given that c-command is a basic predicate of the government-binding theory, we must be able to compute it from the parsing representation. The obvious way to do this would be to use a full tree representation and then design an algorithm to compute c-command from it.

Alternatively, we could build on the fly a representation that makes the calculation of c-command computationally trivial. This is the tack that we shall take. We shall modify an explicitly stored left context so that the computation required for binding will be efficient (at most linear in the length of input sentences) for any single antecedent search. The method we suggest will also allow us to explicitly represent c-command and non c-command relationships between antecedent-anaphor pairs.

The basic idea amounts to a modification of the Marcus parser. Recall that during a parse the Marcus parser builds up a stack of active, or not yet completely built phrases. When a phrase has been completely built, then it is ordinarily dropped into the input buffer, in preparation for attachment to its proper mother node. The notion of phrase completion is grounded upon the satisfaction of the argument structure of the head of that phrase. For example, consider the verb *put*, that obligatorily subcategorizes for an NP and a locative PP. A sentence such as *John put the baby in the basket* will not be judged complete until the locative PP phrase *in the basket* has been encountered and attached to the VP phrase. First, the subject NP *John* is encountered and attached under the S node. Then the VP is started and the verb *put* is attached under it. At this point, if there is no other (presumably optional) material in the input stream that could be attached to the VP, it will be dropped into the input buffer. The next parsing step will be to attach the VP to the main S. The intuition behind the notion of completion is that once we have in hand the obligatory argument structure of a predicate and its optional arguments that can unambiguously be assumed to occur in the same phrase, then semantic interpretation can be carried out in full on that subconstituent.[24]

We must extend Marcus's method somewhat to get actual mimicry of c-command. As is well known, the subject of a clause c-commands everything in a clause and all of the clause's complements. Given our machinery though, the subject would be shunted after completion and would not c-command anything. To fix this, we propose extending semantic completion to the notion "receive or transmit a θ role." That is, an element is not complete until it either receives or transmits its theta role. One mechanism to guarantee this would be to leave a copy of the highest (NP) node in the stack with the same index given during the parse. This indexed NP can then receive a theta role from the following verb in the case of subject. Returning to our previous example, after completing *the guy*, a co-indexed copy NP would be left in the active node stack.

In this model, semantic interpretation works on a nonsyntactic list of propositional structures. As a constituent is completed in syntactic structure, then that unit is shunted off as a basically unordered predicate argument list. We shall call this the propositional list. Note that the syntactic structure may be eliminable given that the thematic roles of a predicate's arguments have already been computed based on the syntactic representation. C-command relations between elements in the propositional list are transparent. If two elements A and B are in the active node stack, then those elements c-command each other; if A is in the propositional list and not in the active node stack and B is in the active node stack, then in the corresponding tree representation, A does not c-command B.

On this view, syntactic and semantic analyses are carried out on distinct representations. This design fits well with evidence about human linguistic memory. Linguistic information seems to be represented in two different memory "stores." The most recently processed constituent can be shown to be stored differently from completely built constituents.[25]

This proposal has the effect of altering the nodes accessible in the
active node stack such that they c-command a constituent about to
be attached. In other words, given this principle of attachment and
node completion, the active node stack extensionally represents the
c-command predicate; c-command need not be separately computed.
To see in detail how this works, let us trace through an analysis of
the modified parser on a sentence such as *The guy that John met likes
him.*

First, as before, the parser will create a toplevel S node. Next, upon
seeing the determiner *the*, it will create an NP node, attaching *the* as
a determiner, and then *guy* as the head of this node.

Next, the parser will detect the beginning of a *that* relative clause,
prompting the creation of an embedded S node (an $\overline{S}$). It becomes the
top of the stack; the original S node becomes the second node down.
That is attached to the $\overline{S}$. The NP subject of the relative clause, *John*,
and its VP will be built in turn. A trace will be dropped as the object
of *met* and bound to *the guy*, completing the VP. The VP is then
attached to the S node, completing the VP and the S. Since it is now
completed, the S is dropped into the buffer, and then immediately
attached to the $\overline{S}$. After the dust settles, things look like this:

Active node stack:

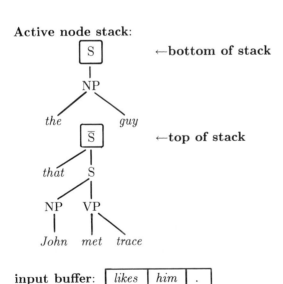

input buffer: | *likes* | *him* | . |

unseen words: (none)

Now the embedded S̄–S is completely built. Following the operating
principles of the parser, it is dropped into the first cell of the buffer,
and then attached to the NP *the guy*. As the completed S is attached to
its proper mother in the syntactic representation, it is simultaneously
shunted to a propositional structure that indicates its local point of
attachment.

Active node stack:

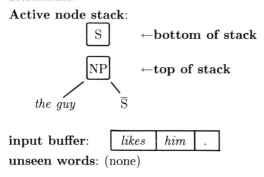

<table>
<tr><td>S</td><td>←bottom of stack</td></tr>
<tr><td>NP</td><td>←top of stack</td></tr>
</table>

the guy   S̄

input buffer: | *likes* | *him* | . |

unseen words: (none)

Note how we have no longer displayed the syntactic structure under
the S̄ in the active node stack. According to the operating principles of
the parser this material is no longer visible to the syntactic component;
it has been transferred to the "propositional" domain. Any material
below the S̄ will no longer be available for any parsing decisions.[26]

Having attached the S̄, the next move of the parser will be to note
that the NP that is currently on the top of the stack is completely
built. As a completed constituent, it too will be dropped into the
buffer, to be attached as the subject NP of the root S. Just as in
the case of the embedded S, the interior syntactic details of the NP
will be lost to future syntactic processing, with the argument structure
being shunted off to the propositional representation. Looking at the
active node stack, we see that the only element visible is the subject
NP below the S. We have assumed that this NP has been assigned an
index, as is standard.

The parse continues in this fashion. Items are attached to constituents
in the active node stack and completed constituents are dropped into
the input buffer with their internal details being lost to syntactic
access. By the time we get to the analysis of the object NP *him*, the
second node in the stack consists of the VP, with *likes* attached; the
third node down in the stack is the S with the attached NP, *the guy
that John met*. Since the NP *him* has now been completely built, it is
time to drop and attach it to the VP as completed.

There is some psycholinguistic evidence that this is the procedure that people use when they are engaged in online processing. Kornfeld 1974 presents evidence suggesting that reaction time tasks are affected by whether or not a probed for item c-commands the last items encountered in a sentence. Kornfeld auditorily presented subjects with sentences and then asked them whether a certain word was actually in the sentence or not. She used structures with pre- and postadverbial clauses, pure complements, relatives, and conjunctive complements. These sentences were varied so that the probed word occurred either in the matrix or the complement clause. Probe latencies (the time subjects took from presentation of the probed word to deciding whether the word was in or out of the sentence) varied significantly between probes in pre- and postverbal complements or relative clauses and the corresponding probes in matrix sentences. Adverbial clauses showed only limited effects from switching the order of the modifying clauses: "there were smaller clause-order differences for stimuli with adverbials than for matched stimuli with relatives and complements" (Kornfeld 1974:84). The structures are given below. Bracketed NPs denote probed words in complement clauses and asterisked NPs, probed words in matrix clauses.

The results were basically these:

(1) Preverbal complement probes (examples A, C, E) took longer than the corresponding matrix probes to respond to.

(2) Postverbal matrix probes (examples B, D, F) took about the same time (and in some cases were even significantly faster than) the corresponding postverbal complement probes for relatives and complements, even though a clause boundary intervenes between these probes and the end of the sentence.

How can we interpret these results in the light of our model? The central idea is that this pattern of different access times correlates with c-command domains. Relatives and pure complements are the only complements that get attached directly to the VP. None of the preverbal complements c-commands the matrix clause. The notion of "completed constituent" can then be used to actually explain these results. Relatives and postverbal complements (as in examples D and F) get attached directly to the VP node. Therefore, the VP is not complete until the complement or relative is entirely built. Given our algorithm, in cases D and F the NP associated with the head of the VP remains in the active node stack until all arguments are completed. This happens only on completion of the complement or relative, the postverbal object and NPs in the complement clause of these examples are simultaneously in the active node stack. Because these NPs are simultaneously available in a single kind of representation, access should be faster in these cases than when the NPs have been shunted into separate stores. In fact, in examples A, C, and E the VP and S dominating the bracketed NP will have been shunted to the propositional representation before the parser begins building the matrix clause A or the main verb C or E. In this case then, access will be delayed. These are exactly the findings. Intuitively, the listener "chunks" utterances into c-command domains and shunts these domains as they are completed. Searching for an element in a non c-command domain demands retrieval communication between different memory stores, and this is what takes extra time. In contrast, elements in the same c-command domain, hence same memory store, produce similar reaction time results.

One caveat. The Kornfeld data, though suggestive, do not set out to test this hypothesis directly. This data is not perfect. There are some instances where even in the postverbal relative and pure complement cases the matrix probe does not c-command. In research to appear shortly, Weinberg (forthcoming) and Garrett and Weinberg (forthcoming) test the c-command hypothesis directly.

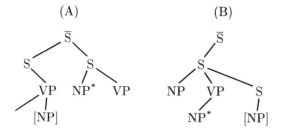

(C)

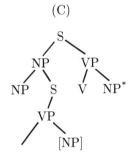

(D)

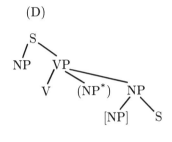

(E)

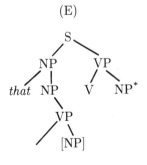

(F)

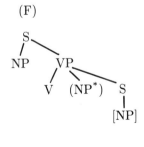

So far we have said nothing about how anaphoric elements are to be bound in this system. *He* can be co-indexed with *John* but not with the NP *the guy*. That this should be so follows from principle (B) of the binding theory. A pronominal must be free in its minimal governing category. The name *John* does not c-command the pronominal *him* in its minimal governing category, and thus it may serve as an antecedent. This co-indexing is also compatible with principle (C) of the binding theory. The name *John* is free with respect to the pronoun *him*, because *him* does not c-command *John*. In contrast the NP *the guy*, the head of the relative clause, transfers its index to the full NP subject, which does c-command *him*. Therefore, *the guy* cannot be an antecedent of *him*. In terms of our machine design, principle (B) of the binding theory translates quite simply as follows. A pronoun seeks its antecedent in the propositional representation within its minimal governing category. We can see then that the notion of completed constituent perfectly mimics the c-command predicate.

A few additional examples should make this mimicry clear. Consider a right branching construction, for example, *John₁ believed that Harry thought ... that John₂ was adorable*. In this case, the topmost S is not complete at the time that the lowest S *John was adorable* is being analyzed. This is because the argument structure of *believe* demands an S, and the S satisfying this argument slot is itself not complete until the lowermost S is finished off. But this means that the NP *John₁* is accessible to *John₂* in the active node stack. According to principle (C) of the binding theory, names must be free. Translated into this parsing system, names in the active node stack may only be co-indexed with names in the propositional representation.²⁷

We have shown that the parser properly distinguishes between c-commanding and non c-commanding elements, but not why antecedent-trace, quantifier-pronoun, and antecedent-lexical anaphor pairs obey c-command but other co-indexing relationships do not. Given one additional natural assumption we can explain this distribution.

Following Aoun 1979 and Chomsky 1981, let us assume a visibility hypothesis for linguistic levels of representation. What visibility comes to is simple. Features of lexical items can be naturally subdivided into those that are relevant for phonetic interpretation, and those that are relevant for semantic interpretation. In addition, each linguistic component has a proprietary vocabulary; it makes reference only to those features that are relevant to the interpretation done at that level. It follows that if an element is not specified for the features relevant for a particular level, that element is invisible at that level. For example, the phonetic component will disregard thematic properties of a given lexical item when figuring out how to pronounce it. Therefore an element that has thematic features but no phonetic features will quite literally be invisible at the level of phonetic interpretation.

Now recall that the propositional structure is the level at which semantic interpretation occurs. To be interpreted as a referential element, a lexical item must have a referential index. To be interpreted as a variable, an item must be linked to an operator. A referential index is required if we presume that one of the jobs of semantic interpretation is to associate with each NP the sets of individuals that it denotes. The notion of variable only makes sense if it can be interpreted as an element in the range of some operator. Therefore let us assume that a referential element must have a referential index and a variable must be linked to an operator in order to be visible at the level of propositional structure. The only way that elements with no inherent referential index or variable status can be made visible is for them to be co-indexed to an element that can transfer its own index, or to fall within the range of an operator. Given this definition of visibility, let us go through the possible cases of antecedent-anaphor relationships, one by one.

Suppose first that an anaphor or variable is encountered before an antecedent or operator. Then that anaphor will have already been put into the propositional representation before its antecedent or operator is analyzed. However, because it has no inherent index or variable status, it will not be visible at propositional structure, and so will never be available for co-indexing and never receive an interpretation. Now suppose that an anaphor or variable is encountered after a non c-commanding antecedent. Then by assumption, the non c-commanding antecedent or operator will have already been shunted into the propositional representation. Therefore, the antecedent/operator will not be accessible to the syntactic representation, and its index cannot be transferred to the anaphor or variable. The anaphor or variable will be shunted into propositional structure without an index, become invisible, and again never receive an interpretation. Finally, if a c-commanding antecedent or operator is encountered, then it will still be accessible in the active node stack at the time the anaphor or variable is to be attached to the parse tree. The index may be assigned

and the anaphor or variable will be visible at propositional structure
and can be properly interpreted at this level.

Turning now to pronominal and nominal co-indexing, recall that
such elements can appear without antecedents; therefore we assume
that they must have an inherent referential index.[28] It follows that
they will always be visible at syntactic and propositional levels. In
turn this means that there is no necessity for pronominal and nominal
anaphors to seek c-commanding antecedents. There is one exception.
Consider pronominal binding to a quantifier. As Chomsky 1977b and
Higginbotham 1980 have noted, a quantifier must c-command a pronoun
that it binds. Chomsky and Higginbotham show that pronouns bound
to quantifiers are properly treated as variables.

(1) *The woman who likes every man$_i$ in the room thinks that he$_i$
     is too rich. (*Every man* does not c-command *he*.)
(2) Every hockey player$_i$ thinks that he$_i$ is the best in the world.
     (*Every hockey player* c-commands *he*.)

From the point of view of the parser, a pronoun can either have an
inherent referential index or be a bound variable with no inherent
index. This is simply to say that things are ambiguous given just the
phonological shape of a pronoun. Given the assumption of determinism,
if a pronoun is assigned a referential index, that index cannot later be
withdrawn. But it is also true that an element cannot be semantically
interpreted as both a variable lacking in inherent reference and as
an element having inherent reference. When the parser encounters a
pronoun then, it first of all has a clearcut syntactic choice. Given
that the pronoun is phonologically present, it can be properly inserted
into the parse tree without any difficulties at all. It is given some
index, but the syntactic representation is neutral as to whether this
index is to be interpreted as a referential index or as a variable index.
This decision is made at the time the clause in which the pronoun is
contained is ready to be shipped off to the propositional representation.
At that time, a search over the active node stack determines whether
there is a c-commanding antecedent or not. This choice is also made
deterministically. Either there is a quantifier in the active node stack or
else there is no such quantifier. In the first case, the parser can choose
the quantifier as the antecedent of the pronoun; in the second case,
the pronoun will be given a referential index and never be interpreted
as a bound variable.[29]

Bounded Context Parsing and Government-Binding Theory

The two stage model described above provides a natural functional account of properties of transformational grammar. Many have argued, however, that transformational grammar cannot fit into a valid model of human sentence processing. For instance, it has been argued that a parser based on transformational grammar cannot possibly be efficient, and so cannot mimic the presumed efficiency of human sentence understanding. In this section we will show that this fear is groundless. The proposed parsing model works efficiently. To be precise, for those sentences that have at most one antecedent-non trace relationship, it will take at worst time n to analyze a sentence n words long; if there are n such relationships (the worst possible case), total time will be n^2.

Our overall goal will be to show that the two stage model can be viewed as a cascade of bounded context (or LR(k)) transducers. The first machine corresponds to what we have called the syntactic analysis of the input sentence, that is, the construction of a syntactic representation with all empty categories, lexical anaphors, pronouns, and so forth inserted, but with no index assignment. As this first stage representation is built, chunks are passed off to a second machine, and indices are assigned. Schematically, the system decomposes like this:

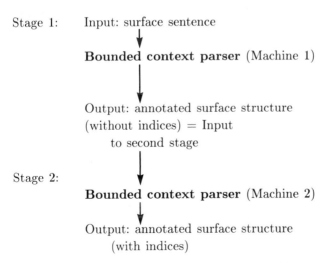

Stage 1:   Input: surface sentence

Bounded context parser (Machine 1)

Output: annotated surface structure
(without indices) = Input
        to second stage

Stage 2:

Bounded context parser (Machine 2)

Output: annotated surface structure
(with indices)

We will "pipeline" the operation of the two machines, so that the second can read the output representation being constructed by the first. In essence, the second, co-indexing machine will be able to look at the stack representation being built by the syntactic parser. All machines are further restricted in that they cannot expand their respective output representations more than a linear amount; that is, the output representations built by each stage cannot be more than a constant times the length of the input to that stage. This constraint played a key role in chapter 4. There we showed that government-binding languages in fact obeyed this property, so that annotated surface structures were in fact just linearly larger than surface sentences.

The first stage of the model is efficient almost by definition. This is because the Marcus type machine we have assumed is deterministic, and outputs just one derivation for every input sentence. We will show that this machine can in fact be modeled by an LR(k) parser. By standard results, such a machine works in time linear in the length of input sentences.[30]

The subsequent stage is also efficient. At worst, we will show that it takes time n for a single antecedent search, and time n^2 for a search for n antecedents. The total time for both stages is proportional to n^2.

One final aside. It is interesting to see just how this model sidesteps earlier objections to syntactic recognition procedures using transformational grammars. For instance, Fodor, Bever, and Garrett 1974 noted two problems with "analysis by analysis" routines that built up parse trees in reverse, like the procedure we are advancing here. First, the number of surface trees compatible with a transformation (or its inverse, if we are parsing) can be enormous. Second, it is not even clear how to invert a transformation, at least given *Aspects* style transformational rules. This is particularly thorny in the case of deletions. If an element is deleted and hence not visible in the input, then the inverse operation of restoring it seems uncontrollable; we can put back the deleted element anywhere.

Recent transformational theories and our parsing model based on them counter each of these objections. Adopting determinism and lookahead, the number of trees compatible with a given input is actually quite small, usually one. Inversion of particular rules is easier, because there is only one general movement rule, indicated by placing traces in the proper locations. Finally, the distribution of phonetically null elements is under tight control. By exploiting the projection principle and other constraints, the parser can know where a trace is to be inserted.

LR(k) Parsing and the Marcus Model

Our first step is to show that the modified Marcus parser is in fact an LR(k) machine, and that it can successfully compute the syntactic representation required by the first stage of the parsing model of the previous section. Let us consider each of these points in turn.

Perhaps the best way to describe the action of an LR(k) parser and associated terminology is to run through a simple example. Consider the following fragment of a grammar:

$Start \rightarrow S$ $S \rightarrow NP\,VP$
$VP \rightarrow V\,NP$ $VP \rightarrow V\,NP\,that\,S$
$V \rightarrow$ *convinced, told,* ...
$NP \rightarrow Det\,N$
$N \rightarrow$ *girl, boy, woman,* ...
$Det \rightarrow$ *a, the*

This grammar will generate (an infinite set of) sentences such as:

The boy convinced the girl.
The girl told the boy that a girl convinced the woman.

Now consider how the second sentence above could be derived by this grammar by expanding the rightmost nonterminal at each step. Sentences are generated by expanding at each step the rightmost nonterminal element. Parsing is just the reverse of this. We must start with the string at the bottom, and work our way backwards to the top, identifying the production we used at each step. Suppose also that we are restricted to read the sentence left to right. We could then go through the rightmost derivation in reverse. We first discover that *the* is a determiner, and so we replace this token with the new symbol "Det."

the girl told the boy that a girl convinced the woman→
Det *girl told the boy that a girl convinced the woman.*

Next we determine that *girl* is of the category N, and replace it accordingly:

Det N *told the boy that a girl convinced the woman.*

What next? There is a rule, $NP \rightarrow Det\,N$. So the first two items in the string form a "complete" NP. We may replace the tokens Det N with a single NP:

NP *told the boy that a girl convinced the woman.*

Because this process bundles up two "lower level" tokens (in this case the lexical items *the* and *girl* themselves) into a higher level node in the derivation tree (in this case an NP node), it is conventionally dubbed a "bottom-up" parse. Intuitively, the assembly of the derivation tree is carried out by working from the fringe of the tree to its root. This is just the reverse of how we generated the string in the first place. What we have done is to locate and construct the leftmost complete subtree of the derivation.

From inspection of this tree we next want the parser to locate and construct the next leftmost complete subtree, namely, a V node with *told* beneath it. Then we must build two complete subtrees, the first being the (subject) NP, the second being the V. Naturally, we must hang onto these pieces of the potentially completed tree. We do so by placing these pieces in a pushdown stack, an ordered list of memory locations such that the topmost element of the list is the subtree most recently built, in this case the V, the next item below it is the subtree next most recently built, and so forth:

Stack of completed subtrees:

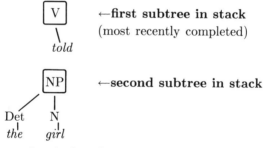

unseen words: *the boy that a girl convinced the woman.*

This processing order is one of the cornerstones of LR(k) parsing. The input string is scanned deterministically left to right, producing a rightmost derivation in reverse. Hence the abbreviation "LR." We shall explain the k portion in a moment.

What next? The next two tokens of the input, *the* and *girl*, can be combined into an NP via the rule $NP \rightarrow Det\,N$, as before. This pinpoints the next complete subtree. The completed NP is placed onto the stack of subtrees, becoming the new first element on this stack. The verb *told* is the second element in the stack, and the NP *the girl* is the third. A snapshot:

Stack of completed subtrees:

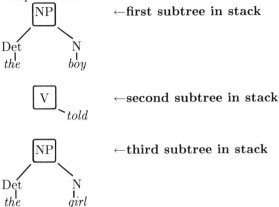

←**first subtree in stack**

←**second subtree in stack**

←**third subtree in stack**

unseen words: *that a girl convinced the woman.*

Now we reach an apparent impasse. Previously we had a unique way to proceed in deciding whether to combine elements in the input stream into a phrase or to continue reading new tokens of the input. Now it seems that there are two equally legitimate paths, corresponding to the two possible expansions of VP as either *V NP* or *V NP that*. We could combine the top two elements on our stack into a single new nonterminal, namely, VP (a so-called reduction); this would mean that we would have in effect decided that the rule $VP \rightarrow V NP$ must have applied to produce the sentence analyzed. Or we could assume that the expansion $VP \rightarrow V NP$ *that* had applied. In this latter case, we should not bundle up the V and the NP alone into a single phrase for we must wait and build the complete subtree corresponding to an S first. If we choose the second path we must keep reading input. Only if we obtain the list of subtrees S–NP–V on the stack, will we know for certain that this latter choice was correct.

There is no way to decide this question based upon only the words analyzed thus far, *the girl told the boy.* Suppose that we pick the first option, that is, we assume that the rule $VP \rightarrow V NP$ must have applied. We reduce the V NP now on the subtree stack to a single nonterminal, the VP on the lefthand side of this rule, and continue. Now VP is the first item on the stack and NP is the second. But the only rule to combine these two items is $S \rightarrow NP VP$. We apply this rule, replacing NP and VP with the single nonterminal S. If the sentence is in fact simply *the girl told the boy*, that is, if in fact the guess we just made is correct, then all is well. The input string ends just as we have reached the root rule $Start \rightarrow S$. Suppose the sentence is rather, *the girl told the boy that NP VP* .... There are no rules to proceed; the only rule accommodating *that* was the alternative VP expansion. We had just ruled it out by choosing the $VP \rightarrow V\,NP$ option. Thus the parse of this sentence fails because we made the wrong guess. Conversely, suppose that we select the $VP \rightarrow V\,NP$ *that* option. Then we shall fail in parsing sentences without a *that* complement, such as *the girl told the boy*. In either case, our only recourse will be to guess and then to undo the effects of our guesses if we are wrong. This means nondeterministic operation. In terms of the LR(k) parsing framework, we may say that the sentences of this grammar cannot be parsed deterministically left to right forming a rightmost derivation in reverse, if we look only at words in the input sentence to the left of the current point of analysis. But then we shall not always be able to analyze sentences efficiently; it is a simple exercise to show that if we must sometimes backtrack and undo the construction of derivations, then parsing will sometimes take longer than time linear in the length of the input sentence.[31]

However, in this case the dilemma is only apparent. We eliminate our troubles by looking at the next input token of the sentence, before we decide what to do. If the token is *that*, then the now unambiguous choice is to assume the rule $VP \rightarrow V\,NP$ *that* has applied. If the token is some end of input marker, then the rule $VP \rightarrow V\,NP$ is the appropriate one; otherwise, the sentence is not well-formed. Thus by looking ahead one token into the input string we resolve the ambiguity in the VP expansion. Because this is the only such ambiguity arising in this grammar, we conclude that sentences generated by this grammar can be parsed deterministically, left to right, forming a rightmost derivation in reverse, given one symbol of lookahead. This is the significance of the parameter k in the LR(k) notation. It denotes the number of symbols of lookahead that the parser is allowed to use in deciding the next move. The grammar above is LR(1). Its sentences can be parsed deterministically left to right using one symbol of lookahead. But it is not LR(0), as we have just seen, because at least one symbol of lookahead is required for deterministic parsing.

The example given above illustrates several key points about LR(k) parsing. First of all, the ability to parse deterministically hinges upon the existence of a unique next move at each step in the backwards rightmost derivation. But an ambiguous grammar is one in which there is more than one distinct rightmost derivation for one and the same sentence. Hence an ambiguous grammar can never be LR(k), for any amount of lookahead. To claim that people parse according to an underlying LR(k) model is to claim that only one derivation is recovered per pass through a sentence, with all potential ambiguities being resolved, perhaps by fiat.[32]

Second, the grammar above included a production ambiguous when considered in isolation, namely, the two possible expansions of VP. The VP expansion is completely deterministic in context because the presence of a trailing *that* determines completely which production must have applied. We may conclude then that the mere existence of alternative expansions, for example, $X \to A$, $X \to B$, $X \to C$, etc., is not sufficient to rule out the possibility of deterministic parsing.

Taking stock, let us see how the Marcus procedure incorporates each of the key features of LR(k) parsing:

1. The Marcus active node stack corresponds to the stack of completed subtrees in an LR(k) parser.
2. The recognition order of a Marcus parse is left to right, bottom-up, just as in LR(k) parsing (but see below for a qualification).
3. The Marcus procedure uses a (finite) lookahead buffer on which to base its next move.
4. The Marcus parser operates strictly deterministically, in that only one rightmost derivation is assumed to be built during the analysis of a sentence; all decisions made are assumed to be correct, just as in the case of an LR(k) parse.
5. The Marcus procedure uses only a finite representation of left context information on which to base its parsing decisions.

This correspondence is qualified for several reasons. First, Marcus 1980 claims that his parser does not parse in a strictly "bottom-up" fashion. In one sense he is correct. At certain points in the parse, the Marcus procedure "predicts" that a higher level phrase forms without having seen all the lower level elements essential to it. For example, upon seeing the "leading edge" of a noun phrase such as *the*, the Marcus parser confidently "predicts" that a noun phrase exists and triggers the rule $NP \to Det\,N$ without having first analyzed the N portion (as would be required in a strict bottom-up parse). But note that this prediction does not change the final order of recognition of complete phrases at all. Not until the N portion of the phrase is analyzed will the Det and N be assembled. At that time the Marcus parser will move the completed NP into its input buffer for later attachment in the parse tree being built. The movement of the NP into the input buffer signals completion of the phrase and final acknowledgment that the rule $NP \rightarrow Det\ N$ must have applied in the parse. The bottom-up order of recognition of completed subtrees is not affected by the introduction of such "predictions."[33]

There is a second qualification. The Marcus parser sometimes bases its decisions not just on lookahead words, or terminal items, but on lookahead nonterminals, that is, whole phrases such as NPs or VPs. Consider, for instance, Marcus's resolution of the problem in parsing *have* as either an auxiliary or a main verb in sentences such as these:

Have the students taken the exam today? (Auxiliary verb)
Have the students take the exam today. (Main verb)

The trees corresponding to these sentences are as follows:

Tree 1:

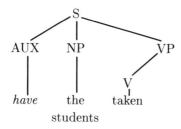

Tree 2:

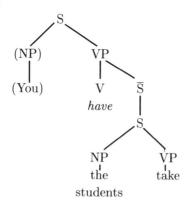

To parse these sentences deterministically we must decide whether *have*
is a main verb. But this resolution is possible only if we look at the tense
marking on the verb later in the string, *take*. If *take* is marked +*ed* as
in *taken*, then *have* is a main verb. Otherwise *have* is an auxiliary verb.
But now observe that the intervening NP could be arbitrarily long in
terms of the number of terminal constituent elements. Therefore, we
cannot decide what to do next based on a finite amount of lookahead
if that lookahead is restricted to terminal (lexical) items. Marcus's
solution is to allow the lookahead to include nonterminals, that is, to
permit a lookahead possibly including complete subtrees, nonterminal
elements such as NP, VP, and the like. Once this is allowed, then in
the "have" case we can write a rule like the following:

IF   lookahead string is:
           have   NP   +*ed*

THEN
           have is an auxiliary verb.

ELSE
           have is a main verb.

This rule violates the strict LR(k) approach of constructing a rightmost
derivation in reverse. *Have* is the leftmost complete subtree. Should we
abide by the canonical parsing order of an LR(k) parse, then we must
decide what to do with *have* before we build the next leftmost complete
subtree, the NP *the boys*. In the case above we violate this constraint by
assembling the NP first and then deciding what to do with *have*. This
is an extension of LR(k) parsing that Knuth 1965 suggested. Instead
of letting the parser assemble only the leftmost complete subtree, let
it choose any one of the leftmost t subtrees to build first, a so-called
LR(k, t) parser. In the case above, $t = 2$; that is, the parser can
build either the first complete constituent found or the second. (In
Marcus's terminology the construction of the second leftmost complete
subtree is dubbed an attention shift, if the phrase is a noun phrase.
Such cases arise when a parsing action depends upon the existence
of a complete constituent as the second lookahead item.)[34] Because
the second subtree may consist of a terminal string with an arbitrary
number of terminal elements, we have in effect enlarged the number
of terminal elements that may be analyzed before we decide upon a

particular parsing action to be potentially infinite. However, only three complete constituents or nonterminals may be used for the lookahead, at least in the parser Marcus designed. Thus any particular parsing action does not depend on an arbitrary lookahead, even though an arbitrary number of elements may be analyzed before the appropriate finite lookahead is finally assembled.[35]

Finally, what about the efficiency of the LR(k) approach? We assume that an LR(k) parser traces through just a single derivation of a sentence. A context-free derivation is linearly proportional to the length of input sentences. This is a straightforward demonstration. So LR(k) machines parse in time kn, where $n=$ the length of input sentences.[36] In our specialized LR(k) parser where traces are inserted (and, in an extended version, other empty categories like Pro), there are two possible outcomes. Should the annotated surface structure not contain empty categories, the parse of the corresponding input sentence will fall under the usual LR(k) analysis, and will take linear time. Suppose, though, that the annotated surface structure does contain empty categories. What difference will this make? First, observe that the insertion of a trace, like all "primitive" operations of the parsing device, presumably takes unit time. Second, because we have assumed that traces cannot be "nested," a trace cannot contain a trace. Therefore, in a sentence of length n there can be at most about n traces. We see then that an annotated surface structure with traces (or other empty categories) will take linear time to construct. We have simply added at worst a linear number of trace insertions to to the overall linear parse. Third, the addition of top-down "predictions" or insertion of phrasal nodes into the node stack before their complete bottom-up recognition, adds at most a linear number of new steps, because the number of predicted nodes must be linear in the size of the input (by the same result showing that the derivation is linear in the input). Finally, what of the extension to whole constituent lookahead (LR(k, t) parsing)? In an LR(k, t) parse, we decide to reduce any of the t leftmost subtrees instead of just the first. Here too it is easy to see that the analysis of a subtree can be postponed at most a finite number of times, t times, in fact (Szymanski and Williams 1976). So an LR(k, t) parser also runs in linear time. The proposed augmentations to the basic LR(k) machine add at worst a linear number of new operations to the parse.[37]

Co-indexing Efficiency

Having informally established the efficiency and correctness of the first stage parser, it remains to show that the second stage, co-indexing, can be carried out efficiently.

To begin, let us divide cases of co-indexing along the constraint fault lines sketched previously. Formally, the second stage co-indexing procedure works as follows.

Its input is an annotated surface structure without indices, its output the same structure with indices. Thus we can think of the procedure as a transduction replacing symbols such as *NP*, *Wh* and *John* with subscripted equivalents NP_i, Wh_j, and $John_k$.

As we discussed in chapter 4, there are two ways to formally regard these new subscripted symbols, with slightly different computational consequences. First of all, we can regard the indices i, j, k, and so forth as actual subscripts attached to linguistic objects. Because the subscripts denote numbers, it takes $\log(n)$ space to store n of them, an additional space factor above and beyond that required for the annotated surface structure without subscripts. That is, should the annotated surface structure without subscripts be of length proportional to n, that annotated surface structure with subscripts is of size proportional to $n\log(n)$.[38] This would mean a greater than linear expansion of the input to the second stage machine, and defeat our mathematical purpose. Second, we can assume that distinctly subscripted constituents are simply distinctly labeled nonterminals, part of the initial stock of grammatical vocabulary. $John_i$ would be regarded as a different nonterminal item from $John_j$, just as NP is distinct from VP. The total number of available subscripts, hence distinct NPs and so on, would be infinite. With this stock of entities, we can satisfy the requirement that the output of the co-indexing stage be at most linearly larger than the input.

The actual process of subscripting can now be viewed as a transduction, with new vocabulary nonterminals replacing unsubscripted nonterminals. For instance, if the NP *John* is to be subscripted NP_1, we want an output rule that rewrites NP(John) as NP-1. If *John* binds a trace downstream in the sentence, then we want that trace, [e], to be rewritten as NP-1 as well, rather than, say, NP-3. By assumption, we have a pushdown stack at our disposal to carry out the transduction.

Let us now consider some possible cases of co-indexing. A trace and its antecedent form a good case study because the antecedent must c-command the trace and the trace must be subjacent to its antecedent. As shown in the previous section of this chapter, at the time that a trace is inserted, the active node stack representation in our parser carries exactly the chain of nodes c-commanding the trace. The second stage machine need only scan this representation to find a trace subjacent to an antecedent. How much of this representation need be scanned? The stack of c-commanding nodes cannot get any deeper than linear in the length of the input string. This is a property of the LR(k) parsing machine (see, for example, Knuth 1965; otherwise, the LR(k) parse itself could not be linear time). There can be only a finite number of accessible NPs attached to any node in this stack. In fact, because a subjacent NP is finitely far away from a trace, we see that it may be found within a constant amount of time. The length of the stage 1 representation that must be scanned may be bounded in advance.

Now consider elements that bind, for example, true quantifiers such as *every*. Here too, the stack representation scanned is at worst linear in the length of the input. Thus the time to carry out any single co-indexing in such a case is also linear. Because there can be at most n such quantifiers in a sentence that is n long, the total time for such co-indexing is bounded above by a function of order n^2.

What of the co-indexing of names and pronouns? A pronoun cannot be bound in its minimal governing category (MGC) by a c-commanding NP; this is Principle B of the binding theory (see chapter 1). So in (1) below, where the governing category of *him* is the S, *him* can refer to *Reagan*, but not *Nixon*.

(1) Reagan thinks [$_{\overline{\text{S}}}$ that Nixon likes him.]

Once we are outside of an S, anything goes. Again, our two stage representation works well here. As the first stage machine parses a pronoun, the second stage machine can check the c-command representation for possible NPs that cannot be bound to the pronoun; it will select an index different from all of these. This process can take at most linear time, because the list of c-commanding NPs can be at most n long. In general, pronominal binding at least will take less time than this, because the minimal governing category does not generally include all c-commanding NPs. It does not in (1), for example.[39] Next, the second stage machine can scan through NPs that can be possible antecedents. Here too there is a readily accessible representation. We may assume that our propositional structure includes a simple list of NPs previously shunted. This list might be useful for other linguistic processes, for example, in discourse. By the way we have designed our first stage machine, each of these NPs cannot c-command the pronoun and thus is a potential antecedent. In addition, the second stage machine must look at those c-commanding NPs outside its MGC. Again, the total number of such NPs cannot be greater than n. Searching both the propositional NP representation and the c-command chain will not take more than time n even if most of the c-command chain lies outside the pronoun's MGC. The stage 2 machine will obviously have to pick an antecedent NP agreeing with the pronoun in number, gender, and so forth. Because a pronoun need not be indexed from within a sentence, the stage 2 machine might fail to find such an antecedent, but this too will take only linear time. One bonus is that because Pros act like pronouns, they also may be processed in this way.[40]

Finally, names are always free. We ensure this by scanning both the c-command chain as represented in the stage 1 machine and the propositional list, whenever a name is parsed. Once again, this can take but linear time, for any single co-indexing or non co-indexing check.

One interesting remaining question centers on our use of a list representation of NPs processed so far. We could dispense with this list and simply rescan the entire parse tree as constructed so far. How much time would this take? For clarity suppose that this information is represented literally as a tree (a singly rooted, directed acyclic graph) though we could choose any of several alternative data structures, for example, a linked list format or an adjacency matrix of 0's and 1's, for an actual implementation. Then, to find a proper antecedent demands an explicit search through this graph until a preceding NP with compatible (exactly the same) features is found. But this can take time $n \log n$ where n is the length of the terminal string, assuming that the graph structure is indeed searched explicitly.[41]

This extra search time for an explicit tree representation may or may not be a real obstacle for the goal of efficient parsability. Let us compare the time it will take against a search that takes linear time. On the one hand, for sentences of "reasonable" length, say 8, and crucially assuming that all constants in algorithmic evaluation are the same, the explicit tree search will take time $8 \log 8$ (base 2) compared to 8. That is, it will take 3 times longer. On the other hand, this result

need not imply that an explicit representation is to be shunned. Either
(i) it might actually take people more than linear time to perform such
a search; or (ii) the constant factors in the relevant algorithms could
dominate small sentence complexity times in such a way as to render
this difference meaningless in empirically relevant contexts. As the
number of co-indexings goes up, then the processing time approaches
n^2 anyway, and this overshadows the extra logarithmic factor. The
lesson of chapter 3 applies. In practice, there might not be any real
difference between these approaches. We will have to wait for concrete
analyses here, not general comparisons.

The Reality of Grammatical Rules and Representations

In this chapter we have seen not only how a modern transformational
grammar can be naturally embedded into an efficient parsing model,
but also how that model can be used to explain some otherwise
mysterious properties of natural languages, the patterning of certain
"locality constraints." Results like this should put to rest the fear,
sometimes raised in the philosophical and computational literature,
that the rules and representations of transformational grammar are
not "real."

What does it mean to say that transformational rules and
representations are "real"? One criterion might be the usual scientific
one. A theoretical entity is real if it contributes to a true description
of the world. It is in this sense that atoms, or better still, the
notion of "atomic valence" is real. Evidently, the same holds for
the transformational operation of Move α. By positing that Move
α exists and that it is engaged in mental computations, we can
actually explain some facts about natural languages, namely, that
they will obey subjacency in certain situations and not others, and
derivatively some facts about human behavior. In contrast, we do
not get the same explanation if we assume other systems of rules
and representations, even some that describe the same set of possible
sentences (for example, the augmented transition network's "hold cell"
model). Even systems written to conform to the same generalizations
as transformational grammar, such as GPSG, but do not use the same
mechanisms fail to provide an explanation for these constraints. This
is then a genuine case in which a particular grammatical rule supports
a particular claim about what sort of mechanism is responsible for a

(mental) computation, just what some have said would be required to show that grammatical rules are "used" in mental computations.[42] Transformational grammar contributes to part of a true description of human behavior in a way that alternative models do not. Perhaps more surprisingly, the Move α rule contributes to a computational account of sentence processing behavior, contrary to the worries of computationalists described in the preface and chapter 2.

There is yet another computational sense in which the representations posited by transformational grammar are real, one that has often been overlooked by computationalists themselves. There is good evidence that the data structures or units of representation posited by theories of transformational grammar are actually implicated causally in online language processing. This, after all, was the burden of Fodor, Bever, and Garrett's 1974 argument. Now algorithms may be thought of as data structures plus some means of control, that is, the representations used are usually written to conform to some algorithmic design. This being so, it would be truly bizarre for the data structures associated with a certain program to be causally engaged in actual computation by accident. If the data structures assumed by grammatical theories are causally implicated in language processing, the simplest hypothesis to make is that they are being used for language processing. Of course, it is not necessary that this be so, but it certainly constitutes a *prima facie* case.

Part of the misunderstanding here may involve just what it means to "use" a grammatical rule, and what "rules" look like in a modern transformational grammar. A transformational grammar need not be embedded in a processing system with rules acting like the directive statements of a programming language because a modern transformational grammar does not consist of program-like rules at all. As chapter 1 indicated, a modern transformational grammar is best thought of as a modular system of constraints, not a set of individual rules. There is no "rule" of passive in such a grammar, but simply the operation of movement plus allowable combinations of constraints on case assignment, head-complement structure, and so forth, giving rise to the constellation of properties called "passive" in English. Chomsky 1981, 1982 has additional discussion of this point. But because there is no passive rule, it is clear that there need be no direct computational instantiation of that rule in a system that "realizes" a constraint oriented grammar. Nor is there reason to compute an inverse of this nonexistent rule in order to parse sentences. Instead, as we have seen, we can simply build a system abiding by the same principles as a transformational grammar, without exhibiting a one rule-one computational operation correspondence. Such a system for English could in fact be described as if it obeyed specific rules, because the interacting constraints in English yield a surface pattern of this kind.

Under these conditions it does not make much sense to say that a model "uses" the passive rule because the rule does not really exist. What does exist is a system of constraints and principles. To use this kind of system all that the computational model must do is operate according to these constraints. The exact implementation of the constraints is left up to the imagination and limitations of the implementor, be it a person or nature.

In at least two senses then, the rules and representations of modern transformational grammar are quite "real," because by assuming that they are actually engaged in mental computations, we can explain part of human behavior. There is a third sense in which transformational grammars are real. They can explain how people learn language. This is the subject of the next chapter.

Chapter 6
Language Acquisition and Transformational Grammar: A Modern View

Perhaps the key goal of modern linguistic theory is to explain how children acquire their first language. Apparently the "evidence" that children receive to learn language is quite impoverished and reinforcement by adults haphazard. Yet first language acquisition seems relatively easy and strikingly uniform. Such robust performance in the midst of raging environmental variation poses a severe challenge for any theory of language acquisition.

Chapter 1 has already sketched the modern answer to this challenge. The idea is to characterize the class of possible human grammars so narrowly that the language learner's burden is eased, perhaps trivialized. In Chomsky's metaphor, hypothesizable grammars should be "sufficiently scattered" from one another so that children can select easily the one corresponding to the language of their caretakers. Restrictions aid the learner because they rule out countless faulty hypotheses about which possible grammar might cover the language at hand. Current theories of transformational grammar are usually motivated and evaluated against the demand of learnability. In these theories, the possible rules of grammar and thus the possible human grammars are restricted as much as possible to just a few actions plus universal constraints on their application.

The metaphor of a child searching through a restricted hypothesis space of grammars has proved to be an enormously fruitful one for modern linguistic theory. However, the study of generative grammar as developed over the past few decades has, for the most part, deliberately abstracted away from a consideration of the actual time course of language acquisition.

This chapter shows how to use generative grammar as a theory of language acquisition. It attacks this question from two points of view.

First, it looks at language acquisition in an explicit computational setting. It presents an implemented computer program based on the Marcus parser (Marcus 1980) that can acquire a substantial number of the parsing rules for English syntax. Importantly the model is plausible in the sense that it uses only simple, positive examples to learn. This acquisition procedure provides graphic demonstration that we can naturally embed a transformational theory of grammar into a working model of language acquisition.

Second, we look at language acquisition in an explicit psychological setting. In a representative case study, we examine how a transformational grammar helps us explain the actual developmental "stages" that children go through when learning their first language. Here too we shall see that by adopting a model based on a transformational grammar we can actually see how children are "driven" from one stage of knowledge to another. Our case study will be the English passive.

We begin by describing how our computer model fits into the generative approach to the acquisition of language, followed with a more detailed look at how the model works. In the next section we present example learning scenarios for the acquisition of a simple phrase structure rule and subject-auxiliary verb inversion. The chapter concludes with a careful examination of how children acquire the passive construction, taking into account both the computer model outlined before and the actual "stages" of development that children go through.

A Computer Model for the Acquisition of Syntax

To begin our computational analysis, we shall adopt a framework for describing "learning" models proposed by Wexler (1982). Wexler observes that there are three parts to any acquisition model: first, the initial state of knowledge of the system; second, the final state of knowledge (the grammar); and third, the acquisition procedure that gets us from initial to final state, along with the input data (the "evidence") the procedure uses to make its inferences.

In our model the final state of knowledge is a representation of a grammar of English, in the form of a modified Marcus type parser. The acquisition of syntactic knowledge is modeled as the acquisition of a series of parsers of increasing abilities. We fix some initial state of knowledge corresponding to an initial set of parsing abilities and a knowledge of what counts as a valid rule of parsing. Then, an acquisition procedure constructs a sequence of new parsers, P_i, incrementally adding to or modifying the knowledge base of parsing rules in response to a set of input data. The sequence of parsers mimics an (idealized) acquisition process by utilizing constraints to approximate ever more closely a "mature" knowledge of syntax. As stated in Chomsky's *Aspects of the Theory of Syntax*:

A child who is capable of language learning must have (i) a technique for representing input signals; (ii) a way of representing structural information about these signals; (iii) some initial delimitation of a class of possible hypotheses about language structure; (iv) a method for determining what each hypothesis implies with respect to each structure; (v) a method for selecting one of the ... hypotheses that are allowed by (iii) and are compatible with the given primary linguistic data. (1965:30)

This [language acquisition] device must search through the set of possible hypotheses G_1, G_2, ...which are available to it by virtue of condition (iii), and must select grammars that are compatible with the primary linguistic data, represented in terms of (i) and (ii). It is possible to test compatibility by virtue of the fact that the device meets condition (iv). The device would then select one of these potential grammars by the evaluation measure guaranteed by (v). (Ibid.:32)

The computer model attempts to relax this idealization of instantaneous acquisition, and pursues the consequences of adopting an explicit developmental approach. There are at least two possible rewards to this approach. First of all, a problem for any "learning theory" is to account for how a learner is "driven" from one stage of knowledge to the next. Some researchers believe that this problem has not received enough attention:

There is, however, a very general problem with practically all studies of language development, whether investigated from the standpoint of rule acquisition, strategy change, or elaboration of mechanism. The problem arises both for accounts that postulate 'stages' of development (that is a finite number of qualitatively distinct levels of organization through which the organism passes en route from molecule to maturity), and for accounts that view development as a continuous function of simple accumulation. The difficulty is this: No one has seriously attempted to specify a mechanism that 'drives' language acquisition through its 'stages' or along its continuous function. Or more succinctly: there is no known learning theory for language. (Marshall 1979:443)

The model described in this chapter is designed to remedy at least part of this problem. It is the parser's attempts to interpret sentences in accordance with its universal constraints that provides a specific driving mechanism for acquisition. In this sense, this model constitutes a true theory of acquisition.

Second, a developmental approach may be useful in its own right as a theory of the actual time course of acquisition. In other words, if we were interested in explaining what actually happens in acquisition, a theory attending to the time course of events seems crucial. Such a theory is important to those interested in developmental processes in and of themselves. Thus those interested in why "truncated passives" are acquired earlier than full passives, or why auxiliary verb inversion appears to be acquired at different times depending on which *wh* question word is involved, must look to an essentially developmental theory. Note that there is no necessary contradiction between the instantaneous and noninstantaneous viewpoints but simply a difference in research aims.

For the developmental approach to succeed we must spell out exactly what is meant by initial parser, input data, and acquisition procedure. As its initial parser, the learning procedure employs a modified version of the Marcus parser as described in chapters 2 and 5. The Marcus parser divides into two parts, a grammar rule interpreter (plus stack and input buffer data structures) and a set of grammar rules comprising the operating rules of the machine. To model acquisition we start with a "bare" interpreter having no grammar rules. The machine learns these rules. As input data the program takes just grammatical sentences, so-called positive evidence, and a rudimentary initial ability to characterize words as objects, actions or unknown. These restrictions aim at a minimally psychologically plausible acquisition model. Children are assumed to have certain initial conceptual abilities in classifying words and little or no access to explicit correction (negative evidence) of their syntactic errors.[1]

The actual acquisition procedure itself is simple. The developing parser attempts to analyze each example sentence supplied by the outside world.[2] The acquisition of new rules is prompted by rule failures during the parsing process. A failure is defined as either (i) the failure of any known grammar rule to apply or (ii) the application of a known rule resulting in a base structure known to be incorrect.[3] Each time a failure is detected in the left to right processing of a sentence and successfully resolved, the system adds a single new parsing rule to its knowledge base or modifies (perhaps reinforces) an old rule.

If the system cannot resolve a local parsing failure, it simply gives up on the analysis of the current sentence and tries to parse the next. This design decision gives the system an incremental behavior; it tends to acquire its knowledge from "clear cases" rather than making large inferential steps. This characteristic enables the system to mimic noninstantaneous development.

What is the initial state of this system? Four kinds of information are known. First, it knows about word segmentation and morphology, for example, that *s* is a plural morpheme in *cats*. Second, it has a crude semantic-syntactic correspondence between lexical items and syntactic categories, for example, that *cat* is a noun. Third, it understands the proper assignment of arguments to verbs, for example, that *John* and *Mary* are the arguments to *kiss* in *John kissed Mary*. Fourth, it knows about the basic data structures of the parser and the proper format for its rules. Three sorts of syntactic knowledge are acquired:

(1) The ordering information implicit in context-free phrase structure rules. The knowledge acquired here corresponds to the basic order and branching structure of (English) phrases, for example, that a verb phrase consists of a verb followed by a possibly optional noun phrase. Note that no commitment is made to precisely how this ordering information is expressed; we need not use explicit phrase structure rules.

(2) Pattern-action lexical insertion grammar rules. This knowledge corresponds roughly to valid contexts for the insertion of terminal elements into a phrase structure tree. This information might also be viewed as local transformations. As a by-product, lexical categorizations are developed during analysis.[4] For example, a rule stating that a transitive verb like *kiss* must appear with a noun phrase object embodies contextual information of this kind.

(3) Pattern-action movement rules. This knowledge corresponds to particular movement operations, inversions, and the like, for example, NP movement, subject-auxiliary verb inversion in questions. Such operations are the parser's counterpart of a general Move α rule.

According to this model new knowledge is acquired by modifying only the rule data base of the parser. The interpreter (working storage and control structure) and knowledge of the valid forms for rules remain fixed.[5] This division is asymmetric, but appears to be a legitimate working assumption. The interpreter and the knowledge of constraints on rules are presumably universal across all languages, hence fixed. There are, however, several details of the interpreter that might be mutable. We can imagine a model where, for example, the working storage of the interpreter expanded over time, corresponding to a general increase in memory or attention span. But no extensive revisions in the control structure of the interpreter are required, in part because the basic execution loop of the "mature" interpreter is already so simple that there is really very little to learn.[6]

In summary, the proposed model for acquisition is quite simple. Knowledge of syntax (a grammar) is identified as a parser; development of that knowledge as a sequence of parsers. The acquisition process itself is driven by the current parser's attempts to interpret positive example sentences prompting changes to its data base of parsing rules.

The Acquisition Model

To understand how the acquisition procedure works in detail, we must develop our picture of the Marcus parser's operation. Remember that for the Marcus machine, parsing simply means executing a series of tree building and token shifting grammar rule actions. Actions, in turn, are triggered by matches of rule patterns against features of tokens in a small three cell constituent lookahead buffer and the local part of the annotated surface structure tree currently under construction.

Grammar rule execution is controlled also by reference to base phrase structure rules. To implement this control each of the parser's grammar rules are linked to one or more of the components of the phrase structure rules. Then, grammar rules are defined to be eligible for triggering, or *active*, only if they are associated with that part of the phrase structure which is the current locus of the parser's attentions; otherwise, a grammar rule does not even have the opportunity to trigger against the buffer and is inactive. This is best illustrated by an example. Suppose there were but a single phrase structure rule for English that gave the canonical order for a sentence as a noun phrase followed by a verb phrase, for example, Sentence $\rightarrow$ Noun Phrase Verb Phrase ($S \rightarrow NP\,VP$).

Flow of control during a parse would travel left to right in accordance with the NP–VP order of this rule, activating and deactivating potentially matching bundles of grammar rules along the way. To illustrate, we start the parse by activating any rules associated with the S packet. These are grammar rules that are always active, rules whose trigger patterns watch for the characteristic signs of English sentences, noun-verb clusters such as *Sue kissed* ...; *for-to* combinations like *for Sue to kiss* ..., and so forth. Now suppose the parser actually detects one of these patterns in the input string. A grammar rule fires to this effect and the parser enters the $S \rightarrow NP\,VP$ phrase structure rule. First, all grammar rules associated with the S remain active, because they must always be ready to trigger even in the midst of assembling a new noun phrase. Second, all grammar rules associated with building the noun phrases at the head of a sentence (in English, the subject noun phrases) would now become active. This would include rules whose job it is to watch out for the telltale "leading edges" of noun phrases (such as *the, any*), and rules specially designed to recognize proper names as nouns, among others. The parser now has the chance to build a noun phrase constituent, eventually advancing in order to construct a verb phrase. This step is marked by deactivating the noun phrase building grammar rules and activating any grammar rules associated with constructing verb phrases.[7]

Together with (1) the items in the buffer and (2) the leading edge of the parse tree under construction, the currently pointed-to portion of the phrase structure forms a triple that characterizes the current state, or instantaneous description of the parser.

Now we can state more precisely just what happens during acquisition. If in the midst of a parse no currently known grammar rules can trigger, acquisition is initiated. The system attempts to construct a single new executable grammar rule. New rule assembly is straightforward. The procedure first tries to see whether the first item in the buffer can be attached to the parse tree under construction in compliance with the conventions of the $\overline{\text{X}}$ theory of phrase structure. If so, it has constructed a new part of the base component, either a lexical insertion rule or a new phrase structure expansion.

If the $\overline{\text{X}}$ restrictions cannot be upheld, the acquisition procedure attempts to build a new transformational-like grammar rule. To do this the procedure simply selects a new pattern and action, utilizing the current instantaneous description of the parser at the point of failure as the new pattern and one of three primitive (atomic) operations as the new action. The local context consists of two parts, (i) a finite left context, the top element in the active node stack, plus additional finite information about the parse tree constructed so far; and (ii) the right context, a finite amount of information in the righthand input buffer.

The primitive actions are (1) switch (exchange) the items in the first
and second buffer cells; (2) insert one of a finite number of lexical
items into the first buffer cell; and (3) drop a trace into the first buffer
cell. These actions turn out to be sufficient and mutually exclusive
so that there is little combinatorial problem of choosing among many
alternative new grammar rule candidates. Each action is subject to a
simple test to see whether it applies in a given acquisition setting.
They work only if some already known grammar rule can apply after
the (tentative) action has been applied.

Should the acquisition procedure find a new grammar rule applying
to the novel sentence, it saves that new rule. First the system determines
whether it must generalize its new rule with an existing grammar
rule that performs the same action in the same packet (same point
in the base phrase structure) as the new one. Translated into the
pattern-action rule format, this means that the system must check to
see whether there is another rule with the same action in the same
packet as the new rule. If the attach action is involved, the effect
of generalization is to form new equivalence classes of lexical tokens.
Class splitting is also allowed should a formerly merged class require
division.[8]

A further constraint is that the acquisition procedure itself cannot
be recursively invoked. That is, if in its attempt to build a single
new executable grammar rule the procedure finds that it must acquire
still other new rules, the current attempt at acquisition is immediately
abandoned.[9]

With this informal sketch in hand, we can now give a step by step
description of the acquisition procedure:

Step 1: Attempt to parse the sentence left to right in a single pass,
using currently known grammar rules. If there are no failures while
processing the sentence (the parser is never blocked because there are
no grammar rules that can trigger) and afterwards (the output is a
complete parse tree with a valid thematic role assignment), read in
and attempt to parse the next sentence. If the parse fails at any point
during the analysis (no currently known grammar rules trigger), enter
an acquisition phase.

Step 2: Acquisition phase. Note instantaneous description (ID) of
the parser at the point of failure (properties associated with the node
on top of the stack and the cyclic (S or NP) node immediately above
the current active node plus contents of the input buffer). Call these

the lefthand context of the current parse (this includes an annotation of these nodes, as described below). Call the input buffer at this point the right context of the parse. Together, right and left contexts summarize all the information about the parse required by the interpreter to make its next parsing decision.

Step 3: Attempt to build a single new (base phrase structure) rule corresponding to the $\overline{\text{X}}$ constituent currently active, by attaching the item in the first buffer cell to the $\overline{\text{X}}$ constituent currently active. If successful, store the new rule as an instantiated $\overline{\text{X}}$ template (via the parser action attach). The success criterion is defined as compatibility with the current features of the $\overline{\text{X}}$ node to which the item is attached, for example, a noun can be attached as the head of a $[+N \ -V]$ phrase; a determiner (marked $[+N \ -V \ -head]$) can be attached as the specifier of a $[+N \ -V]$ phrase but not a $[-N \ +V]$ phrase, and so forth. If the $\overline{\text{X}}$ constituent so built is part of the complement of a head, then annotate the lexical entry of the head accordingly to include this type of complement as obligatory, unless previous examples have shown this complement type to be optionally present.

Percolate the features of the attached item to the top of the phrase under construction, that is, the XP node. This simply means that a maximal phrase will have all the features of its head. Generate a mnemonic name for the new rule. The pattern of the new rule is simply the ID of the parser. In effect, we have performed a reduction, performing the expansion $A \rightarrow a$ backwards. Annotate the currently active node (top of the active node stack) with the name of the rule so formed. Continue with parse; go to Step (1).

If the attach is unsuccessful (the new rule violates the basic constraints of the $\overline{\text{X}}$ theory, for example, that a noun phrase must have a noun head or a known constraint on a verb's subcategorization) the machine must have procedures for deciding whether the current portion of the phrase structure expansion under consideration is optional. If it is, the machine advances to consider the next portion of the $\overline{\text{X}}$ expansion.

If a particular phrase is completed, then drop the entire X phrase into the buffer. Completion is signalled if either (i) known arguments have been attached and the next item in the input buffer is the end of sentence marker or an item that cannot be attached to the current phrase or (ii) predicate-argument knowledge indicates that the phrase is complete. Otherwise, go to Step 4 and attempt to build a new nonbase grammar rule.

Step 4: Attempt to build a single new grammar rule. Select as the new pattern of the rule the instantaneous description noted in Step 2 and as its new action one of the three actions (switch, insert lexical item, or insert trace). The reason for ordering the actions in this way is discussed below. Test each action for successful triggering. The criterion for success is basically that a known grammar rule can execute after the tentative rule has fired, for example, after switch, an already known rule can run. If successful, update the rule database, first checking whether the new grammar rule performs the same action as an already known grammar rule at the same point in a derivation, that is, performs the same operation given the same lefthand context. If so, generalize or refine the grammar rule via one of three methods. Either (1) form an equivalence class of items corresponding to the item just attached or (2) split an existing equivalence class or (3) write a generalized grammar rule. Prompt the user for a mnemonic name for the new rule. Continue with current parse.

If unsuccessful with all three candidate actions, drop the phrase under construction into the buffer and continue. Otherwise, stop the parse of the current sentence and analyze the next sentence. If the sentence as constructed violates the known predication representation, remove any newly created rules from the rule database.

Simple Scenarios

To illustrate how the acquisition procedure works, this section gives scenarios for the acquisition of a range of different syntactic constructs in English.

Acquisition of a Verb Phrase Expansion Rule

As it stands the computer model directly incorporates a "parameter setting" approach to the acquisition of base phrase structure rules, along the lines advanced by Chomsky (1981). Because the computer version is almost a literal implementation of this procedure, we shall only give the briefest of examples here; Berwick (1980, 1982) offers a more detailed discussion.

The key to learning phrase structure is to use the $\overline{X}$ theory. As described in chapter 1, in $\overline{X}$ theory all natural base phrase structure systems reduce to the expansions of just a few templates of the form $XP \rightarrow \ldots X \ldots$ Here, the X stands for an obligatory phrase structure category (projected from the features of lexical items such as nouns or verbs). For instance, if we pick X as a noun, we get a noun phrase.

Given this template filling approach, the problem for the learner is reduced essentially to figuring out what items may go in the slots on either side of the X. It is easy to do this by examining positive examples. Suppose that the acquisition procedure has already acquired a phrase structure rule for English main sentences and now requires information to determine the proper expansion of a verb phrase:

Verb Phrase → ???

The $\overline{\text{X}}$ theory cuts through the maze of possible expansions for the righthand side of this rule.[10] Assuming that noun phrases are the only other known category type, the $\overline{\text{X}}$ theory tells us that there are only a few possible configurations for a verb phrase rule:

Verb Phrase → Verb or
Verb Phrase → Noun Phrase Verb or
Verb Phrase → Verb Noun Phrase or
Verb Phrase → Noun Phrase Verb Noun Phrase
(other combinations of multiple noun phrase constituents)

Now suppose that the learner can classify word tokens as nouns, verbs, or "other" perhaps by initially linking items to some semantic grounding as objects and actions.[11] Then, by matching an example sentence such as *John kissed Mary* against the array of possible phrase structure expansions, the correct verb phrase rule can be deduced quickly; only one context-free tree successfully fits against the given input string. Omitting much detail (see Berwick 1982), the parse proceeds left to right with *John* first built as a noun phrase and recognized as a valid part of the expansion of the already known rule $S \rightarrow NP\,VP$. Note that *John* is attached as a noun by a lexical insertion grammar rule, as discussed earlier.

Now because *kissed* is recognizable as a $[-\text{N} +\text{V}]$ item, a verb, the VP $\overline{\text{X}}$ schema can be entered. The head of the $\overline{\text{X}}$ schema must by definition be a verb; only *kissed* meets this criterion. Consequently, *kissed* can attach as the V portion of the growing tree, again by a lexical insertion rule. Note that we might have required that the insertion of *kiss* be made contingent upon the presence of a noun phrase to the right of *kiss*. This test can be accommodated via the lookahead buffer.

This example rules out at once the options for attaching noun phrases to the left of the head in a verb phrase, assuming that there is a binary choice between head-complement and complement-head order. The only choice left open is whether the given input example is compatible with noun phrase attachment to the right of the head. The next move of the parser shows that it is. *Mary* is recognizable as a name, hence a noun and noun phrase. It is available for attachment to the verb phrase under construction, completing construction of the parse tree. The VP expansion is as desired. A single simple example has provided positive evidence sufficient to establish a major English phrase structure rule. Although this is but a simple example, it still illustrates how phrase structure rules can be acquired by a process akin to "parameter setting." Given a highly constrained initial state, the desired final state can be obtained upon exposure to very simple triggering data. From this point of view, there are no nonterminal categories as classically defined nor any rewrite rules making up a phrase structure "grammar"; rather, these are replaced by the projections of lexical entries. By establishing an order in which parameters may be fixed, the $\overline{X}$ theory also delimits the possible "developmental envelopes" for acquisition, providing a theoretical framework for interpreting actual ontogenetic data. Berwick 1982 gives a general, though preliminary, formal framework to analyze questions of this kind, as well as additional examples of this kind drawn from syntactic and phonological theory.

A Subject-Auxiliary Verb Inversion Grammar Rule
Besides so-called "base" phrase structure rules, natural grammars include also surface forms where arguments have been displaced from their natural position, as well as variance in the standard surface order of constituents. For example, the sentences, *Who will Sally kiss* and *Will Sally kiss John* exhibit these two kinds of variations. How can this knowledge be acquired?

Suppose that the acquisition model has all the base rules and grammar rules to parse *John will kiss Mary*.[12] Now suppose it is given the sentence *Will John kiss Mary*. No currently known rule can fire because all the rules in the phrase structure component activated at the beginning of a sentence will have triggering patterns looking for a noun phrase followed by a verb, but the input stream will hold the pattern [*Will*: +verb +tense][*John*: noun phrase] and so thwart all attempts at triggering a grammar rule. We assume that features such as tense are known in advance. [13] A new rule must be written. The acquisition procedure first tries to attach the first item in the buffer, *will*, to the current active node, S(entence) as the subject noun phrase. The attach fails because of category restrictions from the $\overline{\text{X}}$ theory. Because *will* is not marked as a noun, it cannot attach as the core of a noun phrase. But switch succeeds, because when the first and second buffer positions are interchanged, the buffer now looks like [*John*][*will*].[14] Because the ability to parse declaratives such as *John will kiss* ... was assumed, a noun phrase attaching rule will now match. Recording its success, the procedure saves the switch rule along with the current buffer pattern as a trigger for remembering the context of auxiliary inversion. The rest of the sentence can now be parsed as if it were a declarative.[15]

Later example sentences of this type quickly generalize the required trigger pattern for inversion to something like [auxiliary verb][noun phrase]. Here, the label "auxiliary verb" is actually a gloss for a complex category formed dynamically as an equivalence class of items not taking NP complements. They are partly verbal and are not nouns. Importantly, the grammar rule so acquired also demands no cyclic node be immediately above the current active node. In this case no cyclic node is above an S node at the time the inversion is performed. In other words, the environment in which the rule triggers must be a "root" environment; the subject-auxiliary inversion rule will not trigger erroneously in an embedded environment, just as desired. The ungrammatical sentence, *I wonder did Sue kiss John* should be unparsable given this set of grammar rules for English. The acquisition system would only generalize this rule to nonroot environments if it saw a positive example illustrating inversion in an embedded context, represented by a nonempty cyclic node.

Two computational constraints interact to yield this effect. First of all, the machine cannot use more than a finite left or right context to build its patterns. Specifically, the left context contains at most two phrasal nodes, the top of stack node and a cyclic node above that. The finite bound is independently motivated by our explanation of subjacency and part of a limitation on any finite machine operating with a transparent encoding of $\overline{\text{X}}$ nodes. But why should this barrier fix on the immediately higher "cyclic" node? Again, we appeal to the noncounting character of grammatical representations. Pattern-action rules can refer to the current context and to the adjacent context, but to no more because these are generally the natural predicates of grammatical systems. Interestingly, given this constraint, we can encode only root/nonroot distinctions. A root environment will have an empty cyclic node, and a nonroot environment will not. Grammar rule patterns can pick up this difference. No other distinction is possible because all nonroot environments will otherwise look alike. The machine can tell that a phrase is embedded, but it cannot tell how deeply embedded a node is, because all it looks at is the adjacent context. This limitation contrasts with the power of lexical-functional grammar to encode the predicate "equally deeply embedded" discussed in chapter 4. This result is intriguing because the root/nonroot distinction has been widely noted in natural languages. This contrast falls out directly from a parser design based on finite context patterns plus the noncounting restriction.

In addition to this constraint on patterns, we must appeal to a general learning principle, to hypothesize the narrowest possible language consistent with the positive evidence seen so far. In the case at hand, this has the effect of assuming that inversion is impossible in nonroot contexts unless there is evidence demonstrating it. This "subset principle" discussed in more detail later in this chapter and in Berwick 1982 accounts for a wide variety of specific acquisition strategies useful for language acquisition. Together these constraints guarantee that nonroot inversion is not guessed until seen.

How Passives Are Learned

The first sections of this chapter paint a rosy picture of the relationship between linguistic theory and actual language development. Linguistic theory provides constraints making language acquisition possible. A child selects the grammar of her language from a limited number of choices consistent with environmental input and the innate endowment described by linguistic theory. In fact, the initial constraints are so great that the environmental input can be limited to simple, grammatical sentences.

As noted earlier, this model conveniently abstracts away from the slings and arrows of real language acquisition, such as the "noise" of simultaneous cognitive development, including an expanding memory and developing "semantic" capabilities. Holding this flux constant may be convenient, but it may also obscure the actual time course of acquisition itself. In particular, we have assumed that the child's morphological word formation component is already in place before syntactic acquisition proceeds. This assumes, for example, that the child has already mastered the way that affix attachment modifies the mapping of a predicate's arguments onto syntactic structure before any syntactic knowledge is fixed.

Acquisition is not this simple. Different language "components" might develop at the same time and impinge on the development of other components. The interaction of a number of different modules could lead to apparently complex surface developmental patterns. Far from being a source of confusion, interaction between components might be needed to account for data observed at a given stage.

The Move α rule has come in for particularly heavy fire. Some empirical studies indicate that children go through stages of language development that cannot even be described using the predicates of transformational rules. Many psychologists have presented evidence that early on children apply argument changing rules to semantically well defined subclasses of verbs. This is not predicted by a theory with only syntactically based transformational predicates.

For example, Maratsos (1978) discusses a case where children's early comprehension of the passive is limited to sentences containing "direct action" verbs. That is, children do not learn the passive rule all at once, but first apply it to a subset of all verbs. Maratsos (1978) and Pinker (1982) present two slightly different analyses of this fact. They both point out the inconsistency of their analyses with a transformational system constrained by the "autonomy of syntax" thesis. This hypothesis, at least as sketched in Chomsky (1979:139), suggests that in natural languages, "the concepts of grammar are constructed on the basis of primitive notions that are not semantic." In part this means that transformational rules cannot use a semantic vocabulary. More to the point here, we could not constrain transformational rules to generate passives only from direct action verbs, because this is a semantically defined class. A transformationally organized child should quickly generalize a passive rule from the actional class of verbs to all verbs, as Maratsos states:

Once the child has analyzed a fair number of passives with some success, he should quickly generalize the relation between actives and passives in a way that would be syntactically autonomous and independent of the semantics of the particular verb. (1978:255)

Pinker echoes Maratsos's sentiments, citing the passive case as one of "three facts about language development that are difficult to interpret if language acquisition consists of the child accumulating transformations" (1982:667).

Both authors propose alternative accounts of the acquisition of passive consistent with the lexical-functional theory of grammar (Bresnan 1982b). This success is taken as support for the lexical-functional theory itself: "All three [facts rcb/asw] can be given straightforward interpretations if language acquisition consists largely of the acquisition of lexical entries, each one specific to a grammatical construction that the word enters into" (Pinker 1982:667).[16] On both accounts, it is the nontransformational character of argument structure changing rules that explains the developmental effect.

We shall show that the Pinker and Maratsos accounts are misguided. We can do a better job of explaining things via the interaction of two components of language, the morphological and the syntactic. By carving things this way, we shall arrive at an explanation where each "module" is simpler than one in which the explanatory burden is shouldered by just the syntactic component alone. Importantly, we shall not have to give up the transformational account.

Our first point is that passive rule undergeneralization need not be linked to rules of argument structure change. Rather, it can be linked to the undergeneralization of passive participals like *kicked*. Intuitively, passive meaning associates with passive morphology. Underproductivity of passives tags along with underproductivity of passive participals, even if argument changing rules are fully generalized. Viewed this way, it is the naturally semantically circumscribed character of the morphological component that drives the apparently semantically circumscripted character of passive. In a sense then, we agree with Maratsos in rejecting a purely transformationally based account of passive. But unlike Maratsos, we do not think this is reason to reject the transformational component outright. We think instead that it warrants a deeper look at the interaction between linguistic components themselves.

We begin by reviewing the facts about the development of passive. Next, we turn to a recap of the differences between lexical-functional and transformational grammar that figure in Maratsos's and Pinker's accounts. Our criticisms of their views follows. We conclude with our own analysis and some other experimental evidence that we think supports it. One caveat. Our account is generally compatible with either transformational or lexical-functional grammar. The important point, though, is not that our account directly supports one theory or another, but rather that the interaction between linguistic components may play a key role in the theory of language development.

The Data of Passive Development

Our first job is to describe the "semantic stage" in the acquisition of passive. Here we draw on experimental work by Maratsos, Kuczaj, and Fox 1978. To be concrete, we cite Maratsos's brief description of this experiment:

Actional passives cause comparatively little difficulty [in acquisition rcb/asw], as do a few nonactional passives such as those with *seen* and *heard.* But a number of nonactional passives (*liked, known, remembered, missed,* for example) cause considerable difficulty .... Many subjects comprehend underlying subject-object relations of these even less successfully than for some nonsense passives constructed with nonexistent verbs like *cattered* and *bemoded.* Anecdotal evidence indicates that subjects interpret these nonsense verbs as actional. (1978:256)

This means that there is a stage where children comprehend 1(a) and 1(b) better than 1(c).[17]

(1) a. John was hit.
    b. John was bemoded.
    c. John was liked.

Lexical-Functional Proposals for Passive Development

The lexical-functional treatment of passive diverges from the transformational analysis at key points, and these differences bear on the acquisition story. As mentioned in chapter 2, lexical-functional grammar claims that argument structure changing rules should be stated using grammatical functional predicates, like subject and object. Categorially based argument structure changing rules, basically the Move NP operation, have no status in this theory. Let us review this treatment. According to Bresnan (1982c:8) the lexical rule generating passive in adult English is the universal rule:

(2) Subject $\to \emptyset$ /Oblique

Roughly, this rule associates the grammatical function of object with the NP in the surface subject position.

It is important to remember that in lexical-functional theory it is the characterization of the lexical rules themselves, as opposed to principles of grammar that apply to rules, that is universal. As Bresnan says, "any rule of grammar which changes the grammatical functions of constituents must be a lexical rule. And any such rule will have a universal characterization which reveals its invariant form across languages" (Bresnan 1982c:8).

This fact alone does not explain the developmental data. As Pinker recognizes, rule (2) would also lead us to expect that all direct objects are passivizable from the very earliest stages. This is not the case.[18] Children correctly analyze only direct objects of action verbs.

In fact, Maratsos claims that the rule underlying this early behavior should be "something to the effect that [NP V+*ed* (*by* NP)] = acted on patient + action (+initiator of action or agent)" (1978:256). Pinker tries to square the developmental data with the claims of lexical-functional grammar by introducing two auxiliary assumptions. First, citing Devilliers and Barr (a personal communication), he claims that children only hear restricted examples of passivization, namely, the passives of direct action verbs. On this account, a child reared in this environment will annotate the more general universal rule in the obvious way:

(3) Object → Subject
        ("Oblique" in the sense of Bresnan 1982c)
     only if subject = agent
     only if object = patient

The idea is that rule (3) will cover all sentences the child hears. One problem is that rule (2) does this as well, because all patients are also objects in the sense defined by lexical-functional grammar. This forces the second auxiliary assumption. Rule (3) should be universal to begin with. If the rule were not in the universal inventory it would be difficult to understand why children innately endowed with rule (2), a rule which handles all of the positive evidence in their linguistic environment, would reach outside of the universal inventory to coin an *ad hoc* rule like (3). If on the other hand (3) is a universal, we can automatically explain why it would be chosen first.[19]

This suggestion allows two interpretations. Pinker may want to say there is a universal developmental sequence guaranteeing that the child begins rule formation using semantically circumscribed predicates. These predicates may be "preprogrammed" to drop out of the rule writing vocabulary of natural languages, explaining why we do not see natural languages using these predicates. This is a maturational model. Alternatively, we might think of these semantic predicates as part of the rule writing vocabulary of Universal Grammar, and hope that other (grammatical?) principles will explain when grammars may or may not appeal to them. Pinker seems to favor this second course when he says, "the syntactic units may be said to emerge at a certain maturational state in a (presumably innately specified) reorganization of the child's language faculty" but that this is *ad hoc* and is "to be avoided if possible." (Pinker 1982:679).

The real question, then, is whether we should further extend the rule writing vocabulary of grammatical theory to allow rules like (3).[20] Should the rule writing vocabulary be allowed to mention thematic notions like patient as well as more general thematic notions like theme? Everyone is in the same boat here. Pinker's story will not work unless such narrowly circumscribed semantic notions are allowed into Universal Grammar. Crucial though this assumption is, it is problematic. Assuming that the initial state of knowledge is as in (3), we should expect that the child needs positive evidence (examples of passives of non-direct action verbs) to force a generalization of the rule. The problem is that because (3) is a possibility in Universal Grammar, we would predict that there should be some adult language that this rule describes, a language where only direct actional passives are grammatical. This would be a language where option (3) was in fact selected from Universal Grammar. Then, given that this would be the correct choice for such a language, there would be no subsequent evidence to force a change. The problem is that no such languages exist. It seems then that we must ban this type of predicate from Universal Grammar.[21]

This difficulty undermines Pinker's account. The lexical-functional theory on which Pinker's account is based presupposes that the child has independent notions of grammatical functions at all stages of development. These basic elements are in terms of configuration for languages like English or in terms of Case for languages like Japanese. Assuming that these notions are part of Universal Grammar and thus are available from the earliest stages, it is difficult to understand why the child would circumscribe rules with predicates not in Universal Grammar in the way outlined by Pinker. That is, we would expect the child to modify deep universal principles only when confronted with evidence that existing rules could not handle. But because all agents are also subjects, all of the evidence that the child confronts, even at the earliest stages, is compatible with the more general functionally characterized rule. Therefore, we would expect the child to use the more general rule in the earlier stages. Summarizing, it seems preferable to eliminate the [+patient] option completely as a predicate for rules, relying instead on other principles to describe the early stage discussed by Pinker and Maratsos.[22]

This will be our goal. We shall pursue another account that is consistent with the government-binding theory and that solves the problems just discussed. First though, we shall review the government-binding analysis of passives, because it is central to our analysis.

To begin, remember that the notion "passive construction" has no independent status in the government-binding theory. NP movement is obligatory in passive constructions, but that is related to the passive predicate's quasi-adjectival status. Being quasi-adjectival, such a predicate cannot assign case to the NP that it directly dominates. Because the only structures that will satisfy the case filter are those where passive predicates are followed by nonlexical NPs, the NP must be moved.[23]

The insertion of an empty category in the postparticipial position is likewise forced by the projection principle. Recall what the projection principle says: "Representations at each syntactic level ... are projected from the lexicon, in that they observe the subcategorization properties of lexical items" (Chomsky 1981:29).

Further, there must be a nonlexical NP in the subcategorized position following the verb. Continuing, the linking of the moved NP to the postverbal position is guaranteed by the θ criterion. The moved NP is in a nonthematic position. The θ criterion mandates that every NP must be associated with one and only one θ role. The only way for an NP to get a θ role is to be associated with a θ position. Therefore, the preparticipial NP must be linked back to the postparticipial θ position in order to receive its sought for θ role.[24]

The various constraints, Case theory, the θ criterion, and the projection principle are all part of the child's innate endowment. What the child must actually learn is the formation of passive predicates from their verbal roots. We shall see that comprehension of the passive arises out of the child's inability to give an active interpretation to passive structures while not violating one or all of the above principles.

To summarize, the obligatory movement in a passive structure is forced by the loss of case assigning properties associated with the *en* morpheme attached to a verb root.

Passive participals look strikingly like the past tense forms of the same verbs. However, the past tense morpheme retains the verb stem's case assigning properties. So what the child actually has to learn is that a homophonous morpheme can be associated with two grammatically marked properties. It seems natural to suppose though that the child assumes a unique association between phonetic forms and grammatically relevant properties. This is a natural principle because it forges the tightest possible link between evidence and underlying rule system. Unless positive evidence proves otherwise, the unmarked situation is one in which an affix either unambiguously preserves or modifies the case assigning properties of the lexical item it attaches to. Because *ed* affixation is not unambiguous in this way, it should cause difficulties for the child. The result is a drive to limit the scope of this rule's affixation as much as possible. Hence the initial hypothesis that the rule applies to the most minimal class of verbs consistent with the data that is heard. As Pinker 1982 mentions, parental input is heavily biased towards direct action verbs, so the first hypothesis would be to limit passive predicate formation to these "nonstative" verbs. The child's early rule for passive formation would be:

(4) en:

$$[\text{nonstative}]_{[+V \ -N]} \rightarrow [\quad]_{[+V]}$$

Here, the loss of the "$-N$" feature indicates loss of case assigning power.

The basic idea behind the observed semantic limit on passive is simple. Semantic circumscription follows from the passive predicate's limited application to a semantically circumscribed class of verbs. This limitation, in turn, goes hand in hand with a difficulty in forming passive predicates to begin with, because of a confusion in the morphological component. If a passive predicate cannot be formed, then no well-formed interpretation will be given to the passive sentence.

Consider the "passive" interpretation of sentences where the verb retains its case assigning properties. We derive this representation:

(5)   John$_i$ was liked e_i by Fred.
       +Nom   +Accusative

This representation violates the case filter. *John* gets both nominative case, being governed by the nominative inflection, and accusative case, being linked to a trace governed by the verb. Well-formed structures are possible only by eliminating the case assigning properties of the relevant verbs.[25] Move NP produces a surface form with the appearance of circumscription, because only a small class of predicates mesh with the demands of the case filter. Because affixation rules that eliminate a predicate's ability to assign case are rare in the child's linguistic environment, the rule will be applied conservatively, only to verbs actually heard in this form in adult speech to children. We do not need to also circumscribe the Move α rule in this early stage.

It is important to note that this account does not suffer from the same problems as the lexical "direct approach" discussed above. There are examples of a case-changing affix attaching to a semantically circumscribed class of verbs in adult grammars. For example, the class of English "action nominalizations" is derived by applying the *ing* morpheme to the class of direct action verbs (and only to this class). Complex nominals are the result. Some examples are:

(6)   The hitting (of the ball)
(7)   The singing (of the songs)
(8)   *The liking (of Bill)
(9)   ?The seeing (of the movie)
(10)   ?The hearing (of the story)

Evidently children have good comprehension of these nominalizations in very early stages in their development, from approximately age 3 (see Roeper 1978). Therefore, we may assume that the class of [stative] verbs is a natural class.[26]

This account leaves us with one remaining problem. We have claimed that the passive morphology is first applied to a semantic subclass of verbs. That this option is part of Universal Grammar was justified by the existence of the class of action nominalizations at all stages of development in English. We must now go on to show how this rule generalizes throughout the verbs of passive constructions, and, in fact, why the child is driven to do this. We must then explain why the "action nominalizing suffix" persists in attaching to just a semantically well defined class of verbs in the adult stage.

Semantic Circumscription

We now turn to the explanation of why this semantic circumscription is not observed in adult grammars. Earlier, we presented the rule for forming passive predicates as (4):

(4) en:

$$[\text{nonstative}]_{[+V\ -N]} \rightarrow [\quad]_{[+V]}$$

Lieber 1980 shows that this is the incorrect formulation of this rule. Lieber points out that the passive participle undergoes the same phonological deformations as the perfective form, that is ablaut, substitution of *en* for *ed*, and various infixation processes. This would be explained if passive participles were actually derived from the participial form as opposed to being directly affixed to the verb stem. The derivation would proceed as follows:

(11) en:

$$[\quad]_{[+V\ -N]} \rightarrow [\quad]_{[+V\ -N\ +\text{participle}]}$$

(12) ∅:

$$[\text{en}]_{[+V\ -N\ +\text{participle}]} \rightarrow [\quad]_{[+V]}$$

This derivation predicts that passives and perfectives undergo some phonological processes that nonparticipial forms do not undergo. This is shown in (13) below:

(13)

Tensed form	Perfective	Passive
showed	has shown	was shown
proved	has proven	was proven
saw	has seen	was seen
ate	has eaten	was eaten
rode	has ridden	was ridden
gave	has given	was given
threw	has thrown	was thrown

There is a "zero morpheme" changing the verbal participial form into a quasi-adjectival marker.[27] It seems to be true in general that participial forms serve as the source for passives. This derivation does not commit us to using the same affix ambiguously as both case retaining and case changing. Assuming that this is the correct derivation, we predict that in the adult state there will be no pressure to semantically circumscribe the "passive" word formation rule. So we do not expect to find a semantically circumscribed adult passive.[28] Semantic circumscription in the early stage of acquisition comes from a misanalysis of the relevant word formation rules. This mistake seems natural though because the evidence for the correct derivation comes from inspection of the ablauted forms that differ phonologically from the past tense forms. The past tense derivation is generally simpler.

In most cases there is no evidence to tell the child that the passive form cannot be derived directly from the active verb. The direct derivation from the verb via one word formation rule is simpler than the derivation that first forms participles and then forms passives. The child picks the direct derivation first, revising this decision on the basis of the parallelism of forms noted in (13) above. But once passives and perfectives divide from past tense verbs, the conservative behavior using just one ending to derive case marked forms is no longer in play. Given principles of rule simplification prevalent in the morpho-phonological component of the grammar, the semantic circumscription of the "passive" rule should recede as entries split. Assuming that adult grammars produce passive forms from participals, and that early participal formation is a developmental mistake, we do not expect to find an adult language with a semantically circumscribed passive.[29]

Experimental Support for the Morphological Model

Our model makes several predictions that are actually supported by an experiment reported in Maratsos and Abramovitch 1975. First, we claimed that the structures posited by the child are consistent with the principles of Universal Grammar described by government-binding theory. Consider a passive sentence again:

(14) John$_i$ was liked e_i by Fred.

We could interpret this sentence consistently with government-binding principles by suppressing the closed class preposition and interpreting the sentence as if it corresponded to the active form:

(15) John liked Bill.

If we did not suppress the θ marking properties of the preposition, we would violate the θ criterion because both *by* and *like* would θ mark *Fred*.

Now consider a sentence like:

(16) John was hit.

Hit obligatorily subcategorizes and θ marks a theme. Because the only argument around is *John*, it must be so interpreted. This predicts that short passives and long passives where prepositions are understood as θ markers will be equally good cues for an argument changing operation. Because children vary in their comprehension of closed class items such as prepositions we predict a potential developmental lag for long passives.[30]

Now we can turn to what Maratsos and Abramovitch actually found. Subjects seemed to have stable control over closed class items and equally good control over truncated and nontruncated passives. "The average number of sentences acted out accurately [by the subjects rcb/asw] was 5.00 out of eight possible for full passives and 5.00 for short truncates" (1975:147).

Interestingly enough, this data also support our connection between passive affixes and case assignment. Maratsos and Abramovitch presented children with a series of anomalous passives that would respect both the case filter and the θ criterion if participles were incorrectly analyzed as case assigning. Children were supposed to act out these sentences using toy puppets provided by the experimenters. These were labeled [−prep] passives:

(17) The turtle is licked the cat.

Other "passives," like (18), were missing the copula but not the prepositional phrase. An active interpretation here violates the θ criterion whether or not the predicate is analyzed as a case assigner. These were labeled [−be] passives.

(18) The turtle licked by the cat.

It seems that [−be] passives were treated as passives for some of the subjects. Those subjects who had a stable comprehension of normal truncate and long passives, also had a stable comprehension of the [−be] passives. Maratsos and Abramovitch (1975:150) have the details. In contrast, "removal of the genitive preposition *by* results in children's interpreting the sentence as though it were an active" (Maratsos and Abramovitch 1975:150).

Children's sensitivity to the presence or absence of the prepositional phrase in the experimental situation thus supports the claim that they comprehend long passives by recognizing the postverbal prepositional phrase and its θ marking properties. This is confirmed by similar experiments discussed in Maratsos and Abramovitch 1975. Here children substituted actual θ marking prepositions for semantically null prepositions inserted into sentences previously eliciting "passive" responses. Thus a sentence like (19a) in which the experimenter had substituted an *of* phrase for the passive *by* phrase was repeated either as (19b), (19c), or (19d) but was acted out as a passive.

(19) a. The cat is licked of the dog.
     b. The cat is licked by the dog.
     c. The cat is licked from the dog.
     d. The cat is licked off the dog.

Evidently children realized that a preposition with independent θ marking properties demanded a passive interpretation.[31]

Summarizing, what are the differences between the Maratsos/Pinker model and the transformational model proposed here? For Pinker and Maratsos, semantic predicates circumscribe the argument changing apparatus of lexical rules. We might characterize this as a rule-based account of acquisition. For instance, the rule object → subject may be restricted to apply to only agentive predicates. We showed that once this new machinery is admitted it becomes hard to characterize adult grammars with semantically circumscribed rules. We propose that just word formation uses semantic circumscription. This is required anyway to explain progressive affixation in verbal and "action nominalization" constructions. We are adding nothing new then, unlike the Maratsos/Pinker model. In addition, these restricted predicates are naturally ruled out of the steady state (adult) grammar, once we adopt Lieber's (1980) analysis of passive predicate formation.[32] Finally, we saw that the Maratsos and Abramovitch experiment forces a passive interpretation only when grammatical principles are otherwise violated. This further supports our claim that passive participals are interpreted as case assigners, and bolsters our principle-based account of language development.

Of course, the morphological account is just as well suited to lexical-functional as transformational grammar. By appealing to semantically circumscribed morphological machinery, we can avoid enlarging another component of the grammar. The study of the interactions between the "modules" of word formation and syntax should be a topic for fruitful future research in language development.

Passive and the Computer Model

Our analysis of how passive constructions are learned has thus far been a "standard" psycholinguistic one. We have described several distinct "stages" of knowledge children pass through on their way to mastering passive constructions, and have outlined one way in which the government-binding theory can account for these stages. One thing we have not done so far is make good on our promise to connect a descriptive account like this one to our computational model. That will be the goal here.

A good place to begin is with a description of the target state for the parser. The end rule for the parser's basic passive construction can be written as:

Pattern:
Cyclic node: INFL-max $+be$
Active node: VP $+ed$ +argument
Packet: Parse-complement-VP
Buffer: $[*][*][*]$

Action: *drop trace*

The buffer pattern for this rule contains "wild card" feature predicates that will match against any kind of item in the input buffer. This grammar rule is sufficient to handle cases such as, *Sally was kissed*, *Sally was kissed by John*. The passive rule drops a "dummy" NP node into the first cell of the buffer. Later rules attach this NP to its position in the verb phrase complement, for example, as an object noun phrase. Thus the purpose of this rule is to construct a parse that analyzes a passive sentence as a case of a noun phrase trace, with this element bound to the now displaced NP. For example, in the sentence *Sally was kissed* the noun phrase *Sally* is really the object argument of the verb *kissed* for the purposes of interpretation, just as it is in the straightforward declarative version of the same sentence, *John kissed Sally*.

For this rule to trigger correctly it is crucial for the verb node to be marked with the feature $+ed$ and for the inflection node (here assumed dominating the VP) to be marked $+be$.[33]

The assembly of rules to deal with the passive construction illustrates some important computational points about the acquisition procedure itself. The system is designed to be conservative and incremental in its rule formation, building new rules only when the inference is clearcut. For the reasons discussed above, this has the effect of making the acquisition of so-called "truncated" passives, passive constructions where there is no *by* phrase, as in *Sally was kissed*, easier than the acquisition of full passives in which there is a full passive *by* phrase, as in *Sally was kissed by John*. The computer model also has difficulty here because it cannot acquire both a passive rule and a *by* phrase rule all at once.

For now though, let us turn directly to an example. Given that the rules to handle simple declaratives are known, suppose that a truncated passive is presented to the acquisition procedure, *Sally was kissed*.

The analysis of the first three tokens proceeds normally. The NP *Sally* is attached as the Specifier of Infl-max (S); *was* is attached as the head of Infl, annotating Infl-max in the process. A V-max phrase is formed, and *kissed* attached as its head. Note that *kiss* is coerced to the feature pattern [+V −N +Arg], because the alternative, *kiss* as [+N −V], is not compatible with the NP-INFL-VP schema. Because the head has been attached, the complement packet of the X-max (here, VP) currently active is entered. The feature "+Arg" is the proxy for the subcategorization frame for *kiss*, indicating that an NP must follow. This crucially makes use of the projection principle. No known rules match because the only rule known so far in the Parse-complement-V packet is the rule to attach an object NP to the verb complement. But there is no such object NP. The acquisition procedure is invoked. At this point the parser's state is as follows: The state is annotated with the names of various grammar rules that have been triggered to build the parse so far; this information is used as part of the lefthand context of the parse. "•" denotes the end of input symbol. We have also used feature complexes instead of full category names. So for example, X-max [−N +V −Arg] is actually an S node; [+V −N +Arg] is a VP. On the right we also list the active packet associated with that stack node; for example, for the S node, the packet Parse-complement is active, indicating that we are looking for the complement of an S.

With the acquisition procedure invoked, the system tries to learn one new grammar rule by cycling through its list of possible actions.

Stack:

X-max [−N +V −Arg]
Sally was

Rule subject_NP_attach
Rule be_attach
Packet Parse-complement-X

X-max [+V −N +Arg]
kissed +ed

Rule V_attach
Packet Parse-complement-X
[+V −N +Arg]

[•][   ][   ]

Buffer

An *attach* is attempted, but fails because the end of sentence marker • can never be attached to any node. Note how clearcut this case is. Likewise, *switch* has nothing to switch, and so cannot apply. *Drop trace* is next. An empty NP element is inserted into the first position in the buffer. Now can any known grammar rule execute? Yes, the grammar rule for attaching NP objects looks like this:

Cyclic node: X-max [−N +V −Arg]   **Rule** NP_attach
                                        Packet Parse-complement-X
Active node: X-max [+V −N +Arg]   **Rule** V_attach
                                        Packet Parse-complement-X

Buffer: [NP][•][   ]

This rule does not say that the *be_Attach* rule must be present; therefore, the predicate demanded by this rule pattern triggers against the current machine state. Rule patterns are predicates that must be true of the current parser state before the associated rule action can execute.

   In short, the drop trace rule has succeeded. The new rule pattern is saved. Observe that now the rule pattern for passive will include the triggering predicate *be_attach* annotation on the X-max node above the current active node, because that feature was present at the time the new rule was built. The VP node is annotated with the name of the new passive rule, again to provide a basis for potential semantic differences, if necessary. The remainder of the parse will proceed normally. We have seen previously that the projection principle and the θ criterion guarantee that the trace will be bound to the subject NP.

What about full passive sentences? As far as the parser is concerned, they require a prior ability to correctly analyze prepositional phrases. At the point where PPs can be analyzed successfully, suppose that the system receives the example, *John was kissed by Sally*. At the point where the NP trace should be dropped, the buffer has *by* (marked −N −V +Arg) in its first cell, *John* (+N −V) in its second cell, and • (end of sentence) in its third cell. Assuming that the psycholinguistic insights about the closed class items are correct, we may regard the preposition as misanalyzed. Its θ marking properties are ignored. In this case, the attach operation can attach the immediately postverbal NP directly as the object of the verb *kissed*. This leads to the wrong interpretation, an active interpretation. The attach feature will be the first option attempted in accordance with the subset principle (see below).[34] Once again, a correct analysis will wait until the *by* phrase can be correctly analyzed. If it can, then a trace dropping operation will again be the only action successful at that point. A generalized passive rule will be acquired:

Cyclic node:	INFL-max	**Rule** be‿attach
Active node:	V-max	**Rule** kiss‿attach +ed
		(subcateg. frame [___NP])
Packet:	Parse-complement-X	[+V −N +Arg]
Buffer:	[*][*][*]	

Action:	*drop trace*

This is exactly the target result.

One final remark. An important question to ask is why, having dropped an NP trace, the system does not immediately fire a passive rule once again? For the input buffer now matches once again the pattern of the passive rule just acquired. The annotation of the active node does not help here, so the passive rule will just execute again. If left unchecked, this possibility would lead the machine into an endless loop. There is though a default priority ordering of grammar rules. If two rules in the same packet match the features of the current machine state, the most specific rule gets priority.

This priority is derivable from the subset principle. We derive the particular principle that specific grammar rules trigger before general rules because a more general rule allows a broader range of surface sentences than a more specific one. In our example of passive rule ordering, there is another rule that can execute, namely, the rule that attaches NP objects to the VP (V-max). But this rule demands a more specific pattern match of the input buffer, namely the pattern [NP] [*] [*].

The object attach rule therefore takes priority over the passive rule, attaching the NP trace to the V-max. Now the buffer has the end marker • in its first cell, and the V-max has been annotated with the NP attachment rule. The subcategorization frame for *kiss* is satisfied, and the completed V-max can be dropped into the buffer, deactivating any rules associated with the V-max-complement packet. The remainder of the parse proceeds as in a simple declarative sentence.

Computational Constraints and Language Acquisition

Now that we have seen some examples of the acquisition procedure in action, we can turn to a more important question. How do the computational constraints of the model actually aid acquisition? The answer to this question may or may not be interesting theoretically. The answer would be uninteresting if the model were simply a direct simulation of the government-binding theory. Then the model would contribute no more to an explanation of acquisition than the a-computational government-binding theory itself. The model could still be useful in two ways though. It could provide a working demonstration that a government-binding based theory is compatible with a computational implementation; and it could be a handy bookkeeping device to keep track of the outcome of changes in assumptions in a deductively rich theory.

The answer would be interesting only if the model contained independently motivated computational constraints, not otherwise required by the government-binding theory, but required by the learning procedure. For then the model would no longer be a mere simulation of a government-binding acquisition theory; it would contribute computationally grounded constraints of its own.

We shall show that the computational model adds constraints with no counterparts in government-binding theory. Even more importantly, some of the model constraints justified on grounds of efficient parsability also aid learnability. Given this result, we can answer precisely at least one of the questions that we raised in an abstract way in chapter 3: How do the "functional" demands of efficient parsability and learnability interact? The answer, at least for the government-binding parsing and learning model we have proposed here, is that they are compatible and in fact closely related. Constraints crucial for efficient parsability are also crucial for learnability.

Three of the learnability constraints could be dubbed "locality restrictions"; these are also constraints important for parsability. Three constraints follow from the subset principle, a general requirement for acquisition from positive only evidence. The key locality constraints are:

Bounded context patterns for grammar rules.

Deterministic rule application.

Nonrecursive invocation of the acquisition procedure.

Grammar rules have bounded context patterns because any if-then rule that is learned can refer only to the features of at most three buffer cell nodes and two nodes in the active node stack, the current top of stack symbol and the cyclic node above that top of stack symbol. Further, by the constraint of literal encoding (as discussed in chapter 5), we cannot "pass down" information about the preceding left context in the form of complex nonterminal names. The result is that the "radius of action" of any grammar rule is strictly local. This locality is central to the acquisition procedure sketched above. If we could not say that a rule applied only to a certain bounded context, then when an error occurred we could not pin the blame on a particular rule (or lack of rule) at the current locus of parsing activity. For suppose that a rule three (or n) sentences away could affect the current environment of the parse. Then this rule could be to blame for the current inability to analyze a sentence. There would be no easy way to assign blame when something went wrong, and the repair procedure would be much more complex. Bounded context rules aid local error detectability.

In fact, we can be more precise about what would happen. Suppose that there were no bound on the radius of action of some grammar rule. Then this rule could apply, and yet its effects in terms of the annotated surface structure built would not show up for an unbounded distance in terms of parse tree structure. This means that the child could make a guess as to the effects of this rule and this guess could not be "debugged" except on arbitrarily large structure. We may conclude that unbounded context rules could demand arbitrarily complex data for their successful acquisition, a violation of the psychological plausibility that we have insisted upon.

This restriction bears a close connection to the Wexler and Culicover "Degree 2 theory" (1980) for the acquisition of a transformational grammar. In the Wexler and Culicover model several constraints on transformational grammar are advanced in order to guarantee learnability from "simple" positive data. One key constraint is subjacency. Taken together the constraints roughly amount to the demand that transformational grammars be "debuggable" from simple data. If the learner can detect an error in a hypothesized transformational component at all, there is some simple evidence on which the same error will occur. Similarly, in the acquisition by parsing model, if there is some parsing error that will occur at all (where a parsing error is the construction of an incorrect parse tree) that error must occur (be detectable) on a simple sentence. The two models are quite parallel. It remains to determine the relationship between the bounded context languages defined by the computer model and the languages defined by the Degree 2 theory. For an additional perspective on this issue, see the comparison between the model and Degree 2 theory at the end of this chapter.

Turning now to the second learnability constraint, the deterministic application of grammar rules is the by now familiar condition that at most one correct grammar rule may apply at any given point in the parse of a sentence. A grammar rule is not tentatively applied, with the proviso that it may well have to be withdrawn at a later point in the parse because another rule should have applied. Past parsing decisions are indelible.

From the standpoint of learning, the effect of determinism and the restriction that rules refer only to bounded context is to pinpoint errors to a "local radius" about the point at which the error is detected, where "local radius" is defined as the local context determined by grammar rule patterns. These constraints effectively restrict how one grammar rule could affect another. For one grammar rule to influence another, the prior rule must have triggered within the local radius of the current rule, or else must have labeled some portion of the parse tree under construction so as to "pass along" information. For example, the effect of a rule to analyze *wh* phrases must disappear after the $\overline{S}$ domain in which it was created and any Ss attached to this domain are built, unless we can "pass along" the fact of the rule's firing by means of a trace inserted into the lower S domains. By implication, propositional domains will generally act as opaque barriers.

As another illustration, suppose that the parser's operation were nondeterministic, in that any grammar rule operation could be considered to be a tentatively made decision, retractable on the basis of later evidence. What would happen if a learning procedure with such a parser came to a failure point? There would now be two possible "reasons" for an error. Either its current rule database could be faulty or one of its past decisions could have been mistaken. How could the learning system distinguish a potential error as either a learning error or an ordinary nondeterministic parsing "error"? In general, there would be no way other than to attempt all possible repairs, covering all possible combinations of past decisions affecting the current context. Note that this leads to an exponential tree of combinatorial possibilities. Given parsing decisions $D_1, \ldots, D_n$ with decision D_n ending in failure, then all alternatives at D_1 must be explored, jointly with all alternatives at D_2 and so forth till we arrive at last at the alternatives for D_n, the actual learning opportunity. In contrast, for a deterministic device, none of these alternatives have to be considered, except those at point D_n.

In short, while the assumption of determinism is not a necessary constraint, it saves an extraordinary amount of computation in terms of the number of possible hypotheses necessary for consideration. At each learning step, instead of a number of hypotheses exponential in the length of past parsing decisions, only a constant number of hypotheses must be considered. Intuitively, we must examine globally the computation tree for the parse, precisely the kind of global computation that was to be avoided.

The savings due to noninteraction of the rule effects, the joint result of deterministic operation plus design constraints on features and nodes accessed during parsing, is again the same as that achieved by Wexler and Culicover in their formal model for the acquisition of a transformational grammar. In fact, they rely on quite parallel assumptions. For example, they assume that in a transformational derivation from base to surface structure only the topmost transformation can be hypothesized as being in error; transformations otherwise apply deterministically.

Finally, the acquisition procedure is constrained so that it cannot be invoked recursively. That is, while the procedure is in the midst of attempting to learn a new grammar rule it cannot be invoked again, to attempt to learn another rule. To take a simple example suppose that the acquisition procedure was in the midst of learning a rule to handle a full passive with an agentive *by* phrase when it did not even have a rule to parse prepositional phrases correctly. If the acquisition procedure could be invoked recursively, the system could hypothesize a new rule to parse prepositional phrases at the point when it is trying to build a new rule to parse the passive. While this is appropriate for this example, the problem is that the process cannot be controlled. If the acquisition procedure could be invoked twice, it could be called a third time, and so on. Any combination of these forward hypotheses might be a candidate rule chain. Each would have to be tested. But this would lead to the same computational difficulties that we encountered with nondeterminism, only in the forward direction.

The benefits of each of these constraints for parsability have already been described. Bounded context rules, assuming literal left context storage, are necessary for even implementing an LR(k) type parsing device in a finite way. Determinism is sufficient to eliminate combinatorial backtracking. Recursive acquisition procedure invocation does not apply strictly to the case of parsing because acquisition, not parsing, is involved, but the import of its ban is analogous to the case of left context determinism.

What of the other three constraints? As mentioned, they are purely "learnability" constraints, all corollaries of the subset principle. Briefly, the subset principle demands that a learning procedure should guess the narrowest possible language, consistent with positive evidence seen so far. By hypothesizing as narrow a target language as possible, the acquisition procedure is protected from disastrous overgeneralization. The subset principle is a general, formal condition on the "triggering data" presented to an ideal learner that follows from necessary and sufficient conditions for the acquisition of a language on the basis of positive only, or grammatical input; Angluin (1978) proves this basic result. The gist of the ordering condition is that triggering evidence can be arranged so that the learner can hypothesize the narrowest possible language consistent with evidence seen so far. Otherwise, the learner could be forced to guess too general a language. This guess could never be overturned by any positive evidence if the right target language were smaller, because no positive evidence from the correct target would ever contradict it.[35] But this means that the right hypothesis ordering strategy is to guess the narrowest language consistent with the evidence, just to be safe.

The computational learnability constraints are:

1. Only one new grammar rule is permitted to remedy any single detected error (incremental acquisition).

2. Base phrase structure rules are hypothesized before transformational rules (for any single rule hypothesis).

3. Rules are not marked as optional or obligatory.

Taking each of these constraints in turn, consider first incremental acquisition. The system adds only a single new rule to its knowledge base at a time, rather than hypothesizing and rejecting whole sets of rules or grammars at a time. For instance, when a rule to handle passives is first formulated, it is written in response to the repair of a single sticking point in the parse of some particular sentence. The procedure does not proceed by enumerating the sets of possible parsing rules (or grammars), and testing each for adequacy in turn. Because any grammar rule can contain at most one parsing action, the effect of this constraint is to enlarge the parser's ability to handle different sentences minimally. For example, if a novel inverted auxiliary verb-NP sequence is encountered, then just a single re-inversion rule can be constructed, not a re-inversion plus some sequence of other grammar rules actions such as trace insertions plus attachments.[36]

When a new grammar rule action is hypothesized, it is assumed first to follow existing base phrase structure. Only if this fails will an inversion or movement type action be attempted. A language generated by a base component plus no movement rules is narrower than one generated by that same base plus movement rules.

Finally, this acquisition system can succeed even if it respects the government-binding ban on marking grammar rules, extrinsically, as being obligatory or optional. They simply trigger if they happen to match the current parsing environment. This is fortunate because learning whether a rule should always apply can be difficult. If we assume that a rule is optional, no positive evidence will dislodge this overly generous guess. The evidence will simply suggest that optional application has always occurred.[37]

Four points about the acquisition model deserve further discussion. These are: rule generalization; the order in which rule actions are attempted; the annotation of the active node with the names of rules that build that node; and the order in which rules are executed. Let us cover each of these in turn.

As mentioned, there are basically two situations in which rule generalization can occur. First, new lexical categories can be formed via the collapse of terminal items into equivalence classes. This mode of operation is appropriate whenever the action of the new rule just acquired is *attach*. This is because the attach rule is simply the reverse of the expansion, $A \rightarrow \alpha \ / \ \Phi\underline{\quad}\xi$ that is, α being reduced to A in the context Φ on the left and ξ on the right. Equivalence class formation is based on the notion of "state" from automata theory, a matter taken up in detail in Berwick 1982. Call the state of the parse simply the left context plus the item being analyzed. Parsing actions map between states. Now consider two parser states q_i and q_j, and the succeeding states of the parser prompted by the attachment of the input tokens a or b respectively; call these new states q_{i+1} and q_{j+1}. If the two initial states and the two succeeding states are equivalent $(q_i = q_j$ and $q_{i+1} = q_{j+1})$ then because the parser is deterministic, a must be in the same equivalence class as b with respect to the operation of the parser; such inputs are indistinguishable based on just lefthand context. For example, consider the sentences, *John could kiss Mary*; *John will kiss Mary*. *Could* and *will* are followed by the same lookahead strings and hence must lead the parser through the same sequence of states, leading to acceptance. The parse up to the point where *could* and *will* are encountered is also identical in both cases, so the parse state at the point where each is attached to the parse tree must be the same. Thus the conditions for equivalence are fulfilled, and *could* and *will* should be placed in the same (lexical) equivalence class. Conventionally this is the class of *modals*.

There is a second case where generalization should occur. If the lefthand context and input token attached are the same for two parses, then the succeeding state must be the same in both cases. This is because the parser is deterministic. But the succeeding state is represented by the items of the righthand context, that is, the current input buffer items. Two righthand contexts denote the same state only if the corresponding elements in their buffers are members of the same equivalence classes. For instance, consider the following sentence pairs: *John could take the book*, *John could buy the book*. The parser state after attaching *could* must be the same in both cases; so, *buy* and *take* are members of the same equivalence class. So we generalize the attach rule for *could*:

buffer 1: $[could][take$, verb, tenseless$][the]$
buffer 2: $[could][buy$, verb, tenseless $][the]$
                   $\rightarrow$ intersect features

generalized
rule: $[could][$ verb, tenseless $][the]$

In sum, rule generalization by merger occurs when it is known for certain that the buffer will lead to an equivalent parser state. Note that this second kind of generalization is actually a variant of the first. *Take* and *buy* will be placed in the same equivalence classes via the attachment occurring after *could* has been attached to the parse tree, just as *will* and *should* are merged. This method is simply a variant of a so-called "clustering" or "k-tail" approach to finite state induction (see Fu and Booth 1975). What this means is simply that two tokens are declared in the same equivalence class, hence are denoted by identical nonterminal labels in the acquired grammars, just in case their trailing *k*-cell suffixes, or "k-tails" are identical. If the buffer can hold complete constituents or subtrees as in the Marcus parser, this method actually induces a restricted class of tree automata.

Later examples may force the splitting of a formerly merged class. For example, consider the examples, *I did go* and *I will go*. This example forces *did* and *will* into the same class. However, a later example such as, *I will have gone*, along with the absence of the example, *I did have gone* shows that this merged class must be split. Now, it is generally impossible to tell from positive evidence that an example of a certain type has not appeared. A supplementary principle is required that lets the procedure conclude that if a certain example has not appeared by a certain point in time then it will never appear. If it makes sense at all, this principle of "indirect negative evidence" makes sense for simple sentences that would have an *a priori* high probability of appearing, as in this case.[38] This example underscores two major and often noted problems with purely "inductive" generalization procedures, (1) the requirement for a complete data sample, that is, all and only the positive examples; and (2) the low probability of occurrence of certain positive examples, for example, complex auxiliary sequences.

For the other grammar rule actions, switch and drop trace, no token is attached. Rule generalization must work somewhat differently. The basic equivalence class approach is still used, however. The method is as follows: If the trailing suffix stored in the current buffer is identical for two grammar rules except for the first buffer element and if the lefthand contexts of both rule patterns are the same (thus, in particular, both rules must be associated with the same $\overline{\text{X}}$ context), the rules are merged to yield a new, generalized rule by forming the intersection of the features in the first buffer cell. As an illustration, consider two instantiations of an auxiliary inversion rule. (Here, the "•" marker indicates how far along the parse has moved in the analysis of a phrase structure expansion.)

Rule 1
pattern:

Left context: [S → • NP INFL VP]
Right context
(buffer):   [*Did*, −N +V +Tense][*Sally*, NP][*kiss*, +V...]
Action: *switch*

Rule 2
pattern:

Left context: [S → • NP INFL VP]
Right context: [*Could*, −N +V +Tense][*Sally*, NP][*kiss*, +V...]
Action: *switch*

Because the trailing buffer suffixes are the same in both cases, a merged, generalized rule is formed:

Rule 3
Right context: [−N +V +Tense][NP][+V...]

It is not obvious why these rule generalization procedures should be necessary. Indeed, the claim that class merger can be determined just by inspecting the buffer and the local lefthand context of the parse is a strong one; it is a kind of "locality" principle for learning on a par with the parsing locality principles discussed in chapter 5. Roughly, the claim is that a three constituent buffer plus two cell lefthand context suffices to detect all cases of nonequivalent states.[39]

Turning now to rule action ordering by the acquisition procedure, above it was stated that the acquisition procedure attempts to find a single new action by trying the following sequence of actions: (1) attach; (2) switch; (3) insert specified lexical item (for example, *you*, *there*); and (4) drop trace. Why is this ordering of actions attempted and not some other? This order has been designed to follow the subset principle, which forces the procedure to guess the narrowest possible language first. The tightest assumption possible is that no movement is permitted; that is, all surface strings are base generated unless evidence is provided to the contrary.

Let us now consider the annotation of the active node. As described above, after a grammar rule executes we label the currently active node, the node on top of the active node stack, with the name of the rule just executed. In the case of a newly acquired rule, the name is a uniquely generated name. This is done for two reasons, (1) to mark the current lefthand context of a parse so that certain rules will execute properly and (2) to provide an annotation for a hypothetical semantic translation routine to distinguish between sentence variants, such as declarative and auxiliary verb inverted forms. The name of the rule is simply attached as one of the features of the currently active node.

As an example of the first use of annotation, consider a rule for a passive construction such as *John was kissed*. When the parser reaches the point where it is analyzing the complement of the verb *kissed*, a passive rule triggers. Note that at this point the currently active node is the VP. The snapshot also shows how the maximal $\overline{X}$ phrase, the Infl node, has been labeled with features percolated from its head lexical item (*was*).

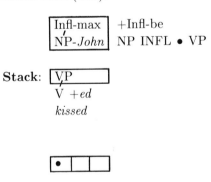

Buffer

The basic action of the passive grammar rule is to drop a trace into the input buffer; the trace acts as a dummy NP, a placeholder for the missing NP object of *kiss*. The pattern for such an action is roughly, an active node of VP, labeled +*ed*, and some record that a passive *be* has been encountered. How is this done? By assumption, the VP node is labeled with the names of rules that attach items to it. In this case, for example, the VP will be labeled with the name of the rule that attached the verb *kissed* to it. Similarly, the Infl node, the maximal projection of inflection, will be labeled with the names of the rules that attached the NP subject and some form of the verb *be*.[40]

As a result, the passive rule will require that the left context of the parser contain an INFL node marked +*be* and a VP node marked +*ed*. Why is this important? Later examples, such as, *Sally was kissed by Bill* force a rule generalization so that passive triggers on a buffer pattern with all "wild cards" in it. That is, the rule will trigger on any kind of element in the buffer. Given just this buffer pattern, the passive rule would trigger erroneously in a sentence such as, *Sally has kissed John*. What prevents it from doing so is the left context of the parse stored as part of the rule trigger. In the case at hand, the cyclic node above the VP, Infl, will not have the proper *be* annotation, thus blocking rule application.[41]

As an example of the second function of annotation, consider the yes-no question, *Will Bill kiss Sally?*. According to the actions of the grammar rules acquired by the system, a *switch* is used to convert this sentence into the form, *Bill will kiss Sally*. Then the parse proceeds as in a simple declarative sentence. But if this is so there would be no way to distinguish between the structure built by this sentence and its declarative counterpart. Therefore, any later or concurrently active semantic interpretation routines would be unable to distinguish between declarative and question forms. Because these sentences obviously differ in meaning, there must be some way that the parser marks them as different. A straightforward marking method is the annotation device. The yes-no question will mark the S node with the name of the switch rule, while the declarative sentence will not. Note that the currently active node at the point where the switch is performed is in fact S.

Conclusion: Computational Constraints and Learnability

In the previous sections of this chapter, we have seen how the government-binding theory can provide a psychologically accurate account of how children actually learn passive constructions. And we have seen how the government-binding theory fits well into a computational model of acquisition. Perhaps most importantly, the same constraints that play a key role for efficient parsability, the bounded context parsing constraints, play a key role in learnability. The bounded context constraint on error detectability appears to be a computational analogue of the restrictions on a transformational system advanced by Wexler and Culicover (1980). In their independent but related formal mathematical modeling, they have proved that a finite error detectability restriction suffices to ensure the learnability of a transformational grammar. By this they mean that if a detectable error in learning occurs at all, it should be detectable on some simple sentence of limited depth of embedding. A detectable error, in turn, is simply visible evidence that a child's hypothesized set of rules is wrong: given a surface sentence s, the tentative rule set maps the sentence's underlying base structure to the wrong surface sentence s'. Wexler and Culicover then go on to propose a whole set of conditions to guarantee finite error detectability: subjacency, the raising and "freezing" principles, and many others.

The Wexler and Culicover model lends support to the basic design of the acquisition model. Wexler and Culicover guarantee that their acquisition procedure will converge in finite time by keeping the number of possibly hypothesized rules small. This property is forced by restricting the context of rule application and interactions with other rules. Besides subjacency (which they call the binary principle), Wexler and Culicover also adopt a whole raft of constraints whose joint effect is to limit the scope of a rule to a small radius about the rule's point of action. This is quite similar in spirit to bounded context parsing. Both the Wexler and Culicover model and bounded context parsing insist on the property of being able to tell whether a rule has applied correctly within a finite radius of that rule's triggering. Apparently then, the exigencies of language processing are intimately connected to the abstract constraints advanced by current theories of grammar; many of the same constraints that ease parsing, forcing decisions to be made locally, also aid the cause of acquisition.

So we have come full circle. We began this book promising to join together modern linguistics and computation, *what* and *how*. Chapters 2 and 3 showed us how to go about this job. Things were not as grim as they seemed for the modern theory of transformational grammar. In chapters 4 and 5 we saw how far from grim things were. In fact, transformational grammar fits quite well into an efficient, natural parsing model, a model that even explains some mysteries about why natural languages look the way they do. Finally, the same constraints that contribute to the efficiency of our parsing model and its success in explaining the character of natural languages also underpin our learning model, a learning model that can explain observed developmental stages in language acquisition. So revived, the modern theory of transformational grammar is all that it was promised to be: a computationally grounded theory of natural language.

Appendix A
The Constant Growth and Linearity Theorems

Theorem. Given a government-binding grammar G and its corresponding language $L(G)$, for every sentence w_k in $L(G)$ larger than some predefined constant M, there exists (a distinct) sentence $w_{k'} \in L(G)$ such that $|w_k| = |w_{k'}| + c$, where c is a member of a finite set of constants depending on $L(G)$.

Proof. Our plan of attack is to take an arbitrary sentence w_k from $L(G)$, and then construct an associated sentence $w_{k'}$ that meets the conditions of the theorem. The basic idea is to break any w_k into two parts. The first part is that portion of the terminal string (surface sentence) corresponding to material associated with the matrix or topmost S (cyclic) domain. The second portion is that terminal material associated with all other embedded S or NP (cyclic) domains. By making certain assumptions to be later relaxed we can show that the matrix material is bounded in length from above by a constant. Further, the embedded material can be replaced by a possible surface sentence of the same length. This becomes our $w_{k'}$. Assembling these two facts, we obtain the desired result. The proof proceeds by cases on the possible transformational interactions between the matrix S and the embedded material. This depends on whether there has been movement at all, whether movement is NP or *wh* movement, and so forth.

We will first assume that Kleene star repetition of adjectives or adjective phrases, prepositional phrases, and free placement of adverbs is not permitted. Further assume that no NPs in the matrix (topmost) S exhibit recursion. All of these assumptions guarantee that the matrix sentence can be at most a fixed number of terminal elements long dependent on the grammar. The reason for this should be clear. If no true adjuncts or NP recursion are permitted, then the terminal material at just the topmost (matrix) S level is at most finite, because context-free rules without recursion can generate at most a finite number of terminal symbols. Call this finite upper bound K. We shall show later that the restrictions to prohibit Kleene star adjunction or NP recursion, which are not realistic, can be relaxed without violating the constant growth property. Intuitively, Kleene repetition does not violate the constant growth property due to the very nature of this kind of process. If five adjectives or prepositional phrases are allowed, then so are four. As a result, the length of possible sentences must be "close together." Roughly, NP recursion in subject or object position is handled by converting relative clauses into full sentences, and then forming a new sentence via conjunction.

With the assumptions of the preceding paragraph in mind, we can write w_k as follows:

[matrix S   [embedded S (possibly null)]]

Our general plan of attack will be to show that because the matrix S is bounded in length by a constant, we can construct an example that meets the conditions of the theorem by taking that constant as the constant of the theorem and constructing $w_{k'}$ from the embedded S (if necessary). Depending on its structure, the analysis of the embedded S splits into three cases:

Case 1. The embedded S is empty. This means we have a simple sentence, or else there has been movement within the S, for example, passive or topicalization. Let us call these latter kind of sentences "S transformed." What we must show is that there is a shorter simpler sentence, $w_{k'}$, such that this sentence is a constant shorter than the given matrix simple sentence. But by our assumptions any simple or S transformed sentence can be at most K long. This means that any two such sentences are at most $K - 1$ apart in length. Simple or S transformed sentences, then, meet the conditions of the theorem, with the set of constants ranging between $(1 - K)$ and $(K - 1)$ depending on whether the matrix S is so short that the next possible surface sentence is larger than it or not

Case 2. The embedded S is nonempty, but there have been no movements from the embedded S to the matrix S.

Subcase (i). The embedded S is a full sentence, for example, *Bill knows that John is a fool.*

Note that the embedded S may itself contain embeddings. The form of such cases is [matrix S [Comp NP INFL VP]]. Comp may be present or not; INFL may be realized as tense or not as in, *Bill knows John to be a fool*. What we must show is that no matter what the terminal length of the embedded S, there is some valid matrix sentence of the same length. We show this by building a valid matrix sentence out of the very same Comp NP INFL VP terminal string given by the sentence itself. For example, consider the case when Comp is optionally absent, and INFL is realized as a tensed verb (in English). Then the embedded S is itself a possible surface sentence, for example, *John is a fool*. Note that we need not continue our reconstruction below this level of embedding into the possibly recursive structure of the embedded S itself. If the embeddings of the complement S were properly formed originally, then altering the complement S so that it is a valid matrix S does not change this well-formedness. For example, *John wants to be a fool* is a valid surface sentence. If Comp is present, it is one lexical item, for example, *that*. But this means we can add 1 to the constant K and proceed as if no Comp had been lexically present, $|w_k| = c + 1 + |\text{Comp}| + |w_{k'}|$, where $w_{k'}$ = the surface sentence constructed as if Comp were not present, and c must be a number between 1 and K. Similarly, if INFL is realized as a tenseless infinitive (for example, *to be*), then we can change it to a tensed counterpart with the loss of at most a constant number of lexical items (in this case, 1). So this adjustment also makes no difference. We will frequently use this ability to adjust for a constant number of lexical items.

Crucially, because we need not continue this process of building $w_{k'}$ down into embedded structure any further, the constant adjustments that we make to build $w_{k'}$ are fixed.

Subcase (ii). Controlled Pro.

These are examples such as *The boy tried to win*. On the government-binding account the embedded S contains a Pro subject that is not introduced by any kind of movement, but is "controlled" by a matrix subject. To handle this situation we imagine moving the NP back to replace the subject Pro. This leaves behind a matrix S that was again at most K long. The matrix S must be some constant number of terminal items long, where the constant is between 1 and K. For example, the embedded S in *the boy tried to win* becomes, *the boy to win*. Now as before we must adjust the INFL element of the embedded S to form a proper matrix S, as in *the boy won*. This adjustment again only alters K by a fixed finite number. Again note that we need not continue this process beyond one level of embedding, because the sentence we get will be a valid surface sentence no matter what any embeddings look like. For example, if the original sentence is *the boy with blond hair tried to force Bill to want to win*, then we can convert it to *the boy with blond hair forced Bill to want to win*.

What of the example of long distance controlled Pro, as in *John thought it was certain that feeding himself was dangerous*, where the subject of *feeding himself* is a Pro controlled by *John*? Because in this case the Pro can be arbitrary in reference (always an option), we can simply take the embedded S as a valid surface sentence, and we are done.

Case 3. Constituents have been moved from the embedded S to the matrix S. There are four subcases, depending on the kind of movement or deletion.

Subcase (i). NP movement.

The case of actual NP movement is handled exactly the same as that of Pro, with the difference that long distance movement is not permitted. Thus, *John seemed to want to win* has an associated $w_{k'}$ of *John wanted to win*. Details of this demonstration are omitted.

Subcase (ii). *wh* movement.

The idea here is to build w_k by moving the displaced *wh* constituent back one cycle into the Comp of the embedded S. As usual, constant adjustments may have to be performed. Because the *wh* sentence had to have been derived by such movement, it must always be possible to undo this movement and obtain a valid surface sentence. For example, consider the sentence *Who did Bill think that Mary wanted to see?* We can move *who* back one cycle to obtain *Who Mary wanted to see* and then insert tense markers as appropriate to yield *Who did Mary want to see?* Note again that we need only move backwards by one step. Further, because COMP cannot hold more than one lexically realized *wh* element, we only have to do this once.

Subcase (iii). Other cases of material deleted under identity, for example, VP deletion, gapping, and conjunction.

We describe just the case of conjunction; the other cases are similar. First, note that we have deliberately restricted conjunction to just two conjoined phrases, because Kleene star repetition has been temporarily prohibited. Consider then a sentence such as, *the meat is ready to take out of the fridge and serve to our guests*. Here there are two gaps linked to *the meat* along with a Pro controlling the subject of the embedded S. We can move back the first NP and replace the second with a pronoun; the Pro can also be replaced with a pronoun, as in *we will take the meat out of the fridge and serve it to our guests.* At most a constant number of lexical items is added to $w_{k'}$.

Subcase (iv). Parasitic gaps.

These sentences are problematic because one NP is linked to two different gaps. An example is *the book that people read without buying.* These can be handled by first moving the NP back to occupy the position of the first gap after *buy*, and then inserting a pronoun into the second gap, increasing the length of $w_{k'}^*$ by 1. This means we must subtract 1 from K in this case. For instance, in the sample sentence we obtain a $w_{k'}$ of *people buy the book without reading it.* Here the deletion of the Comp actually adds 1 to our modified K, so the two alterations to K balance out. In point of fact, because this sentence is an NP it goes under the analysis of recursion through NPs, described below.

This exhausts the possible kinds of surface sentences; in each case, we are able to construct a $w_{k'}$ meeting the conditions of the theorem. It remains to relax the earlier assumptions banning Kleene repetition and NP recursion.

Consider NP recursion. First of all note that by the way we have built up $w_{k'}$, we need only handle the sentences where NPs are recursive in the matrix S and there are no links with these NPs back to any embedded S. This is because if there are such links, we can build up $w_{k'}$ by moving back the NPs. Hence, whatever recursion these NPs exhibit becomes a part of $w_{k'}$, and is therefore unproblematic. Suppose on the other hand that the recursion is exhibited by NPs that are in thematic positions just at the matrix S level. Because we are now permitted to add PP adjuncts, adjectives, and adverbs, we can do so freely, and obtain a new sentence $w_{k'}^*$ that is at most some constant longer than the original sentence w_k. This means that the set of constants C will include some finite set of negative integers as well as positive integers. For instance, we can convert *the book which is on the table beside the lamp* to a similar length sentence by adding just a single adjective.

Genitive constructions such as *Fred's brother's book* may be handled by postposing the genitive adjective and inserting two lexical items, a specifier and *of*, yielding *the book of Fred's brother.* This is just another case of a constant adjustment to K. These two subcases exhaust the possible problems with recursion through NP.

Finally, consider relaxing the restriction on Kleene star PPs, APs, and conjoined Ss, as well as unlimited numbers of adverbs. We claim that sentences with such repetitive elements can never violate the constant growth property by the very nature of such adjunct phrases. This is because wherever one adjunct phrase is permitted, so are two or more as well. Therefore, suppose we have a sentence with some series of adjunct phrases that is n terminal items long. We can build a new sentence that is close to it in length by simply selecting enough adjunct phrases of the same type that form this n length terminal string, but each of a fixed length, for example, three.[1]

Because for all possible surface sentences we can find a constant drawn from a (fixed) finite set of constants (depending on the language) and a $w_{k'}$ meeting the conditions of the theorem, the theorem is established.

We can now move to the linearity theorem.

Theorem. Let G be a government-binding grammar, and $L(G)$ the language it generates. Let AS_i be the annotated surface structure associated with sentence w_i in $L(G)$. If there is more than one such annotated surface structure, then AS_i is a set of annotated surface structures. AS_i is a singleton set if there is just one annotated surface structure. For all sentences w_i in $L(G)$ and for all annotated surface structures AS_i underlying w_i, $|AS_i| < k|w_i|$.

Proof. The proof proceeds by induction on the number of cycles (S or NP domains) in a derivation of a sentence in $L(G)$.

Basis step. $i = 1$ (bottom cycle, no embedded sentences or NPs.) Given a surface sentence w_i, we consider the length of the corresponding annotated surface structure. Let $s =$ the length of the surface sentence. There are four cases.

Case 1. No movements in the S or NP cycle, and no specified lexical deletions. Assume a context-free base with no useless nonterminals or cycles, and with rules where the length of the longest righthand side is p. If $m =$ the number of nonterminals in the derivation of a sentence in this grammar, then $m \leq cs$ for some fixed positive integer c as may be easily verified by induction. In addition, to write down the annotated surface structure, we must add two bracket labels for each nonterminal symbol. Thus $|AS_i| = 2m + s \leq 3cs$. Note that if we wanted to establish a relationship between debracketed annotated surface structures and surface strings, then this last step would be unnecessary.

Case 2. A finite number of specified lexical deletions, e.g, *that*, an imperative, or Pro. Let the maximum number of these deletions be K. Then $|AS_i| < 3cs + 3K$. For $s > 1$, $3cs + 3K < 3cs + 3Ks = (3c + 3K)s$. Let $c' = 3c + 3K$. Then $|AS_i| < c's$. Again, we can omit the $2K$ factor for the debracketed case.

Case 3. Movements within this cycle, for example, passive or topicalization. Any such movement leaves behind an empty category. But by the constraints of the government-binding theory, all places where such constituents can "land" must be possible base generated constituents, for example, Comp for *wh* elements; subject position for NPs. There are a finite number of such positions in a single S or NP. Let K bound this number from above. Then $|AS_i| < c's + K$; using the same approach as in case 2, the righthand side of this inequality is less than $c''s$. Clearly, combinations of cases 2 and 3 cause no problems because we can add together a constant number of deletions together with the constants obtained from within cycle movements to obtain a new constant factor.

Case 4. Movements out of this cycle (into cycle 2). If movement leaves behind empty categories, displacing terminal material into a higher cycle, then we must subtract some material from cycle 1's terminal string. This decreases s. However, the empty category left behind is just 1 symbol long. Thus the annotated surface structure is just a constant longer than the original base generated annotated surface structure minus the terminal material subtracted via movement. This completes the basis step.

Induction step. Suppose that up through cycle i, $|AS_i| \leq ks_i$, where s_i is the terminal length at the ith cycle, and k is a constant. We now must show that this relation holds for cycle $i + 1$. Again, the demonstration will proceed by cases, depending on the possible syntactic operations allowed on this cycle. There are five possibilities.

Case 1. No movements in cycle $i + 1$. The terminal string associated with this cycle consists of two parts, terminal material introduced in cycle $i + 1$, and material moved into the current domain from cycle i. But there are a finite number of landing sites for material moved into the current domain. By the inductive hypothesis any of these constituents themselves meet the condition that their annotated surface structures are bounded above by a linear multiple of their terminal strings. Thus the total annotated surface structure for the current cycle is at most a constant times this bound, plus a constant for material introduced at this cycle. So we have:

$$AS_{i+1} \leq d \sum\nolimits_{j=1}^{i} AS_j + d'$$
$$\sum\nolimits_{j=1}^{i} AS_j \leq K \sum\nolimits_{j=1}^{i} s_j$$

Substituting the second sum in the first we get,

$$AS_{i+1} \leq K \sum\nolimits_{j=1}^{i} s_j + k'' s_{i+1}$$
$$\leq k s_{i+1}$$

Case 2. Specified deletions. If there are a finite number of specified lexical deletions, this plainly does not affect the linearity bound, as in the basis case.

Case 3. Movement strictly within cycle $i + 1$. The demonstration proceeds as in the basis case.

Case 4. Movement to cycle $i + 2$ from cycle $i + 1$. Again, like the basis case.

Case 5. VP deletion, conjunction reduction, or gapping. This is the only new situation that arises in the induction step as opposed to the basis step. Suppose we have a conjunct formed by deleting material from each of n conjuncts. An example is *the meat is ready to take out of the fridge, heat, and serve*. The example is from Rounds (1975:137) attributed to E. Bach. But because of the nature of conjunction, each cyclic domain of the the associated annotated surface structure contains a constant number of empty "gaps," denoted [e]. Therefore, the total number of gaps in the conjoined structure is bounded from above by a constant times s_{i+1}, the length of the terminal string. There can be at most a linear number of such empty elements.

Finally, consider deletion type operations such as gapping, VP deletion or conjunction reduction. If these involved actual deletion of deep structure material, then problems could arise. But under an interpretive approach governed by the "across the board" conventions of Williams 1978 we can derive the appropriate results without actually copying large sections of the deleted terminal and nonterminal string. For example, a sentence like *the meat is ready to heat, serve, and eat* is factored as:

The meat$_i$ is ready   to heat e_i

            1   eat   3

                      serve

                      2

We can represent this by denoting term (2) as an unordered set of lexical items, for example, *heat, eat, serve*. Plainly, this representation cannot be more than linearly larger than the surface sentence. This exhausts the range of possible cases, completing the induction and the proof.

Notes

Chapter 1

1. The description here is taken from Hopcroft and Ullman 1979:148.

2. Note that once we adopt anything like a binary alphabet, we can easily encode any more complex symbol system. For example, we could make $a = 1$; $b = 2 = 10$ in binary; $c = 3 = 11$ in binary, and so on. This will affect the exact length of the input. If we used a decimal encoding instead of a binary one, then z would be 1110 in binary or 4 digits long but only 2 digits long in decimal. In general the compression factor would be logarithmically proportional to the size of the alphabet involved. Below we shall see why this does not matter in most cases. The reader should think about what would happen if we shifted to a *unary* (one digit) alphabet. Then z would take 26 digits to write down.

3. If the length of the input is included in the space count, then a TM cannot use less than space n for an input of length n. If we allow the TM to have "scratch" tapes in addition to its input tape, forbid writing on the input tape (maybe it is a valuable Elvis recording), and do not count the input tape as part of the space calculation, then the amount of space a TM could use could be less than n, or less than linear space. All TMs use at least one cell regardless. $S(n)$ is at least 1.

4. Hopcroft and Ullman (1979:290) contains a standard proof of this "speedup" theorem. The TM must have at least two tapes for this construction to work.

5. To hint at one subtlety here, the effects of recoding might be visible "at the surface". If every primitive move of the new machine involves units that are k long, then anything smaller might be computationally opaque in the sense that any potentially visible computational process (errors, for example) would not be made at a grain size of less than k. So empirical cognitive studies could provide constraints on the kind of recoding we could carry out. For a concrete case study of this possibility, see chapter 2.

6. Formally, we say that a function $f(n)$ is *of order* $g(n)$ if the ratio $f(n)/g(n)$ approaches a constant as n approaches infinity.

7. What if the machine is nondeterministic? As it turns out, the class of languages recognizable by a nondeterministic TM in real time is the same as the class recognizable in linear time (Book and Greibach 1970). The same equality does not hold for deterministic machines.

8. We can even quantify just how much harder parsing is than recognition (see below).

9. There is one note of unreality here. No real machine can store a number of arbitrary size without cost. This suggests a modification where the size of the number stored is factored into the complexity score. For most of our purposes, this distinction will not matter.

10. This is a standard result. See Machtey and Young 1978 for one proof.

11. More precisely, the number of wires leading into and out of interconnections must not be arbitrarily large, and the circuitry engaged to solve ever larger versions of some problem must not vary arbitrarily. The circuit to solve some problem of size $n + 1$ must not be too different from the one used to solve the nth sized problem. Cook 1980 has formal definitions of these terms.

12. Even though the polynomial might be so large, like n^{100}, as to be bigger than 2^n for practical values of n. This point is also discussed in chapter 3.

13. We can use the complexity class definitions to illustrate one point that we hinted at earlier: parsing is harder than recognition. Context-free language recognition takes at most cubic time. But the problem of recognizing whether a sentence is in the language generated by a given general context-free grammar is as difficult as any problem requiring deterministic polynomial time (Jones and Laaser 1974). Parsing is much harder. This is an important point because parsing is also psychologically more relevant than mere recognition. Human sentence processing involves associating a meaning with a phonological string. This demands parsing, not just recognition. Therefore, recognition results for classes of grammars might not be of psychological relevance though they might indicate boundary conditions, since parsing is at least as hard as recognition. Chapter 3 explores this point in more detail.

14. This restriction entails no loss of generality (see Hopcroft and Ullman 1979, chapter 12) because this restricted format has the power to express any CNF formula.

15. Note that the grammar and string so constructed depend upon precisely what formula is under analysis. For each different CNF formula, the procedure presented above outputs a different lexical-functional grammar and string pair. In the case of lexical-functional grammar it is important to remember that grammar really means grammar plus lexicon, as one might expect in a lexically based theory.

16. Our debt to these authors will be clear to any reader familiar with these works.

17. Of course, we expect the logical theory to shed light on "real" acquisition. This is what we shall do in chapter 6.

18. There is another line of research claiming that the degeneracy argument paints too bleak a picture. This work has tried to show that adults are more careful when speaking to their children than when they engage in normal conversation, the so-called "motherese" hypothesis. This Berlitz-like assumption has not fared too well under careful scrutiny. Newport, Gleitman, and Gleitman 1977 found that this careful speech does not facilitate language learning. In fact it might even retard it. Deficiency remains an enormous problem which the availability of motherese does not even begin to remedy. Wexler and Culicover 1980 and White 1981 contain further discussion.

19. These questions are formed by moving the subject or object from the pre- or postverbal positions leaving a gap in place. The resulting structures are:

(a) Who$_i$ e_i finally issued a statement?
(b) Which statement$_i$ did Ronald Reagan finally issue e_i?

20. The detailed explanation for this set of phenomena is given in Chomsky 1982 and need not concern us here. We are more interested in the form of the problem that such facts create.

21. This, of course, is the plight of the linguist who without conscious access to this tacit knowledge must rummage around an extensive class of data before being able to argue for the superiority of one analysis over another.

22. Most of the core constructions have been acquired by age 5.

23. Transformational grammar claims that deep structure is the level of representation at which an NP's (thematic) role, like agent or patient, is determined. *John* in (a) and (b) expresses the semantic or thematic role of patient, encoded in transformational grammar via its postverbal appearance at the deep structure level.

(a) Bill hit John.
(b) John was hit.

The relevant deep structures are (c) and (d):

(c) $[_S$ Bill $[_{VP}$ hit John]]
(d) $[_S$ [e] $[_{VP}$ was hit John]]

24. Informally, a quantificational condition is a condition on terms in a structural description or structural change using quantifiers. A Boolean condition is one in which terms may be defined using a disjunction or negation. For example, a rule such as $\{A\,or\,B\}\,XY \rightarrow 2\,3\,1$ (a rule that uses disjunction to signal that either A or B may undergo some change) is a rule using Boolean terms.

25. Furthermore, the more possibilities of choice, the more possibly wrong hypotheses open to the child. Experimental evidence does not underwrite

the enormous amount of testing that would be needed if so powerful a framework described the child's linguistic knowledge.

26. The adjacency of the potentially preposed NP to the verb is derived from considerations that we will not discuss here (but see Hornstein and Weinberg 1981).

27. The use of quantificational terms in the statement of transformational rules is motivated if one believes that identity between a triggering context for a rule and its target has to be stipulated in every individual rule where such conditions of identity apply. There are rules that invoke this identity between trigger and target. For example, deletion rules apply only when this condition is met. Nonetheless, Chomsky 1965 shows that we may allow these rules to apply freely with no mention of this stipulation in their structural descriptions if we subject their output to a general condition that guarantees the recoverability of deletion.

28. Lasnik shows that disjunction is the only Boolean condition that ever did any real work in grammatical theory. Conjunction and negation never even successfully captured the generalizations that purportedly motivated them.

29. See Chomsky 1977b, 1981 for details and evidence that this analysis extends to a broad class of languages.

30. The domain of binding theory remains controversial. Empirical reasons suggest that the notion minimal governing category should be replaced by the notion of first accessible Subject. Chomsky 1981 has details.

31. See Chomsky 1973 and Dresher and Hornstein 1979 for details; Pullum 1980 has an attempted counterargument. Also see May 1981 for a counterreply to Pullum, exploiting principles discussed in Dresher and Hornstein's article. It should be noted that trace theory is motivated by other considerations as well; see Chomsky 1981 and the discussion of the projection principle below.

32. Given this theory, we might wonder why (a) is grammatical since the *wh* movement superficially crosses many S nodes.

(a) Who$_i$ do you believe [$_S$ Mary claimed [$_S$ Bill said [$_{\overline{S}}$that Fred liked e_i?

The reason is that the movement is not accomplished in one step. Bresnan (1972) argues that *wh* movement is to the complementizer ($\overline{S}$) position. In the above example, the *wh* element moves through the complementizer of each clause thus obeying the subjacency condition. In contrast, even successive movement through the complementizer of a relative clause yields a subjacency violation because one of the movements will have to cross both the NP of the complex noun phrase and the S of the sentence that dominates the relative clause, as (30) shows.

33. (35) is the deep structure source for (36). For arguments that *John hit Bill* should not serve as the deep structure for (36), see Bresnan 1972.

34. That VPs and PPs share case assigning properties is not surprising because they form a natural class (Jackendoff 1977).

35. Rather than providing a formal definition of government we shall simply list the structures where case is assigned under government. Chomsky 1981 gives a definition of government.

36. Baltin 1982 and Chomsky 1981 contain a discussion of passive participles. The tests of adjectival status are from Wasow 1977. There are many other diagnostic tests for the adjectival status of these elements. Wasow 1977 and Baltin 1982 have a complete analysis.

37. Binding theory (see above) explains why the NP cannot move to a case position lower in the tree.

38. Generative grammarians use the idea of strict subcategorization to encode the elements in a verb's argument structure. For example, the obligatory co-occurrence of *hit* with an NP capable of being interpreted as its patient is encoded by the grammar in the lexical entry associated with this verb. The verb is inserted in this entry along with a lexical frame indicating that it obligatorily occurs with a postverbal NP, an NP to be interpreted as its patient. For details, consult Chomsky 1981 chapter 2.

39. Given this condition, we may wonder why passive is possible at all since the subject position is usually associated with some thematic role. The reason is that passive predicates allow dethematicization of the subject position. Independent evidence for this comes from examples of athematic lexical items (dummy markers that have no thematic role) occurring as subjects of passive but not active sentences, just when the object does not require case. Contrast (a) and (b):

(a)   *It* was believed that John was crazy.
(b)   *It believes that John is crazy.

This allows passive with no θ criterion violation.

40. Fodor (1979) claims that this means that the parser "parses only deep structures" because in earlier theories, subcategorization information is made available only at this level. Strictly speaking, this cannot be correct. The parser is not given the deep structure directly but must construct it. It uses the surface structure information to accomplish this task. If lexical information is needed to succeed, then it must be available at this level of representation as well.

41. Actually, each of these categories is a feature bundle. There is some dispute about the proper characterization of features. Chomsky 1970 and Jackendoff 1977 give differing approaches to this question.

42. Bresnan 1976 suggests that we can use the feature notation provided by the $\overline{\text{X}}$ system to restrict the class of possible rules. Bresnan claims that rules that are written by combining features that are not natural in the

$\overline{X}$ framework are not attested in natural languages. Therefore we can ban Boolean combinations of such features, replacing them with unary terms defined by the $\overline{X}$ theory.

43. We cannot explain this by claiming that *say* does not co-occur with infinitives because of the grammaticality of (a):

(a) I said[$_S$ Pro to get a grant.]

Chapter 2

1. There are exceptions. Jerrold Katz (1981), for example, insists that linguistics deals with a mathematical entity "language." Hence questions of "psychological reality" are irrelevant to the description of this entity. Katz does claim though that informant judgments and even psycholinguistic evidence could count in the evaluation of a grammatical theory.

2. Wasow agrees: "A minimal condition for the attribution of psychological reality to a grammar is that its assignments of grammaticality conform with the judgments of native speakers" (1978:84).

3. Lightfoot 1979 section 7.2 has independent arguments along these lines about the role of historical derivations.

4. This is not to say that grammatical theory should not be responsible to such experimental data, but rather that this responsibility might not constrain the choice of grammatical theory to a great degree.

5. Sometimes type transparency has been taken as a necessary condition on psychological explanations:

Grammars are descriptions of languages; constraints on grammars which do not constrain the set of languages generable limit only the sorts of descriptions available. Hence, if one wants to draw psychological conclusions from such constraints, one must assume that the linguists' grammars stand in a very close correspondence with portions of the speaker's mental representation of the language. (Wasow 1978:83)

6. As noted earlier, there are some such as Wasow who insist that this condition is too strong on account of weak psycholinguistic evidence, and demand only that the processing theory specify an acceptor for the surface language:

One initial cause for skepticism towards claims for the psychological reality of grammars is the lack of convincing psycholinguistic evidence in support of such claims. The past 15 years have seen investigators employ numerous experimental paradigms to test the match between the linguist's grammars and the mental operations involved in language use. The results of such work should not encourage proponents of the G[rammar] view. (Ibid.:85–86)

But Wasow fails to note that these same research results provide overwhelming evidence for the "reality" of structural descriptions of sentences, the "data structures" on which grammars are based. What is in doubt is the mapping between sentences and mental descriptions. Thus attention to just language is far too weak; we already know something about the grammar.

The grammar furnishes multiple structural descriptions in the case of sentences that are structurally ambiguous, and perhaps incomplete or no descriptions for those sentences that are not members of the language. It even seems likely that a parser can analyze successfully ungrammatical sentences. Thus structural descriptions of such sentences are available for further analysis, and judgments of grammaticality can be made.

7. See Fodor, Bever, and Garrett (1974:322) and Bresnan (1978:2).

8. By "candidate grammar" we mean a grammar that is otherwise explanatorily adequate, that is, adequate for providing solutions to other psychological problems, such as the acquisition of language.

9. Fodor, Bever, and Garrett (1974:229):

Further, the data suggest that the transformations may produce a linearly additive complication of the stimulus sentences: for example, sentences which involve both the negative and passive transformations appear to require a time approximately equal to the sum of the average time required for negative or passive applied separately.

10. This possibility is also mentioned by Valian (1979:6).

11. Emonds 1972 and 1976; Chomsky and Lasnik 1977 have a comprehensive discussion of this issue.

12. See Ross 1967. The motivation for this analysis was the assumption that phrases that have the same meaning should have the same deep structures (a basic assumption of the branch of transformational grammar called generative semantics). Because phrases such as *the red door* and *the door which is red* have the same meaning, they presumably derive from the same underlying deep structure source. Chomsky 1970 has theoretical and empirical arguments against this assumption.

13. For example, he presents cases where a grammatical prenominal adjective has no grammatical transformational source.

14. Bresnan 1972 and Chomsky 1977a contain the evidence. Given this, even a transformational grammar embedded directly in a serial processing model would predict the data that Watt cites.

15. There are other alternatives to deal with "local" movement rules in a parsing model; Marcus 1980 has some examples.

16. Gough 1965 showed that the same reversibility effects were obtained in the picture matching task even when presentation of the picture was delayed for three seconds after presentation of the linguistic stimulus (Garnham forthcoming). Gough interprets this to show that Slobin's task does not really reflect online parsing.

17. Fodor, Bever, and Garrett recognize that their perceptual strategies make no contribution to a theory of **language acquisition**. This leads to the

perhaps strange view that the knowledge speakers have of their language as specified by a grammar is never used in language processing. Recognizing this possibility, Fodor, Bever, and Garrett attempt to show that grammars are somehow involved in parsing. Their first suggestion is that the grammar could serve as a kind of "backup routine" when parsing heuristics fail:

That is, there exist some well formed sentences to which they [the heuristics rcb/asw] will not assign the correct structural descriptions. Such sentences must be recognized by resort to "brute force"... problem solving routines in which the grammar is concretely employed.... The function of the grammar is to provide a library of information about the structure in a language and the function of some of the heuristics is to access the grammar. (1974:370–371)

On this account there is still no sense in which the parsing mechanism is a reflection of the grammar rules. Rather, the grammar rules and parsing heuristics form two unrelated systems, an oddly redundant state of affairs. It is preferable to assume that we could eliminate one of these systems, that is, assume that there is one system that governs, albeit in an indirect way, both language use and language acquisition. Fodor, Bever, and Garrett provide such an alternative suggestion that the grammar provides the functions that the parsing algorithms must compute:

Recognition procedures can be constructed by a simple and general algorithm from grammars.... The process of learning a (first) language involves internalizing the grammar and applying this algorithm to construct the corresponding recognition procedure. (Ibid.:371)

This alternative will be discussed in the main body of the text. The point is that an adequate psychological theory of language must contribute to both theories of language learning and language use.

18. We should stress that the approach presented in Bresnan 1978 (what she calls the extended lexical grammar (ELG)) has been modified and formalized in Bresnan 1982b (and dubbed lexical-functional grammar). We focus on the 1978 version because it is the most concise statement of this position. The two theories are not significantly different in the areas that concern us. We shall indicate relevant distinctions as we proceed.

19. For example, passive, so-called "raising" constructions, the NP movement rule associated with *there* insertion, and the like.

20. In the Extended Standard Theory the direct object status of this phrase is also captured at the level of surface structure through the mechanism of trace binding.

21. Transformations or their interpretive counterparts are retained for *wh* movement via the device of binding.

22. As Bresnan writes, "But there is another way to establish a correspondence between the argument structure of a verb and its syntactic context.... For example, the argument structure of *eat* can be converted from a two-place relation into a one-place relation. A logical operation that has precisely this

effect is the variable binding operation of quantification" (1978:16).

23. As Noam Chomsky has pointed out to us, the term "existential" should be loosely interpreted here. Nothing should be claimed to exist in a sentence such as (a):

(a) Advantage was taken of Bill.

24. To quote Bresnan and Kaplan:

Because the outputs of these lexical redundancy rules already exist in the stored knowledge component of the model, the processor need not perform the operations specified by these rules as the model decodes the grammatical relations of a sentence. If we further assume that all lexical forms are accessed in parallel, then in this model the complexity of syntactic computations will... reflect only the complexity of the analysis of the surface phrase structure tree. (1982:xxxiii–xxxiv)

25. Note that for this prediction to go through we must also assume that lexical retrieval takes "unit" time no matter how complex the passive form entry is relative to the active form entry.

26. As recognized by Bresnan and Kaplan:

Assume that the arguments of lexical forms can be accessed both by the functions they select (SUBJ or OBJ, etc.) and by their semantic properties. Then the process of extracting the grammatical relations of a sentence could be facilitated by semantic information that differentiated the arguments of a lexical form.... In this model, Model II, the complexity of syntactic analysis could be reduced by asymmetries in the semantic structure of the predicates. Thus, Model II would produce "nonreversibility" effects like those reported by Slobin 1966. (1982:xxxiv)

27. In the most recent version of this theory, lexical-functional grammar, *wh* movement is also computed directly from the surface representation. Transformations are completely eliminated from the rule writing system. The relevant point for this discussion is that *wh* movement cannot be stored as part of the entry of a given lexical item. *Wh* movement is not defined over local lexical configurations, but over potentially unbounded syntactic domains. This is true in two senses. First, the cue given by the *wh* word itself cannot be what is stored because these lexical items appear unboundedly far away from the position in which they are thematically interpreted. Secondly, the verb itself may not serve as a locus for storing the effects of movement because any verb may or may not co-occur with a *wh* element. The effects of *wh* movement are read directly off the surface structure representation by using the "bounded domination metavariable" notation described in Kaplan and Bresnan (1982:235).

28. An ambiguous sentence would have two or more such associated annotated surface structures; in these cases, the Marcus parser by definition computes just one of these at a time.

29. Chapter 4 has a formal analysis of the computational complexity of this process.

30. Because the number of features that a node like a noun phrase might have is by assumption finite, the total amount of information the parser has available at any given step in order to decide what to do next is also finite.

31. The left-right seriality of the order in which words enter the input stream allows us to mimic the left-right seriality of speech. Other components of the parser need not operate in this serial manner though they certainly must wait upon the process that reads words into the input buffer. That is, in principle the machine computations on the input string may be effected in several different ways. For example, rules can operate in parallel over the items in the input buffer.

32. Lance Ripps (personal communication).

33. We could easily modify the procedure just outlined to accommodate the Forster and Olbrei 1973 results, given that they seem to be a more valid account of active/passive complexity differences than the Slobin experiments. Forster and Olbrei observed that all passives take significantly longer to parse than their active sentence counterparts. Further, Slobin's reversibility effects were not found. To handle this possibility, we could assume that the preverbal NP is attached to the sentential subject position. Later movement to postverbal position could cause extra complexity. Chapter 5 discusses this possibility in detail. Similarly, in an EST model, neither reversible or nonreversible passives would be marked with a binding index. Finding the right antecedent would take roughly the same amount of extra time in either case.

34. Another way to look at this effect is that it is technically much like the linear speedup theorem of automata theory described in the first section of chapter 1. By recoding two unit operations as one, we can "speedup" any computation taking time cx to one taking time $(1 + \eta)x$, simply by expanding the instructional repertoire of the underlying machine to include all finite combinations of actions composed of previously primitive elements. For example, (i) attach and (ii) locate becomes a single "attach and locate" operation.

The calculation of concurrent processing complexity is less straightforward than that of serial computations and has been subject to some dispute in the psychological literature. We take up this matter below and in note 46. The problem is this: suppose we have many operations working at once, say n. Each operation has some chance of completing in mean time t, according to some specified probability distribution. To ensure mathematical tractability, the distribution is generally assumed to be exponential, with mean t and variance t^2. These distributions are easily added together. Finally, suppose that all n operations must finish for the overall computation to succeed. As the number of independent concurrent operations, n, increases, the individual completion probabilities overlap in such a way that it appears that overall completion time increases in time $\ln nt$ ($\ln = \log$ to base 2). Note that a strictly serial model would exhibit an overall completion time of nt. From this analysis we could conclude that a concurrent processing model such as the one we have just described could actually behave like a serial model, for appropriate values of n and t. For a recent review of this matter, see Snodgrass and Townsend 1980.

The catch in the comparison lies in the clause "for appropriate values of n." In our analysis, there are only 2 concurrent operations. Completion time should behave like $\ln 2t$, approximately t. But this means that the speedup works. A serial completion time of $2t$ is reduced to t.

We emphasize that this calculation is meant only to be illustrative. There are numerous assumptions possible in a parallel model concerning the distributions for completion times, resource allocation, and completion rules; these are reviewed in Snodgrass and Townsend 1980. But the central point still stands.

35. In fact, this version of *there* insertion is illicit in current versions of transformational grammar. It assumes that transformations can be "compounded," and compounding is not allowed. First this rule moves the subject NP to the right. Because *there* can be inserted only into NP positions, we must simultaneously leave a copy of the NP node in the subject position. Finally, we must insert *there* into the empty NP node. Obviously such rules are not highly valued. If compounding is allowed, then the number of possible derivations for a given sentence increases exponentially.

36. We know this because *there* is not a thematic element appearing in a θ position in these cases. Given the θ criterion, we predict a thematic element, in this case the postposed subject, linked to this position. This is, of course, another case of a local dependency.

37. The parse of sentences such as (6c) could proceed in the following way: *There* is recognized in the subject position. It attaches to to the S as the subject of the sentence. The postposed NP *an apple* must later be linked to this position. We can accomplish this in several ways, either by passing down an index through the verb phrase until this noun phrase is encountered, or by using the method in Marcus 1980. The true subject must always be present in a neighboring position. In the passive sentence the passive morphology on the verb will tell the parser that *the apple* also triggers the insertion of a trace after the verb *eaten*, yielding the correct interpretation for this case.

38. This assumes that there is a dative transformation like this:
Structural description and change:

X	V	NP	NP	Y	$\rightarrow$
1	2	3	4	5	
X	V	NP	*to*	NP	Y
1	2	4	6	3	5

39. This assumes that the parser must mimic the operations of a transformational grammar in a one-for-one fashion. This is not the only possibility. For example, we can imagine a system in which rules of "passive" and "dative" are acquired separately and yet are combined by a mechanical procedure to yield possible interactions; these interactions are then "sped up" to unit time complexity. The parser will now make finer distinctions than the grammar. It will have a rule of "passive-dative." There would be no such rule in the basic system of knowledge that is acquired. In this particular case how language is put to use would be a refinement of "knowledge of language."

40. This point was already made in Berwick and Weinberg 1983, the article to which Bresnan and Kaplan's comments are directed.

41. This definition of concurrent computation should not be confused with others that are current in the psycholinguistic literature. For example, Cooper and Cooper 1980 raise the issue of "parallel computation." But for them "in parallel" means that parsing is not strictly top-down, that is, we can build a clause and the dependent of a clause simultaneously. The Marcus parser is not strictly top-down in this sense. Whether the Marcus parser actually parses top-down is a separate issue from whether it can compute two levels of representation concurrently (the sense of "parallel" that is exploited in the model above). These different interpretations lead to some difficulty in interpreting experiments purporting to show that people can or cannot compute "in parallel"; we discuss this matter later on in this section.
In the case of the Extended Standard Theory, this parallelism amounts to carrying out two grammar rule "actions" at the same time. It does not hinge upon there being two separate structural descriptions, that is, concurrently constructed deep and surface structures.

42. We have chosen the case of passive for concreteness, but the same logic applies to the realization of many other rules investigated under the rubric of "DTC experiments."

43. As far as we can tell, this also holds true of the theory espoused in Bresnan 1982c. There is one lexical entry for the active form of a verb and one lexical entry for the passive form. It is quite easy to show that in this case the recognition time complexity for some lexical-functional languages must still be so hard that there is at present no known serial Turing machine algorithm for recognition that runs in time that is less than exponential in the length of input sentence lengths; further, it is highly unlikely that a polynomial time algorithm for recognizing such languages exists (see chapter 4 for discussion and proof, and chapter 1 for a definition of "polynomial time recognizability").

44. Consider a recent series of articles debating the possibility of finding evidence to distinguish between propositional and imagistic theories of mental representation (Anderson 1978, Pylyshyn 1979, Hayes-Roth 1979, and Anderson 1979). Anderson replies to the point that the propositional

mimicry of an image might take exponential time and hence perhaps be distinguishable from an imagist theory on the grounds of a detectable increase in externally measured processing time by invoking parallel machinery. He cites a result based on work by Borodin 1977, among others. See also note 34.

45. These are chiefly assumptions that one is able to expand the required hardware and its associated wiring arbitrarily or, perhaps, manipulate in parallel vectors of numbers of arbitrary length.

46. As discussed immediately below, we should not confuse this kind of synchronous parallelism with the perhaps more familiar case of asynchronous parallelism. In asynchronous parallelism, two or more quite different typically intermodal tasks operate simultaneously. The speedup results refer only to the former sort of concurrency in which a single function has been designed to be computable in parallel. This is just the sort of parallelism involved in the passive analysis discussed in the previous section.

We should realize that there is no paradox between the inherent seriality of the speech stream and the possibility of parallel computation over those tokens. The Marcus parser is designed precisely to resolve this paradox. Tokens are read groups at a time into an input buffer, and then rules may operate, in parallel, if need be, over the entire set of tokens. There is then a limit to the amount of parallelism that is allowed. The buffer is of finite "bandwidth." As we demonstrated in the previous section, this limited bandwidth is sufficient to handle the parallelism required at least for the passive case.

Note 34 in this chapter has a discussion of parallel-serial distinguishability.

47. See Borodin 1977, Cook 1980, and Ruzzo 1980. Chapter 1 describes details of the construction of these circuits.

48. Even if resources are unlimited, it is possible to prove quite specific theorems about bounds on the speedup possible when a single problem is solved by asynchronous parallelism.

49. Of course, we have not even considered here the possibility of overlapping distributions of completion times; note 34 has a discussion.

50. That is, NPs can only be moved into phrase marker positions where phrase structure rules of the grammar can generate NPs.

51. Emonds 1976 offers an alternative analysis; Freidin 1978 and Chomsky 1977b argue that Emonds's first hypothesis was correct.

52. The story is actually more complicated than this. Bresnan (personal communication) points out that in a theory such as transformational grammar allowing successive cyclic movement into complementizers we might think that the *wh* element in Comp would also be in a strictly local domain, and could thus employ the speedup technique in this case as well. Under these assumptions we would not capture the purported difference between *wh* movement and passives with respect to psycholinguistic timing results. To enforce this distinction should it be relevant, we must appeal

to another principle. We should repeat that Slobin's results are extremely controversial and that under the assumptions of Forster and Olbrei 1973 we would expect *wh* movement and passive to take the same amount of time. Our additional constraint is the parsing principle motivated by the design stipulation that only completed constituents may be attached to the parse tree under construction. In the relevant cases, before we could bind a *wh* element to its trace, we would attach all the material to the S node dominating the trace, then attach this node to the $\bar{S}$. Only after this attachment could we bind the trace to the *wh* element in the $\bar{S}$. This constraint exists because grammar rules are only sensitive to material in the immediate dominating cyclic node (NP or S). Chapter 5 discusses this same constraint from another point of view, showing how it actually explains certain constraints of grammar. By this account, the parser must wait for the S to attach to the $\bar{S}$ before binding to the $\bar{S}$ is possible. Otherwise the $\bar{S}$ is not easily accessible. Given this story, we might expect timing distinctions between *wh* movement and passive cases. The passive trace can bind immediately to an element within the parser's "window," but a *wh* trace must wait on the completion of the S. It would not be necessary for a timing distinction to exist; this argument only says that there are enough differences to account for one.

The design principle itself is not completely *ad hoc*. The decision to attach S and $\bar{S}$ separately and to govern the attachment of S to $\bar{S}$ by a principle that says, "first complete constituents, then attach them" is not an arbitrary decision. There are cases where it is crucial that this procedure be followed; Marcus 1980 has details. Moreover, this assumption of uniformity figures crucially in the overall learnability of the system as discussed in chapter 6.

53. The situation is a little more complicated, as shown by sentences like this:

It was believed that Nory was too shy.

The correct generalization is that a trace will be inserted if the parser is sure that the postparticipial material is an NP. This complication makes no difference for the discussion above.

54. Recall that one grammar is weakly equivalent to another grammar if it can generate the same set of terminal strings, the same sentences, as the second grammar. In this case it need not generate the same structural descriptions at all.

55. By "parsing" we simply mean "recover structural descriptions." We have abstracted away from a consideration of time and space resource use. It well might turn out as will be shown below that two grammars equivalent with respect to parsing could be radically different with respect to their computational efficiency.

56. In fact it will take only a fixed number of steps per individual rule used in the derivation.

57. This result is a significant one for those who study models of language

use because it illustrates how a parser can be nontransparently related to the grammar it instantiates. This is not just a theoretical possibility. The study of "transformations" from one grammar to another that preserve recoverability of structural descriptions and improve amenability to parsing is a longstanding area of research in formal language theory and programming language analysis. (See Kuno 1966, Kurki-Sunio 1966, Foster 1968, and Hammer 1975.)

For a concrete example consider Kuno's Harvard Syntactic Analyzer (Kuno 1966). As Nijholt 1980 observes, Kuno's basic aim is exactly that of finding grammatical transformations ensuring parsing efficiency while at the same time preserving recoverability of structural descriptions. Kuno even includes a diagram just like the one above as the framework for his research. More specifically, Kuno attempts to find mappings from arbitrary context-free grammars for natural languages to grammars that were efficiently handled by a particular top-down parser he had constructed, based on non left-recursive context-free grammars. A non left-recursive grammar contains no productions of the form, $A \to \ldots \to A$ where A derives itself by one or or more rules. The important point is that top-down parsers can be guaranteed to work only if they incorporate non left-recursive grammars. Kuno compiled a list of ways to change a context-free grammar with left-recursive productions into a non left-recursive one and hence one amenable for top-down parsing. In so doing he obtained a grammar that (right)-covered the original.

Nijholt has shown that every context-free grammar (without single "erasing" productions of the form $A \to$ empty) can be right-covered by a grammar in Greibach normal form, a canonical representation of a context-free grammar where every production is of the form $A \to bB$, where b is a terminal symbol and B is a string of nonterminals (possibly empty). Note that Greibach normal form is non left-recursive. Nijholt's result thus provides one way to convert "almost any" context-free grammar into a form that can be used by a top-down parser.

A covering grammar provides an easily computed mapping between the structural descriptions of a Greibach grammar and the structural descriptions of its associated grammar of origin.

58. Chapter 6 describes a computer model that explicitly connects a model of language use, the Marcus parser, to a model of language acquisition.

Chapter 3

1. We should be very clear that an argument about the computational benefits accruing from a restriction to context-freeness need not be the only reason, or even the primary reason, for preferring grammars that generate only context-free languages. Gazdar (1979:1981) has argued that his nontransformational theory of grammar is superior primarily on the standard linguistic grounds, namely, that the theory does a better job of accounting for linguistic generalizations than the theory of transformational grammar. See Williams 1982 for a partial reply to these arguments. In a personal

communication, Gazdar has informed one of us that the original motivation for the theory was a desire to eliminate the transformational component of transformational theory entirely. Only afterwards was it realized that this move, because it permitted the generation of only context-free languages, might also have computational import. In this context, it is interesting to note that the generative grammars proposed in Chomsky 1951 were in fact context-free systems that used the indexed phrase structure mechanisms described by Harman 1963 and Gazdar 1981. In this chapter we shall focus attention on just the question of efficient parsability, leaving these other questions aside.

2. Later in this chapter we give examples of strictly context-sensitive languages that are recognizable in real time. See also chapter 5 for a discussion of parsing algorithms.

3. Chapter 4 and Lapointe 1977 contain discussions of the significance of the Peters and Ritchie results. Matthews 1979 and Chomsky 1980b have summaries.

4. This result is also proved in Hopcroft and Ullman 1969 or Harrison 1978, 430–437. Slightly "better" functional speedups are possible, reducing the n^3 time to nearly $n^{2.5}$. The best current result as of 1980 was about $n^{2.52}$.

5. We are holding all other potential sources of variation, for example, the grammar, constant.

6. Note that Gazdar 1981 also assumes the class NL to be a proper subset of the class of context-free languages, as evidenced by the quote at the beginning of this chapter. The intent of his restriction is presumably to rule out the "unnatural" context-free languages, perhaps using the criteria suggested above. According to Gazdar's argument, a powerful reason that the restriction to just the CFL languages pays off is that of parsability. But, as we have just seen, because we have to look at a restricted class of languages anyway, one not coinciding with any of the Chomsky hierarchy classes, it makes little sense to exclude in an *a priori* fashion just those strictly context-sensitive languages that are also efficiently parsable, simply because they do not happen to meet some other mathematical condition.

7. Postal 1964 has putative examples of strictly context-sensitive constructions in natural languages. Higginbotham (personal communication) has recently constructed some apparently legitimate examples for English.

8. As chapter 1 observed, stronger recognition time constraints in conjunction with restrictions on the assumed underlying reference machine can be quite potent in eliminating certain classes of languages. For example, if we imposed a linear time recognition constraint so that recognition can take only time kn, where n=the length of the input sentence and in addition limited the machine to only one tape, then the string sets so recognizable are regular (Hennie 1965). Furthermore, some languages known to be recognizable in real time on one kind of reference machine, a random access machine, are not recognizable in real time on a Turing machine. Not surprisingly, if we adopt this finer grained complexity analysis, we can distinguish between

various brands of machines. The problem then becomes one of justifying the machine restriction and the grain size of the complexity analysis. What evidence can be adduced that people are one tape Turing machines, as opposed to random access machines, or two tape Turing machines, or even k tape Turing machines? What evidence is there that people process sentences in real time, as opposed to, say, linear time?

9. Except, of course, in the case where $f(n) = n$, where the ratio of the functional forms is 1 for all values of n. In this case, the constant terms will still predominate.

10. There is no reason to suppose that parsing has been "optimized" according to our sense of machine design, of course; worse yet, evolution is known to be opportunistic, not optimizing. This is not just idle speculation. As researchers in evolutionary biology know, there are many examples of evolutionary "designs" that are quite inefficient by certain engineering standards but nonetheless survive because there is now no way to "rechannel" whole enzymatic systems into new ways of doing things. For instance, the photosynthetic machinery of plants is apparently ill-designed because the oxygen generated as a by-product acts as a competitor for the enzyme sites used in the fixing of carbon dioxide. Wheat would grow 20 per cent more if the oxygen content of the air was 2 per cent instead of 20 per cent (Moore 1981). Certain plants have evolved clever ways to sidestep this defect by getting rid of the excess oxygen, but there is apparently no way at this late date to redirect the enzymatic pathways to a completely different system. The reason for the difficulty is apparently that the photosynthetic system evolved hundreds of millions of years ago, when the oxygen content of the atmosphere was in the 2 per cent range. It is important to keep in mind, whenever casual evolutionary arguments are offered as "functional explanations" for one or another aspect of some cognitive faculty or, for that matter, any biological competence, that the systems of an organism cannot be evaluated in isolation from one another. For example, it cannot be assumed without additional argument that the syntactic parsing machinery, if such exists, has been "optimized" independently of other cognitive subsystems or even independently of the entire organism of which it is a part.

11. It might of course still turn out that asymptotic measures are appropriate. But this cannot be determined in advance of empirical investigation.

12. For example, with $n = 9$, $n^3 = 729$, but $2^n = 512$, so the exponential form is still "better"; whereas with $n = 11$, $n^3 = 1331$, but $2^n = 2048$, and the exponential form takes almost double the time of the polynomial. It must be stressed that we do not mean to imply that the rough trade-off described above accurately depicts what is the case in human sentence processing. Rather, the tradeoff scenario is meant to be illustrative, showing how the range of sentence lengths that the cognitive machinery actually deals with is what is crucial to the practical functional evaluation of an algorithm, and not necessarily its asymptotic behavior. The tradeoff discussed above is

unrealistic because, among other things, if the measure of length includes grammatical formatives, then the "break-point" where an exponential time method would begin to take longer than a cubic time method might be different. As we shall see below, whether anything of functional import hinges on the inclusion of formatives in the length count depends in part on the size of the constants in front of the functional forms, and because this cannot be determined in advance of a detailed formulation of the complexity of human sentence processing, it would seem premature to advance any detailed argument along these lines.

13. It might be an interesting exercise to examine the actual range of input sentence lengths in spoken and even written language; one's initial impression, in fact, is that the bulk of sentences are shorter than the 10–12 word length breakpoint that conceivably separates cubic from exponential time. This simple breakpoint is almost certainly not correct, because it ignores the effect of constant multipliers in front of the relevant functional forms.

It is well known that it is not so much length as it is structural factors such as degree of nesting or more potently, degree of center-embedding that contribute to sentence processing difficulties (Chomsky 1965).

14. In general, if the constant factor for the cubic method is c times larger than the constant factor for the exponential method, then we can expect the exponential method's superiority range to be extended by $\log_2 c$ words. $\log_2 1000$ is approximately 10.

Presumably, part of the job of the cognitive psychologist is to try to find out whether people use cubic or exponential time algorithms. What would seem to distinguish between these alternatives is which algorithm supports the right counterfactuals. This is the ability to formulate statements such as, "If we increase sentence length by, say, one word at the point where exponential methods begin to take longer than cubic methods, does the time for analysis rise rapidly, thereby lending credence to the internalization of an exponential time method, or does it increase only modestly, indicating a cubic time method?" The problem is that the crucial test points may be well outside the range of psycholinguistic access. If the relevant simple sentences are thirty or more words long, then other cognitive factors such as attention span, memory, and the like may intervene so as to render these test cases problematic. On the other hand, it may well be that suitable test sentences can be constructed. This is a matter that can only be settled by empirical work.

15. There is another familiar result in complexity theory that might mean that constant factors "do not matter" in the analysis of algorithms, and hence that grammar size may be safely ignored in the determination of parsing efficiency. This is the theorem of chapter 1 stating that any algorithm that runs in time $kf(n)$ can be recoded so as to make the constant k as close to 1 as desired ($f(n)$ must be a linear time function or larger). Because grammar size $|G|$ is just another "constant," this result would seem to indicate that we can recode an algorithm and eliminate the effect of

grammar size.

However, a more careful analysis of the implicit assumptions of this theorem shows that it is actually inappropriate to invoke it for the analysis presented in the text. The reason is that the theorem demands an ability to manipulate what are assumed to be the underlying "primitive operations" of the reference computer model. Intuitively, what this amounts to is that instead of being able to examine and execute one rule per time step or one input token, by recoding k symbols into new "complex symbols" we are now permitted to examine and execute C rules or read C tokens at a time, where C is a constant that depends on the constant k incorporating grammar size. Thus we must change the basic "unit operations" of the finite state control of the Turing machine. This alteration of underlying primitive operations is permissible in the case of Turing machines because we can program them at our whim. It is much less clear what we are allowed to do in the cognitive analogue. As pointed out above, it is probably the case that the underlying computational machinery is more or less fixed, though we do not know what the "primitive operations" are. Consequently, it would not seem valid to allow recoding of the sort required by the linear speedup theorem. The conservative approach is to assume that the constants matter. As a final postscript on this issue, it is worthwhile to point out that the trade-off between constant factors and asymptotic complexity arises even in the realm of computer science. It is widely known that the asymptotically "fastest" context-free recognition algorithm involves such large constant factors that it is impractical for actual use. This is Valiant's method; Harrison 1978 has details.

16. This fact has been noted by many researchers in computer science. Pratt 1975 and Graham, Harrison, and Ruzzo 1980 give excellent analyses of the issues.

17. Earley's algorithm is based on the "tabular" parsing methods of Cocke and Schwartz 1970, Kasami 1965, and Younger 1967. Numerous variants of Earley's method have been proposed. These include chart parsing (Kay 1967) and well-formed substring table methods such as that in Kaplan 1973.

18. It is interesting to compare this complexity result with that of the older Cocke-Kasami-Younger (CKY) algorithm (Younger 1967). See also Hopcroft and Ullman 1979. The CKY algorithm runs in time that is proportional to the size of the grammar and the cube of the length of the input sentences. Why then is the CKY method inferior to the Earley algorithm? The reason is that the CKY method works only on grammars in Chomsky normal form, that is, grammars producing only binary branching trees, with rules of the form $A \rightarrow BC$ or $A \rightarrow a$. Earley's algorithm works on any context-free grammar. The best known algorithm for converting an arbitrary grammar into Chomsky normal form in the worst case also squares the size of the grammar. From this standpoint the two methods seem to be on a par. In fact, it is easy to show, as observed in Ruzzo 1978, that the Earley algorithm involves a kind of "hidden" transformation of an arbitrary context-free grammar into Chomsky normal form. The conversion involves

"splitting" the right hand sides of rules of the form A→BC...D into binary branching form by introducing new nonterminal names and expansion rules that incorporate "complex symbols" formed by all the possible ways of dividing a right-hand side up into two sets of non-terminals; for example, A→BCD becomes A→ •(BCD), A→(B) • (CD), A→(BC)•(D), A→(BCD)• In the worst case this expansion squares the size of the grammar.

19. Input sentence length will not dominate the complexity equation until $n =$ approximately 63 ($63^3 = 250047$).

20. If the relevant range of input sentence lengths is 10 or less, then even a reduction from a cubic to a linear time function of n will not necessarily outweigh the gains of succinctness. For example, suppose that we can obtain a linear algorithm at the price of expanding the number of grammar rules to 6000 or so, a twelvefold increase. Then the complexity of the new grammar with the new "faster" algorithm and a maximum input sentence length of 10 will be 3.6×10^8, whereas under the old, "slower" algorithm it was only 2.5×10^8.

More generally, assuming the Earley algorithm as a basis functional form, if G_0=the size of one grammar, and G_1=the size of another grammar, then efficiency gains from succinctness outweigh gains from a reduction of the exponent on input sentence length from n^j to n^k if $G_1/G_0 > \sqrt{n^j/n^k}$. In the example in the main text, with $j = 3$ and $k = 1$, this will occur when the ratio of grammar sizes exceeds the square root of n; for $n = 10$, this is approximately 3.16, and $1600/500 = 3.2 > 3.16$.

We should emphasize that these examples are meant to be purely illustrative in nature. Still, order of magnitude blow-ups in grammar size of the sort described here are not atypical. As we shall see below, even exponential expansions in grammar size are theoretically possible if we opt for a "weaker" formalism instead of a stronger one.

21. On the other hand, it can also be shown that there exist languages for which there is no gain in succinctness by moving to a more powerful descriptive formalism. The question of interest for linguistics is whether the use of more "powerful" descriptive machinery, for example, transformational grammar, permits more succinct descriptions of natural language. This was one of the arguments made for transformational grammar in *Syntactic Structures*.

22. Here we assume on-line recognition so that at least n time steps are required to just read an input of length n. On this assumption, recognition cannot take less than time n.

23. More pertinent succinctness results have been obtained. Joshi, Levy, and Yueh 1980 show that there are context-free languages whose context-sensitive phrase structure grammars are exponentially more compact than any weakly equivalent context-free grammar. They show further that this sort of grammar can be incorporated into the the Earley parsing framework, though with a modified polynomial bound, thus demonstrating that substantial efficiency gains are in some cases possible by moving from a context-free

phrase structure system to context-sensitive phrase structure rules. This result is actually a particular subcase of the more general Meyer and Fischer theorems.

It remains to be seen whether the formal devices that Gazdar introduces, slashed categories as complex symbols and metarules, actually lead to efficiency gains for parsing; this would depend upon just how much larger a slashed category grammar is than an equivalent transformational grammar, the computational bookkeeping required, and so forth. The one worked out example of such a context free grammar the authors are familiar with is the slashed category grammar of Harman 1963. Harman claimed that this grammar generated the same language as the transformational grammar of *Syntactic Structures*, using about the same number of rules. An up to date comparison might yield different results. Superficial study of implemented versions of generalized phrase structure grammar. in fact shows that the number of slashed rules increases tremendously in a working generalized phrase structure parsing system so much so that it is more efficient to keep the rules in their unexpanded, implicit form. The 1983 Association for Computational Linguistics Proceedings has a number of reports on this topic. In other words, we do not "write out" all possible phrase structure rules indicating where constituents may be moved, but retain an implicit rule determining possible movements. Again, it has turned out that "precomputing" the results of movement transformations and then looking up the answers is not as advantageous as doing the computation at the time it is needed. In any case, it does not immediately follow that conversion to the slashed category notation is computationally advantageous.

24. Some storage representations admit efficient "preprocessing" operations on the presumably now fixed grammar that are just not available in other formats. For instance, given a fixed grammar we might compute in advance of the parse of any input sentence a table that tells us which non-terminals can be derived from other non-terminals. For example, in the grammar $S \to AB$, $A \to C$, we would store the "lemma" that S can derive A, B, or C; and that A can derive C. These finite step "lemmas" can possibly shorten parsing work later on, if they can be integrated in an efficient manner into the parsing algorithm as a whole. It turns out, although we cannot demonstrate this fact here, that tradeoffs between preprocessing operations, alternative grammar representations, and different parsing algorithm organizations can be quite subtle.

To get some idea of the subtlety of "real" implementations, see the variants proposed by Graham, Harrison, and Ruzzo (1980:437, 440, 441, and 442; figures 4, 6, 7, and 8). Each variant provides a slightly different way of stating which rules are related to which other rules given a particular input sentence and different ways of organizing the actual parse of a sentence. Without grasping in detail just what these different formats are supposed to do, we can still note that they entail quite different ways of storing and manipulating rules of the grammar, and hence make quite different assumptions about just what "primitive operations" are available.

25. Because we are looking only at parsing efficiency, let us say that there is a "cognitive analogue" of the parallel operations if the cognitive machinery can simulate the requisite operations while preserving the "unit time" execution character of the parallel operations. This is roughly the account that we gave in chapter 2.

26. We leave open the question as to whether resource complexity more generally is an appropriate measure for the finite sized problems that the brain computes. It may well be that the alternative measures of program size or Kolmogorov complexity are more suitable. Gewirtz 1974 is a good summary of this approach. The theory of program size complexity attempts to find the shortest program it takes to compute some function, irrespective of the amount of time or space it may take to do the actual computation. There are obvious connections between the notion of shortest program and simplest theory, as classically described, that deserve further study.

27. Much recent work has gone into showing that the human parsing system in fact uses principles borrowed rather directly from linguistic competence theories. In fact, much of the work previously thought to be accomplished by independent parsing strategies seems more adequately handled by grammatically-based devices. We take up this matter directly in chapter 5.

Chapter 4

1. Wasow 1978 has a contrary view. Wasow insists that it is the study of constraints on languages, not grammars, that is central to the linguistic enterprise.

2. We could argue that the theory of lexical-functional grammar is but a format for writing theories of grammar, and it is these particular theories, rather than the lexical-functional metatheory, that will capture the notion of a "natural" grammar. In this view it would not be surprising to find, say, a natural language like Dutch demanding rule machinery that, combined in other ways, would lead to an unnatural rule system. It would be up to an as yet incomplete theory of substantive constraints on grammars written in the lexical-functional style to tell us just what counts as natural. This theory would also presumably rule out the deadly combinations leading to unnatural grammars. There is nothing really objectionable to this approach. It is just that the same escape hatch is even open to an *Aspects* style transformational system. Peters 1973 noted that all naturally written transformational grammars somehow obeyed the Survivor Property, a particular property of derivation sequences guaranteeing that the languages so generated will be recursive. Evidently, there is some unnamed collection of constraints on natural transformational grammars preventing them from being able to simulate arbitrary Turing machines. Lapointe 1977 and Wasow 1978 explore this point in some detail. Analogously, there must be some unidentified constraints limiting the lexical-functional grammars. What is more important is that modern transformational grammars do not permit us

to write the unnatural grammars that are possible in the lexical-functional system and it is clear why they do not. We will discuss this issue in more detail below.

3. The proper generalizations here might be stated in terms of grammatical functions instead of categorial notions like NP, VP (Bresnan 1982a).

4. More generally, the assembly directive is specified via the notation, ($\uparrow$ feat1) = ($\downarrow$ feat2), where *feat1* and *feat2* are metavariables specifying a subfield of the functional structure immediately above or below the node to which the annotation is attached. If no field is given, then the entire functional structure is assumed. For example, the notation, ($\uparrow$ subject number=$\downarrow$) attached to a node X means that the number subfield of the subject subfield of the functional structure associated with the node above X is to be filled in the the value of the entire functional structure below X.

5. It seems difficult to find a real example of a language that cannot be generated by a lexical-functional grammar, not built by some kind of diagonalization technique. We conjecture that the language $w_1 c w_2 c \ldots w_n$, where $w \in \{a, b\}^*$ cannot be generated by any lexical-functional grammar.

6. There is some disagreement over how much structure should dominate the remaining NPs. Bresnan et al. argue for structure (3). Whatever the right answer turns out to be, it is consistent with the government-binding theory and is not directly relevant to our point.

We should also point out that here we are not talking about the problem of parsing Dutch sentences or recovering S-structure, given the input string. Rather, we are talking about the abstract problem of defining well-formedness for a string given a grammar. This is precisely what Bresnan et al. are discussing; as they observe, their f-structure algorithm is not a parsing procedure.

7. It is possible to write other kinds of lexical-functional grammars with these same devices and obtain similar results. For instance, we can control an object NP from a more deeply embedded subject position in a complement clause, a case of reverse control. This is true because the functional structure unification procedure is defined to be adirectional.

8. One technical detail is that this linearity property holds if we assume an unlimited stock of alphabet symbols for NPs in lieu of subscripts like NP_1, NP_2, etc. This is because the subscripting itself takes logarithmic space (n subscripts would take $\log(n)$ space to store), violating linearity. But if we are allowed to generate new alphabet symbols for NPs, then we can use the symbol NP-1 to stand for NP_1, NP-2 for NP_2, and so forth. Note that Kaplan and Bresnan 1982 must adopt this same assumption in order that lexical-functional language recognition take linear space. They also use the co-indexing of NPs to indicate co-referentiality, and there could be proportional to n such subscripts in a sentence n words long. Kaplan and Bresnan 1982 ignore this possibility in presenting their claim, but it is essential, because otherwise the resulting f-structure cannot even be written

down in linear space.

9. It is possible to get rid of the $\log n$ factor if we are willing to assume an indefinite stock of distinct NPs, as if each NP_i is a different vocabulary item. This will become crucial later on, when we establish the linearity of annotated surface structures. The same assumption is made in the lexical-functional theory; see note 8.

10. We could substitute "deep structure" for "annotated surface structure" in the theorem. This is because the mapping from annotated surface structure to deep structure essentially involves just interchanging traces and displaced NPs. Pros remain where they are. Therefore deep structures are also just linearly larger than their associated surface sentences.

11. These include feature agreement, the lexical analogue of subject or object "control," lexical ambiguity, and a garden variety context-free base grammar.

12. This grammar will have to be slightly modified in order for the reduction to work, as will become apparent shortly.

13. See for example Pinker 1982 where this claim is made for lexical-functional grammar. Still, it is most natural to assume that there is a potentially unbounded number of lexical items. This is all that is required for the reduction.

Chapter 5

1. As discussed in chapter 3, the divergence between the generative capacity of the competence system and its embedding into a parsing model could emerge in one of two ways. (1) There could be sentences that are grammatical, but not parsable (acceptable) and (2) there could be sentences that are parsable, but not grammatical. As noted above, multiply center-embedded sentences exemplify the first sort of case. Examples of the second type will be given below. These are cases where a complete syntactic parse tree can be built successfully, but where co-indexing violates grammatical principles, for example:

*Pictures of the men_i pleased each $other_i$.

2. An ambiguous sentence would have two or more such associated annotated surface structures; in these cases, the Marcus parser by definition computes just one at a time.

3. It should be pointed out that current theories of transformational grammar substitute the rule Move NP (plus general restrictions) for the individual rules of passive, raising, and the like. There is no longer a one rule-one construction correspondence. This is also true of the Marcus parser; see Marcus 1980:94–96.

4. It is well known that in the worst case such backtracking is computationally expensive. Consider an example provided by Hopcroft and Ullman (1972:299).

The grammar is $S \rightarrow aSS$, $S \rightarrow$ empty string. As Hopcroft and Ullman observe, for every string a^n the number of possible ways to derive the strings of the language generated by this grammar exceeds 2^n. To see this informally note, as Hopcroft and Ullman do, that any particular a could have been derived from either the left S or the right S and that any pair of Ss can be derived entirely from the left S, the right S, or from both, and so on multiplicatively. Any parser that backtracks might have to examine all these possibilities and thus take exponential time.

Another problem with backtracking parsers is that any semantic interpretation that might have been done on the assumption of tentatively constructed phrases might have to be withdrawn. We will return to discuss the problem of "online" semantic interpretation in the context of the Marcus parser below.

5. There are clearly cases where there is simply no way for a deterministic parser of this sort to be right all the time. For example, consider cases of global ambiguity (more than one possible structural analysis for a sentence) or so-called "garden path" sentences where a legitimate local analysis is globally ill formed. Marcus asserts that these cases are not a problem for this theory. Global ambiguity is accommodated by claiming that people simply obtain one parse at a time, embedding a single, deterministic procedure in a loop, as it were. In effect, such a machine is allowed to backtrack by throwing away the analysis of the input sentence completed so far and starting over. In contrast, a nondeterministic device or its deterministic simulation via a backtracking control structure trivially subsumes this kind of behavior, but in addition can do more than this, because at any point it can choose to backtrack and undo only part of the structure built so far. Garden path sentences are actually, Marcus claims, evidence that the deterministic approach is cognitively faithful. If parses were carried along in parallel, there should be no evidence of processing difficulty in garden path sentences. Marcus further claims that garden path sentences strongly support this model but this claim is somewhat more controversial.

Of course, we could simulate deterministic operation within a weaker, nondeterministic model, because the nondeterministic model subsumes the deterministic one. But it seems more reasonable to adopt the stronger theory until it is disproved.

6. By "left to right" we mean that the parser handles builds up syntactic structure as the input stream of lexical items is coming to its attention and that its decisions are affected by the sequence in which these tokens are encountered. This is to be contrasted with, for example, a parsing scheme that waited until the whole input stream was terminated and then began analysis at any arbitrary point in the stream.

7. For this to work we must assume that modifier phrases are attached to NPs before the status of the complement is fixed. This is done via the "attention shifting" mechanism discussed by Marcus 1980.

8. Traces but not Pros are governed by the subjacency condition. We shall

explain this difference below.

9. This is a basic assumption of the design of abstract computational models, from finite state automata to Turing machines. Each consists of a finite state control device (the operating rules of the automaton) along with (optional) auxiliary storage, for example, a pushdown stack, a linearly bounded tape, etc. Crucially, the rules of a finite state automaton, pushdown automaton, or Turing machine operate by looking at only a finite number of symbols in any given step. For example, a Turing machine examines just a single symbol at any one step and consults its control table to decide whether to move left or right, write a symbol, etc. Thus the control table rules can specify only a finite number of context symbols; they cannot themselves be algorithms, as a search procedure would be.

10. One historical note. This was the approach used in the first attempt to define general left to right, deterministic parsing, that of Floyd 1964. In Floyd's model, parsing decisions were made via triggering patterns that consisted of finite strings of symbols to the left and to the right of the current analysis point in the input string. This was dubbed "bounded context parsing." LR(k) parsing is a generalization of bounded context parsing to the case where left contexts can be arbitrarily long in terms of the literal number of context symbols, but form a regular set and hence can be generatively encoded into the finite control of the parser. We shall see that the model we have adopted is closer to a bounded context parser.

11. There is one subtlety to overcome here. One clause might have an indefinite string of adjuncts of the same type, such as prepositional phrases. The trace and antecedent would be unboundedly far apart in terms of constituent material. Such a string of adjuncts may be represented in a principled way as a single set of constituents of unspecified number but of the same type, roughly, the Kleene star notation XP^*. Note that this does not enlarge our constituent category inventory. We cannot make up arbitrary complex regular expressions like $(S\,NP\,VP)^*$.

12. What about wh movement? To force it to be local we can successive cyclically encode wh, say by leaving a trace in comp. This allows the parser to exploit the bounded search procedure. Marcus (1980:161–162) proposes such a mechanism and we shall assume the parser uses something similar. The wh moved structures will reflect successive cyclic movement as described by Chomsky (1973, 1981).

13. See Chomsky 1955, 1965 for further discussion of the noncounting character of grammatical rules.
It might be argued that a predicate like "seven" could be obtained by the combination of two natural predicates, adjacency, plus compositionality. But the point is that such predicates are not observed in natural rule systems. There may be a reason for this. If we could combine two available predicates to get counting predicates, it would be difficult to see how to stop at 15 rather than 150.

14. Grammars clearly exploit the predicate "adjacent" in other situations.

For example, Case assignment is generally restricted to adjacent categories. We can say, *I kissed Mary* but not *I kissed quickly Mary*. See Stowell 1981 for additional discussion.

15. Noam Chomsky (personal communication) observes that there are dialects of English in which at least the pleonastic *it* can be moved more than once (*contra* Dresher and Hornstein's description). Some speakers find sentences such as (a) grammatical:

(a) It seems e_i to appear e_i to be obvious that Bill will win.

Each of the traces in this sequence can be "dropped" during parsing on the basis of "local evidence." How could we extend our account to cover both (a) and sentences such as (13) and (14) in the text? Suppose we annotate a dropped trace with a feature indicating that the trace is either thematic (as in (13)) or athematic (as in (14)). Then we can distinguish between (13) and (14) and cases like (b) and (c):

(b) Jody Powell was believed $[_S$ $e_{i,+\theta}$ to have been asked

$[_{\overline{S}}$ $e_{i,+\theta}$ whether Carter would go back to the farm]]

(c) It$_i$ was believed $[_S$ $e_{i,-\theta}$ to have been asked

$[_{\overline{S}}$ whether Carter would go back to the farm]]

Alternatively, we could claim that traces directly encode the features of their antecedents. This commits us to layered traces, encoding all the features of complex antecedents. In chapter 4 we assumed that layered traces were disallowed; an assumption that was crucial to assuring the constant growth property for government-binding theory. Therefore, we cannot take advantage of this alternative.

16. Passive morphology's failure here to make the relevant distinctions on its own in no way compromises the account of simple passives discussed in chapter 2. This account relied both on the parser's ability to access the passive morphology and the local prenominal environment in one time step. Whether this access should be extended to access of subjacent prenominal NPs depends on psycholinguistic facts that are not presently known. Does NP raising add any time complexity to online processing? The important point is that the account of simple passive cases remains as before. Passive morphology tells the parser to look at the prenominal subject position before deciding whether to drop a trace.

17. It should be noted that GPSG is a theory of grammar and is not to be taken directly as a parsing model. In the following sections we shall be talking about a fictional parsing device that is based directly on the types of rules proposed in GPSG.

18. A key property of context-free grammars is that the left contexts of rightmost derivations of every context-free grammar form a regular set, and hence can be stored in a finite state control. To see this informally consider the successive lines of a rightmost derivation of a context-free

grammar. We can see that each line is in the form αx, where α is some string of as yet unexpanded nonterminals and x is a string of terminals. But working backwards, successive lines of the rightmost parse in reverse can be generated by a grammar containing no self embedding, a finite state grammar. Note that while this result holds for all context-free grammars, it also holds for some strictly context-sensitive grammars (grammars that generate strictly context-sensitive languages), namely, those whose successive rightmost derivations contain no self embedding.

More generally, GPSG is roughly the usual simulation of a pushdown automaton via a complex symbol encoding of its state and stack information; see Chomsky 1959 for discussion.

19. This is not to say that a subjacency-like constraint cannot be written in the GPSG framework. The problem is simply that the functional grounding sketched above cannot be used in this framework.

20. We would have to argue that without a learnability analogue of subjacency we cannot learn a GPSG from "simple" data of limited embedding. In the Wexler and Culicover transformational framework, this constraint is demanded. Otherwise a single transformation could make reference to unbounded context. But it is not clear that unboundedness has the same force in GPSG because the whole point of the complex nonterminal exercise was to make all unbounded movements easy to compute.

21. This method may be employed to insure efficient context-free parsing (see Earley 1968).

22. The machine is therefore a transducer. In fact one way to look at it is as a machine implementation of Chomsky's notion of levels of linguistic representation (Chomsky 1955). Berwick 1982 contains a more detailed study.

23. There seems to be some tendency to take the intransitive reading in a neutral context, as is predicted on our account. On encountering an ambiguous case, the parser would first look in the subjacent domain, and then, not finding an antecedent, assume that the verb is intransitive. Only later during interpretation would it be possible to determine that the transitive reading is satisfactory.

There are sentences in which a transitive parasitic gap reading is preferred after an optionally intransitive verb. Interestingly though, it seems that distance in terms of terminals and nonterminals from the true gap influences preference for this reading. Apparently, distance has some kind of perceptual effect in this case as well. As an example, (to our ears at least) (a) seems to take a transitive first reading while (b) does not.

(a) What did Bob cook $(e)_i$ without eating $(p)_i$?
(b) What did Bob cook while telling Nory about
    the great electronics toys you could get cheap without eating?

24. Marcus 1980 adopts this strategy. NPs are shipped off for semantic interpretation before an entire complement structure is built.

25. See Fodor, Bever, and Garrett 1974. A more extensive discussion of this psycholinguistic evidence appears below. Berwick and Wexler 1982 have an earlier discussion of c-command in a two stage model.

26. The same shunting procedure is followed when any constituent is completed, not just S nodes.

27. This approach will also handle the case of preposed constituents, for example, *After he showers, John feels refreshed.* See also note 40.

28. So far we have not been able to explain why a nominal or pronominal element is obligatorily not c-commanded. Higginbotham 1983 offers an explanation in terms of "referential dependencies."

Finally, one apparent problem for this approach comes from sentences where elements c-commanded at D-structure are displaced so that the c-command relation is destroyed in the representation that the parser receives. These cases may require a process of reconstruction, where these constituents are literally returned to their D-structure positions. Importantly, the clauses that need to be reconstructed have distinguishing phonological shapes (comma intonation or a copular or *wh* head). Relevant examples include:

(a) It is each other that Mary believes that Sheila thinks
    that the representatives will talk to.
(b) Each other, Sheila believes that Doris thinks
    that the representatives respect.

29. Recall that the phonological distinction between traces and pronouns or lexical anaphors allows us to derive the requirement that traces obey a bounding condition while pronouns and lexical anaphors need not. The insertion of traces, a parsing decision, depends on the presence of an actual antecedent; in addition, traces are inserted by actual rules of the parser, which must be stored in a finite control table. In contrast, the insertion of lexical anaphors and pronouns into the parse tree does not depend on the existence of an antecedent. Rather, the parser simply attaches them to the parse tree in the appropriate place. Only later is binding carried out.

The bound variable interpretation is not obligatory when the pronoun is c-commanded by the quantifier. In this situation it is possible to obtain either of two readings for a sentence such as (2). This is analogous to the case of a globally ambiguous sentence. Presumably in such cases the deterministic parser is embedded in a loop that first obtains one reading and then (perhaps using the same parse tree, perhaps not) reanalyzes the sentence to obtain the other readings.

30. Knuth 1965 has a discussion of LR(k) parsers and these results.

Of course, the requirement of no backtracking operation means that garden path sentences will not be accepted by the parser, even though these are grammatically legal.

31. This happens because there may be a multiplicative cascade of choices worthy of reconsideration. In the example above, our only choice was between the alternative VP expansions. But NP or S could also have alternative

expansions, these in turn containing new alternative VP expansion choices, and so on. We obtain the usual kind of nondeterministic computation tree with branches as follows:

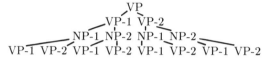

In the worst case, we must explore each of these possibilities, and there can be approximately 2^n for them, for a sentence of length n.

32. Thus we can attempt to parse an ambiguous grammar via an LR(k) parsing procedure, but then conflicts about how to proceed must be resolved by means other than the structure of the grammar itself. For example, we might use semantic preference information. This approach has proved useful in the design of programming languages, as discussed in Aho and Ullman 1972.

33. It is true that the predicted nodes (say, NP) will become part of the lefthand context of the parser's state, available for encoding information about what has been encountered thus far. This is precisely the information that is contained in an LR(k) parser's finite decision table. Just where the Marcus machine has a predicted NP node, the LR(k) machine has a distinct "state." Note that the left context of a Marcus machine is, in fact, finite (as we have noted many times). The corresponding LR(k) encoding is therefore feasible. A detailed examination of the correspondence between the Marcus machine left context and an LR(k) machine's states would take us too far afield at this point. Berwick 1982 contains more details.

34. One way to think of the LR(k,t) extension is to imagine that a duplicate of the first LR(k) parser is set to work on a "mini phrase" beginning at the left edge of the subtree in question. Indeed, this is the metaphor that Marcus used. For example, the parsing of the second leftmost subtree in *Have the boys...* can be carried out by setting the LR(k) parser loose on the phrase starting with *Have the boys...*, noting that this submachine should eventually find an NP. Hammer 1975 has a related approach.

35. We can illustrate this additional power of nonterminal lookahead more precisely by presenting a formal analogue of the *Have the boys...* case:

$Start \to S$ $S \to ADF$ $S \to BDG$
$A \to a$ $B \to a$
$D \to Dd$ $D \to empty$
$G \to g$ $F \to f$

This grammar generates basically two kinds of sentences, one with a leading a followed by an arbitrary number of d's, then a trailing f; the other just like the first, but ending in a trailing g:

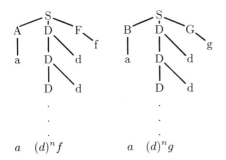

$$a \quad (d)^n f \qquad a \quad (d)^n g$$

This grammar is unambiguous. There is only one derivation for any sentence. Still it causes problems for an LR(k) parser. The problem is exactly the one faced in the *Have the boys...* case. Upon seeing an a the parser must decide whether to reduce it to A or B (via the rules $A \to a$ or $B \to a$); it is the leftmost complete subtree of any derivation. This is analogous to the decision to parse *have* as either a main verb or an auxiliary verb. We can determine the correct reduction to make by looking at the telltale f or g at the very end of the sentence, just as we can see by the *take-taken* alternation what kind of rule must have been used to produce *have*. Unfortunately, an arbitrary string of d's intervenes, just as the potentially long NP is interposed in *Have the boys....* Therefore, this grammar is not a strict LR(k) grammar, for any value of the lookahead k.

But, we can parse the intervening string of d's deterministically. Suppose we do so, temporarily "shifting our attention" to this second leftmost subtree. We ignore the first terminal element a, and focus instead on the second terminal element d, as if we were starting the parse all over again, but now beginning with a d. The existence of a d in the terminal string means that we must have applied the rules $D \to Dd$; $D \to$ empty. Therefore we may predict safely that this rule has been applied, just as in the case of *Have the boys...* the presence of *the* leads to the definite prediction of the start of an NP. The parse of the entire d subtree now proceeds. Eventually, we successfully parse the entire subtree, and return with that subtree now filling the second position in the input string:

Input
Buffer:

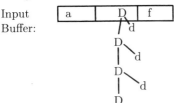

Now we can tell what a should be. A finite lookahead, based on nonterminals, expands the grammars that can be parsed deterministically, left to right.

Note that Marcus 1980 seems to equate arbitrary lookahead with a vitiation of the notion of deterministic parsing. In a sense this is true, but we must be careful to realize that cases where an arbitrary number of terminals must apparently be viewed before deciding what to do next do not necessarily constitute an insurmountable barrier for deterministic parsing.

What constitutes a violation of the LR(k) condition then? Basically, any kind of arbitrarily extendable global ambiguity leads to a non LR(k) grammar. For instance, the following grammar is not LR(k), for any k:

$$S \rightarrow Ab \qquad S \rightarrow Bc \qquad A \rightarrow Aa$$
$$A \rightarrow \text{empty} \qquad B \rightarrow Ba \qquad B \rightarrow \text{empty}$$

Once again, there are basically two sentences and two sorts of trees derivable from this grammar. There is a telltale flag at the end of each sentence, b or c. However, this time there is no way to get to the b or c by attention shifting, because at each step we are faced with the decision between producing an a via the rule $A \rightarrow a$ or via $B \rightarrow a$. Thus we cannot plunge ahead, no matter which subtree we look at. Note that this grammar is nonetheless unambiguous.

This grammar is "unnaturally" parsable deterministically, left to right. We could just store all the a's, wait till we see a b or a c, and then start announcing the right derivation structure for the string. This is an unnatural parse because the parser's operation would not be connected in any transparent way to the derivation of sentences in the grammar. The parser would in essence have figured out the proper derivation by reading the sentence and counting the number of a's, as if it were a puzzle. Global sections of tree structure are ambiguous. That is why this grammar is not LR(k). Still the tree structure generated by the alternative rules has the same shape without category labels. We might be yet able to "parse" sentences of this language by building a skeleton tree and supplying the labels afterwards.

More precisely, there are two conditions that must be fulfilled for a grammar to be LR(k). The first is unique invertibility. We must be able to determine which production $X \rightarrow Y$ or $Z \rightarrow Y$ has applied. Note that this condition is met if no two rules have the same right hand sides. The second is unique phrasing. We must be able to locate uniquely the boundaries of phrases. The first condition is also clearly met if we ignore nonterminal labels when we parse.

36. Aho and Ullman 1972 contains details.

37. This demonstration is not quite complete. We must still handle cases where input sentences are not in the language accepted by the parser. This could pose a problem. There could be an ill-formed input string causing the parser to loop endlessly without consuming any input. One conventional way to sidestep this difficulty is to first see how long the input string is by copying it and then use this length to define a clock that shuts off the parser when it begins to run longer than it should (longer than time Cn, where C is a fixed number taking into account all the constant factors of

the parsing machine. Because the operating rules of the machine are known in advance, we can fix C beforehand.)

38. This is true under most interpretations of an index. For example, suppose that an NP index is regarded as a "pointer" or "address" indicating the location of a (mental) representation of the object denoted by the NP. Pointers and addresses also take logarithmic space to store.

39. In most cases, the MGC is strictly local. We leave open the question of the exact process by which the minimal governing category is to be computed for all examples. The exact formulation of the MGC is still an open question. It cannot be worse in length than the c-command chain as we have defined it.

40. There is a remaining subtlety we have not described. Sometimes a pronoun's co-indexer occurs after it:

(a) Near him, Dan saw a snake.

But then, by the time *Dan* is encountered, *him* will be in the propositional list with an inherent index, because no antecedent could have been found. As mentioned, this causes no failure. Now the NP *Dan* must have an index. Because we must search the propositional list anyway to find potential co-referential NPs (suppose we had the sentence, *Near Dan, Dan saw a snake*), in the normal course of looking for co-referential items for *Dan* we will pick up *him* again.

41. Suppose that we must search depth first a balanced binary tree with n terminals. If it takes $T(n)$ steps to search a tree with n terminals, the tree with $2n$ terminals will at worst take time $2T(n) + 4$ steps to search, $n - 1$ steps to search each half, plus four steps to choose between the branches. The total number of computational steps will be defined by the inductive formula $T(2n) = 2T(n) + 4$, which has the solution $n \log n$.

42. See Stabler 1983 for an attempt to distinguish between "program using" and "hardwired" computational systems in an effort to show that rule based grammatical theories must assume some kind of program for language use whereas a wired, non rule based system might suffice. The argument seems flawed for several reasons. As we have seen, by positing machinery grounded on the specific rules of transformational grammar, we can actually explain external behavior. Stabler also argues that a rule is "used" if it is causally efficacious under some encoding in actual linguistic behavior. But this behavior would include language acquisition. Thus if the representations of modern linguistic theory account for language acquisition, as they are supposed to, then they are causally efficacious, even if no literal "rules" remain in the adult grammar. In fact, because modern transformational grammars do not even have "rules" in the traditional sense, this possibility even seems likely. The principles of grammar are used to acquire a system of abilities that need not bear any direct resemblance to specific rules.

Chapter 6

1. Brown and Hanlon 1970 and Newport, Gleitman, and Gleitman 1977 have a discussion of the apparent weak effect of negative evidence in child language acquisition.

2. A characterization of what exactly is the primary data that children receive to learn language has been a topic of vast dispute over the past several years. The ordering of examples actually provided to children is probably neither completely random nor so structured as to provide possible encodings of grammars. Yet despite the immense possibility for individual variation in data input, the course of acquisition is remarkably uniform. This uniformity can only come from two sources, the external world or the child. In light of the controversy over what is input to the child the current research has opted for a strong assumption about external order, namely to assume no external ordering of input data. All structure is imposed by the internal structure of the acquisition model itself. Note that even with this assumption there is a device whereby the effects of randomness can be partially "filtered" so as to ensure that by and large simple sentences are acquired before more complex examples. We might call this the principle of data focus. The competence of the system at any given point in time imposes an intrinsic filtering of the input examples, in that examples "too complex" for the parser to either (1) handle directly or (2) easily acquire rules for (in a sense of "easily acquire" that will be made precise later) are simply ignored. The first sentence of *Finnegan's Wake* might be input first, but it will simply not be completely and successfully interpreted, and thus not figure prominently in acquisition. See chapter 1 for additional discussion.

3. This second failure introduces a contact with a crude kind of semantic interpretation, in the sense that incorrect base structures can be detected in simple cases via the recovery of thematic roles such as agent, instrument, theme, etc. independently of linguistic context. This assumption is comparable to that of Wexler and Culicover 1980, who posited that base structures were somehow inferrable "from context." It is weaker than their assumption in that only the assignment of arguments to thematic roles is assumed to be reconstructible, not the entire base structure. In fact, as will be discussed, this difference is not so great because the constraints of phrase structure theory ($\overline{X}$ theory), adjacency requirements on arguments, and so forth almost ensure that the base structure is superfluous aside from thematic argument structure.

4. Chomsky 1965 n. 18 to chapter 2 contains a discussion of local transformations. Joshi and Levy 1977 has a formalization of the notion of a local transformation.

5. We might well question whether the model's identification of grammatical knowledge with a set of rules is the right approach. As Chomsky (1982) has noted, there has been a shift in recent years in generative grammar away from the study of rule systems and toward the study of systems of principles. In this newer view, rules are just the "surface" epiphenomena

of deeper systems of constraints that underly grammatical systems. Thus, there is no "rule of passive" as such but rather a cluster of properties arising out of the interaction of a single movement rule and a number of quite general constraints on grammars.

6. There are some organizational modifications obviously worth investigating. For instance, the ability to handle the "interrupts" characteristic of the processing of recursive phrases (especially, given Marcus's framework, the parsing of noun phrases as separate entities), is a plausible candidate for maturational change.

7. This scheme was first suggested by Marcus (1980:60) and implemented by Shipman (1979). The actual procedure uses the $\overline{X}$phrase structure schemas instead of explicitly labeled nodes like "VP" or "S."

8. This process of rule generalization and splitting corresponds in simple cases to the induction of a finite state automaton from positive examples, and in complicated cases, to the induction of simple tree automata. Lexical classes are therefore defined dynamically, by their insertion contexts as determined by grammar rules. There are no categories such as determiner, modal, or noun as such, but rather the classes determined by an invariance relation defined over the behavior of the parser, namely, equivalence classes of parser states. Formally, this may be viewed as the definition of nonterminal labels. See Berwick 1982 for details.

9. Obviously, a later attempt at the same sentence could lead to different results, if in the meantime the additional missing rule had been acquired by exposure to some other example sentence.

10. This point was first discussed in Williams 1981 and Chomsky 1970.

11. As Berwick 1982 shows, it is quite easy to extend this rudimentary initial categorization into a full set of lexical categories for English, including adjectives, adverbs, articles, quantifiers, modal verbs, prepositions, and particles.

12. This does not mean that such a system could produce such a sentence. For example, children's use of (unstressed) *do* in declaratives apparently appears after its occurrence in yes-no questions (Fletcher 1979:272). On the other hand, *do* sometimes appears as a main verb before its occurrence in the inverted forms and might therefore be presumed marked as +verb. In any case, the early (2 yrs., 3 mos.) appearance of sequences such as, Adult:*Shall I put your watch on?* Child: *no, I will* (Fletcher 1979:267 from Leopold 1949) at least suggests that rules exist to handle the declaratively positioned modal (or auxiliary?) verbs at or about the time the inverted forms are to be parsed.

13. More accurately, *will* is marked [+verb −noun +head −arg] as a member of a more abstract "verb like" category that includes the modals such as *could* or auxiliary verbs such as *have* or *do*, but excludes main verbs. There is, of course, considerable complexity to the English auxiliary verb system that is being glossed over here. auxiliaries and modals can appear only

in certain orders and in certain combinations. See Berwick 1982 for more extensive discussion on the acquisition of these relationships.

14. This procedure clearly presumes that an entire constituent, in this case, a noun phrase, has been made available for switching into the first buffer cell. Following Marcus (Marcus 1980:175), the parser does this by temporarily "shifting its attention" to the processing of the noun phrase starting with the token *John*. In the case at hand, the noun phrase analysis is simple. But because English noun phrases may themselves contain Sentential forms (hence other noun phrases), this approach leaves open the possibility of an infinite forward chain of attention shifts and lookahead. There are several obvious restrictions that deal with this problem. One adopted by Marcus is to note that no "plausible" (descriptively sufficient) grammar rule for English ever requires more than five buffer cells total; any shifting beyond this local radius is prohibited and leads to apparent processing difficulty. This restriction will be called the total buffer cell limitation; it is also adopted here. Secondly, we might deliberately disallow recursive invocation of the acquisition procedure; this would push most complex noun phrases beyond the reach of the early parser, the recursion limitation. The relationship between these two restrictions awaits further investigation. However, both seem independently necessary. Because the buffer cell limit is required by even a "mature" parser, it seems clear that the first restriction is not entirely subsumed by the second; the no recursion condition also appears warranted for other, independent reasons, again to ensure locality of acquisition.

15. The triggering of a switch is also recorded permanently at the appropriate place in the parse tree so that a distinction between declarative and inverted sentence forms can be maintained for later "semantic" use. In general, the "active" node, the one currently being built, is annotated with the names of the rules that build it.

16. We shall deal with the acquisition of the passive construction in this chapter as it is the most difficult case to handle. For a more complete discussion of this construction and other so-called "semantically circumscribed" developmental sequences see Weinberg forthcoming. The other two "problematic" cases are those involving *whiz* deletion and gapping. As mentioned in chapter 2, there is no good evidence that prenominal adjectives are generated using *whiz* deletion or any other transformation. The same holds for gapping, at least if we assume the analysis of Williams 1978. In addition, Maratsos 1978 claims that the acquisition of the "Equi NP" construction is a problem, but see Rizzi 1981 who shows that the developmental sequence associated with "Equi" is predicted by transformational assumptions.

17. An extension to nonsense "actional" verbs is intriguing because it is evidence for a productive rule. It would count against a purely conservative model of acquisition, where a construction is acquired on a verb by verb basis according to frequency of contact to a particular verb.

18. This is because the characterization of object in English is as the first

NP under VP. Any NP directly dominated by VP should be passivizable. For complete details about how grammatical relations are assigned in different languages, see Bresnan 1978, 1982b.

19. The reason for this has to do with the assumption that children must learn natural language without the benefit of negative evidence. As mentioned in footnote 1, psychologists have shown that children do not seem to take the corrections (negative evidence) of their caretakers into account when hypothesizing alternative grammars for their language. Indeed, there does not seem to be much negative evidence to begin with. If this is true though, we might predict that children will always choose the most conservative option that their rule system allows to handle data in their linguistic environment. In the case at hand, suppose passives in a target language L_1 were generated by rule (3). Further suppose however, that the child hypothesizes rule (2) first. Rule (2) will overgenerate. The only way that a child could realize her mistake would be to be corrected by the caretaker. But given the ban on negative evidence, this cannot be built into the acquisition procedure. It follows that the narrowest possible target language, that generated by rule (3), should be tried first and jettisoned only if positive evidence demands it. This ordering principle is not part of the grammatical theory, but rather part of the theory of learning. It and other cases like it may be formalized as a more general subset principle of learning, namely to hypothesize the narrowest possible language consistent with evidence seen. The subset principle seems to account for a wide range of observed examples of hypothesis ordering in language acquisition. This principle is discussed in more detail below and in Berwick 1982.

20. This alternative was explored in Weinberg 1979 where it was ultimately rejected because there was no natural way of barring it at a later stage.

21. The claim that such adult languages do not exist is made in Marantz 1983 and by Kenneth Hale (personal communication). In contrast, Pinker asserts that "In some languages, rules may apply only if certain thematic conditions are first met" (1982:711). He claims, although no cases are cited, that there are rules that refer to just the [+patient], [+agent] categories needed in the early stage. Unfortunately, a survey reveals no such languages. Therefore we shall assume that they are not attested.

Marantz 1983 provides another argument against the direct approach. Marantz claims that notions like "subject" and "object" have no independent status in grammatical theory. Rather these notions are defined as "relations" with respect to how they combine with functors to form predicates and propositions. This much is uncontroversial. Marantz argues that thematic terms should also be relationally defined. For instance, a "theme" is an element that combines with a verb to form a complex predicate. This approach does not supply the proper predicates for Pinker's annotation approach. More controversially, Marantz wants to claim that there is a stage where thematic roles (as opposed to relations) do play a role in the early stages of acquisition. He claims that this correlates with children's incorrect categorization of verbs as functors. And there is even some evidence for this.

Children seem to have difficulty picking out the proper class of functors in their language. In particular, the so-called pivot class of functors includes many expressions that do not serve as functors in the adult grammar.

There are two main problems with Marantz's positive proposal. First, at the stage when the passive construction is acquired there is a good deal of evidence that the "functor like" character of verbs has stabilized. The pivot class has stabilized to the verbal and adjectival class. Thus it would be difficult to use Marantz style arguments to explain this set of cases. The second problem is that evidence from Goldin-Meadow 1979 suggests that the "functor like" character of verbs is available from very early on. In particular, Goldin-Meadow notes that even in the two word stage we can predict which of a verb's arguments is likely to co-occur with it. If the verb is transitive, we can predict that its object (obligatory) argument will be expressed. If it is intransitive, it will co-occur with its subject. This suggests that even from the earliest stages children know that the argument structure centers around the verb and that "verbal" elements in the adult stage are the predicates of these argument structures. Weinberg (forthcoming) treats this matter in greater detail.

22. The inclusion of semantic notions, while not allowed in the transformational component, is permitted in a government-binding theory as a whole. Wasow 1977 and 1980 provides evidence that grammars must not treat passives as a unitary phenomenon. He claims that two very different kinds of rules handle the full range of passives, described by Wasow as a transformational passive and a lexical passive. The transformational passive is stated using categorial predicates (like NP). But there is also a lexical rule that uses other kinds of predicates. Anderson 1977 and Williams 1981 suggest that thematic notions like theme and actor are appropriate for this type of rule. The lexical rule encodes a theme of a verb via an argument external to the verb phrase:

(a) en:

$$[\quad]_{[+V\ -N]} \rightarrow [\quad]_{[+V]}: \text{theme} \rightarrow \text{external argument}$$

The motivation for additional rules of this kind is twofold. First, there seem to be languages of the world where only themes are passivizable. Second, even in English, lexical passives seem to be distinguished from verbal passives by a host of criteria quite characteristic of lexical phenomena. The point is that once such lexical rules are embraced, then obviously, they may be annotated in the same way that the rules of lexical-functional grammar are. That is, we can have a rule like:

(b) en:

$$[\quad]_{[+V\ -N]} \rightarrow [\quad]_{[+V]}: \text{patient} \rightarrow \text{external argument}$$

The learning story would then proceed exactly as in the lexical-functional framework. The child would start out with a rule like (b). This would be the most conservative rule that could handle the passives that the child actually hears. On further exposure to nondirect actional passives, the child would generalize the rule to (a).

Two important comments should be made here. The question is not whether lexical rules should be allowed. Both theories allow lexical rules stated over thematic categories like theme. The question is whether phenomena not handled by such rules are best stated as transformations respecting a strong autonomy of syntax thesis or whether another kind of lexical rule, one allowing the use of grammatical function notation, should also be allowed. Such a system would be consistent with a weaker autonomy thesis, because it would limit the use of semantic predicates to lexical rules that are listed in a predicate's dictionary entry. Both systems are equally restrictive in terms of the number of different types of rules allowed.

23. The case filter says:

$$*[NP_{lexical}] \text{ unless } NP = (+case)$$

24. The mechanism linking the subject position to its trace is the Move α rule. This representation would still violate the θ criterion if we assumed that preverbal positions are inextricably linked with agentive thematic roles. The interpretation would accord with the principles of grammar only on the assumption that this position could be "athematic." However, as Williams (1981) notes, this athematic option seems to be part of the Universal Grammar of the morphological component. We assume that the child makes use of this option upon realizing that this is the only way to give the sentence an interpretation. More generally, as noted by Burzio 1981, verbs that do not assign Case to objects do not assign a thematic role to subjects.

25. Principles of the binding theory (Chomsky 1981) will also serve to rule out passive structures with case marked postverbal objects.

26. One problem with the interpretation of these results is that two different populations were used. One population established that subjects had control over closed class items, the other, that full and truncated passives were acquired at the same time. The population tested for closed class control was slightly older (median age 3 yrs. 7 mos.) than the other (median 3 yrs. 3 mos.). Subsequent work by Maratsos (1978:255) reveals confidence about the main conclusion. Truncates are either as good or better as full passives, in terms of acquisition:

Comprehension too appears to develop for short passives as early as or earlier than for corresponding long one.... Thus, short passives appear to be acquired at least as early as long passives, if not earlier.

Incidentally, Maratsos (Ibid.:254–255) takes the co-occurrence of truncated and full passives as a problem for transformational grammar:

What kind of initial acquisition can be expected if children hold the classical transformational hypothesis that grammatical deep structure of sentences represent logical relations uniformly?... Given such a theory, two predictions are reasonable. First, the analysis of short passives, in which the logical subject is not represented in surface structure, should cause more difficulties than that of long passives. Second, once the child has analyzed a fair number of passives with some success, he should quickly generalize the relation between actives and passives in a way that would be syntactically autonomous and independent of the semantics of the particular verb and accompanying NPs.... What is known about children's acquisition of passives fails to support those predictions in a number of ways.

The argument presented here answers these objections.

27. The interesting thing about this class is that the presence of an overt determiner acts as clear evidence that these are nominal phrases. Most importantly, it also no longer has the ability to assign case to the postverbal NP, as can be seen by the obligatory insertion of the preposition *of* between the head nominal and its object. Roeper presents evidence that, from very early stages, children understand these structures as nominalizations. Given that this construction is restricted semantically and given that it is one of the only other cases of category changing rules encountered at the early stages, we are not surprised to find that children similarly restrict the "passive" affixation particularly given the facts about parental input discussed in Devilliers and Barr (see above).

Compare these cases with gerundive NPs that are also formed by adding a possessive NP to a verbal head. Semantic circumscription like the action nominalizations is not observed.

(a) [$_{NP}$ John's hating mathematics so much] is surprising.
(b) I was surprised that [$_{NP}$ Mary's loving John] did not bother her old boyfriend.

We might suggest that gerundives are not derived from the same source as action nominalizations. So for example, note that we do not get action nominalizations in cases where we do not get corresponding progressives:

(c) *John was liking Mary.
(d) John's liking Mary disturbed his mother.

We might therefore suggest that action nominalizations are formed by a "zero derivation" from the progressive form, the rule being:

(e) [   ]$_N$:
[ing]$_{[+V -N]}$ (verb) → [   ]$_{[-V +N]}$ (noun)

Under this analysis we do not directly put a [nonstative] interpretation on the morphological rule. Rather, we assume that "progressive meaning" is compatible with stative verbs, so progressives will only be licit with statives. Because action nominalizations apply to the output of the progressive forming affix, they will *de facto* only apply to statives. The problem with this account is that there are some statives that can be given a "progressive" meaning but cannot be "action nominalized." For example, take the pair:

(f) The sun was shining for two hours.
(g) The executive was shining his shoes for two hours.

Only the second describes a real activity. Interestingly enough, only the second allows a (perhaps marginal) action nominalization:

(h) *The shining of the sun went on for two hours this morning.
(i) The shining of the executive's shoes went on
     for two hours this morning.

The result is that we must actively apply the [nonstative] restriction, even to a "zero derivation" analysis of this construction.

28. "Zero derivation" is a change of category without addition of an overt affix. It is quite common. Nouns, for example, are often derived from verbs by this process; *a hit* from *hit*.

29. The markedness principles governing word formation dictate that the simplest rule (the rule written using the least features) must be preferred. The noncircumscribed case will be picked as the first option.

30. As mentioned, the principle of one-to-one mapping is designed to guarantee that evidence from the speech stream will encode a unique class of grammatical information. The idea is that we want the affix to serve as a unique determinant of the categorial status of a word so that the child does not have to search for independent evidence of the affixed form's category on every encounter. We also would not want a child who had learned that *ation* was a nominalizing suffix in, e.g., *nominalization,* to have to test extensively whether it had the same function in, e.g., *verbalization.* But with zero derived forms we must always have independent evidence of categorial status. We cannot distinguish these forms from their roots because there is no phonological affix. The conclusion is that we would not expect the uniqueness restriction to apply to zero affixation.

31. There may also be semantic factors of the type noticed in Slobin 1966 pushing children to the correct interpretation of long passives. In particular, Slobin pointed out that certain long passives are "irreversible." The "subject" of a passive sentence is anomalous as the subject of the corresponding active. Thus we can only derive a semantically anomalous active interpretation (b) for a sentence like (a):

(a) The flowers were smelled by the cat.
(b) The flowers smelled the cat.

This predicts that irreversible short passives, violating both structural and semantic conditions, should be the best exemplars for a passive rule.

32. Steven Pinker (personal communication) notes that this argument succeeds only if we can assume that the loss of an argument in surface structure does not prompt the child to create a new intransitive form for the homophonous transitive verb. We believe (as we shall show below) that there is a general principle inhibiting the use of an homophonous element for a different, grammatically salient function. If this is correct, then such strategies will not be tapped until other methods like the one we describe in the text are used. Interestingly, there is some personally

communicated experimental evidence (D. Finer and T. Roeper) suggesting that children do first try a passive interpretation for legitimately optional transitive/intransitive verbs. For instance, children try to interpret *John* as the theme in a sentence such as (a):

(a) John pushed.

33. As mentioned in footnote 22, Wasow suggests expanding the grammatical devices of transformational grammar to include lexical rules that can use predicates like theme. Given this power, we must explain how the child moves from a narrow thematic characterization to a Move α rule. The jump can be explained by a ban on Boolean conditions. Assume a lexical rule stated in terms of theme. The only possible way to incorporate a sentence where the preposed NP has no thematic connection to the verb is either to assume a move NP rule, or to write a rule using a Boolean disjunction. That is, to derive a sentence like (a):

(a) John is believed [e] to be a fool.

our rule would have to have the disjunctive theme or subject of predicate in its structure description. However, this type of rule is banned by the principle of Universal Grammar that prohibits rules with Boolean conditions. Such conditions have been ruled out on linguistic grounds, as mentioned in chapter 1. The only general predicate that applies across all thematic domains is the categorial notion "NP." We assume that the child adopts this option.

As an aside, it is striking that all attempts to show that Boolean conditions are necessary in the statement of linguistic rules have come up empty handed, at least so far. Even the most recalcitrant of complex surface patterns like that of dative alternation have succumbed to explanations that do not appeal to Boolean conditions. In the case of dative, Hoffman (1980) shows how general conditions on particle movement interacting with Case theory suffice to describe those verbs that allow dative alternation and those that do not. In brief, the correlation is that verbs that occur with particles, for example, *give–give up* also exhibit dative, and those verbs that do not, such as, *donate–*donate away* fail to. Hoffman demonstrates that this general approach, decomposing the apparent surface complexities of dative into several interacting parts, is actually superior to a lexically based, verb by verb approach. It would be interesting to apply his study to developmental analyses of dative acquisition for this reason.

34. Note that this pattern will also trigger on NP-*be*-Adjective +ed constructions such as, *The boy was unlearned*, unless some restriction like "+argument" is included in the rule pattern. But this is precisely what is known because *unlearned* never appears with a surface direct object, as in **John unlearned the boy*. Thus, the subcategorization frame for *unlearn* will not include a direct object, and the drop trace rule will never be built to handle such cases. Rather, *unlearned* will be attached as an adjective, just as in the comparable case, *John was sick*. As a result, the drop trace rule

will never be (over)generalized, and always retain its initial "+argument" marker in its triggering pattern. Alternatively, this distinction could be encoded by means of distinct packet names. A verb demanding a direct object could activate the packet Parse-object, but a predicate adjective that cannot take a direct object could activate a different packet. The passive rule is cached in the packet Parse-object and thus would never be triggered by the predicate adjective construction.

There are other auxiliary verbs in English that allow passive (Baker 1979), for example, *got*:

John got arrested.

The acquisition procedure also acquires this alternative construction.

35. Berwick (1982) advances a slightly different explanation for this phenomenon. Interested readers may refer to this work for details.

36. Actually, overgeneralization is permitted if it is recoverable, if there is possible positive evidence that will tell the learner that overgeneralization has occurred. If the only evidence is positive example sentences, if one language is a proper subset of another, and if we guess too large a language, then there is no such saving grace. On the other hand, in particular cases there may be other grammatical constraints that act as positive evidence prompting recovery from pernicious overgeneralization.

37. Incremental acquisition may well prove to be far too strong a theory in the case of child acquisition. If there can be dramatic "radical reorganizations" of grammars, for example, the abandonment of one whole set of phrase structure rules for another the model proposed here will not suffice, but may form part of this more general theory. It may be the case that language acquisition is an either/or type process with either incremental acquisition or radical restructuring as the two options. See Bowerman 1973 for discussion of cases of radical reorganization. On the other hand, incremental decisions, such as the decision that heads follow complements, can have significant impact on the appearance of surface strings.

38. Each new parser P_i is determined by the current input example sentence plus the previous parser, P_{i-1}. This implies that the acquisition procedure does not store previous example sentences it has encountered (though it does so indirectly via the knowledge in its rule base). Conclusions about the structure of a new rule are made by drawing upon knowledge of past rules, the current example sentence, and specific constraints about the form of all rules. Thus the acquisition procedure is intensional, in Chomsky's sense (1975:119–122). The current parser plus the new input datum fixes the next parser rather than the next language.

39. For additional discussion, see Berwick 1982, where the relationship between indirect negative evidence and hypothesis ordering is discussed.

40. It is also not clear whether the three cell limit is psycholinguistically significant or not. Given the assumption that an S consists of NP INFL VP, then the input buffer can hold an entire S. In addition, grammar rule

patterns can access two nodes of the active node stack, the current active node and one cyclic (S or NP) node above the current active node. At most then a grammar rule can access an S as the cyclic node, an S as the current active node, and the constituents NP INFL VP in the input buffer. This is roughly a two sentence range, the current S being parsed plus the S dominating the current S.

41. This annotation is automatic. By convention, and in accord with ideas developed in Chomsky 1970 and Williams 1981, the features of the head of a phrase are percolated through to the projections of that phrase. For instance, the features of Infl, by assumption the head of the sentence phrase, are automatically passed through to the S node; the features of a verb are passed through to label the VP node. This percolation mechanism has also been adopted in recent theories of word formation; see Lieber 1980.

Appendix A

1. We simply supply the integer part of $n/3$ such phrases; we will be within $n \pmod 3$ of the actual length n. This meets the conditions of the theorem. For example, in the case of PP adjuncts, a string of PPs that is 50 terminal items long can be replaced with a set of 16 three-word PPs, *with the* ⟨*Noun*⟩, with 2 words left over.

Why not use this property to establish the constant growth property directly? Note that our proof is somewhat more natural, because we just use indefinite repetition exactly where it is needed to handle another case of indefinite repetition.

References

Aanderaa, S., 1974. On *k*-tape versus *k-1* tape real time computation. *SIAM-AMS Colloquium on Applied Mathematics* vol. 7. *Complexity of Computation*, R. Karp, ed. pp. 75–96.

Aho, A. and J. Ullman, 1972. *The Theory of Parsing, Translation, and Compiling.* Vol. 1. Englewood Cliffs, NJ: Prentice-Hall.

Anderson, J., 1978. Arguments concerning representations for mental imagery. *Psychological Review* 85:249–277.

Anderson, J., 1979. Further arguments concerning representations for mental imagery: a response to Hayes-Roth and Pylyshyn. *Psychological Review* 86:395–406.

Anderson, S., 1977. Comments on the paper by Wasow. In *Formal Syntax*, P. Culicover, A. Akmajian, and T. Wasow, eds. New York: Academic Press, pp. 361–378.

Angluin, D., 1978. Inductive inference of formal languages from positive data. *Information and Control* 45:117–135.

Aoun, Y., 1979. On government, case marking and clitic placement. MIT Department of Linguistics, unpublished ms.

Armstrong, J., 1979. Recursive solution to the equations of motion of an n-link manipulator. *Proc. 5th World Congress on Theory of Machines and Mechanisms* Vol. 2 pp. 1343–1346.

Baker, C.L., 1979. Syntactic theory and the projection problem. *Linguistic Inquiry* 10:533–581.

Baker, C.L., and J. McCarthy, 1981. *The Logical Problem of Language Acquisition.* Cambridge, MA: MIT Press.

Baltin, M., 1982. A landing site theory of movement rules. *Linguistic Inquiry* 13:1–38.

Berwick, R., 1980. Computational analogues of constraints on grammars. *Proc. 18th Meeting of the Association for Computational Linguistics* pp. 49–53.

Berwick, R., 1982. Locality principles and the acquisition of syntactic knowledge. PhD dissertation, MIT Department of Computer Science and Electrical Engineering.

Berwick, R., 1983. How to use what you know: a computer science perspective. *The Behavioral and Brain Sciences* 6:402–403.

Berwick, R. and A. Weinberg, 1982. Parsing efficiency, computational complexity, and the evaluation of grammatical theories. *Linguistic Inquiry* 13:165–191.

Berwick, R. and A. Weinberg, 1983. The role of grammars as components of models of language use. *Cognition* 13:1–61.

Berwick, R. and K. Wexler, 1982. Parsing efficiency and c-command. *Proc. First West Coast Conference on Formal Linguistics*, pp. 29–34.

Bever, T., 1968. A survey of some recent work in psycholinguistics. In *Specification and Utilization of a Transformational Grammar*, W.J. Plath, ed. Scientific Report No. 3, IBM Thomas J. Watson Research Center.

Book, R. and S. Greibach, 1970. Quasi-realtime languages. *Mathematical Systems Theory* 4:97–111.

Borgida, A., 1983. Some formal results about stratificational grammars and their relevance to linguistics. *Mathematical Systems Theory* 16:29–56.

Borodin, A., 1973. Computational complexity: theory and practice. In *Currents in the Theory of Computing*, A. Aho, ed. Englewood Cliffs, NJ: Prentice-Hall, pp. 35–89.

Borodin, A., 1977. On relating time and space to size and depth. *SIAM Journal of Computing* 6:733–744.

Bowerman, M., 1973. *Early Synactic Development: A Cross Linguistic Study With Special Reference to Finnish*. London: Cambridge University Press.

Bresnan, J., 1972. The theory of complementation in English syntax. PhD dissertation, MIT Department of Linguistics.

Bresnan, J., 1976. On the form and functioning of transformations. *Linguistic Inquiry* 7:3–40.

Bresnan, J., 1978. A realistic transformational grammar. In *Linguistic Theory and Psychological Reality*, M. Halle, J. Bresnan, and G. Miller, eds. Cambridge, MA: MIT Press, pp. 1–59.

Bresnan, J., 1982a. Control and complementation. In *The Mental Representation of Grammatical Relations*, J. Bresnan, ed. Cambridge, MA: MIT Press, pp. 282–390.

Bresnan, J., 1982b. *The Mental Representation of Grammatical Relations*. Cambridge, MA: MIT Press.

Bresnan, J., 1982c. The passive in lexical theory. In *The Mental Representation of Grammatical Relations*, J. Bresnan, ed. Cambridge, MA: MIT Press, pp. 3–86.

Bresnan, J. and R. Kaplan, 1982. Introduction: grammars as mental representations of language. In *The Mental Representation of Grammatical Relations*, J. Bresnan, ed. Cambridge, MA: MIT Press, pp. xvii–lii.

Bresnan, J., R. Kaplan, S. Peters, and A. Zaenen, 1982. Cross-serial dependencies in Dutch. *Linguistic Inquiry* 13:613–636.

Brown, R., 1973. *A First Language*. Cambridge, MA: Harvard University Press.

Brown, R. and C. Hanlon, 1970. Derivational complexity and the order of acquisition in child speech. In *Cognition and the Development of Language*, J. R. Hayes, ed. New York: John Wiley, pp. 155–207.

Burzio, L., 1981. Intransitive verbs and Italian auxiliaries. PhD dissertation, MIT Department of Linguistics and Philosophy.

Chomsky, N., 1951. Morphophonemics of modern Hebrew. M.S. dissertation, University of Pennsylvania Department of Linguistics.

Chomsky, N., 1955. *The Logical Structure of Linguistic Theory*. New York: Plenum Press.

Chomsky, N., 1959. On certain formal properties of grammars. *Information and Control* 2:137–167.

Chomsky, N., 1963. Formal properties of grammars. In *Handbook of Mathematical Psychology*, R.D. Luce, R. Bush, and E. Galanter, eds., vol. 2. New York: John Wiley, pp. 323–418.

Chomsky, N., 1965. *Aspects of the Theory of Syntax*. Cambridge: MIT Press.

Chomsky, N., 1968. *Language and Mind*. New York: Harcourt, Brace, Jovanovich.

Chomsky, N., 1970. Remarks on nominalization. In *Readings in English Transformational Grammar*, R. Jacobs and P. Rosenbaum, eds. Waltham, MA: Ginn and Co., pp. 184–221.

Chomsky, N., 1973. Conditions on transformations. In *A Festschrift for Morris Halle*, S. Anderson and P. Kiparsky, eds. New York: Holt, Rinehart, and Winston, pp. 232–286.

Chomsky, N., 1975. *Reflections on Language*. New York: Pantheon.

Chomsky, N., 1977a. Conditions on rules of grammar. In *Essays on Form and Intepretation*, New York: North Holland, pp. 163–210.

Chomsky, N., 1977b. On Wh-movement. In *Formal Syntax*, P. Culicover, T. Wasow, and A. Akmajian, eds. New York: Academic Press, pp. 71–132.

Chomsky, N., 1979. *Language and Responsibility*. New York: Pantheon.

Chomsky, N., 1980a. On binding. *Linguistic Inquiry* 11:1–46.

Chomsky, N., 1980b. *Rules and Representations.* New York: Columbia University Press.

Chomsky, N., 1981. *Lectures on Government and Binding.* Dordrecht, Holland: Foris Publications.

Chomsky, N., 1982. *Some Concepts and Consequences of the Theory of Government and Binding.* Cambridge, MA: MIT Press.

Chomsky, N. and M. Halle, 1968. *The Sound Pattern of English.* New York: Harper and Row.

Chomsky, N. and H. Lasnik, 1977. Filters and control. *Linguistic Inquiry* 8:425–504.

Cocke, J. and J. Schwartz, 1970. *Programming Languages and Their Compilers.* New York: Courant Institute, New York University.

Cook, S.A., 1980. Towards a complexity theory of synchronous parallel computation. University of Toronto Department of Computer Science Report No. 141/80.

Cooper W.E. and E.C.T. Walker, 1979. *Sentence Processing: Psycholinguistic Studies Presented to Merrill Garrett.* Hillsdale, NJ: Lawrence Erlbaum.

Cooper, W. and J. Paccia-Cooper, 1980. *Syntax and Speech.* Cambridge, MA: Harvard University Press.

Dresher, E. and N. Hornstein, 1979. Trace theory and NP movement rules. *Linguistic Inquiry* 10:65–82.

Earley, J., 1968. An efficient context-free parsing algorithm. PhD dissertation, Carnegie-Mellon University Department of Computer Science.

Earley, J., 1970. An efficient context-free parsing algorithm. *Communications of the Association for Computing Machinery* 14:453–460.

Emonds, J., 1970. Root and structure preserving transformations. PhD dissertation, MIT Department of Linguistics.

Emonds, J., 1976. *A Transformational Approach to English Syntax.* New York: Academic Press.

Evers, A., 1975. The transformational cycle in Dutch and German. PhD dissertation, Department of Linguistics, Rijksuniversiteit, Utrecht, Holland.

Fletcher, P., 1969. The development of the verb phrase. In *Language Acquisition*, P. Fletcher and M. Garman, eds. New York: Cambridge University Press, pp. 261–284.

Floyd, R., 1964. Bounded context syntactic analysis. *Communications of the Association for Computing Machinery* 7:62–66.

Fodor, J., T. Bever, and M. Garrett, 1974. *The Psychology of Language: an Introduction to Psycholinguistics and Generative Grammar.* New York: McGraw Hill.

Fodor, J. and M. Garrett, 1967. Some syntactic determinants of sentential complexity. *Perception and Psychophysics* 2:289–296.

Fodor, J. D., 1979. Superstrategy. In *Sentence Processing: Psycholinguisitc Studies Presented to honor Merrill Garrett,* W. Cooper and E. Walker, eds. Hillsdale, NJ: Lawrence Erlbaum.

Forster, K., 1976. The autonomy of syntactic processing. Paper presented at the Convocation on Communication, MIT.

Forster, K., 1979. Levels of processing and the structure of the language processor, In *Sentence Processing: Psycholinguistic Studies Presented to Honor Merrill Garrett,* W. Cooper and E. Walker, eds. Hillsdale, NJ: Lawrence Erlbaum, pp. 27–86.

Forster, K. and I. Olbrei, 1973. Semantic heuristics and syntactic analysis. *Cognition* 2:319–347.

Foster, J., 1968. A syntax improving program. *Computer Journal* 11:31–34.

Freidin, R., 1978. Cyclicity and the theory of grammar. *Linguistic Inquiry* 9:519–550.

Fu, K. and T. Booth, 1975. Grammatical inference: introduction and survey. *IEEE Transactions on Systems, Man, and Cybernetics* 4:95–111.

Garnham, A., forthcoming. Why psycholinguists don't care about DTC: a reply to Berwick and Weinberg. *Cognition.*

Gazdar, G., 1979. English as a context-free language. unpublished report, University of Sussex.

Gazdar, G., 1981. Unbounded dependencies and coordinate structure. *Linguistic Inquiry* 12:155–184.

Gazdar, G., 1981 forthcoming. Unbounded dependencies. In *The Nature of Syntactic Representation,* P. Jacobson and G. Pullum, eds. Dordrecht, Holland: Reidel Publishing Co.

Gewirtz, W., 1974. *Investigations in the Theory of Descriptive Complexity.* New York: Courant Computer Science Report No. 5.

Goldin-Meadow, S., 1979. Language without a helping hand. In *Studies in Neurolinguistics,* vol. 4, H. Whitaker and H.A. Whitaker, eds. New York: Academic Press, pp. 125–209.

Gough D., 1965. The verification of sentences. *The Journal of Verbal Learning and Verbal Behavior* 5:107–111.

Graham, S., M. Harrison, and W. Ruzzo, 1980. An improved context-free recognizer. *ACM Transactions on Progamming Languages and Systems* 2:415–462.

Gray, J. and M. Harrison, 1969. Single pass precedence analysis. *IEEE Conference Record of the 10th Ann. Symp. of Switching and Automata Theory* pp. 106–117.

Greibach, S., 1965. A new normal form theorem for context-free grammars. *Journal of the Association for Computing Machinery.* 12:42–52.

Grimson E. and D. Marr, 1979. A computer implementation of a theory of human stereo vision. *Proceedings of the Image Understanding Workshop* Palo Alto, CA., pp. 41–47.

Halle, M., J. Bresnan, and G. Miller, 1978. *Linguistic Theory and Psychological Reality.* Cambridge, MA: MIT Press.

Hammer, M., 1975. A new grammatical transformation into deterministic top-down form. Cambridge, MA: MIT Project MAC TR-119.

Harman, G., 1963. Generative grammar without transformation rules: a defense of phrase structure. *Language* 39:597–616.

Harrison, M., 1978. *Introduction to Formal Language Theory.* Reading, MA: Addison-Wesley.

Hayes-Roth, F., 1979. Distinguishing theories of representation: a critique of Anderson's "Arguments Concerning Mental Imagery." *Psychological Review* 86:376–382.

Hennie, F., 1965. One-tape, off-line turing machine computations. *Information and Control* 8.6:553–578.

Higginbotham, J., 1980. Pronouns and bound variables. *Linguistic Inquiry* 11:679–708.

Higginbotham, J., 1983. Logical form, binding, and nominals. *Linguistic Inquiry* 14:395–420.

Hintikka, J., 1974. Quantifiers vs. quantification theory. *Linguistic Inquiry* 5:153–177.

Hoffman, C., 1980. Phrase structure, subcategorization, and transformations in the English verb phrase. PhD dissertation, University of Connecticut Department of Linguistics.

Hopcroft, J. and J. Ullman, 1969. *Formal Languages and Their Relation to Automata.* Reading, MA: Addison-Wesley.

Hopcroft, J. and Ullman, 1979. *Introduction to Automata Theory, Languages, and Computation.* Reading, MA: Addison-Wesley.

Horn, B. and Raibert, M. 1978. Configuration space control. *The Industrial Robot,* June, 1978, pp. 69–73.

Hornstein, N. and Lightfoot, D., 1981. Introduction. In *Explanation in Linguistics*, N. Hornstein and D. Lightfoot, eds. London: Longmans, pp. 9–31.

Hornstein, N. and Weinberg, A. 1981. Case theory and preposition stranding. *Linguistic Inquiry* 12:55–92.

Jackendoff, R., 1977. $\overline{X}$ *Syntax: A Study of Phrase Structure*. Cambridge, MA: MIT Press.

Jones, N.D. and W.T. Laaser, 1974. Complete problems for deterministic polynomial time. *Proceedings of the 6th Annual Symposium on the Theory of Computation*, pp. 40–46.

Joshi, A.K., 1983 forthcoming. How much context sensitivity is required to provide reasonable structural descriptions: tree adjoining grammars. In *Natural Language Processing: Computational, Psycholinguistic and Theoretical Perspectives*, D. Dowty, L. Karttunen, and A. Zwicky, eds. New York: Cambridge University Press.

Joshi, A. and Levy, L. 1977. Constraints on local transformations. *SIAM Journal of Computing* 6:272–284.

Joshi, A. Levy, L. and Yueh, K. 1980. Local constraints in programming languages, part I: syntax. *Journal of Theoretical Computer Science* 12.3:265–290.

Kaplan, R., 1973. A general syntactic processor. In *Natural Language Processing*, R. Rustin ed. New York: Courant Science Symposium, Algorithmic Press, pp. 193–241.

Kaplan, R. and Bresnan, J., 1982. Lexical functional grammar: a formal system for grammatical representation. In *The Mental Representation of Grammatical Relations*, J. Bresnan, ed. Cambridge, MA: MIT Press, pp. 173–281.

Kasami, T., 1965. *An Efficient Recognition and Syntax Algorithm for Context-free Languages*. Bedford, MA: Air Force Cambridge Research Laboratory report No. AF-CRL-65-758.

Katz, J., 1981. *Language and Other Abstract Objects*. New York: Rowman-Littlefield.

Kay, M., 1967. *Experiments with a Powerful Parser*. Santa Monica: Rand Corporation RM-5452-PR.

Kayne, R., 1981. ECP extensions. *Linguistic Inquiry* 12:93–133.

Keyser, S.J., 1968. Review of Sven Jacobson, adverbial positions in English. *Language* 44:357–374.

Knuth, D., 1965. On the translation of languages from left to right. *Information and Control* 8:607–639.

Kornfeld, J., 1974. The influence of clause structure on the perceptual analysis of sentences. PhD dissertation, MIT Department of Psychology.

Koster, J., 1978. *Locality Principles in Syntax*. Dordrecht, Holland: Foris Publications.

Kripke, S., 1976. Is there a problem with substitutional quantification? In *Truth and Meaning*, J. McDowell and G. Evans eds. Cambridge, England: Oxford University Press.

Kuno, S., 1966. The augmented predictive analyzer for context-free languages—its relative efficiency. *Communications of the Association for Computing Machinery* 9:810–823.

Kurki-Suonio, R., 1966. On top-to-bottom recognition and left recursion. *Communications of the Association for Computing Machinery* 9:527–528.

Lapointe, S. 1977. Recursiveness and deletion. *Linguistic Analysis* 3:227–265.

Lasnik, H., 1980. Restricting the theory of transformations: a case study. in *Explanation in Linguistics*, Hornstein, N. and D. Lightfoot, eds. London: Longmans, pp. 152–173.

Lasnik, H., 1981. Learnability, recursiveness, and the evaluation metric. In *The Logical Problem of Language Acquisition*, C. Baker, and J. McCarthy, eds. Cambridge MA: MIT Press, pp. 1–29.

Lewis, H. and Papadimitriou, C., 1980. *Elements of the Theory of Computation*. Englewood Cliffs, NJ: Prentice-Hall.

Leopold, W., 1949. *Speech Development of a Bilingual Child: a Linguists' Record*. vol.3. Evanston, IL: Northwestern University Press.

Lieber,R., 1980. On the organization of the lexicon. PhD dissertation, MIT Department of Linguistics and Philosophy.

Lightfoot, D., 1979. *Diachronic Syntax*. New York: Cambridge University Press.

Machtey, M. and P. Young, 1978. *An Introduction to the General Theory of Algorithms*. New York: North-Holland Publishing Co.

Marantz, A., 1983. Grammatical relations and language acquisition. In *Studies in Generative Grammar and Language Acquisition*, Y. Otsu and H.van Riemsdijk, eds. Tokyo: Monshubo Grant for Scientific Research Conference Proceedings, pp. 29–48.

Maratsos, M.P., 1978. New models in linguistics and language acquisition. In *Linguistic theory and Psychological Reality*, M. Halle, J. Bresnan, and G. Miller, eds. Cambridge, MA: MIT Press, pp. 247–263.

Maratsos, M.P. and R. Abramovitch, 1975. How children understand, full, truncated, and anomalous passives. *Journal of Verbal Learning and Verbal Behavior* 14:145–157.

Maratsos, M.P., S. Kuczaj II, and D. Fox, 1978. Some empirical studies in the acquisition of transformational relations: passives, negatives, and the past tense. In *The Minnesota Symposium on Child Psychology* W.A. Collins, ed., vol. 12. Hillsdale, NJ: Lawrence Erlbaum.

Marcus, M., 1980. *A Theory of Syntactic Recognition for Natural Language.* Cambridge, MA: MIT Press.

Marr, D., 1982. *Vision.* San Francisco: W.H. Freeman.

Marr, D. and E. Hildreth, 1979. The smallest channel in early human vision. *Journal of the Optical Society of America* 70:868–870.

Marr, D. and T. Poggio, 1977. From understanding computation to understanding neural circuitry. *Neuroscience Research Program Bulletin* 15:470–488.

Marr, D. and T. Poggio, 1979. A theory of human stereo vision. *Proc. Royal Society London B* 204:301–328.

Marshall, J., 1979. Language acquisition in a biological frame of reference. In *Language Acquisition,* P. Fletcher and M. Garman, eds. New York: Cambridge University Press, pp. 437–453.

Matthews, R., 1979. Do the sentences of a natural language form a recursive set? *Synthese* 40:209–224.

May, R., 1981. On the parallelism of movement and bound anaphora. *Linguistic Inquiry* 12:477–483.

McMahon L., 1963. Grammatical analysis as part of understanding a sentence. PhD dissertation, Harvard University Department of Psychology.

Mehler, J., 1963. Some effects of grammatical transformations on the recall of English sentences. *Journal of Verbal Learning and Verbal Behavior* 6:335–338.

Meyer, A. and M. Fischer, 1971. Economy of description by automata, grammars, and formal systems. *Proceedings of the 12th Annual ACM Symposium on Switching and Automata Theory,* pp. 185–194.

Miller, G. and N. Chomsky, 1963. Finitary models of language users. In *Handbook of Mathematical Psychology* vol. 2, R. Luce, R. Bush, and E. Galanter, eds. New York: John Wiley, pp. 419–491.

Moore, P., 1981. The varied ways plants tap the sun. *New Scientist,* February 12.

Newport, E., H. Gleitman, and L. Gleitman, 1977. Mother, please, I'd rather do it myself: some effects and non-effects of maternal speech style. In *Talking to Children: Language Input and Acquisition,* C. Snow and C. Ferguson, eds. New York: Cambridge University Press, pp. 109–150.

Nijholt, A., 1980. *Context-free Grammars: Covers, Normal Forms, and Parsing,* New York: Springer-Verlag.

Oehrle, R., 1974. The grammatical status of the English dative alternation. PhD dissertation, MIT Department of Linguistics.

Peters, S., 1973. On restricting deletion transformations. In *The Formal Analysis of Language*, M. Gross, M. Halle, and M. Schutzenberger, eds. Holland, The Hague: Mouton, pp. 372–384.

Peters, S. and R. Ritchie, 1973a. Context-sensitive immediate constituent analysis—context-free languages revisited. *Mathematical Systems Theory* 6:324–333.

Peters, S. and R. Ritchie, 1973b. On the generative power of transformational grammars. *Information Sciences* 6:49–83.

Pinker, S., 1982. A theory of the acquisition of lexical interpretive grammars. In *The Mental Representation of Grammatical Relations*, J. Bresnan, ed. Cambridge, MA: MIT Press, pp. 655–726.

Poggio, T., and B. Rosser, 1982. The computational problem of motor control. MIT Artificial Intelligence Laboratory Memo 687.

Poggio, T. and V. Torre, 1980. A theory of synaptic interaction. In *Theoretical Approaches in Neurobiology*, W. Reichardt and T. Poggio eds. Cambridge, MA: MIT Press, pp. 28–38.

Posner, M. and R. Mitchell, 1967. Chronometric analysis of classification. *Psychological Review* 74:392–409.

Postal, P., 1964. *Constituent Structure*, Bloomington, Indiana: Indiana University Linguistics Club (also Mouton).

Pratt, V., 1975 LINGOL—a progress report. *Proceedings of the 4th International Joint Conference on Artificial Intelligence*, pp. 422–428.

Pratt, V. and L. Stockmeyer, 1977. The power of vector machines. *Journal of Computer and System Sciences* 12:198–221.

Pullum, G., 1980. Languages in which movement does not parallel bound anaphora. *Linguistic Inquiry* 11:613–620.

Pylyshyn, Z., 1979. Validating computational models: a critique of Anderson's indeterminacy of representation claim. *Psychological Review* 86:383–394.

Reinhart, T., 1976. The syntactic domain of anaphora. PhD dissertation, MIT Department of Linguistics.

Reynolds, J., 1968. *Grammatical Covering*. Chicago, Illinois: Argonne National Laboratory TM 96.

Richter, J. and S. Ullman, 1980. A model for the spatio-temporal organization of X and Y-type ganglion cells in the primate retina. MIT Artificial Intelligence Laboratory Memo 573.

Roeper, T., 1978. Linguistic universals and the acquisition of gerunds. In *Papers in the Structure and Development of Child Language*, H. Goodluck and L. Solan, eds. Department of Linguistics, University of Massachusetts Occasional Papers, pp. 1–36.

Rosenberg, A., 1967. Real-time definable languages. *Journal of the Association for Computing Machinery* 14:645–662.

Ross, J., 1967. Constraints on variables in syntax. PhD dissertation, MIT Department of Linguistics.

Rounds, W., 1973. Complexity of recognition in intermediate-level languages. *Proceedings of the 14th Ann. Symp. on Switching Theory and Automata*, pp. 145–158.

Rounds, W., 1975. A grammatical characterization of the exponential time languages. *Proceedings of the 16th Annual Symposium on Switching and Automata Theory*, pp. 135–143.

Rouveret, A. and J.R. Vergnaud, 1980. Specifying reference to subject. *Linguistic Inquiry* 11:97–202.

Ruzzo, W., 1978. General context-free parsing. PhD dissertation, University of California at Berkeley Department of Computer Science.

Ruzzo, W., 1980. On uniform circuit complexity. *Proceedings of 20th Annual Conference on the Foundations of Computer Science*, pp. 312–318.

Savin, H. and E. Perchonock, 1965, Grammatical structure and the immediate recall of English sentences. *Journal of Verbal Learning and Verbal Behavior* 4:348–353.

Schank, R. and K. Colby, 1973. *Computer Models of Thought and Language*. San Francisco: W.H. Freeman.

Shipman, D., 1979. Phrase structure rules for Parsifal. MIT Artificial Intelligence Laboratory Working Paper No. 182.

Silver, W., 1981. On the representation of angular velocity and its effect on the efficiency of manipulator dynamics computation. MIT Artificial Intelligence Laboratory Memo 622.

Slobin, D., 1966. Grammatical transformations and sentence comprehension in childhood and adulthood, *Journal of Verbal Learning and Verbal Behavior* 5:219–227.

Snodgrass, J. and J. Townsend, 1980. Comparing serial and parallel models: theory and implementation. *Journal of Experimental Psychology* 6:330–354.

Stabler, E., 1983. How are grammars represented? *The Behavioral and Brain Sciences* 6:391–402.

Stowell, T., 1981. Origins of phrase structure. PhD dissertation, MIT Department of Linguistics and Philosophy.

Szymanski, T. and J. Williams, 1976. Noncanonical extensions of bottom-up parsing techniques. *SIAM Journal of Computing* 5:231–260.

Tyler, L., 1980. Serial and interactive parallel theories of syntactic processing. MIT Center for Cognitive Studies Occasional Paper No. 8.

Ullman, S., 1979. *The Interpretation of Visual Motion.* Cambridge, MA: MIT Press.

Valian, V., 1979. The wherefores and therefores of the competence/performance distinction. In *Sentence Processing: Psycholinguistic Studies Presented to Honor Merrill Garrett,* W. Cooper and E. Walker, eds. Hillsdale, N.J.:Lawrence Erlbaum, pp. 1–26.

Walker, E., et al., 1968. Grammatical relations and the search of sentences in immediate memory. *Proceedings of the Midwestern Psychological Association.*

Wasow, T., 1977. Transformations and the lexicon. In *Formal Syntax,* P. Culicover, T. Wasow, and A. Akmajian eds. New York: Academic Press, pp. 327–360.

Wasow, T., 1978. On constraining the class of transformational languages. *Synthese* 39:81–104.

Wasow, T., 1980. Major and minor rules in lexical grammar. In *Lexical Grammar,* Hulst, T. et al. eds. Dordrecht, Holland: Foris Publications, pp. 285–312.

Watt, W. C., 1970. On two hypotheses concerning psycholinguistics. In *Cognition and the Development of Language,* J. Hayes, ed. New York: John Wiley, pp. 137–220.

Weinberg, A., 1979. Grammatical theory and parsing theory. unpublished paper delivered at the 1979 GLOW Conference, Nijmegen.

Weinberg, A., forthcoming. Grammar and the theory of language use. PhD dissertation, MIT Department of Linguistics and Philosophy.

Weinberg, A. and M. Garrett, forthcoming. C-command domains and the language processor. MIT Department of Linguistics and Department of Psychology ms.

Wexler, K., 1982. A principle theory for language acquisition. In *Language Acquisition: The State of the Art,* L. Gleitman and E. Wanner, eds. New York: Cambridge University Press.

Wexler, K. and P. Culicover, 1980. *Formal Principles of Language Acquisition.* Cambridge, MA: MIT Press.

White, L., 1981. The responsibility of grammatical theory to acquisitional data. In *Explanation in Linguistics.* Hornstein, N. and D. Lightfoot, eds. London: Longmans, pp. 241–283.

Williams, E., 1975. Small clauses. in *Syntax and Semantics,* J. Kimball, ed. New York. Seminar Press, pp. 249–274.

Williams, E., 1978. Across-the-board rule application. *Linguistic Inquiry* 9:31–43.

Williams, E., 1981. Argument structure and morphology. *Linguistic Review* 1:81–113.

Williams, E., 1982. Transformationless grammar. *Linguistic Inquiry* 12:645–653.

Winograd, T.,1974. A procedural model of language understanding. In *Computer Models of Thought and Language*, R. Schank and K. Colby, eds. San Francisco: W.H. Freeman, pp. 152-186.

Woods, W., 1970. Transition network grammars for natural language analysis. *Communications of the Association for Computing Machinery* 13:591–606.

Younger, D. 1967. Recognition and parsing of context-free languages in time n^3. *Information and Control* 10:189–208.

Index

Aanderaa, S., 13
Ablauted form
in passive acquisition, 221, 222
Abramovitch, R., 222, 223, 224
Acceptance
and computational complexity, 4–6
distinguished from parsing, 252 n. 13
by Turing machine, 4
Acquisition
of action verbs, 213, 220, 286 n. 17
conditions for initiation of, 220
incremental, 201, 203, 225, 304 n. 37
instantaneous, 202
logical problem of, 17
of nonsense passives, 215
of passive rule, 212–229, 292 n. 34
of subject-auxiliary inversion rule, 210–212
Acquisition model
as problem for transformational grammar, 286 n. 16
and computational constraints, 229–241
and computer example, 208–212, 225–229
and computer model, 202–208
of dative rule, 292 n. 33
and description of initial state, 203–204
description of, 203–208
and do, 285 n. 12
and Equi NP rule, 286 n. 16
and Marcus parser, 200
and modals, 285 n. 13
new rule acquisition, 203, 207, 211, 226
and passives, 225–229
role of environment in, 203

scenarios (computer examples), 208–212
subject-auxiliary inversion, 210–212
Across the board constraint
and complexity of government-binding languages, 124
and linearity, 249
Action nominalizations, 220
and passive acquisition, 219–220
Active and inactive grammar rules
in Marcus parser, 204–205
Active node stack, 8, 151
as account of c-command, 173–180
as encoding of left context in Marcus parser, 151
Active phrase (Marcus parser)
and c-command example, 152
definition, 151
Adjacency
and case assignment, 276 n. 14
in explanation of root/non-root distinction, 212
as principle of natural grammars, 158–160, 276 n. 13, 276–277 n. 14
and subjacency, 158
Adjectives
distribution of, 27
prenominal and whiz deletion, 46
Adjunct phrase
and constant growth property, 246, 247
in linearity proof, 294 n. 1
and parsing, 276 n. 11
Adverb movement, transformational description, 47–49
Adverbial clause, preposed, 283 n. 40

Preposition
case marking properties of, 27–28
thematic properties of, 222
Prepositional phrase, 164
as bounding node, 25, 155
movement from, 164
placement of in tree, 206
Primitive (atomic) parser actions, 206
Principle A (of binding theory), 24
Principle B (of binding theory), 24, 197
Principle C (of binding theory), 24, 180
Priority
of grammar rules, 229
and subset principle, 212–228
Pro (empty pronominal)
and c-command, 180
and constant growth, 129–130
explanation of unboundedness, 170
and parsing, 170, 171
and subjacency, 275 n. 8
ungoverned, as parsing cue, 171–172
Probe
online, 177
problem of, 103
Processing time, and sentence length,
266, n. 12
Processing. *See also* parsing
bottom-up, 202
depth of, 68–69
efficient, 5ff.
online, 9, 51
parallel, 66–73
parallel, asynchronous, 11, 12, 71
parallel, intermodal, 70, 71
parallel, synchronous, 12
serial, 12, 39, 45
and theory of grammar, 40, 80–82
top-down, 202
Program size complexity, 272 n. 26
Projection principle, 30–31, 65, 162
definition, 30, 77
parsing analogue, 31, 44, 153, 161
and passive acquisition, 218
and theory of phrase structure, 30
Pronominal binding, 181–182
explanation of unboundedness, 170–172
in parsing, 170–172
Pronouns, binding of, 24, 145, 156, 203
and c-command, 180, 182
locally cued to parser, 170–171, 215

Proportionality, constant of, 11, 94–99,
267 n. 9
Propositional list, 174, 176
Psycholinguistic evidence
and c-command, 279 n. 25
for morphological model, 291 n. 32
for passive model, 226
Psychological reality, 36ff., 37ff., 256 n.
2, n. 5, n. 6
of grammar 38ff., 283 n. 42
of transformational grammar, 143, 199–
200
Pullum, G., 254 n. 31
Putnam, H., 127, 130
Pylyshyn, Z., 262 n. 44

Quantificational terms, in transforma-
tional rules, 253 n. 24
Quantifier binding, 142, 182
Quantifier, binding of, 203
Quasi-adjectival construction, 218
Question formation, 22

Racial memory, as component of innate
endowment, 38
Raibert, M., 67
Raising transformation, 258 n. 19
Random access machine, 11, 12, 13
and realtime recognition, 266, n. 8
Reaction time, 7, 37, 66
Reagan, R., 18, 19, 253 n. 19
and contradictory statements by, 18–19
Realtime, 9-10, 36
Reciprocal, 24
Recoding, and efficiency, 268 n. 15
Recognition, 8
vs. parsing, 270 n. 22
of transformational grammar, xii
Recognition complexity, 267, n. 8
Reconstruction, and c-command, 279 n.
29
Recursion
and constant growth, 153
NP, 242ff.
Recursion limitation, in acquisition, 286
n. 14
Recursive enumerability, 10
Reduction, 14ff.
and computational complexity, 131–139
proof sketch of, 134ff.